American Sherlock

American Sherlock

Remembering a Pioneer in Scientific Crime Investigation

Evan E. Filby

ROWMAN & LITTLEFIELD
Lanham • Boulder • New York • London

Published by Rowman & Littlefield
An imprint of The Rowman & Littlefield Publishing Group, Inc.
4501 Forbes Boulevard, Suite 200, Lanham, Maryland 20706
www.rowman.com

6 Tinworth Street, London SE11 5AL, United Kingdom

British Library Cataloguing in Publication Information Available

Library of Congress Cataloging-in-Publication Data

Names: Filby, Evan E. (Evan Everett), 1943- author.
Title: American Sherlock : a forgotten pioneer in scientific crime
    investigation / Evan E. Filby.
Description: Lanham : Rowman & Littlefield, [2019] | Includes bibliographical
    references and index.
Identifiers: LCCN 2019005457 (print) | LCCN 2019009642 (ebook) | ISBN
    9781538129197 (electronic) | ISBN 9781538129180 (cloth : alk. paper)
Subjects: LCSH: May, Luke S., 1892-1965. | Criminologists—United
    States—Biography. | Forensic sciences—United States.
Classification: LCC HV6023.M39 (ebook) | LCC HV6023.M39 F55 2019 (print) |
    DDC 363.25092 [B]—dc23
LC record available at https://lccn.loc.gov/2019005457

♾™ The paper used in this publication meets the minimum requirements of American
National Standard for Information Sciences—Permanence of Paper for Printed Library
Materials, ANSI/NISO Z39.48-1992.

Contents

Introduction and Acknowledgments   vii

1   Scientific Detection   1

2   A Criminologist Is Born   17

3   The Early Casebook of Luke May   29

4   Moving to Greener Fields   43

5   Centralia Deaths Spark Career Surge   57

6   Education, Innovation, and More National Renown   71

7   Fame Grows, at Some Cost   89

8   Notoriety Follows a Lull   103

9   Work and Play   117

10   Tool Marks Are the Key   131

11   Chicago Calls   141

12   Spreading the Word   155

13   Chief of Detectives and Criminologist   169

14   Riding the Crest   183

15   War Clouds Gather   197

16   Naval Intelligence Duty   213

17   The Game Has Changed   229

18   Playing Out the String   243

Retrospection   255

Appendix: Cases Overview   261

Notes   267

Bibliography   291

Index   295

Introduction and Acknowledgments

Figure I.1. Pioneer Criminologist Luke S. May.
Source: **May-Reid Records.**

𝒫rivate detective Luke S. May, our "American Sherlock," practiced scientific crime detection for more than fifty years early in the 20th century. He came long before TV shows like *CSI, NCIS, Bones,* and many other crime lab spin-offs and imitators. Back then, May was a "celebrity detective" and pioneer crime fighter.

When he was on a case, newspaper reports typically read, "Luke S. May, Seattle criminologist." They did not explain who he was or why he mattered. Writers simply assumed their readers would know all about a man who had been linked to so many thrilling cases. He earned sobriquets such as "America's Sherlock Holmes" and "a real-life Craig Kennedy." The latter was a U.S. equivalent of the fictional Holmes.

May handled numerous cases, with an impressive record of success. In the process, he advanced the state of the art in the use of science and technology in crime detection. Through his lectures and writing, he trained many police officers and other detectives in his advanced methods. He also served as a consultant in the creation of crime laboratories supported by public funding in the United States as well as Canada. With all this, May tried to broaden the use of "criminology," roughly, the scientific study of crime and criminals. Over time, other terms came into use—"criminalistics," "forensic science" and more specialized subdisciplines. But May always considered himself a criminologist, so I will stick with that terminology.

When May started as a detective around 1909, the use of science to solve crimes was rudimentary, to say the least. Some European universities had laboratories that could handle evidence, but it's not clear how much actual crime scene work they did. So far as we know, there were no such labs in this country. In 1910, the city of Lyon, France, agreed to sponsor the first police crime lab in the world. There would be nothing like it in the United States until the mid-twenties. So May's "full-service" lab was a decade ahead of its time in this country.

However, May eventually "worked himself out of a job." Police and justice departments gained access to public labs and no longer needed private facilities like his. Still, in July 1965, newspapers all over the country picked up a death notice that noted his "innovations in crime detection." But as the years passed, memories of Luke May's place in the history of forensic science began to fade. After awhile, only his descendants and a few with special interest in the field knew his name.

Around 1979, his daughter, Patricia Helen (May) Reid, recorded her childhood memories in a brief journal. She worshipped her father and thought about creating a longer memoir about him. Sadly, that never happened. Still, the journal proved to be a valuable resource for this project. The "baton" passed next to May's granddaughter, Mindi Reid. Ms. Reid cherishes fond childhood memories of her grandfather's gentle humor and deep urge to teach. Along with her mother's journal, she has a vast collection of newspaper and magazine clippings about her grandfather. She has produced two published articles about him.

Mindi was kind enough to authorize my access to the Luke S. May Papers held at the University of Washington. Here, I must give kudos to the staff at the UW Special Collections Reading Room. When I made an extended visit there, they worked diligently to haul boxes—there are sixty-five of them—from offsite storage for me. I recorded more than a thousand images of case log sheets, letters, reports, newspaper clippings, and photographs. To go with all that, I have collected more than eighteen hundred clippings myself.

Reid introduced me to Mr. Jan Beck, a retired Questioned Documents examiner. He too has produced an article about May, which was published in the *Journal of Forensic Sciences*. Although Beck never met Luke May, he considers himself a disciple of May's. He focused his interest on the technical side of May's career. We have had many valuable conversations about May's work, and Mr. Beck critiqued the entire first draft. Mindi also put me in touch with her cousin, Terrence May. Terrence and Luke May had a common ancestor in Timothy Franklin May II: Luke's grandfather, Terrence's great-great-grandfather. Terrence has done and continues to do much genealogical research on his family. My genealogical research on the Mays has focused more on Luke May's direct line, but the two of us have shared a number of ideas and "finds" along the way. I myself rather "came in a side door" to the topic. May lived in Pocatello, Idaho, for only about five years. But in that brief span, he earned a place in the four-volume *History of Idaho* edited by James Henry Hawley. I read May's short biography there and decided to do an article about him for my Idaho history blog. More research uncovered the significant role Luke May played in the development of forensic science. I was, in fact, amazed that no one had done a complete biography of the man . . . hence, this book.

Here, as usual, I must credit my wife, Caroline. She encouraged me to pursue this project and waited patiently in the motel with our two miniature schnauzers while I spent days in Special Collections. Plus, she handled more than her share of the day-to-day chores of life, allowing me to focus on my research and writing. I cannot thank her enough.

I have built the story around May's cases because he worked almost obsessively hard at his profession until just months before his death at age seventy-two. Yet along the way he did make some time for a life outside of work. That included hunting, fishing, boating, raising horses, and training a succession of beloved pet dogs. He also endeared himself to his daughter and then granddaughter. Moreover, he made friends who sent him warm, chatty letters long after they had worked with him regularly or had seen him face-to-face.

Sometimes I want you to feel like you're looking over the shoulders of the participants. These events I have written as "you are there" scenes. In these scenes, I never make up actions or dialogue. I use only material that was recorded by a participant or witness. Settings—physical layout, weather conditions, and so forth—are derived from photographs, maps, and records of the time.

Sadly, the Luke May Papers do not include much material not strictly related to his work. I have made do with the few of his letters that were preserved and what his friends and other contacts said about him. Not perfect—two wives preceded his final life mate—May fashioned a productive career with enough "play" to stay sane. He was one of the giants upon whose shoulders modern forensic scientists stand to see the future.

Scientific Detection

He bowed in perfunctory fashion as Holmes mentioned my name, and then with a masterful air of possession he drew a chair up to my companion and seated himself with his bony knees almost touching him.

"Let me say right here, Mr. Holmes," he began, "that money is nothing to me in this case. You can burn it if it's any use in lighting you to the truth. This woman is innocent and this woman has to be cleared, and it's up to you to do it. Name your figure!"

"My professional charges are upon a fixed scale," said Holmes coldly. "I do not vary them, save when I remit them altogether."[1]

Thus did writer Sir Arthur Conan Doyle open the meeting between his great fictional sleuth Sherlock Holmes and a new client, J. Neil Gibson. Gibson's wife has been shot to death. Police have leveled murder charges at the beautiful governess living in the household. The plot shows many of the key aspects of a standard Holmes case. In turn, those would be typical features of a Luke May investigation.

Holmes began his study with a general overview of the episode. The police had the key facts. A gamekeeper found the wife, Maria, sprawled at one end of Thor Bridge, dead from a gunshot to the head. They found no weapon beside the body. Maria's hand clutched a note, signed "G. Dunbar," that said, "I will be at Thor Bridge at nine o'clock." Grace Dunbar was the name of the governess.[2] The bridge was located almost a half mile from the manor house. It spanned the narrowest part of a long pond.

Holmes then reviewed the personalities involved. The characters would become stereotypes in British detective fiction. They were not, however, when Sir Arthur used them a century ago. Neil Gibson, the husband, was a hard-charging American millionaire. Five years earlier, he had moved to England and bought a country estate. Observers respected his strength and business acumen but deplored his ruthless tactics. Maria was the hot-blooded Latin beauty he married as a youthful gold miner. She was loving and passionate but "had nothing—absolutely nothing—in common" with her mature husband. Dunbar was the pure young lady "with a noble figure and commanding presence."[3]

Holmes carefully explored the relations among these three. The husband had long since fallen out of love with Maria. She, however, remained fervently devoted to him. Gibson admitted that he was strongly attracted to Dunbar. He told Holmes, "All my life I've been a man that reached out his hand for what he wanted, and I never wanted anything more than the love and possession of that woman."[4]

He offered to make her his mistress, but she flatly refused. In fact, Dunbar remained in the household only because she had people dependent upon her and needed the job. She also felt that her presence nudged Neil toward his better nature. The millionaire agreed: "She found that I listened to what she said, and she believed she was serving the world by influencing my actions."[5]

However, key clues strongly implicated Dunbar as a murderess. That clearly included the note clutched in Maria's hand. A motive was obvious. Worse yet, police found a once-fired pistol of the right caliber buried in Dunbar's wardrobe. Yet Holmes questioned the psychology of that. Why would even the most inept killer hide the likely murder weapon where it was sure to be found?

Holmes and Watson then met with the local police sergeant, who had been called to the scene right after the body was found. The officer admitted that he was in over his head and needed help.

They went together to examine the death scene. There was not much to see, aside from a stone the sergeant had placed to mark where the body had been. The hard ground showed no footprints or signs of a struggle. The fatal shot had been fired at close range and hit just behind Maria's right temple. Holmes studied the scene, "his quick gray eyes darting their questioning glances in every direction." A white scar in the dull gray of the bridge parapet caught his attention. Scrutiny with his pocket lens showed it to be a fresh chip in the hard stone. Being "at least fifteen feet from the body," the mark had no obvious link to the tragedy.[6]

Holmes and Watson next interviewed Dunbar. That revealed much. Maria, in fact, had set up the meeting at Thor Bridge. When they met, she revealed her bitter hatred for the governess. Dunbar had fled in horror from a raging torrent of vitriolic curses. Holmes learned more from the governess and then fell into his famous deductive pose, trying to fit the pieces into a coherent picture. Then he sprang into action.

"Come, Watson, come!" he cried.

They hurried back to Thor Bridge. There, Holmes borrowed Watson's revolver and tied a length of cord to the handle. On the other end, he tied a large stone. He hung the weight over the edge of the bridge and walked to where Maria's body had been found. Finally, Holmes lifted the revolver high beside his head. When he let go, the weight of the stone yanked the weapon against the parapet and then on over the edge. The impact left a mark just like the one already there. A grappling hook would easily retrieve both Watson's revolver and the death weapon from the pond.

Maria, despairing of ever regaining her husband's affection, had shot herself. The event had been cunningly staged to implicate Dunbar as a murderess. Maria had even planted a matched pistol in the wardrobe. Had Holmes failed to solve the puzzle, the wife might have dragged the governess down with her.

Sir Arthur published this story, "The Problem of Thor Bridge," in *The Strand* magazine in 1921. His narrative provides a protocol for "scientific crime detection." That is, the detective first collects information and evidence, anything that might relate to the case. He, or she, then analyzes the situation to figure out what probably happened. Finally, where it makes sense, the investigator tests the validity of the hypothesis. At each step, he or she uses applicable scientific tools to enhance the process.

Naturally, we must allow for dramatic license. For a real case, the cycle may be repeated several times, and some lines of inquiry won't go anywhere. Still, Conan Doyle's story shows the basic model used by Luke S. May to investigate actual cases. This book will frame May's life story through a selection of his cases because, for better or for worse, his cases *were* his life.

To start our chronicle, let's leap forward about a decade in time, deep into the Prohibition era in the United States. Span an ocean and a continent to Hoodsport, Washington, a rustic hamlet about thirty miles northwest of Olympia. It is located on the Hood Canal, a natural waterway, or fjord. The canal runs some fifty miles from its entrance on upper Puget Sound deep into Washington State. In 1930, smugglers often ran bootleg liquor from Canada down the channel. And moonshine produced by illegal stills was something of a "cottage industry" in and around Hoodsport.

Sunday morning, November 23. Harry Markland tramped along a side road about a quarter mile off the main highway. He carried a Winchester model 1895 rifle, the U.S. Army version chambered for a .30-06 cartridge. He and a friend, George "Curly" Simmons, had arranged to go deer hunting together. But Curly had not arrived at the expected rendezvous.

Rounding a slight bend, Harry saw a car parked on the road. As he drew closer, he realized the Ford Model A roadster belonged to Simmons. Perhaps Curly had misunderstood the plan. Markland walked up beside the vehicle and glanced inside. He was shocked to find his buddy slumped behind the wheel, dead. Curly's overcoat had a large, ragged tear on the front, stained with blood. His rifle, also a .30-caliber army version, lay across the body's lap. Markland rushed to inform the Mason County sheriff.

As in the fictional case, officers did a great deal of work to start with. They quickly noted that the fatal bullet had passed completely through the body. They also observed a bullet hole through the left door of the car. The rifle held a fired cartridge in its chamber.

The sheriff summoned two local physicians to examine the body. Neither had any experience in forensics work. Yet the situation seemed quite simple. The hole in the back was small and relatively neat, while the chest wound was larger and the flesh was mangled. That jibed with Curly's torn and bloody front clothing. "Everyone knew" that an exit wound could show more damage than the entry. Neither wound showed any powder burns or tattooing.

The doctors conclude that George has been shot in the back from outside the car, with a soft-nosed slug. The weapon found in the car contained hard-nosed bullets. The *Daily Olympian* noted that County Attorney Joseph W. Graham "believed the slaying was either a cold-blooded murder or else a hunting accident in which the killer attempted to avoid responsibility by making it appear the victim had committed suicide."[7]

A hunting accident seemed plausible, since authorities knew of no obvious motive for murder. Still, heavy forests clogged the rugged western shore of Hood Canal. These could provide cover for an uncountable number of illegal stills. And moonshiners sometimes did resort to violence to hide their equipment. Deputies questioned everyone living within five miles of the shooting scene but found not even a hint of trouble.

Simmons was a relative newcomer to the area. He and Markland both worked on a construction project for the City of Tacoma electric company. Curly, twenty-three years old and boyishly handsome, had been popular and well-liked in the community of company employees. His two brothers insisted that he had no enemies. As for suicide, they knew of no personal or financial problems that might have been bothering him. Searchers did find a cryptic note near the car, signed by Curly, that said, "I will pay for it if Bill don't."[8]

The demand for answers mounted. Officials began to hear hints that Curly might have been *too* popular in one particular instance. Early on Saturday evening, Curly had gone to a meeting about a twenty-minute drive from Hoodsport. He then returned to attend a party at a friend's house. There, the guests included Harry Markland and his pretty wife, Effie. Curly, who seemed "gay and carefree," had danced several times with Effie.[9] This was apparently not unusual.

Now the rumor mill conjured up notions of a love triangle among the three. After all, she was only twenty years old, having married Harry—seventeen years her senior—as a child bride of fifteen. Jealousy always worked as a motive. And how convenient that Markland had been the one to find the body. Officers already had Harry in jail as a material witness and stepped up their interrogation. He vehemently denied any problem with Simmons. Curly was one of his best friends, he said. Harry did say that his rifle had been loaded with soft-nosed ammunition. This "admission" only convinced interrogators that they were on the right track.

With a prime suspect who denied culpability, authorities needed proof beyond rumors and innuendo. Deputies searched again and again around the death scene. At last, they found what they believed to be bullet fragments, which might somehow be connected to the shooting. No trace of a bullet had been found inside the car. However, because of the medical opinion, they clung to the notion that the shot came from outside. The body had been sent to a facility equipped with an X-ray machine to see if bullet fragments remained inside.

Finally, locals asked for help from Captain John S. Strickland of the Tacoma police department. Strickland, in turn, knew of Luke May's expertise. He called on May to compare the cryptic note to other samples of Curly's handwriting. The wording did vaguely support a suicide scenario. He also reviewed the other evidence with May. Then they studied the death car. May later wrote that their proper attitude was to "dismiss from our minds everything that had been related to us about the case, including the opinions of the two physicians."[10]

They saw right away that the rifle shot had originated inside the vehicle. May and the captain removed the upholstery for testing. They also sampled inside and around the bullet hole in the door. The presence of blood in those samples verified that the slug had passed through flesh *before* puncturing the metal. This bolstered the suicide theory. But how to make sense of the torn clothing on the front of the body? A jacketed slug should have punched a neat hole. Also, they saw no obvious powder burns, which one would expect from a close-range shot. As May said, "It all seemed very confusing."[11]

As the data piled up, May surely paused at some point to reflect on what it all meant. Like Sherlock Holmes, he would have reviewed the evidence and tried to visualize how all the pieces fit together. From that, he could deduce what other clues might exist. Time to test the theory that Simmons had shot himself. May read *everything* that could apply to his work. Military researchers had been studying what they called "wound ballistics" for more than a half century. Still, May's exercise might have been a first for a civilian case. He designed a test using Curly's rifle and ammunition, plus similar clothing

Figure 1.1.   Death Car of George "Curly" Simmons. *Source*: **May-Reid Records.**

on a simulated human torso. In the key trial, May pressed the muzzle right against the target.

When the rifle fired, most of the powder residue and other debris drove deep into the wound, following the slug. However, the simulated body could not contain the blast of expanding gases. Those blew back, shredding pseudo-flesh and tearing the cloth on the entrance side. This dramatic result virtually duplicated the actual damage observed. Later, May and Strickland had a deputy similar in size and build to Simmons stage the setup. That showed clearly how Curly would have held the rifle against his chest and fired it with his thumb.

May always seemed to get as much, if not more, satisfaction from using his approach to free an innocent suspect as he did from convicting a guilty crook. Of course, more than half of May's cases involved private clients, not law enforcement. Most of those, and even some of the criminal cases, remained confidential. Thus, key details were not retained in the Luke S. May Papers, noted in the introduction as being stored at the University of

Washington. Files in the Luke May Papers range from one-page log sheets to thick stacks of reports, photographs, and other materials.

May's most active stretch occurred from about 1920, when his reputation blossomed, until his fame peaked shortly before the U.S. entry into World War II. During that period, his firm logged, on average, one or two new cases *every week*. Those included about one death case every month. In his entire career, he handled more than twenty-two hundred cases. (The Cases Overview Appendix provides a summary of what we know about May's career workload.)

May's case files focus mostly on the evidence. Only a few provide context for the overall episode. Thus, for most of them, we must link the data to other published accounts. One such publication was May's own book, *Crime's Nemesis*, released in 1936. Intended to explain scientific criminology to a popular audience, the book used many of his cases as examples. Beyond that, we must look to magazines and the larger newspapers. Fortunately, I found accounts of nearly 330 of his cases (including more than two hundred murders, suicides, and accidental deaths) in those media. From these, I have selected the most interesting and important cases to tell the Luke May story.

Because of his scientific approach, some articles chose to call May "America's Sherlock Holmes." That was certainly justified from a technical point of view. However, May almost never had the luxury of working on just one case at a time, the norm in fictional detective stories like the Holmes series. During his heyday, May always had five to eight case files open at the same time. His career was more akin to what modern publishing calls a "police procedural" story. (Fittingly, over the years, numerous jurisdictions granted May deputy sheriff status.)

On criminal cases, he tried to view the crime scene himself and collect evidence. For complex events, that might take several days. Meanwhile, work on other cases would proceed: agents interviewing witnesses and technicians running routine assessments. Other personnel might be logging and storing evidence submitted by law officers for yet more cases. However, May kept his staff as small as possible to limit costs, so some tasks had to wait until he returned to his office.

Back at headquarters, May would review the backlog of new and partially analyzed evidence. When necessary, he ran complex or specialized test methods himself. Then, with observations and data in hand, he would craft a report explaining the analyses that had been run, and what—in his professional opinion—the results meant. Through all this, the demand for quick action was intense and relentless, especially for criminal cases. In due course, May might need to testify at an inquest or in court. Especially after his reputation soared, attorneys wanted May to appear himself, rather than sending an agent. Thus, during his career, May spent hundreds of hours on the witness stand (and many more hours waiting to be called).

The rapid pace and the legal ramifications made May's technical operation quite different from a normal academic or industrial research lab. No written standards existed for forensic methods, but May knew he might be required, in court and under oath, to defend his results. And the opposition could hire their own experts to dispute his findings. Thus, May depended upon methods he had verified for himself, with perhaps small adaptations for a specific situation. Seldom, if ever, would he have had time to develop and prove a completely new approach for an active case. His results and testimony would simply reflect a higher level of uncertainty if a technique proved inadequate.

But May was not one to be satisfied with deficient methods. Somehow, he made time to improve techniques that had fallen short and to verify them for possible future use. That, by the way, is absolutely typical of the kind of "service" lab that May had. Research is driven mostly by problems with the routine methods. Similarly, May would have tested and, when necessary, improved techniques he learned about in his extensive self-education.

We know that May exchanged ideas with several forensic specialists and at least one generalist like himself. All, of course, had an interest in improving their methods. In the process, they sought answers to a question that must have plagued even the earliest human tribes: What's the best way to track down people who commit crimes but leave no eye witnesses? Various civilizations rose to power around the world. Yet over those millennia, no record of a systematic approach to what we call criminology or criminalistics surfaced.

Finally, around 1248 AD, a Chinese judge published the treatise *Hsi Duan Yu* (The Washing Away of Wrongs). The title referred to the prevention or correction of judicial errors. The author felt a wrongful conviction was as bad as letting someone get away with a crime, which we tend to think of as a modern concept. The writer combined his own work as a crime scene investigator with prior accounts. The text urged coroners to be observant and painstaking in examining victims. Other chapters discussed patterns of *rigor mortis* and much more. Early on, the treatise's lessons spread to nearby countries. So far as we know, it was not translated into English until 1855.

Yet even when they possessed this knowledge, detectives had to use it correctly. And that would never change. Luke May said, "The human factors of observation, logical deductions and knowledge of men are still the groundwork of criminology."[12]

But for more than five hundred years after *Hsi Duan Yu*, observers had to depend mostly upon their unaided senses. Worse yet, some of their practices were downright dangerous. Tasting an unknown substance—a common alchemical test—is generally a bad idea and can be fatal. Matters began to change after the scientific and industrial revolution in the eighteenth century. The new methods were first called upon to detect poisoners.

Poison has been a weapon of politics, inheritance, and hatred as far back as recorded history and surely before. By the late Renaissance period, poisoning had been raised to an art. The most skilled masters claimed to offer customers specific forms of death for the victim. The end could be quick and peaceful for a relative who was simply in the way, or slow and painful for a despised enemy. Medical practice of the time, such as it was, really had no way to tell for sure that someone had been poisoned. Practitioners had to rely mostly on symptoms observed as the person died. These often mimicked one of the many ways that sufferers perished from natural causes.

Spaniard Matthieu Orfila made the first systematic study of the various poisons in common use. Orfila had moved to Paris in 1807 to study medicine and pharmacy. He received his degree after four years and later became a professor at the University of Paris. In 1814, Orfila published his results as a *Traité des poisons* (Treatise on Poisons). The book became hugely popular and earned Orfila the title of "The Father of Toxicology."

The text gave key symptoms known for each poison. When possible, it described changes in the body that might be seen during an autopsy. At the time, chemists could not directly measure poisons or their residues in the body. That would soon change, but the observer had to be both trained and motivated. Many years later, May described a poisoning where neither criteria was met. He declared that the case "might have been less of a murder mystery if a country coroner had not failed in his duty."[13]

In Orfila's time, the most popular poison was arsenic, in its oxide form. The material was easy to slip into foods. Better yet, its symptoms are much like those for many deadly intestinal disorders. Early in the century, chemists sought better ways to detect arsenic in the body of someone who might have been poisoned. This work culminated in the famous "Marsh Test," devised by the Scots chemist James Marsh in 1836. Highly sensitive, a positive test leaves a silvery-black mirror on a ceramic or glass surface. That result provides a long-lasting and visually dramatic bit of proof to show a jury. The frequency of probable arsenic poisonings reportedly declined sharply when the Marsh Test came into common usage.

About the time of Marsh's work, a landmark inquiry involving firearms took place in London. The case might not have been *the* first, but it's the first for which we have reasonable records. Even at that, accounts are vague on certain details. The detective was one Henry Goddard, a Bow Street runner. The runners were a police force supported by a combination of public and private funding.

A homeowner had been shot and killed, purportedly by a burglar. An autopsy recovered the fatal ball and scraps of paper wadding. Goddard noticed that the missile had a visible flaw. Then he found a ball mold among the effects of a household servant (the butler, in some accounts). A defect in the mold looked just like the flaw in the deadly slug. Moreover, he discovered paper that matched the wadding found during the autopsy. Confronted with these physical traces of his guilt, the servant confessed.

Despite this early start, the use of firearms evidence evolved slowly. More than forty years would pass before people began to look beyond gross differences in bullet type. Now vastly improved, such assessments are still a vital tool for the crime investigator. Also, as suggested by the Simmons suicide case, Luke May would become one of its most skillful practitioners.

London was also the scene of a notorious forgery case in 1843–1844. That brought handwriting analysis into play with what we now call a Questioned Documents (QD) examination. This field involves the detection of forged wills, deeds, checks, and other documents. Like the study of poisons, document assessment has ancient roots. However, the pursuit of rigorous methods is of relatively more recent vintage. Justice officials needed experts because, in 1634, the English Parliament made forgery a capital offense. Over roughly the next two centuries, it is estimated that English courts sent well over a thousand convicted forgers to the gallows.

The 1843 documents case concerned the purported will of spinster Anne Slack. She lived on income from a bequest of long-term bonds held in a Bank

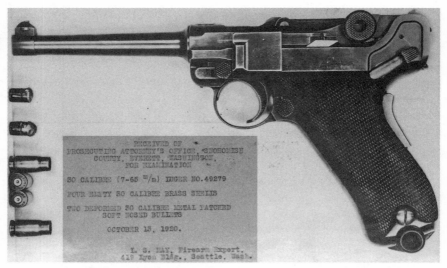

Figure 1.2.   Firearms Evidence for May Case, 1924. *Source:* **May-Reid Records.**

of England account. Her earnings of about £200 per year were double those of what a fairly well-paid clerk might make at that time. With some surplus to invest, in 1843 she instructed her broker to make a purchase of more bonds. Imagine his surprise to learn that the bank had marked her account with a "deceased" notation. The subsequent inquiry exposed the infamous "Will Forgeries."

A small gang of clever men obtained a list of dormant—long inactive—accounts from a clerk at the bank. (Whether the clerk was blackmailed or took an active part was never clearly determined.) They then forged wills giving the money in the dormant accounts to gang members. Their forgeries were apparently only so-so. However, the chance of them being challenged was minimal because many of the holders actually were deceased. In any case, the gang supported each will with a death certificate that seemed legitimate. At that time in England, one obtained death certificates from the "Doctors' Commons," an association of doctoral-degreed lawyers. The petitioner only needed to make a verbal statement. No supporting documentation was required.

Anne Slack was their key mistake. The spinster had *two* accounts at the bank. Besides the one she lived on, there was another containing £3,500. For unknown reasons, Anne never learned about the second bequest. It therefore went dormant. As Luke May observed, "Events that occurred months or perhaps years prior to the crime, unknown to the criminal, may bring themselves into play."[14]

A lawyer representing a gang member presented the death certificate and fake will and collected £3,500 for his client. Quite naturally, the bank also marked the active Anne Slack account with the deceased tag. Parties to the fraud were soon tracked down and jailed. After a fevered trial, three culprits were sentenced to transportation (to Australia, two for life). Two others spent two years at hard labor. In this, the crooks could consider themselves lucky. In 1837, Parliament had finally rescinded the law that decreed the death penalty for forgery of a will.

In this case, the quality of the forged signature was a relatively minor issue. More commonly, however, cases turned on the authenticity of the handwriting and especially the signature. Thus, around the middle of the century, specialists began to emerge in the field.

Through all this, scientists, engineers, and inventors produced a vast range of groundbreaking discoveries. They ranged from items as far-reaching as the steam engine to the lowly safety pin. That heady success inspired some to apply the new tools of science to understand crime and criminals. Italian Cesare Lombroso spent years studying deviant behavior and even had a stint as director of an insane asylum. In 1876, he became a professor at the University of Turin. That same year, he published the first edition of his *L'uomo*

Delinquente (The Criminal Man). The text and its later revisions were hugely influential.

Initially, Lombroso asserted that most criminals were born that way, being throwbacks to primitive savages. He also thought they shared observable physical traits. That was clearly wrong, and those notions were eventually discredited. Still, Luke May said, "His great contribution to this science was in drawing attention to the possibilities for studying the criminal class."[15] That is, Lombroso's work led criminologists to pay more attention to the psychology and motivation of the lawbreakers themselves.

Of course, police departments focused on the practical matter of catching crooks. Over time, they sensed that many criminals, perhaps even most, were repeat offenders. However, unless a police officer or judge happened to know a suspect, the person need only use an alias to escape notice. Alphonse Bertillon, a records clerk for the Paris police, devised an answer. For each criminal, he measured a specific set of bodily dimensions. These included the head length, size of the left foot, and about eight more. (The exact number seemed to vary over time.) This was the first known use of anthropometry—human measurement—in police work. Bertillon also tallied markings such as scars and tattoos, and recorded front- and side-view photographs.

The measurements and these other items were recorded on a card. Clerks then filed the cards according to a complex system of cross indexes. A new set of numbers for the same individual should track through the system to arrive at the same file location. A quick glance at the photos would reveal a previous offender, even if he or she used a new name. Thus, in 1884, Bertillon extracted the identities of more than two hundred repeat offenders from his files.

Bertillon also devised equipment and methods to systematically photograph a crime scene. We take this for granted now, but this was a major advance at the time. Those early cameras were large and awkward, and only a skilled operator could obtain useful images. Nor were those Bertillon's only contributions to the field. Luke May asserted: "Many of Bertillon's exploits in the scientific investigation of crime outrival those of Sherlock Holmes."[16]

The lowly clerk-turned-criminologist became an international celebrity, and his system was widely adopted. His type of anthropometry, however, enjoyed only a brief period of ascendancy. The measurements are hard to make, change with age, and do not uniquely identify an individual. Anthropometry soon gave way to fingerprints, which are unique and much easier to record. Moreover, a perpetrator may leave fingerprints as a clue at the scene of the crime. That being said, we retain a legacy of Bertillon's system in our use of mug shots and records of telltale physical marks.

Fingerprints were used at least as far back as ancient Babylon. They are specifically documented in Chinese writings from more than two thousand years ago. They came into greater use in China after the invention of paper there. It is unclear when the practice appeared in India. But that was almost certainly before European ships began arriving there around 1500 AD. Records suggest that only the highest Indian castes used them, however. Historians are unsure if these early users considered fingerprints unique.

European anatomists seem to have begun studying skin patterns on their own. Some may have heard of the Asian usage, but that cannot be verified. In any case, the study of hand and footprints was well established in Europe by about 1700. After centuries of collecting data, scientists accepted that such prints are unique to an individual.

However, for many years, only medical people showed much interest in the field. That changed in the latter half of the nineteenth century. Sir William James Herschel, a colonial administrator in India, is generally credited as the first European to use fingerprints as a means of identification. As Luke May wrote, "Even before the criminologist made use of the fingerprint, Herschel himself had used it for seventeen years in . . . India."[17]

The English scientist Sir Francis Galton included fingerprints as part of his research on human physiology and heredity. To organize his results, he identified features that could be used to classify most fingerprints—mainly loops, whorls, and arches. His book, *Finger Prints,* published in 1892, is considered the first comprehensive text in the field. Galton's results arrived at just the right time for Juan Vucetich, an officer with the Argentinian police. Vucetich secured a murder conviction that is thought to be a first using fingerprint evidence.

Sir Edward Richard Henry made the next key advance. As Inspector-General of Police in Bengal, he was quite familiar with the use of fingerprints. He exchanged ideas with Galton and then led the development of a system to classify fingerprints by their key features. With that, officials could file prints for later search and identification. Thus, by the 1890s, fingerprints were becoming an accepted tool for police work.

During this same period, *The Strand* magazine began publishing short stories that featured Sherlock Holmes. Arthur Conan Doyle first used the Holmes character in a novel, *A Study in Scarlet,* published in 1887. It was surely not happenstance that he created his character when and how he did. He earned his MD degree from the University of Edinburgh in 1885. By then, major advances in science and technology had transformed life in Western Europe and North America and, to a lesser extent, in other parts of the world.

Doyle was entranced by science. He decided to use his literary leanings to pursue those interests. He published a second Holmes novel, *The Sign of the Four,* in 1890. The books were not particularly successful at first. Then the short stories in *The Strand* introduced Holmes to a wider audience. That readership was equally enchanted by the wonders of science. The brilliant and enigmatic Holmes, with Watson as narrator, led them through that new world. The mysteries became wildly popular, and their influence was profound. Luke May himself said, "I believe the writings of Conan Doyle have done more than any other one thing to stimulate active interest in the scientific and analytical investigation of crime."[18]

In 1893, Austrian Hans Gross published what some call the founding document of criminology. The book was *Criminal Investigation: A Practical Handbook for Magistrates, Police Officers and Lawyers*. Gross was a magistrate and professor of criminal law. He urged officers to use the tools of science to collect and assess physical evidence. Beyond that, he wanted to study criminal psychology scientifically. Considered the "Father of Criminalistics," he later expanded his approach in several highly influential books.

Other fields of crime work began to come to fruition during this period. That included questioned documents examination. Now, in addition to direct handwriting assessment, examiners analyzed the ink and paper used in a document. The same year that Gross's *Handbook* came out, a New Jersey court accepted testimony based on the unique features of a typewriter. The field would flourish, and more than half of Luke May's cases would involve questioned documents.

Another field that had made great strides was what we now call "forensic serology," the study of blood and other bodily fluids. Aside from a body, the most common sign after a crime of violence is blood. Not only does blood appear where the assault occurred, but often the attacker ends up spattered with it. Luke May devoted two chapters of *Crime's Nemesis* to the topic, one of which he titled "Cursed by Blood." In his experience, May said, "Truly the curse of blood is on every murderer."[19]

But first, the investigator must prove that a stain is really blood. Toxicology researcher Matthieu Orfila published a test for blood in 1827. He mentioned work by previous researchers, but his was the first method that became widely known. However, there were doubts about the specificity of his test. Finally, in 1853, Polish physician Ludwig Teichmann found a way to reliably identify blood. Unfortunately, the test could not tell the difference between human and animal blood.

Almost a half century passed before Paul Uhlenhuth, a German bacteriologist, solved that problem. In 1901, he described a version of the so-called precipitin test that could specifically identify human blood. Uhlenhuth's test was a major breakthrough. Still, criminologists wondered if there was more they could learn from such a ubiquitous clue. Karl Landsteiner, a medical researcher at the University of Vienna, gave the world the beginnings of an answer. Also in 1901, he published results that defined the A-B-O human blood groups. However, many years would pass before his lab results could be adapted for forensic cases.

The year before Landsteiner's publication, a physician in the United States published a landmark article about firearms identification. Dr. Albert L. Hall first read the paper to a medical conference in Syracuse, New York. The text was then published in the *Buffalo Medical Journal* as "The Missile and the Weapon."[20]

One should first look for foreign matter clinging to the surface of the bullet, he said. That might include blood, fabric, or even grains of unburned powder. Next, every marking on the missile itself must be assessed. That is, "Those originally present and due to manufacture, should be differentiated from those produced by bruising, as well as those caused by the rifling of the weapon."[21] Hall's paper was not widely distributed, but the breadth of his treatment indicated how far the field had come. Within a couple years, courts began to accept expert testimony about rifling marks and test fired bullets.

Criminology continued to advance in other areas. A new leader at Scotland Yard replaced anthropometry with fingerprint records. As noted above, they did retain other features of the Bertillon system. About the same time, fingerprints were adopted in the United States. Thus, around the dawn of the twentieth century, detectives had the beginnings of a tool kit for scientific crime investigation. Luke S. May was one of the pioneers who used and improved those resources.

A Criminologist Is Born

Luke Sylvester May was born December 2, 1892, in Hall County, Nebraska, on a homestead located roughly twenty miles southwest of Grand Island. His parents were William Patrick and Mary (Engelmann) May. He was surely delivered at home, since the area had no general hospital. The nearest settlement was the village of Prosser. The tiny town is in Adams County, less than a mile from the Hall County line. Country doctors from Hastings, the Adams County seat, made regular trips through the area. They could ride the train to Prosser, then hire a buggy and make their rounds. (More than eight years would pass before an Adams County resident owned an automobile, a steam car.)

Family memories recall no particular drama about the birth, aside from the usual risk to mother and infant. Even the weather cooperated, although locals were concerned because they were about 15 percent low on precipitation. For this was grain country, mainly corn and wheat, and almost none of the land was irrigated. Luke was born on a clear and mild day, with light breezes and temperatures in the high thirties, somewhat above normal. So there were no portents at the time to suggest that this newborn would become one of the most effective, and famous, detectives and criminology teachers of his day. Nor did his lineage offer any prophecy of such eminence. For many generations back, his forebears had been farmers and manual workers.

The first of May's ancestors to come to the New World arrived in 1825. They emigrated from Ireland to Canada with an expedition financed, oddly enough, by the British government. Many Irish had been thrown upon hard times by a combination of forces: failed crops, splintering of family holdings, and conditions imposed by absentee landlords. Fearing unrest, the British government decided to relocate some of the poorest to Canada, where voluntary immigration rates had been disappointing.

Canadian-born Peter Robinson, a veteran of the War of 1812, was selected to organize the effort. After a small initial effort, Robinson chartered nine ships in 1825 to transport more than two thousand immigrants across. He aimed to settle them in a sparsely populated area called Scott's Plain, about sixty-five miles northeast of Toronto. By Herculean efforts, Robinson got the newcomers to their settlement locations before winter set in. He later wrote, "The first party I ascended the river with consisted of twenty men of the country, hired as axe-men, and thirty of the healthiest of the settlers; not one of these men escaped the ague and fever, and two died."[1]

The immigrants barely had enough time to construct rough cabins before the first snow flew. A few years later, the region's name was changed to Peterborough County in Robinson's honor. Luke's great-grandfather and great-grandmother, on his grandmother's side, were among the passengers listed on different ships of the 1825 expedition. Unfortunately a fire destroyed the local Roman Catholic Church and all its early records, so we don't know exactly when they were married. Luke's grandmother, Ellen Mahoney, was born about a decade after the immigrants settled in the area.

However, the relocation program proved too costly and was not repeated. Yet the problems in Ireland continued and many people yearned to leave for something better. Hope for a few came in 1831 when the English Parliament created a program meant for military pensioners. To get them off the pension roles, the government offered them a lump sum and a land grant in Canada. Billed as an economy measure, the consequences were mostly disastrous. Few such pensioners had the temperament or skills to settle in what was largely wilderness. Most had no concept of how to handle money. In fact, many drank up their allotment and never even went to Canada. Complaints about retired soldiers thrown on the poor rolls led to termination of the program after two years.

But as it happened, Luke's great-grandfather, Timothy Franklin May was one of those who qualified for the offer. He had served for a time in the Sligo Militia, raised in County Sligo, Ireland. Fortunately, about four years before the pensioner program began, the government had made key legal changes that allowed cheaper fares for passengers on trans-Atlantic ships. Thus, while the program was active, Timothy moved his family to Peterborough County. Included in the group was Luke's grandfather, Timothy May Jr., who would have been ten years old in 1836 (the year his future wife was supposedly born).

These settlers faced a daunting task. Unlike the Robinson contingent, they had to buy and transport their own tools and initial food supplies to their plots. Then, after felling enough trees to build a rough log cabin, settlers had to continue hacking productive fields out of the forest. Thus, in 1839 the provincial Lieutenant Governor asked the British government to help a long list of commuted pensioners, all of whom were poverty-stricken. Timothy May was among the names on that list. It took more than a year, but May did receive an additional grant of one hundred acres. Timothy Sr. and his wife were able to live out their lives in Peterborough.

In 1853, Timothy May Jr. married Ellen Mahoney at St. Joseph's Catholic Church in Douro, Peterborough County. Luke's father, William Patrick May, was born in November 1858. By the end of the American Civil War, the couple had four sons and two daughters. And that posed a problem, because the supply of good farmland around Peterborough was limited.

Hope for something better loomed to the south. In May 1862, President Abraham Lincoln signed into law the Homestead Act. Under the act, pioneers could claim 160 acres of public land. All they had to do was file on it, live there for five years, and make certain specified improvements. Filing and other fees cost just $18. The offer was open to U.S. citizens *and* to immigrants who formally declared their intention to become citizens. States with large expanses of public land touted the new law, taking out advertisements in the East and even in Europe.

During this period, Luke's grandfather moved his wife and their large brood to Brookfield, in Clinton County, Iowa. The township is about ten miles north of De Witt, Iowa, where there was a thriving Roman Catholic Church. By the time of the 1870 U.S. census, the family included five sons and three daughters, the last two children being born in Iowa. However, during the decade, the family began to drift westward. That included a spot north of Des Moines, Iowa, where another daughter was born. From there, the family continued on into Nebraska.

No family documents exist to tell us why they did not stay put. However, railway companies were trying to encourage settlement in Nebraska by extending branch lines all over the state. The town of Hastings came into existence as the junction for several railroads in 1872. After a stiff political fight with Juniata, six to eight miles west, it became the county seat in 1878.

Two years later, Luke's father, William, married Annie Mary Engelmann in Hastings. Annie was born in Luxembourg in 1862. Her father, Urbanus, had traveled alone to the United States that same year. He listed his occupation as blacksmith but took up farming in Illinois after he brought his family over. Some time after about 1874, they moved to Cottonwood Township, located roughly ten miles southwest of the Adams County seat. The ceremony for William and Annie took place in the Roman Catholic Church of St. Cecilia, which had been completed in Hastings the year before.

Luke's grandmother died in 1883, and the family began to scatter as the children reached their majorities. The Nebraska state census of 1885 found

Grandfather Timothy farming in Barada, a village about sixty miles south of Omaha. Only three of his children remained at home. William had also left Cottonwood Township, moving into Hastings. According to the census, he and Mary had two children: a daughter, Mary Evelyn; and son, Vincent. William's brother was boarding with them. They had both found work as blacksmiths.

Family history states that William was "quite a hell-bent-for-leather character" and often away from home.[2] He supposedly took part in the famous Oklahoma Land Rush on April 22, 1889, when "Sooners" became notorious. But William May's name does not appear among the land claimants for the Oklahoma rush. Still, he perhaps earned a stake as an itinerant carpenter during all the subsequent building activity. That would have allowed him to buy or rent property in the country north of Prosser, where Luke was born three years after the Rush. Luke was the fourth of William and Mary's children. Another sister had been born in 1885. Her given name was Margaret Lena, but the family always referred to her as "Maggie." Luke's years in Nebraska are recorded only in snippets of family memory. No one left a full diary or memoir for that period. We do know he had a fairly typical childhood for that time and place.

First and foremost, young Luke surely worked hard almost as soon as he could walk. Anyone who rhapsodized nostalgically about old-time country life either never lived it or had a remarkably selective memory. And during that era, farm families always had a vegetable garden. Produce that could be stored for long periods was crucial: onions, potatoes, carrots, pumpkins, and more. These went into a root cellar to be stretched through a long winter. Soon enough, the heavy garden work—hoeing and raking to prepare the ground and so on—would have probably been assigned to Luke. And he learned his lessons well. Many years later, his daughter said, "Daddie was a good vegetable gardener."[3]

Hunting and fishing were other sources of food. Thus, Luke learned to hunt and fish at an early age. Of course, settlement had drastically reduced the variety of game he could pursue. But deer could be found in the bottomlands. Also, a boy with a shotgun could bag doves, quail, prairie chickens (a kind of grouse), and other small game birds. But ammunition cost cash money, which forced the young hunter to place his shots carefully. Luke became an excellent marksman with both rifle and shotgun.

If he was like most boys, the family dog probably accompanied him on these forays. Luke had an abiding love of dogs and an amazing ability to train them to do clever and useful things. He distrusted cats, however. One he thought was friendly scratched him severely when he was a kid.

Oddly enough, besides these normal boy things, Luke also learned to sew from his mother and sisters. This was another lesson he learned well. His daughter later said he could "produce a very mean stitch both by hand and on the sewing machine."[4] She also said, "He often regaled me with descriptions of the masterful items of apparel his sisters whipped up in their younger days."

Had his father's venture into farming been a long-term success, Luke might possibly have taken up that occupation himself. But the 1890s proved to be a bad time to be a farmer in Nebraska. Off and on through the decade, the area suffered moderate to severe drought. The summer of 1894 proved especially bad. The *World-Herald* in Omaha published a long report on the damage with the headline "May Yield Half of a Crop."[5] The report first noted, "The week has been unprecedentedly hot and dry, with hot south winds, which have been very disastrous to all vegetation."

For Adams County, the paper said, "Corn destroyed by hot winds. Corn probably will not yield the seed planted in the spring."

Hall County was much the same: "Corn an entire failure, except a few fields along the Platte river. There will not be much grass large enough to cut."

To make matters worse, farm areas across the country were still reeling from the impact of the "Panic of '93," a severe financial recession. Hundreds of banks failed all over the country. With no one to lend them money against their future crops, farmers couldn't buy seed, much less pay their other expenses. By around 1898, the May family had moved into Shelton, a village about twenty miles northwest of Hastings. Shelton was primarily a grain shipping point, being a station on the main east-west rail line. Yet it was also the center for a noted horse breeding area, which might have encouraged May's later interest in raising horses himself. An early county history said, "Some of the finest stallions in the state are owned by Shelton parties and kept for breeding purposes."[6]

With a population of a bit over 800, Shelton had grain elevators, the usual stores, a local newspaper, two banks, and five churches. It even had a library. However, that institution had a very limited inventory of books, having only opened in 1896. The little town also had a long tradition of public schooling, starting in 1866. By around 1900, the school offered classes at all twelve grade levels.

Luke, who proved to be an avid student, took full advantage of the opportunity. During the census that year, the recorder noted that "Lukie" had attended school eight months during the past year. That was a month more than his sister Maggie. All of Luke's siblings were still at home at the time of the census. Census records strongly suggest that Grandpa Timothy was living in a Shelton boardinghouse not too far from William and his family.

Figure 2.1.   May Family, circa 1898. Luke center front. *Source*: May-Reid Records.

Two of Luke's uncles were widely scattered. However, another uncle and two married aunts now lived in Utah. That would soon be a factor in Luke's life.

People in Shelton and surrounding areas saw the usual ups and downs for an agricultural economy. Overall, the situation seemed favorable as the new century opened. The *World-Herald* bubbled with optimism, asserting that, "Nebraska's development in land values has only commenced. It is not unreasonable to predict a doubling of land values in Nebraska within the next twenty years."[7]

Of course, William May no longer operated a farm and had committed to carpentry and the construction business. It seems likely he used the home in Shelton as a base to find work in all that growth. In the meantime, what might have been a pivotal moment in Luke's life occurred. The *World-Herald* first trumpeted the event on June 29, 1902. An advertisement said the newspaper had "secured at large cost the exclusive right in this territory to Conan Doyle's new story, 'The Hound of the Baskervilles.' It is another adventure of Sherlock Holmes."[8]

The next day's issue provided more details under the headline "Sherlock Holmes at His Best."[9] Luke would have probably *heard* of Sherlock Holmes by this time. Newspapers often invoked the name when a policeman had done some particularly clever detective work. A reporter might also suggest that officials needed a Sherlock Holmes when they had an especially puzzling crime.

But it is highly improbable that Luke had actually read any of the Holmes stories. The family could not afford books, certainly not books of light fiction. Nor was the tiny Shelton library likely to have them. And a check of issues for those years turns up no prior mention of any newspaper in the state buying the rights to a Holmes work. Thus, this *World-Herald* serialization was most likely Luke's first exposure. A regional history makes it clear that Shelton was within the distribution area of the newspaper, and chapter 1 appeared on Sunday, July 13, 1902. The narrative continued to run through the September 28 issue.

Many fans consider *Baskervilles* to be the best of all the Holmes novels. Certainly, it had the elements to fire the imagination of a bright boy of nine going on ten. As usual, Holmes made brilliant deductions based on clues that others did not see or thought insignificant. Then the narrative added outdoor action in a memorable setting, physical danger, and a touch of horror. Moreover, Sir Arthur had long been a master of the cliffhanger. He ended chapter 2, "The Curse of the Baskervilles," with:

> Dr. Mortimer looked strangely at us for an instant, and his voice sank almost to a whisper. "Mr. Holmes, they were the footprints of a gigantic hound!"[10]

Of course, the editors who serialized the material also knew how to exploit that device. They chose a dramatic moment in the final chapter to end the segment published on September 21, 1902:

> With long bounds the huge black creature was leaping down the track, following hard upon the footsteps of our friend. So paralyzed were we by the apparition that we allowed him to pass before we had recovered our nerve. Then Holmes and I both fired together, and the creature gave a hideous howl, which showed that one at least had hit him. He did not pause, however, but bounded onward. Far away on the path we saw Sir Henry looking back, his face white in the moonlight, his hands raised in horror, glaring helplessly at the frightful thing which was hunting him down."
> (Concluded Next Week.)[11]

A week later, this final episode ended with a burst of physical action and a wrap-up. That was followed by "A Retrospection." In that, Holmes explained how he followed a chain of clues so they would be there on the dank, foggy moor to rescue Sir Henry from the hound of the Baskervilles. Of course, the notion that Luke experienced the narrative in this way is conjecture. Still, May left no doubt that Sir Arthur Conan Doyle's creation inspired him to take up his life's work.

As noted above, Luke's father had a brother and two married sisters in the Ogden-Salt Lake area at that time. Thus, he had surely heard about the building boom in Salt Lake City. In late 1902, a writer for the *Telegram* there noted, "The growth of Salt Lake during the past year has been unusually noticeable."[12]

That positive news was surely a factor in the many changes Luke would experience over the next year or so. It had already begun several months earlier when his oldest sister, Mary, married James E. Britcher, a young ex-soldier. Mary was pregnant with their first child when sister Maggie married David Thompson, who might have been a railroad worker. Family recollections do not say how or where either couple met.

In June 1903, James and Mary gave Luke a nephew, Theodore J. Britcher. David and Margaret—she always used her given name after her marriage—returned to David's home state of Missouri and, three years later, gave Luke a niece, Evelyn. Margaret would live out her life in Missouri.

That fall, the *Telegram* reported, "Building operations in the various portions of Salt Lake since January 1st of this year have exceeded by far those of any corresponding season in the history of the city."[13] And the boom would continue. The *Telegram*: "The outlook for 1905 is the best in the history of Salt Lake."[14]

During this furor, William May moved his family to the city. Having been through the chancy boom-and-bust farm cycle, Luke's father perhaps decided that Salt Lake City offered a more certain future. Luke later told interviewers he was eleven years old when they moved. That places the date probably sometime in early 1904.

A whole new world opened up for Luke in Utah. Where the Shelton library had a few hundred books, the Salt Lake City library had more than twenty-five thousand. The institution's budget included money to add twenty-five hundred volumes to its holdings each year. Moreover, in October 1905, the library moved into a fine new building, paid for by mining magnate John Q. Packard.

Soon enough, Luke began working for his father in the construction business. However, he also made time to check out books on topics that might be relevant to criminal investigation. That included not only the hard

Figure 2.2.   Downtown Salt Lake City, circa 1905. *Source*: Library of Congress.

sciences—physics, chemistry, biology, and so forth—but also psychology, sociology, history, and more (hitting topics related to crimes and criminology). As opportunities arose, he studied photomicrography, handwriting analysis, firearms identification, fingerprint technology, and other possible police techniques.

During his studies, he encountered the names of Cesare Lombroso and Hans Gross (both mentioned in chapter 1). By then, a couple dozen Lombroso articles had been translated into English and published in the United States. May found even more guidance in the *Criminal Investigation* handbook published by Hans Gross in 1893. Over the years, the text had gone through several editions, with translations into French, Danish, and other languages. May said that he had had a friend translate the German version for him. One hopes the translator got more than just a simple thank you. The original text spanned more than five hundred pages and discussed everything: maintaining the crime scene, evidence collection, interrogation of suspects, and much, much more.

With all his self-study, May was a busy fellow since he was working for his father and also taking classes. There must have been some disruption in his schooling, but an article in the *Salt Lake Tribune* for June 3, 1908, lists a "Luke S. May" among those receiving eighth-grade diplomas from the Jordan School District.[15]

After that, he squeezed in time to attend the Gordon Academy, a preparatory school founded by the Congregational Church. In early 1908, the *Telegram* noted how well the current term had gone: "Gordon Academy has just closed its first semester with the most promising outlook for a larger enrollment for the second."[16] Best of all, from May's perspective, "A large addition to the laboratories has facilitated the work in the sciences."

May attended the academy for at least two years but did not attain the equivalent of a high-school diploma. Clearly, however, his self-studies in relevant topics went far beyond a normal high school or college-preparatory curriculum. Later, May had to go undercover at a business school. He took advantage of the assignment to learn bookkeeping and other business subjects.

As it happens, 1908 saw a number of important milestones in criminology. In Europe, the British Home Office appointed Bernard Spilsbury (later, Sir Bernard) to be its chief pathologist. Son of an industrial chemist, Spilsbury attained a natural science degree from Oxford University in 1899. Spilsbury would dominate the field of scientific criminology in England for nearly forty years. Luke May almost certainly followed his career with great interest.

In this country, the Justice Department established yet another milestone. The U.S. Attorney General assembled a team of former Secret Service agents to handle cases that required a national level of jurisdiction. A new

Attorney General called the force the Bureau of Investigation, which eventually became the Federal Bureau of Investigation, the FBI. The unit soon ballooned from ten to more than three hundred agents.

Washington, DC, was also the site of an event involving one of the most famous American pioneers in criminology. That man was Albert S. Osborn, a questioned documents specialist from Rochester, New York. A native of Michigan, Osborn had gone to work as a penmanship instructor at the Rochester Business Institute in 1882. He was then about twenty-four years old. A series of major cases established his reputation as the best documents examiner in the country.

In April 1908, Osborn was called to testify before a U.S. House of Representatives committee investigating charges of influence peddling that George L. Lilley (Republican, Connecticut) had made against some of his colleagues. The resulting committee report said that Lilley had been "used" by a government contract bidder and, in several instances, had made deceptive statements to bolster his assertions. News reports said he escaped expulsion only because he was then the leading party candidate in the race for governor of Connecticut.

Two years after this case, Osborn published the book *Questioned Documents*. That text was considered *the* definitive reference in the field for generations of document examiners. Naturally, May himself acquired a copy of the book. Osborn would continue to lead his field for nearly forty years.

The scene for our significant events now shifts west to highlight a surprising fact. Even today, far more people live east of the Mississippi than there are west of Salt Lake City, Utah. In 1908, the ratio was more than eleven to one. Yet for the next half century, most of the well-known criminologists would be based in the far West.

One of them was Edward C. Crossman. In 1908, he placed several hunting articles in *Western Field* magazine and at least one in *Arms and the Man* (today's *American Rifleman*). A Midwesterner like Osborn, he had moved west from Iowa to California. Crossman was a notable marksman; and the articles initiated his long career as a writer and as a recognized authority on guns, ammunition, and shooting. He would also be one of Luke May's favorite writers and a good friend.

In the spring of 1908, the city of Oakland, California, obtained a Bertillon identification system. Besides equipment for mug shots and forms to keep track of identifying marks, it also had everything needed to record fingerprints. A few months later, the *Morning Republican* in Fresno reported, "the Bureau of Identification is in charge of Harry Caldwell, who is rapidly mastering the details of the several systems in use."[17] A native of Nebraska, born in 1872, Henry H. "Harry" Caldwell had joined the Oakland police force five years earlier. He moved up rapidly through the ranks and was assigned to the detective division. Caldwell remained in the Bureau of Identification until his retirement and did much to broaden and improve that subfield of criminology.

Unlike Caldwell and the other pioneers just mentioned, Edward O. Heinrich would become a generalist. Originally from Wisconsin, he lived in Tacoma, Washington, for nearly fifteen years before enrolling at the University of California at Berkeley. He graduated in 1908 with a bachelor's degree in chemistry, when he was twenty-seven years old. He then landed a job with the city of Tacoma. Heinrich also began to broaden his background in topics relevant to scientific crime detection. In many ways, Heinrich's career would parallel that of May's, and both would become highly successful.

A final 1908 milestone also took place in Berkeley, California. There, August "Gus" Vollmer initiated the first police school in this country. Born in New Orleans, Gus lost his father in 1884, when he was eight years old. Two relocations later, the family was living in Berkeley. Like May, Vollmer had no formal education beyond some vocational courses at the high-school level. After service in the Spanish-American War, he worked for a while as a mail carrier.

Voters elected Vollmer town marshal for Berkeley in 1905, and he continued as chief when the city of Berkeley was incorporated four years later. Ironically, given his own lack of schooling, Vollmer believed that police officers should be well educated. But, like Luke May, he also knew how hard it could be to gain that education by self-study alone. His police school began with a relatively limited set of classes but expanded over time. Chief Vollmer would introduce many innovations in police work and attain international renown.

Of course, in this milestone year, Luke May was still building the foundation for his own career in scientific criminology. On the personal side, his sister Mary (May) Britcher died April 25, 1909, in Salt Lake City. She and her son had rejoined the family three years earlier and then she divorced her husband in July 1907. After her death, Luke's parents raised Theodore.

As the end of the decade neared, May had made friends with officers at the local police station. He also became a spectator during court trials, where he could see how evidence was presented to a judge and jury. May would later tell interviewers that he considered himself a practicing detective by around 1909. Also, based on skills he soon exhibited, he must have set up an examination bench, a crude laboratory. There, he gained firsthand experience studying various materials that might figure as evidence, such as hair and inks.

The next year would see May's career as a scientific criminologist take off. Yet his first contact with a major crime would not feature any esoteric methods or specialized knowledge. Instead, he used the investigator's prime tool: keen observation of the crime scene.

· *3* ·

The Early Casebook of Luke May

The trolley car rumbled along a broad residential street in east Salt Lake City. Light winds from the northwest still brought clouds in over the Great Salt Lake, but the morning showers had passed. Midway through the lunch hour, the car carried few passengers. Suddenly Conductor Robert Spiller noticed a stir in front of a house off to the side. A slender figure in shirtsleeves stumbled across the lawn, then tripped over a low wall onto the sidewalk. A passenger near the rear cried out, "He's been hurt!"[1]

Spiller hurriedly signaled his motorman to stop. One passenger scrambled out the rear. Another leaped from the front platform; he carried a small satchel. Spiller followed as soon as the car had fully halted. The injured boy was groaning and breathing heavily. The forward passenger quickly prepared a needle from his kit. Dr. J. Lloyd Woodruff later told the *Telegram* that he had tried to give the boy a strychnine stimulant. "But really," he said, "before I could administer a hypodermic injection he was dead."[2]

The physician verified that the boy had died, noting two gunshot wounds high in the chest. Other than that, he tried to leave the body undisturbed for the coroner. A neighbor told them the youth's name was Thomas Karrick. He lived in the house with his mother and three older siblings. Thomas was fourteen years old and had come home from school to have lunch.

Police investigators tried to reconstruct the crime. The house sat near the edge of an elevated terrace, and a basement window was visible along one side. It was unlocked and open, so police assumed that someone had simply climbed in. The untouched meal sitting on the kitchen table indicated that Thomas had heard the burglar and confronted him. The intruder sprayed him with bullets from a .45-caliber revolver, which, police learned, had been stolen from an upstairs bedroom. Besides the two fatal chest wounds, a slug

29

had hit Thomas in the wrist. On his way out the kitchen door, the killer had tossed the weapon into the coal scuttle. Fresh tracks in the damp ground of the backyard suggested that the fugitive had been a man.

As it happened, the victim was the nephew of District Judge Thomas D. Lewis. And, by this time, October of 1910, Luke May had been pursuing his interest in detective work for at least a year. That, of course, included visits to court. Perhaps that linkage is what brought May into the case so quickly. He said, "I was called into the case by a friend of the family."[3]

He heard everything the police knew and then, accompanied by one of the Karrick brothers, made his own examination of the premises. Besides some cash, the most valuable property stolen from the house appeared to be Mrs. Karrick's gold watch. They finally made their way down to the basement. Nothing much struck May, although he did notice a handsaw on the floor. It had been there long enough to show a heel mark and scattered dirt on its surface. May had "a fondness for tools," so he said to the brother, "You really ought to hang up that saw . . . before it gets rusty from the dampness."[4]

The brother and police had supposedly searched the house thoroughly. Karrick stared at the tool in surprise and then declared that the saw did not belong to them.

After verifying that the brother was not mistaken, May surmised that the intruder might have dropped it there. After all, he asked, "Who else could have left it?"[5]

A day after the murder, the *Telegram* ran a follow-up article under the headline, "Few Clues for Police to Follow."[6] Still, the chief of detectives did tell reporters that a "saw was found there that cannot be accounted for by the Karricks. It does not belong to them and may have been brought there by the burglar."

"You bet I remember a man with a saw," a streetcar conductor said when police tracked this lead.[7] The crew recalled him because the customer had held the saw between his knees while he found a coin for the fare. He had exited the streetcar within a block of the Karrick home. The witnesses provided a complete description of the rider. With that, police backtracked him to Murray station, located about eight miles south of where the murder occurred. But there, in the town of more than four thousand people, the trail faded out.

Another day passed. Then the Salt Lake County sheriff's office received a phone tip from a caller in Murray. That afternoon, there had been some excitement locally when a man who boarded with neighbor John Kropf tried to kill himself. But the attempt failed, and a local doctor was called to treat him. Naturally, word got around, and neighbors gathered to see what was going on. During a conversation with the caller, Kropf mentioned that he'd lent the man, a Hungarian immigrant named Julius Sirmay, a saw. Sirmay had landed a job cutting some wood in Salt Lake City.

That evening, the tipster finally made the possible connection. Might this be the saw mentioned in the newspaper? The next morning, officers escorted Kropf and his son to the police station where they identified the tool as the one loaned to Sirmay. Shortly before noon, Sheriff Joseph C. Sharp and his deputies arrested Sirmay and locked him in the county jail. Later, *The Telegram* reported, "Fearing mob violence, Saturday night Sheriff Sharp . . . hustled Szirmay [*sic*] to the state prison for safekeeping."[8]

On Sunday, officers grilled him about the murder. The borrowed saw put him at the crime scene, with eyewitness testimony as indirect support. The immigrant finally admitted that he had been in the Karrick home. He maintained, however, that he had never left the basement. A purported confederate had planned the burglary, and only he had gone upstairs. Sirmay fled when he heard the boy come home. In his haste, he left the handsaw behind. That was why he had tried to kill himself. He was sure the tool would lead police to him.

Deputies found nondescript possibly stolen items, like a specific brand of razor blades, among Sirmay's effects. (The gold watch was apparently never recovered.) Still, officials were confident of their case. The Hungarian went on trial in January 1911. At no point could Sirmay's defense produce any evidence for a partner in the crime. The jury brought in a guilty verdict, and Sirmay was sentenced to death.

The usual appeals followed, but they failed. Sirmay chose death by firing squad rather than the gallows and was executed about nineteen months after the murder. A few hours before the execution, he finally admitted that he alone had burglarized the Karrick home. Hard up, he had discovered the open basement window and couldn't resist climbing in. He had shot young Thomas in a panic at being caught.

Later in his career, May kept separate files for each case he and his detectives worked on. However, folders for these earlier jobs—if he kept them back then—did not survive moves first to Pocatello and then on to Seattle. He included the Karrick case in *Crime's Nemesis*, where he focused on the key point in the investigative process: the discovery of the handsaw. May made it clear that the significance of the tool did not spring—full-blown—into his thoughts. However, as a matter of routine, he identified its presence as an anomaly, something out of place. How much longer might it have laid there while the trail grew cold? Someone might have put it away without realizing it didn't belong.

The 1910 *City Directory* for Salt Lake City showed Luke as a "student" who was a "boarder" at his father's address. Apparently, he was not then ready to make his interest in detective work official. Also, Luke's data for the U.S. census, recorded in April, did not include an occupation. He was, of course, listed as being seventeen years old.

It's not clear when May began to claim he'd been born in 1886, adding six years to his age. Back then, young professionals often used that ploy to attract customers who might not hire a mere boy. In any case, despite his youth, May had begun to take part in the Salt Lake City social scene. Within months after the Karrick murder, Luke May was acknowledged as a member of the "First Nighters," those who regularly attended openings of the latest theatrical shows.[9]

Besides plays, May surely would have been interested in the newfangled medium of motion pictures. During the late summer of 1910, moviegoers in Salt Lake City could view the semidocumentary *Ranch Life in the Great Southwest*. Although stars were not then named, one of the players in the

Figure 3.1.   "First Nighter" Luke May, 1911. *Source*: May-Reid Records.

film was cowboy wrangler Tom Mix. Mix would go on to become the first Western movie megastar of the silent film era.

May also continued to expand his education. An accused embezzler was being escorted back to Memphis, Tennessee. To avoid the expense of shipping his personal library, and for some ready cash, he sold the books for what he could get. Sadly, the article in the Ogden *Evening Standard* did not provide an inventory. But it did report, "Among the purchasers of the volumes were Herman Bauer, secretary to Chief Barlow, Luke S. May, a private detective, and others."[10]

May reached a new stage in his life early the next year. On January 7, 1911, the *Telegram* published the following tiny notice, tucked away at the bottom of a page: "Filed with the county clerk: Maylon Detective service, to carry on a general detective business; capital stock, $10,000, in $10 shares; Luke S. May, president and general manager; William May, secretary and treasurer."[11]

William's association with the startup suggests that he paid for the venture at some level. Although not shown as an officer, Luke's brother Vincent also had a role in the agency. The situation offers an instance of a classic immigrant experience in America. Recall that Luke's father was born and raised in a poor farming area that had been essentially transplanted from Ireland to Canada. In such communities, the normal expectations were that sons would follow their fathers into farming or other closely related lines of work.

After the family moved to the United States, William's first job off his father's farm was in a blacksmith shop. That was still within the norm, as was his next stint as an itinerant carpenter. Then, of course, he tried farming himself. But by the time William moved his family to Salt Lake City, he saw himself, to some extent, as a building contractor. That is, he had moved beyond a limited father-to-son progression. Now, with Luke's venture into a field outside of any normal expectation, William was helping realize a May family version of the American Dream.

For two or three years, May had already been representing himself as something akin to the Maylon agency (he never explained the name). Now, he was *officially* in business as a detective. He had enough capital, and perhaps cash flow, to rent a separate office space. Moreover, the 1911 *City Directory* for Salt Lake City contained a listing for the service, which directed readers to an advertisement on the back cover. That ad cannot have come cheap.

Of course, as a private investigator, most of May's work was, of necessity, private. Thus, several months passed before one of his cases made the newspapers. The episode began in early April. Someone had apparently burglarized a fashionable home not far from the University of Utah campus. The home belonged to Malcolm A. Keyser, son of a wealthy stock rancher and real estate investor.

Keyser and his wife had lived in the house less than a year. The thief made off with around $700 worth of cash, jewelry, and expensive clothing. Aside from the missing items, the intruder had left few signs of his (or her) search through the home. That suggestion of a professional job contrasted with the apparent method of entry, a battered lock on the front door. A pro would have surely favored a more discreet approach.

Reports didn't say how May entered the case. But he saw right away that the blows to the lock, while dramatic in appearance, would not have forced it open. May immediately suspected an inside job and suggested that police thoroughly search the live-in maid's quarters in the basement. The Keysers, and the police, vehemently rejected the notion. Neither May's account nor later newspaper stories say what the girl claimed to be doing at the time of the supposed break-in. But whatever it was, her convincing story and ingratiating manner totally deflected suspicion.

May spent most of the next two weeks tracking her movements and associations, both before and after the break-in. If she was guilty, she was also being very clever. None of the stolen items appeared in the usual channels. May did discover that she had been born in Salt Lake City but educated at an Eastern girls' school. She had then worked as a manicurist in Chicago and was supposedly engaged to a young man there. However, she had also been discharged from two previous domestic positions, one for stealing household items, the other for undisclosed reasons.

This evidence, along with the lack of real damage to the lock mechanism, helped May convince the Keysers that they should confront the maid. She quickly confessed and was jailed on a charge of grand larceny. For the first time, May's name appeared in the news in connection with a case. The article in the *Telegram* began: "After working quietly on the case for ten days, Private Detective Luke S. May . . ."[12]

All of the missing items were, in fact, hidden among the maid's belongings. May also found a claw hammer in her room. The young detective then made a comparison that presaged a hallmark of his career: tool mark identification. He examined the door latch and the hammer under strong magnification. This showed that the marks on the lock "fit identically similar microscopic imperfections on the face of [the] claw hammer."[13]

The next issue of the *Telegram* mentioned May again. It also stated that the girl said she had taken the items because "she intended to be married and wanted the things for her home."[14] Because all of the stolen items were recovered, and for reasons of their own, the Keysers declined to press charges. Without elaboration, the *Telegram* reported, "The girl will be given another chance."[15]

May had other cases where the newspapers barely referred to him or his agency. One such was a bank robbery in Tooele, a town located about thirty-five miles southwest of Salt Lake City. In early June, thieves had robbed the Commercial Bank there, getting away with nearly $10,000 in cash, gold, and silver. A report in the *Telegram* said, "Officials of the Pinkerton national detective agency and of the Maylon detective agency of Salt Lake City are working on the case."[16]

The bank cashier, Sylvester I. Shafer, said that the two men, dressed in mining outfits and heavily armed, had invaded the bank right near closing time. The crooks bound him tightly, dumped him in the bank's lavatory, and then made off with the loot. The bank president, Frank E. McGurrin, offered a reward of $1,000 for the recovery of the loot. What happened over the next few weeks took place entirely behind the scenes. But the amount stolen would be equivalent to about $240,000 today. May surely began to ask around the city for news of large, unexplained financial transactions. Events would also show that he suspected an inside job and followed leads for that.

Finally, a headline in the *Telegram* blared, "Stolen Money is Returned to Bank."[17] Yet the article carried only bare facts, with no explanation. President McGurrin did say, "I always keep my word, but I cannot say at this time to whom the reward was paid." That money probably went to the private detectives, including Luke May. Like his case files, May's financial records for the period before 1920 are rather sparse, so there is no way to verify this inference.

In the end, this case profited from an element May cited in his writing: "The carefully planned crime is usually much easier to unravel than the accidental crime."[18] At first thought, this seems counterintuitive, since you might expect the perpetrator of an unplanned crime to make mistakes and leave more clues. However, as May explained, the activities in an elaborately planned crime "are predictable, and the various steps in the crime are easily traced after a clue has been found."

And so it proved in this case. Shafer turned out to be the inside man for another bank employee and that man's brother-in-law. Perhaps because the money was returned and the robbers were first-time offenders, they received jail terms of only one year.

While the Tooele case played out, May probably noticed a brief item in the *Telegram* that said, "In an address to the Paris Academy of Sciences, Professor Balthazard contends that when a leaden bullet traverses cloth, characteristic marks are left upon it, which are not obliterated by the subsequent passage of the bullet through flesh, provided that it does not strike bone."[19]

Victor Balthazard was a professor of forensic medicine at the Sorbonne in Paris. Born near Paris in 1872, he received his medical degree in 1903 and was certified as an expert witness in pathology and forensic science within three years. Like May, Balthazard was a generalist. Thus, in 1910, he published *Le poil de l'homme et des animaux* (The Hair of Man and Animals), one of the most influential texts in early criminology.

At some point, May surely obtained a copy of Balthazard's book. Later, he would observe, "Hair can tell the criminologist a great many things. . . . However, exhaustive research must precede any such determination, for, as in other sciences, a little learning is a dangerous thing."[20]

Several months passed with no mention of Luke May in the newspapers. Then on November 21, 1911, the *Telegram* reported, "Luke S. May of this city and Miss Florence McCullough of Logan were married in the office of the county clerk by 'Cupid' J. U. Eldredge, Sr., Saturday afternoon."[21]

Miss McCulloch (a more common spelling) was indeed from Logan, but she lived in Salt Lake City at the time. May was not quite nineteen years old, so Florence was almost two years older than her new husband. One suspects that he had already begun to claim those extra six years. Family memories do not say how the two met. Florence had moved to Salt Lake City around 1909 and briefly worked as a housemaid at a fancy home in the Avenues neighborhood. She then found a job as a telephone operator.

The article about the couple's marriage went on to say, "Mr. and Mrs. May took quarters at the New Grand hotel and did not notify their friends of their marriage until a day or two later. So well were their plans prepared that Mr. May's brother, V. B. May and other associates in the office knew nothing of his decisive step until Sunday."[22] Soon enough, Florence and Luke set up housekeeping in an apartment in downtown Salt Lake City, less than two blocks from the Maylon offices. Three months after his marriage, another May case hit the newspapers.

May and the two plainclothes police officers ambled casually along the street. They tried not to pay too much attention to the Maylon operative striding along the other sidewalk. The late February evening was chilly and clear, with a crescent of waxing moon adding to the glow of the streetlamps. The agent, going under the name of Kelly, slowed as he neared the fashionable apartment building. The followers tried to blend into the shadows.

Their target, a young man named Arthur Edwards, stepped out to meet Kelly as he neared the front entrance. After a moment of low-voice conversation, the two walked toward the end of the building. Edwards must want a less public spot to make the exchange. May and the officers quietly followed, taking up a position where they could continue the surveillance. Edwards and Kelly stopped, and then the young man took a small envelope from his pocket and handed it to the agent. That should be the packet of cocaine they had agreed upon.

The two exchanged a few words, and then Kelly reached up to nudge his hat back on his head. Alerted by the signal, the watchers hurried across the street. May hung back as the officers arrested both men. After Edwards had been booked into jail, officers searched the young man's apartment. They also arrested his two roommates, who worked for the same drug company. Officials suspected they were members of a drug ring being run by the young man. Police also hauled a large steamer trunk off to headquarters so they could inventory its contents.

May and his operative had entered the case about three weeks earlier. Reports gave few details, but officials of the Smith-Bailey Drug Company had hired Maylon to investigate shortfalls in their product stocks. Suspicion soon fell on Edwards. He had the best access to the drug supplies, by far the most valuable of the missing materials. Operative Kelly struck up an acquaintance. After awhile, he suggested that he might like to obtain some drugs without the formality of a doctor's prescription. Edwards admitted that he could get some. He'd be willing to supply them to Kelly for a suitable price. When they were ready to set up a buy, May contacted his friends in the police.

After the booking, police quietly released Kelly, keeping the packet of cocaine as evidence. The marked money the agent had given Edwards for the drug assured his guilt. Under interrogation, the young man admitted that he had been pilfering stock for about five weeks. The *Telegram* reported that he said, "I carried the stuff out in my pockets as I went home at night and did not know that I was suspected."[23] He also said, "I had no other confederates." The two other suspects "did not know what I was doing."

The other two men were quickly released after May and the police determined that Edwards was indeed telling the truth. The steamer trunk turned out to be a treasure chest, stuffed with more than a thousand dollars worth of drugs and druggists' sundries. The drugs included a couple of cocaine formulations, several forms of morphine, an opium solution, and ten ounces of Argyrol. The news report noted that Argyrol "is so costly that the average drug store seldom carries more than one or two ounces in stock."[24] Given the high value of what was stolen, Edwards might have spent considerable time in jail. However, the judge took his lack of a criminal record into account and sentenced him to just three years in prison.

Despite this positive activity, the next couple of years proved to be up and down for May. On the plus side, he later said that 1912 was when he began to seriously study tool mark identification. At the time, he was "engaged in designing and perfecting an instrument for the recording of sound to be used in detective work."[25] He completed that task using "a small but fully equipped machine shop."

As a side question, he wondered if he could identify the specific blade "used in a screw-cutting lathe to cut fine threads on parts of a scientific instrument."[26] (He does not explain what prompted this query.) Soon, his studies "conclusively proved that practically every tool used in the shop could be positively identified." This discovery would later guide one of Luke May's major technical contributions to criminology. On a family note, Luke gained a sister-in-law in June 1912. That's when brother Vincent married Laura Koontz, a young lady from Salt Lake City. That meant that both May brothers now had wives to support. A few months later, their grandfather, Timothy May (II), passed away in Salt Lake City. Two years earlier, Timothy had been staying with a son in California. The fact that he had two sons, a daughter, and eight or nine grandchildren living in Utah likely drew him there. He was eighty-six when he died.

Meanwhile, income from the detective business—despite the occasional good news in the papers—must have seemed too chancy for the new family men. Thus, about six weeks after Vincent's wedding, the two became officers—Luke as vice president and Vincent as treasurer—of a new firm founded by inventor William Hoppie. Hoppie had devised and patented a number of electrical devices. One was a telephone repeater, and he formed this company to commercialize it. The brothers probably invested in the startup, but how much is unknown.

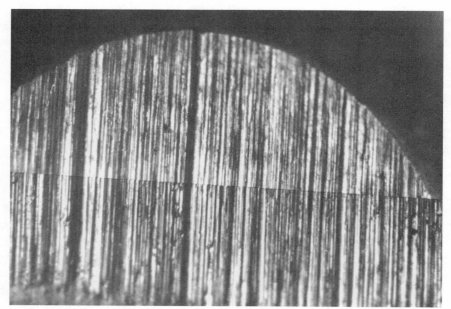

Figure 3.2.   Comparing Tool Marks on Cut Wire. *Source*: **May-Reid Records.**

The Hoppie venture seems to have done well for a time. Late in the year, May had the wherewithal to join in a hunting trip that spanned nearly three weeks. He made the *Telegram* with the headline, "Six-Prong Buck is Evidence of Skill of Local Nimrod."[27] He and four other men had taken an extended vacation in the country twenty to thirty miles northwest of Tooele. The article said, "The largest deer killed was shot by Mr. May. The big buck is one of the largest ever brought into Salt Lake City." The reporter interviewed May and then wrote, "He says that game is plentiful and that coyotes are numerous and particularly daring."

However, Hoppie's company went into tax default in March 1913 and lost its license to operate. After that, the brothers had only the detective agency to generate income. Then, in June, Florence gave birth to a daughter, Florence Dorothy May. Luke was a bit over twenty years old when he became a father, with another mouth to feed. Thus, in July he became vice president of another venture created by William Hoppie.

Again, the purpose was to manufacture and distribute innovative products. One such device was the sound recorder for detective work that May had developed in 1912. May's association with the inventive Hoppie probably reinforced his later tendency to design and build his own equipment.

Throughout all this, Luke retained his connection with Maylon. But in early January 1914, a Japanese detective with the agency was arrested on extortion charges. The *Telegram* reported that the evidence against him included "marked coins, five gold pieces of the denomination of $10 each . . . two in the prisoner's pockets and three in the bureau drawer in his room."[28] A Japanese businessman told police that the agent had demanded a bribe to suppress what he claimed was damaging evidence against the businessman. Officers then set up a "sting" operation with the marked coins.

Less than a week after that report, another article in the *Telegram* said, "L. S. May has severed his connection with the Maylon Detective agency. . . . His brother, V. B. May, succeeds him as head of the detective agency."[29] The item also said that Luke had been promoted to a general manager position in the Hoppie firm. The company prospered for a while, reaching a peak value of 75¢ per share in early March, according to a paid spread in the *Telegram*.

In the interim, news from the world of crime science surely caught May's attention. During the first quarter of 1914, newspapers across the country published an article with the headline (or a variation), "Identifying Crooks by Pores of Their Skin." Even the *Standard*, in Anaconda, Montana, carried the item. The article began, "That your pores will tell who you are is the assertion of Dr. Edmond Locard, director of the police laboratory at Lyons, France."[30]

An overview of "poreoscopy" and fingerprints followed. Locard felt that his method had a major advantage over fingerprints because it could work from a small patch of skin. Fingerprinting needed a record of most of the end of the digit. (Actually, poreoscopy depends too much on ultrafine detail and never became widely used.)

Frenchman Edmond Locard is generally considered the first forensic scientist. Born in 1877, he obtained his doctoral degree in 1902. He then took a position at the University of Lyon and began a broad study of forensic medicine. Work on other criminological techniques followed. He even made time to study with Alphonse Bertillon for a while. Some of his most wide-ranging work concerned fingerprints. He is credited with reducing the fingerprint classes defined by Sir Francis Galton to a set of systematic rules for the practitioner. Thus, along with his poreoscopy paper, Locard also produced a treatise on *The Legal Evidence by the Fingerprints.* There seems little doubt that May would have soon got his hands on a copy.

Locard had set up a small laboratory in 1910 to help the Lyon police with scientific crime investigation. Two years later, the city formally recognized it as the *Laboratoire de Police Scientifique.* This unit is considered the first official police lab in the world. Locard is best known to the interested layman for the "Locard Exchange Principle." Simplistically, the principle declares that every contact leaves a trace. That is, when you or an object touches another person or object, material from one will transfer to the other. While basically true, use of the notion cannot be pushed too far. The key question is whether an observer can actually detect what has been exchanged.

Along with the widely published Locard item, an intriguing classified advertisement appeared in the *Salt Lake Tribune.* It was posted shortly before the triumphant "75¢ per share" Hoppie announcement appeared. The item said, "We shadow individuals. Recover jewelry, papers . . . Retainers reasonable and results guaranteed. Finest equipped and only absolutely confidential offices in the West. . . . Revelare International Secret Service."[31] Contact was to be through a mailbox because the advertisement did not include a telephone number or any specific person's name.

The usual Maylon ad appeared two slots below that for Revelare. Maylon seems to have struggled along for another year. After that, their ads disappeared from the newspapers. In any case, the Revelare posting was the work of Luke May. The item must have been a trial balloon to gauge interest in another detective service. Clearly, his desire to pursue the field had not changed . . . and his confidence in Hoppie had most likely waned. As a matter of fact, the firm's stock would drop to 16¢ per share a year later.

Two months after the trial balloon, the *Telegram* reported that "L. S. May . . . has been made district chief of the Revelare International Secret Service of Paris, France. Mr. May will have supervision over the district between Omaha and San Francisco. He will make his headquarters in Salt

Lake."[32] In reality, Revelare existed only in May's imagination. Even so, ads for the new firm immediately appeared in various Utah newspapers. He also tried to lend some credibility to the company by recruiting agents around the country. The item that appeared in the *Evening Star* in Washington, DC, was typical: "Wanted—Detective Representatives: Local young men for special work; credentials of authority given if accepted."[33]

Sadly, about that same time, Florence (McCulloch) May filed for divorce from the young entrepreneur. She gave nonsupport as grounds for the complaint. Details to back up the nonsupport claim were not retained in the case file. May must have spent a good deal of money for that "small but fully equipped machine shop" mentioned earlier. Plus, he had almost certainly invested in those successive electrical equipment businesses. Still, Florence was probably happy when Luke traded his position with Maylon for a real job with Hoppie. She most likely saw that as a sign that Luke was ready to settle down.

But now, he had ventured back into detective work. Florence apparently decided enough was enough. She asked for custody of infant Florence Dorothy, $15 a month child support, and $50 for attorney fees. Luke did not contest the action, and the court issued the interlocutory decree on June 18, 1914. Barring any changes in the situation, the divorce was considered final six months from that date.

So, at twenty-two years of age, May found himself single, yet responsible for the support of a young child. He left nothing to tell us directly how he felt about this situation. However, subsequent events show that he did keep track of his ex-wife and little girl. And life went on. May scraped up enough business to advertise regularly in the Utah papers. At least into the fall, he held to the notion that they were just the local agent for a worldwide firm. Their regular ad in the Ogden *Standard* said, "Revelare International Secret Service. We handle Ogden business through head office, 315-16-17 McIntyre Building, Salt Lake City. L. S. May."[34]

His campaign to recruit agents who could give his firm at least a national reach went fairly well. Revelare would soon be able to claim the company had agents coast-to-coast. But toward the end of the year, May must have decided they could not maintain the pretense that Revelare had its headquarters in France. On December 10, 1914, the *Telegram* announced, "Salt Lake City is now the capital for an international organization of detectives."[35]

He also had a new investor, J. Clark Sellers. Born in Wasatch County, east of Salt Lake City, Sellers was working as a shoe salesman in the city in 1914. Luke's claim of an extra six years made him seem older than Clark, but Sellers was actually older by more than a year. In a memoir written many years later, he said his investment in May's venture was $400 (equivalent to about $20,000 in today's valuations). Sellers had taken many business courses but no science beyond elementary school. May tutored him on detective techniques and encouraged his interest in questioned documents assessment.

Sellers introduced May to a friend of his, John L. Harris. Although Harris did not then become part of Revelare, he would eventually join the venture. Sellers became vice president when they reorganized Revelare as a Utah corporation. Papers were filed to show that "the concern has a paid up capital of $10,000 and 500 representatives scattered through the United States."[36]

They claimed to have divisional offices stretching from Boston to San Francisco, with cities like Omaha in between. The same issue of the paper contained a large—not full-page, but quite eye-catching—advertisement about the new company. They even claimed to have an office in Ogden. May had apparently learned to think big from promoter Hoppie.

But as the year ended and May's divorce went final, events were about to turn his future in a new direction. That new course would lead to notable successes and national recognition.

· *4* ·

Moving to Greener Fields

*I*n early December 1914, the *Telegram* published an article about the new Bertillon identification system the Salt Lake City police had purchased. The latest version of the kit now included fingerprinting components, a flash unit and tripod for taking photographs, and much more. The *Telegram* said, "No longer will the habitual criminal who visits Salt Lake be able to hide his identity under an alias when arrested."[1]

The Bertillon system was the culmination of changes made in the Salt Lake City police over a period of five or six years. Around 1909, the department started buying motorcycles and automobiles as patrol vehicles, and other advances followed. Police Chief Brigham F. Grant, appointed in 1912, put his secretary, Frank S. Spooner, in charge of the new identification unit. That spring, Spooner traveled to Oakland for further training under Harry Caldwell, whom we met in chapter 2. In the fall, Spooner attended a meeting in Oakland organized by Caldwell. There, twenty-two men founded the International Association for Criminal Identification.[2] Caldwell was elected president, while Spooner became second vice president.

Then, in early 1915, the city purchased space needed to house the Bertillon system and allow other improvements, including a laboratory. The report of the transfer stated that the necessary renovations should be complete around the first of March. Even that early in his career, May's vision for the future included the sort of services the police in Salt Lake City had just acquired for themselves. Events would soon show that he began to consider nearby Idaho as a fertile area for his skills.

Coincidentally, on March 1, 1915, Idaho Governor Moses Alexander signed into law a liquor prohibition bill. The law was to go into effect on the first of the following year. By this time, many counties in Utah had already gone "dry." So, jurisdictions there got an early taste of the rampant law-breaking the ban caused. It seems likely that May expected similar results from Idaho's new law.

He had also landed what became his first highly publicized case in the state. Solon B. Clark, the newly-elected prosecuting attorney for Custer County, Idaho, hired him to investigate a very suspicious death. And May soon provided evidence that backed the prosecutor's hunch. The events had unfolded a year and a half earlier in the mining town of Mackay, located just over eighty miles northwest of Idaho Falls. Rich copper mines in the mountains nearby had turned Mackay into a boomtown. It also had the only railroad connection between the county and the outside world, a branch line from Blackfoot.

The late September day had been a fine one in Mackay, with temperatures in the high seventies. Still, towering mountains to the west brought early darkness and a coolness to the air. Ed White, a prosperous sheep rancher and a bachelor, came to town seeking some company. Around seven o'clock, he wandered into the Big House, a well-known dance hall, where "the girls" also provided other services.[3] Ed had a few drinks and then danced for a while with a young woman named Mamie Regan.

But when Regan took him up to her room, White said he would only pay two dollars rather than the usual three. She refused and then they bickered some. Finally, she led him back downstairs. He had a few more drinks and danced with her and then another woman. Finally, the madam, who went by the name of Rae Moore, told the two women that she was going to drug his next drink. He could then be safely relieved of whatever bankroll he had . . . and would remember nothing. Later, Regan heard that the other woman had taken $250 from him.

The next time she saw White was in the parlor, where he was passed out on the couch and breathing heavily. A bit later, Moore had the house piano player and another man haul White out the door. She cried, "Don't let him die in the house."[4] The men thought she was overreacting, but he was found dead the next morning in the lumberyard across the street. The coroner made a cursory examination, and the coroner's jury attributed his death to unspecified natural causes. Originally from Ohio, White had no family in Idaho to pursue the matter.

Prosecutor Clark had wondered about the case for some time. Soon after being elected county prosecuting attorney in 1914, he began to make quiet inquiries. That led him to engage Luke May. May, in turn, secured a crucial toxicology analysis that said White had died from a massive dose of morphine sulfate. With that as a lever, May collected a number of depositions. Thus, one witness heard Rae Moore say, "I was drunk and I gave him too much."[5]

After several weeks, May and various law officers tracked down suspects and jailed them in Challis, the county seat. Then, on March 30, the *Idaho Register*, in Idaho Falls, reprinted news of the arrests under the headline "Five Arrested on Murder Charge."[6]

Oddly enough, on that same day, May got married again, in Blackfoot, Idaho. The bride was Miss Clara Douglas. Born in Tennessee, Clara had re-located to Utah in 1909–1910. A dressmaker, she lived first in Ogden before moving to Salt Lake City around 1914. As with Florence, we do not know how the two met. Blackfoot was a junction station between the main north-south railroad line and the branch to Mackay. It is also the county seat of Bingham County, so the county clerk performed the ceremony.

A few weeks later, the *Idaho Register* reported, "Woman's Death Ends Trial."[7] Margaret Conway, alias Rae Moore, had been transported to the Challis hospital, where she died. Many people, including May, suspected she had committed suicide. The *Register* article concluded, "The death of the woman brings to an end one of the most sensational murder cases in central Idaho." Solon Clark told May, "The evidence that you obtained against Rae Moore was without doubt the most conclusive I have ever seen, and I wish to thank you for your personal handling of the case."[8]

May was also collecting other testimonials from Idaho. On June 1, 1915, he received a letter from the prosecuting attorney for Bannock County. The attorney first thanked him for the services performed by May and his opera-tives. He said, "The work done by your company is perhaps the best and most complete that it has been my privilege to observe during my two terms as public prosecutor."[9]

All these favorable prospects in Idaho, plus the potential loss of business in Salt Lake City, must have persuaded May to move. In August, the *Idaho Statesman*, in Boise, said, "Pocatello will have a detective agency, says L. S. May of the Salt Lake agency of the Revelair [*sic*] Detective company."[10]

The arrangements took some time, but in early January 1916, the *Statesman* reported the incorporation of Revelare, "with the principal place of business at Pocatello. . . . The incorporators are L. S. May, J. C. Sellers, C. S. May, L. B. Matthews and A. Bartlett."[11] It is interesting, and perhaps significant, that Luke's new wife was among the incorporators. She would remain an officer of the corporation for the next six or seven years. Perhaps, after his experience with his first wife, May wanted to "keep peace in the family" by giving Clara a role in the business.

The agency soon made an impact. In February, the *Twin Falls Chronicle* published a remarkably clear photograph of the fingerprint of a suspected burglar. May recovered the image from a letter, where it had been "invisible to the naked eye."[12] He used a special camera and film, after regular fingerprint methods failed to reveal anything useful. Based on the fingerprint image, "The man was connected with several robberies in the city, the largest of which was that of furs and other valuables from Mrs. E. O. Key."

The following month, May began another of his most notable early cases, one that called on several different skills and sent him all over the region. Mid-to-late March had been fairly mild in the Idaho Falls area, with temperatures reaching into the high fifties. Farmers had felt encouraged enough to prepare for spring planting. Managers of the New Sweden Irrigation District had crews checking headgates, cleaning out debris, and otherwise getting ready for the watering season. (The New Sweden area is a few miles southwest of Idaho Falls.)

But on March 23, temperatures dropped after midnight, and a big snowstorm moved through the valley. The weather bureau in Pocatello reported that the snow "was the heaviest ever recorded at this office" for a twenty-four hour period.[13] On the following day, the high temperature was just 38°. Thus, the four men of the New Sweden District crew were surely glad to pack it in for the day, sometime after 9:30. They had just settled into their bunks when the door flew open, and two men marched in. A large, heavily built man held a flashlight in one hand and a big revolver in the other. His smaller accomplice brandished two guns. Both wore masks, overalls, and gloves.

Actual photograph of finger print made with special finger-print camera, this print was taken from a letter and was invisible to the naked eye, the regular powder ordinarily used failed to bring it out, but by using Chief May's special process the result shown above was obtained.

Figure 4.1.   Enhanced Fingerprint Image, 1916. *Source:* May-Reid Records.

The smaller intruder moved from man to man to tie their hands while the big bandit threatened them with his gun. One old-timer, Dave Evans, thought maybe it was all a prank by some other hands. He tried to kick the hand tier, but the big man was too quick. He belted Evans with his gun barrel and fired a warning shot. After binding everyone to their bunks, the robbers took nearly an hour searching for loot. Then they told the men to stay quiet and left. The victims had started stretching their bonds when perhaps a half dozen gunshots exploded in the distance.

Almost an hour passed before they could free themselves and notify the sheriff. Searchers then found the body of Wilbur Breckenridge, the company foreman, about fifty feet from the bunkhouse. He had been shot five times. Originally from La Grande, Oregon, Breckenridge had worked for the District for about ten years.

The tracks of the killers, clear in the snow, led onto the main road, where they were lost. Dave Evans thought he recognized the larger bandit as one "Coyote Bill" Banty, a trapper who had worked streams in the area. However, all he had to go on was the man's voice, build, and body movements. Police thought the killers might try to escape on the night train, which would head south at one o'clock in the morning. They placed two officers, men who claimed to know what Coyote Bill looked like, at the station. But the watchers did not see him among the passengers who boarded the train.

In town, authorities detained a few suspects who couldn't account well for their time but soon released them. Aside from the weak tip about Coyote Bill, officials had just one clue. The barrel of the big crook's .41-caliber revolver had broken off when he clubbed Evans. It was found on the bunkhouse floor.

Seeing the police come up empty, a citizen's committee from the New Sweden area took up a collection the very next morning to hire Revelare. May arrived that afternoon. An autopsy revealed that Breckenridge had been shot with guns of two different sizes, one .41 caliber, the other .38. The broken .41-caliber weapon had sprayed considerable raw powder onto the victim's body. May felt sure the shooter would discard such a damaged weapon, probably by throwing it somewhere. He extended his search further from the tracks in the snow and quickly found the gun.

Then they got a major break. Schoolchildren found parts of a watch the bandits had stolen from Dave Evans along the main rail line headed south. So at least one of the killers had probably left on the train. May decided to pursue the notion that Evans was right about Coyote Bill being involved. Perhaps the officers didn't know Bill as well as they thought, or the man changed his appearance somehow. Many years later, May did an "as told to" feature on this case for *True Detective Mysteries* magazine. He observed, "A few bitter experiences had also taught me that the more positive an officer is, the more liable he is to be mistaken."[14]

A lot of necessary drudgery followed. May discovered that Coyote was probably part Indian and had trapped all over the Northwest. He also found that Coyote and a partner had last shipped furs from Salmon, Idaho, in February 1916. A trip there unearthed evidence that put the likely death weapons in the hands of Coyote Bill and his partner. May's search in the Salmon area also provided him with a sample of Coyote's handwriting. He used that to trace the men to a Montana railway station and then to Idaho Falls. They had registered at a rooming house there on the day before the robbery-murder, using false names.

May next traveled to Salt Lake City. After a long, dogged search, he found that Bill and his partner had registered at a hotel there the day after the murder. They signed in with the same names they had used in Idaho Falls. But then the trail went cold for many, many weeks. A report in the *Idaho Register* at the end of June suggested little progress: "The Breckenridge murder case was reported on by the committee appointed some time ago, and also by Mr. L. S. May, chief of the Revelare International Secret Service."[15]

Yet, within a week, that changed. More than a month earlier, two men had been jailed in Rexburg for petty theft. One, a young man of about nineteen, was soon released. With such a minor offense, no one paid much attention to the older prisoner . . . until he cut his way out. In the follow-up, authorities realized that their prisoner had been Coyote Bill. Bill had disappeared again, but officers quickly recaptured the young partner, a man named Alfred Metzner. (Several alternative spellings of his name appeared in the newspapers.) He led May and sheriff's officers to their camp, which held an arsenal of rifles and handguns, with plenty of ammunition. Later, the *Salmon Herald* reported, "L. S. May . . . was in Salmon on business Sunday, driving through in his car, and his wife accompanying him. He brought with him a grip full of guns."[16]

The Lemhi County sheriff identified several of the weapons as having been stolen or otherwise procured around the county. With that information and other tips, May was able to reconstruct the activities of the crooks in the area. At first, Metzner claimed he had only been with Bill during the petty theft episode. But then officers laid out the evidence they and May had collected. The *Idaho Register* reported the resulting confession: "The boy under arrest denied the charge until the happenings of the past few months were recited to him almost day to day."[17]

When his case came to trial, lawyers for the youngster convinced the jury that the evil influence of Coyote Bill had led their defendant astray. He escaped the death penalty with a conviction for second-degree murder. The court sentenced him to ten to twenty-five years in the state penitentiary. Years later, when the "as told to" article came out, Coyote Bill had not been found. Fragmentary evidence suggested he had escaped into Canada, married an Indian woman, and lived out his life among her people.

Of course, the Revelare agency had much more going on besides the New Sweden investigation. While Luke May dug for basic facts about Coyote Bill, the *Idaho Register* reported, "The Revelare Secret Service located in Pocatello has done some very quick and effective work in that city in the way of detecting and capturing criminals, so much so that men of that type and class are giving Pocatello a wide berth."[18]

Not only had agents foiled two planned robberies, but they were a veritable plague on bootleggers and moonshiners. The article went on, "The secret service department works with the county attorney in such a way that over two hundred arrests for liquor law violations have been made and sentence passed without taking a case into court."

Luke May's next headline-grabbing case surfaced in the spring. Newspapers back then routinely printed stories, some of them spiced with over-the-top hyperbole, about what they called "fiendish" crimes. But the rapist who murdered seven-year-old Alice Empey truly was a fiend. She was last seen in mid-April 1916, on a road near her home about three miles east of Idaho Falls. Her savagely mutilated body was found about a month later after heavy rains washed away the debris used to hide it.

The perpetrator was surely a "degenerate," a child molester. But May's exhaustive investigation also suggested someone who mostly lived off the land and seldom came in sight of settled people. He used that pattern, what we now call "profiling," to assess every suspected degenerate in the region. He finally caught up with one, Edward Ness. Dubbed the Idaho Wild Man, Ness lived mostly in the backcountry, dressed in poorly-cured animal skins, and had filthy hair hanging down to his waist.

With careful questions and comments, May convinced the suspect that the detective knew even more than he did. Ness finally confessed that he had, indeed, raped and murdered Alice Empey. However, authorities chose to prosecute Ness for another case where they had more evidence. They feared, rightly, that he would repudiate the confession. Ness was convicted and sentenced to twenty to forty years in prison.

Throughout this period, Revelare pursued many routine cases that generally did not make the newspapers. And they continued to collect testimonial letters. District Judge James M. Stevens had followed May's career both as a judge and in his private practice. Stevens wrote, "I regard him as the cleverest man I have ever known in this class of work. . . . He does his work quietly and quickly, and never fails to get results."[19]

Besides collecting testimonials, May also tried to publicize his agency, with an emphasis on the scientific tools they could bring to bear. Thus, an article appeared in the *Electrical Experimenter* magazine that named several devices built by "Mr. L. S. May, Chief Electrician," of the detective agency.[20] The item had no byline so it's not clear whether May wrote it himself or gave an interview. By this time, May had adapted the sound recorder mentioned in the previous chapter to capture telephone conversations. He had also developed a "wireless telephone"—actually a radio transceiver set—that could "be carried about in a suitcase." Another setup could snap simultaneous photographs from three different angles for his mug shot files.

May also expanded his possible business contacts by joining the Pocatello Masonic Lodge. This must have come after considerable thought, given his Roman Catholic background and baptism. For centuries, the church has viewed Freemasonry with deep suspicion, despite the number of Catholics who have joined the society. And he was an active member. His biography in the *History of Idaho* said, "He is a Mason and devotes a great deal of time to Masonic work."[21] Luke would remain a member for the rest of his life.

Figure 4.2.   May in His Pocatello Office, circa 1918. *Source*: **May-Reid Records.**

Meanwhile, in March 1917, *The Oregonian,* in Portland, reported events that presaged May's next big murder case. The article said, "Sheriffs of two counties are hunting for the slayer of Thomas Cavanaugh, a prominent young rancher of the Brownlee district, who was last seen on March 12."[22] Cavanaugh's spread was located about thirty-five miles north of Weiser, Idaho, near the border with Oregon. Authorities had found no body, but a cousin in Weiser had become worried after Tom missed a planned meeting.

About three weeks later, Dan Ruth, another cousin of Cavanaugh's, was jailed for forging the missing man's signature on a check. But he told a plausible story and was released on bond. The body was finally found in mid-May. He had been shot through the skull. Ruth and another man were immediately arrested. A week or so after the body was discovered, officials hired May to investigate.

Although the killer had tried to clean up the cabin, May quickly determined that traces found there were human blood. May discussed this mystery at some length in *Crime's Nemesis.* He wrote, "I discovered evidence of blood on the inside of the oven door; also on the inside of the oven. A portion of the bullet that had passed through the victim's head, entering the base of the skull and making its exit through the eye, was also found melted in the oven."[23]

We now take blood-spatter and bullet-trajectory analysis for granted. But recall that this was 1917, when such methods were practically unheard of in this country. May concluded that the victim "had been kneeling in front of his stove, in the act of either putting something into the oven or taking it out, at the time he was shot."[24] Backtracking the low trajectory suggested that the shooter had been sitting on the bed across the room. So, the killer was probably someone known to Cavanaugh. That and testimony collected earlier by authorities pointed the finger directly at Dan Ruth.

In May's considerable experience, the results of a detailed crime-scene assessment often had a profound impact on a guilty suspect. That was particularly true for a perpetrator who thought he had successfully covered his tracks. As May said, "To him it seems weird and uncanny that almost every action at the scene of the crime is accurately reconstructed."[25] And so it proved in this case. At the end of May, the *Idaho Statesman* reported, "In a confession made by him in the presence of several officers of the law, Dan Ruth acknowledges that it was an act of his which caused the death of Thomas Cavanagh [*sic*] on March 12, but insists that the fatal shot was accidental."[26]

The defense brought in a hotshot attorney from San Francisco, and the subsequent trial was an Idaho sensation. The *Statesman* observed, "L. S. May of Pocatello, an important witness in the case, arrived in Weiser Sunday night."[27] Despite a fight to deny its use, Ruth's statement to law officers was admitted as evidence. (It was deemed an "admission" not a "confession," in lawyerese.) In the end, Ruth was convicted and given a life sentence by the judge. In a subsequent letter to May, the prosecuting attorney said, "That jury was fairly stunned at the web woven by you about the accused, backed up by such logic, such science, that one simply had to believe."[28]

The science would have included an explanation of what the pattern and shapes of the bloodstains had to say. As noted in chapter 1, blood has always been a prime clue in crimes of violence. Of course, most of those early scientific studies of crime-scene blood were concerned with whether it *was* human blood. Even so, according to the text *Bloodstain Pattern Analysis*, "Scattered throughout these discussions are references to patterns observed at scenes."[29]

Eduard Piotrowski is generally credited with the first definitive treatise on the analysis of bloodstain patterns. He worked at an institute of forensic medicine in Krakow, Poland. In 1895, the University of Vienna published his *Uber Entstehung, Form, Richtung und Ausbreitung der Blutspuren nach Hieb-wunden des Kopfes* (Concerning the Origin, Shape, Direction and Distribution of Bloodstains Following Blow Injuries to the Head).

His use of live test subjects (rabbits) repulses modern sensibilities and perhaps disturbed even those of his day. He laid the groundwork for such analyses, but few seemed to have followed his experimental example. Also, many years passed before even parts of his results were translated into English. A few other academic papers discussed the topic, but most of those were published in Eastern Europe.

Hans Gross did include a section on blood and bloodstain patterns in his *Criminal Investigation* handbook. That was probably where May learned of the techniques. May seems to have been far ahead of his time in the practical use of blood-spatter evidence. The technique would figure in several of his most celebrated cases.

Two days after the judge passed sentence on Dan Ruth, the United States declared war on Austria-Hungary. (The country had been formally at war with Germany since April 6.) Now U.S. troops could be sent to the Italian theater, where they might face Austrian units. On that same day, J. Clark Sellers signed up for military duty at Fort Douglas, near Salt Lake City. May and Clark had both registered for the draft in June. Of course, Sellers was single, while May had a wife and was paying child support. Revelare had to do without Sellers until his discharge after a year of service.

The company now had informants, if not actual agents, all over Idaho. Besides his usual criminal work, May contributed to the war effort by watching for possible violations of the Espionage Act of 1917. The act made it illegal to interfere with the draft or otherwise hamper the war effort. No headline-grabbing murder cases came Luke May's way for the next year or so. Still, Revelare made the newspapers for thwarting a couple of robberies and for breaking up a burglary gang in south-central Idaho. May and his agents also continued to help officials enforce Idaho's prohibition laws.

Meanwhile, on July 18, 1918, May sent a letter to the clerk of the District Court in Salt Lake City. He enclosed his monthly child-support check and asked for verification that he was fully paid up. He also wrote, "I will be pleased to have you furnish me with copies of all the papers in my case."[30] Below, in an all-caps postscript, May also said, "I would like very much to receive the address of Florence May."

Significantly, the case folder contained an envelope, postmarked January 5, 1918, that had gone to two different addresses for Florence in Los Angeles and then to a small Arizona mining town before being returned to the clerk's office in Salt Lake City. A deputy clerk answered May's letter on July 27. The note told May that he was all paid up and gave the cost for certified copies. It also said, "Address of Mrs. May is not known at this office. . . . Delay in replying to your letter was caused by waiting for her to come in for her alimony, at which time it was expected that her address could be learned."[31]

So for a period of more than six months, Florence had been out of touch with the clerk's office. Where was the child during this period? Touring the West with her mother, or perhaps living with an aunt in Utah? Family memories suggest that after her divorce Florence had found work as some sort of performer, perhaps a dancer or stage assistant in a road show. May could have, and probably had, tracked the two through his extensive network of affiliate detectives. It's hard to escape the notion that May's request for Florence's address was merely *pro forma*, based on advice from a lawyer.

Florence must have heard about Luke's interest. In mid-August, her lawyer began a series of actions to have the court substantially increase her monthly allowance. For reasons known only to themselves, May and his lawyer did not respond to any of this. Finally, on November 12, they received a stern show cause order and were forced to act. Thus, on the very same day, Luke's attorney filed a document titled "State of Utah in the Interest of Dorothy May."[32] That complaint served to put the child's future in the hands of the Juvenile Court.

Confidential hearings continued through the following two days. Then the judge declared Dorothy to be, legally, a dependent and neglected child. As a result, the judge decreed that Dorothy was made a ward of the Juvenile Court. She was to be placed "in a good home, said home to be agreed upon by the two attorneys."[33] May would pay a $5 per week support allowance, as well as a full clothing stipend. Of course, all such payments would be handled through the county office. Presumably, Luke would have no direct contact with the child. But then, neither would Florence . . . and that was perhaps Luke's purpose.

A little over a week after the decree, Florence had her attorney sign a final statement. It said, in part, "For good and valuable consideration," she "acknowledges full satisfaction" of all her claims in the case.[34] The records do not describe the settlement that gained Florence's agreement. After this final break, her whereabouts become difficult to trace. The announcement of her brother's death in 1933 gave her location as New York City.

With the files sealed, it is even harder to find out what happened to Florence Dorothy May. Some records connect her with a family that lived in the Chicago area for a while. That particular Florence Dorothy May moved to Logan, Utah, in the late 1920s. She finished high school there and married a local in 1929. There is no way to judge the accuracy of these final conjectures. Still, May almost certainly had no direct contact with his first wife or daughter after these court actions in late 1918.

While those events played out, May was very busy in Idaho. Four days after the armistice in Europe, seven suspects escaped from the Lincoln County jail. Four of the men were burglars arrested on evidence provided by Revelare, so May and his agents joined the pursuit. Yet even with all that going on, in the fall May began to show increased interest in expanding his operation into the state of Washington, specifically Seattle. That interest was confirmed by an item in the *Idaho Statesman* that said Clark Sellers had been discharged from the army and had returned to Pocatello. The brief note then said, "Mr. Sellers left Thursday for Seattle, where he will be the manager of a branch office of the Revelare detective work."[35]

A couple months later, May recruited Clark's friend, John L. Harris, for the Pocatello office. Recall that Sellers had introduced Harris to May before the war. Born in Missouri in 1894, Harris had moved to Salt Lake City around 1915. After a bit of looking around, he found a job as an auto mechanic. Like Sellers, he enlisted in the army in December 1917 and went into an aero squadron. Harris was discharged in March 1919. Corporate records show that Revelare commenced business in Washington on May 2, 1919. Officers included Luke and Clara May, J. Clark Sellers, and John L. Harris. Advertisements for the firm appeared in the *Seattle Times* by the end of the month.

Then Revelare got some publicity that must have seemed like a godsend to May's attempt to open the new office. *The Investigator,* published in Chicago, billed itself as "The world's greatest detective magazine."[36] It filled its pages with articles by and about detectives all across the country. A feature in the issue for July 1919 asked, "Who of us have ever thought that the profession flourished to the point of fame and accuracy amid the great, extensive and lofty mountains of the far West?"

The item was a highly laudatory description of Luke May and his agency. The article outlined several key cases, including the murders of Breckenridge,

Cavanaugh, and Alice Empey. It also described some of the fingerprint and photography techniques May had developed. But its rhetorical question was actually a bit ironic. For, as we saw in chapter 2, most of the top scientific detectives worked in the Far West.

In fact, during the period right after the war, Albert Osborn was the only well-known criminologist who was based in the East. Of course, Osborn specialized in questioned documents and very few such cases make headlines or end up in court. Osborn's one headline-grabbing case for 1919 took place in Topeka, Kansas, not quite the West but far from his base in the East. Osborn joined with a regionally known documents expert to declare a purported will to be a forgery.

Oddly enough, one of our western-based pioneers was working in the East in 1919, although not as a criminologist. As World War I heated up, the U.S. Army had promoted gun expert Edward C. Crossman from the enlisted reserve to the rank of captain and called him to active duty. He was sent to Camp Perry, in Ohio, although he retained his home in Los Angeles. The army had to process great swarms of soldiers entering basic training. Crossman's job was to prepare the needed rifle instructors. After the war, Crossman found himself in charge of organizing a rifle marksmanship competition in New Jersey. Three years later, he would resign from the army for health reasons.

Also in 1919, the International Association for Identification held its annual convention in Berkeley. As noted earlier, Harry H. Caldwell had led formation of the association, which dropped the word "Criminal" from the name at the 1918 annual convention. Interestingly enough, Luke May joined the association a few months later.

Besides Caldwell, the list of speakers included criminology pioneers August Vollmer and Edward O. Heinrich. (May was not slated to attend the Berkeley meeting, quite possibly because he was tracking one of the burglars who had escaped from the Lincoln County jail.) Besides his conference talk, Chief Vollmer initiated many advances in Berkeley during the year, including psychological and intelligence testing of prospective police officers.

Heinrich had moved to Tacoma after gaining his BS degree from UC-Berkeley in 1908. Over time, he did more and more criminological work. After about nine years in Tacoma, he attained a position as chief of police for the city of Alameda, California. But after five or six months, a substantial raise lured him to Boulder, Colorado, as its city manager. Then handwriting expert Theodore Kytka died suddenly in San Francisco. Kytka was a good friend of Heinrich's and had a considerable clientele. Within a few months, Heinrich moved to San Francisco and assumed Kytka's practice. His move might well have had an indirect impact on May's career.

At the time, all of Revelare's business came from Idaho, Montana, and Utah. There is no evidence that the company's advertisements in the Seattle newspapers had attracted any work. Yet there were credible business reasons to pursue that venture. For one, Seattle and the other Puget Sound cities had a greater combined population than the entire state of Idaho. Simple arithmetic suggested the area would generate more business.

His decision was almost certainly helped by another factor. On January 29, 1919, the Eighteenth [Prohibition] Amendment to the U.S. Constitution was officially ratified. As mentioned earlier, Revelare had developed a steady, lucrative sideline helping Idaho officials enforce state prohibition laws. The heavily populated Puget Sound area had close ties to Canada. Did May foresee the huge illegal import industry that would spring up? One suspects he did.

And finally, there was Heinrich's strong commitment to the Bay Area. Up to that point, there was always a chance that he might resume his detective business in the state of Washington. But now, Heinrich was firmly settled in California. Did May decide to "fill a vacuum" in the Northwest? We have no way of knowing, yet it seems not unlikely.

Whatever the reasons, Luke May was about to step onto the stage where he would have his most famous triumphs. There, he would forge a national and international reputation as one of the greatest detectives of his day.

• 5 •

Centralia Deaths Spark Career Surge

"*R*eturned Heroes Slain by I.W.W.," screamed the front-page headline of the *Salt Lake Tribune* for November 12, 1919.[1] Similar headlines about an attack the day before in Centralia, Washington, appeared all over the United States and, indeed, around the world. Details were limited, but the reports agreed that four army veterans had been gunned down by members of the Industrial Workers of the World union, often called the "Wobblies." The incident would be a major turning point in Luke May's career.

To that point, May's attempt to gain a foothold in Washington had gone slowly. Neither his records nor the newspapers noted any Revelare cases in the region for five or six months after the Seattle office opened. During that period, May handled publicized cases in both Montana and Idaho. In Montana, he investigated the clubbing death of Philipsburg storekeeper Frank Lambert. Evidence pointed to the wife as at least an accomplice. However, deputies had not properly secured the crime scene, which hampered May's later assessment. She was acquitted when the case came to trial. This was the first known case where improper handling of evidence might have negated May's efforts.

In mid-October, the Bannock County prosecutor called on him to examine a weapon. The defendant was Pocatello police patrolman Don De Shirlia, who had shot and killed moonshine still operator Charles Atkins during a raid. The officer first alleged that another moonshiner had shot Atkins but switched to a self-defense claim when May's evidence cast doubt on that story. On that basis, his attorney obtained an acquittal from the jury. Still, the county prosecutor later wrote a testimonial letter to May. In it, he said, "Your fire-arm work in the De Shirlia case was especially valuable to the State."[2]

Through all that, events were fermenting in Centralia, located a bit over twenty miles south of Olympia. In Centralia, as elsewhere, painful wage and price adjustments after the war inflamed the face-off between employers and unionized workers. Some of the bitterest conflict involved the Wobblies, who have deep Radical and Anarchist roots. They strongly opposed U.S. involvement in World War I, a stance that angered many people. Thus, in the spring of 1918, a mob wrecked the IWW union hall in Centralia. Despite threats, the union reopened its Centralia headquarters in the summer of 1919. By then, the American Legion provided a strong focus for hostility to the radical union.

Toward the end of October, the American Legion post in Chehalis, just south of Centralia, took up the notion of a parade of remembrance. The *Seattle Times* noted that the Chehalis post planned to confer with the Centralia group. Members would meet "to arrange a joint celebration by both posts of Armistice Day, November 11."[3]

Right away, word on the street claimed that veterans would use the occasion to smash the IWW hall. In early November, a Wobbly leader met briefly with Elmer Smith, the only lawyer in Centralia who supported their cause. What should they do if the Legionnaires attacked? Later testimony stated that Smith equated a break-in at the hall to a home invasion. In such a case, he said, you were entitled to defend yourself.

On November 11, the parade stepped out about two o'clock in the afternoon. Members of the Elks Lodge and a Boy Scout patrol led the way. The Legionnaires marched at the rear of the three-block-long procession, those from Centralia at the very end.

The Centralia contingent included four men marked for death. Post Commander Warren Grimm led them. A star football player in high school and at the University of Washington, Warren later went into law. He then volunteered and spent the war as a lieutenant in the Siberian campaign. He resumed his practice in April 1919. Widowed young, he had remarried and fathered a daughter, born while he was overseas. Marching in the formation behind Grimm were Arthur McElfresh, Ben Cassagranda, and Dale Hubbard.

McElfresh and Cassagranda had served in the 91st Infantry Division. The unit had seen hard action in the Meuse-Argonne offensive and then on the Belgian front. After his discharge, McElfresh became a druggist in Centralia. He was about twenty-five years old and unmarried on the day of the parade. Also about twenty-five, Cassagranda owned a shoeshine parlor in Centralia and had been married for a few months. Son of a lumberman, Dale Hubbard served in France with the forestry engineers. His unit provided timber products for the armies. Around twenty-six years old, he had been married about a month.

The parade route ran north on Tower Avenue, keeping to the right (east) side. Tracks down the middle of the street helped the marchers keep their alignment. As it happened, the line passed the IWW hall, which was on the west side of Tower, about fifty yards past the Second Street intersection. At Third Street, the marchers doubled back on the route, returning along the west side. Most of the procession came back past the hall with no problem. But as the head of the Centralia contingent neared the Second Street intersection, Grimm saw that the group had separated as they made their reversal at Third Street. Grimm called out, "Halt" to the front lines, then ordered those further back to "Close up."

From here, partisan accounts split drastically. Wobbly supporters said the Legion contingent charged the hall. Only when the attackers broke down the doors, the Wobblies claimed, did they open fire. Conversely, Legion witnesses said there was no such move before the firing started. With so much conflicting testimony, it's possible, perhaps even probable, that a small group of Legionnaires did break away from the parade and rush the hall. Yet even on the witness stand, none of the armed Wobblies said they had given any warning before they began firing wildly. At this remove, no one can confirm or deny those variations. A hail of gunfire killed Grimm, McElfresh, and Cassagranda. Five other Legionnaires were wounded.

The Legionnaires scattered, helping the wounded as best they could. Then, after arming themselves, they rushed the hall and overpowered the shooters. Some Wobblies fled, and one of them shot and killed Hubbard before being captured. That evening, vigilantes lynched that shooter from a nearby bridge. No attempt was ever made to identify those responsible. The final victim of this incident was rancher and Deputy Sheriff John M. Haney. Four days later, during the search for other Wobbly escapees in the hills, he was accidentally shot and killed by another officer.

By early December, authorities had jailed a dozen suspects, including Elmer Smith. Because of all the local publicity, a Superior Court judge granted a change of venue for the trial. It would take place in late January at Montesano, located about thirty-two miles west of Olympia. And, at some time after the shootings, authorities hired Luke May and Revelare.

One may well ask a key question: How did Revelare land such a high-profile case? Possibly they had handled enough cases in Washington to pay expenses, but if so, none had made the news. Perhaps someone in law enforcement recalled the article in *The Investigator*. Their complex case, with so many people involved, might benefit from May's expertise. Of course, it's possible authorities *preferred* a little-known agency. Rumors suggested that militant Wobblies might try to disrupt the trial. A new firm might have better success in placing undercover agents at union gatherings.

Either way, they took a chance. May's commitment to objective, scientific evaluation of data was total. He refused to skew his results to fit anyone's preconceived notions or a hoped-for outcome. More than once, over the years, his results would disappoint the police.

The Mays might have still been living in Pocatello at this point. Or they were perhaps in the process of moving to Seattle. In any case, Luke found himself spending a lot of time in Centralia in the weeks and months after the attack. This first major case on the Pacific Coast would clearly involve a great deal of work. So May brought John L. Harris with him from Idaho and made him the office manager for the Seattle branch. That freed up Sellers for more legwork. Harris would collect and organize the agent accounts that began showing up in Revelare files by mid-December.

Besides assigning men to watch the Wobblies, May launched a detailed study of the physical evidence. His investigators tracked many of the guns used by the union men, but it was never clear how many weapons they had. Agents also waded through reams of conflicting witness accounts.

From all this, May and the local officials reconstructed what happened. Grimm had died from a rifle shot, the death wound slanting downward through his torso. The external blood spray showed that he had been standing out in the street, facing away from the IWW hall. The *Idaho Statesman,* in Boise, described part of May's results: "Tracing up the side of the angle, the exact location of the man who fired the . . . rifle was located in the Avalon hotel."[4] The Avalon was located on the east side of Tower, south of the Second Street intersection.

Cassagranda was killed by a handgun. He was shot on Second Street, probably by a revolver fired also from the Avalon Hotel. McElfresh was hit in the head by a high-powered .22-caliber rifle. Blood evidence showed that he had been out in the street when hit. He was the only victim within even twenty yards of the union hall. Shell casings and testimony showed that the small-caliber rifle had been fired by one of three IWW members stationed on a ridge four to five hundred yards to the east of the hall. The men posted there had been told to open fire if they heard shots from near the hall.

The Wobblies had not only armed themselves, they had set up an ambush. Besides the sniper positions in the Avalon Hotel and on the ridge, later testimony showed that they had shooters in the Arnold Hotel, located across Tower Avenue about thirty yards northeast of the hall. Whatever their purported right to defend a meeting hall as their home, they had clearly gone well beyond anything Elmer Smith could have imagined. Eventually, ten men were indicted for the killings in Centralia. That included Smith, who was charged as an accessory. Jury selection for the trial took until February 6, 1920.

As an indication that Revelare still had a presence in Idaho, May was in Boise on that day. He was there for a peace officers' convention, convened by the state commissioner of law enforcement. May gave a talk titled "The Peace Officer and [the] Private Detective."[5]

The Wobbly trial proceeded, with fireworks on both sides. May's experience and training surely guided a lot of the prosecution's courtroom preparation. And his special expertise proved crucial, including the bullet-tracking skill he displayed in the 1917 Cavanaugh case. Three years after that case, May was still ahead of his time in using the technique.

The court released one of the accused early in the trial. Another was institutionalized after being judged not guilty by reason of insanity. The jury verdict acquitted Elmer Smith. Despite his ill-advised assertion about "home" defense, his pacifist views about nonviolence were well known. The other seven were convicted of second-degree murder. The judge then imposed the maximum sentence for the crime, twenty-five to forty years in prison. Most served only about ten years before they were paroled. May would eventually handle a great many murder cases, but none would be more controversial than this one. Stories about the event were laced with harsh partisan propaganda. One side called it the "Centralia Massacre." Others used the more low-key "Armistice Day Riot."

The case solidified May's decision to reposition Revelare to focus more on the coast. And his success at Centralia generated much more work behind the scenes for May's agency. Not long after the verdict, the *Idaho Statesman* reported on a reorganization. Clark Sellers had been reassigned such that "all offices in Utah, Idaho, Montana and Wyoming are under his direction. He will make his headquarters at Pocatello."[6]

May would run the main office in Seattle. By this time, Revelare had clearly recruited many local sources. Those contacts supplied Luke with a key tip about a major sawmill fire in Chehalis at the end of March. *The Oregonian*, in Portland, reported, "The fire undoubtedly was of incendiary origin."[7] Not only had there been a reek of gasoline, but the nearest firehose had been slit. The report also said, "C. L. Brown, one of the pioneer lumbermen of southwest Washington, is the principal owner of the mill."

Four days after that report, May sent a letter to Brown. Most of the message concerned other business. Then he urged the lumberman to launch a hush-hush search for a second gasoline bomb. "I have reason to believe that there was another place where the fire was intended to start among the lumber piles."[8] That follow-up did not appear in the newspapers.

But May's next big case—a firearms assessment—did make a splash in the news. It opened with a headline in the *Seattle Times* for April 5, 1920: "Outlaw May Have Murdered His Companion."[9] Two crooks had been stopping cars in southeast Seattle and robbing the occupants. Although they tried to keep moving, law officers finally caught up with them. In the resulting shootout, Deputy Sheriff Robert Scott was killed. The bandits escaped by forcing a robbery victim to drive them into downtown Seattle. The driver heard a shot just before one bandit disappeared into the waterfront area. The other crook, one Elmer Cady, lay dead in the back seat. According to May's account, police found a handgun next to the body.

May began receiving evidence for the case nine days after the killings. These included a mix of bullets, empty shell casings, and several unfired cartridges. The King County coroner sent three .38-caliber slugs, two extracted from Scott and one from Cady. Eventually May received two .41-caliber Colt revolvers, "one 38 caliber Colt Army Special revolver No. 434364," and another .38-caliber weapon (the record of its make and model do not appear in the case file).[10]

May's interest in firearms identification dated from at least eight or nine years before this and the Centralia cases. In chapter 3, we learned about Frenchman Victor Balthazard, who gave a paper about bullets passing through cloth and then flesh. In research papers that followed, the professor introduced the use of enlarged photographs to highlight marks on bullets. Firearms testing methods had also spread to the United States. However, the bullets from the Centralia fusillade were apparently too distorted or damaged to match with any particular weapon, other than the caliber and general type.

For the Scott-Cady case, May compared the weight and caliber of several test bullets to the death bullets. He also painstakingly measured the width and depth of the grooves on the surface of each slug. From all this, May determined that *all* the fatal bullets had almost certainly come from the .38-caliber weapon found in the escape car. Still, to check every possibility, May also fired several test shots from the Army Special and observed that the weapon "marks the bullets in a very clean-cut matter."[11] However, he also found that the groove widths and other features were quite different from those of the death slugs. Thus, he reported, "We can definitely determine that the Revolver No. 434364 did not fire the bullets that were taken from the bodies of Cady and Scott."

May noted that the murder weapon "had been handled by more than thirty persons" so the fingerprints on it were "just a jumble."[12] Linking it to a particular suspect seemed hopeless. However, he also noticed that the gun had been altered to improve its trigger pull. His detective curiosity aroused, May examined the inside of the weapon. There, he found a clear set of fingerprints. Although the suspected killer, known only as "Blackie" in news reports, stayed free for several years, police did eventually track him down. At first, he disclaimed any knowledge of the murder weapon. He was stunned when May showed him images of his fingerprints inside the gun. A confession quickly followed.

Luke May's next newsworthy case came in mid-May. The headline in the *Seattle Times* read, "Father Shot and Killed by Stepson."[13] The article began, "Robert Friedman, 22, is held in jail today pending action of the authorities on the death of his stepfather, Phil B. Friedman, prominent jeweler and sportsman."

The stepson claimed the two had quarreled, not for the first time, about the stepfather's abuse of Mrs. Friedman. The older man had purportedly produced a gun, which the two fought over. The gun then went off and inflicted a fatal shot to the head. Revelare received the death weapon, a .45-caliber Colt automatic, on May 22. May was not, however, allowed to visit the crime scene until two days after that. (The house had been under a scarlet fever quarantine.) By then, he later reported, "All of the blood in any quantity had been washed up and all physical traces removed with the exception of some few spots on the floor."[14]

The police had discovered bullet fragments, along with a slug embedded in a piece of board. Three empty shell casings had also been recovered. In his crime scene inspection, May was able to locate a number of bullet scars, which gave him a reasonable idea of most of the trajectories. He concluded that two shots had been fired at the elder Friedman as he had turned to run. Then the attacker clubbed him three times on the back of the head. The autopsy revealed that the blows were such that "any one . . . would have been sufficient to have incapacitated" him.[15]

May's tests showed that the large automatic pistol would deposit clear powder burns "at anything under 25 inches." However, the coroner found no such marks. Thus, the fatal head shot had probably been fired while the old man was sprawled on the floor. Bullet scars supported this scenario, but the lack of blood stains made it difficult to confirm. May's report concluded, "In my opinion the element of self defense entering into this case is preposterous. This could all have been definitively determined however, could I have been on the ground and been able to make my investigation with all the elements as they should have been."[16]

Several months later, the prosecuting attorney finally gave up. He had the court drop the murder charge because there was "insufficient evidence to convict."[17] This would not be the last Luke May case where law enforcement personnel compromised a crime scene.

Revelare's work in the logging camps and lumber mills continued through all this. In May, the county prosecuting attorney in Chehalis sent him a letter that referred to "the matter we were talking about the last time in Chehalis."[18] They had evidently discussed an expansion of May's network

EXHIBITS STATE OF WASHINGTON
vs
ROBERT FRIEDMAN.
RECEIVED OF CORONOR SHAVER, PIERCE CO.
ON MAY 22 1920, FOR EXAMINATION.

Figure 5.1.   Friedman Death Weapon. *Source:* **May-Reid Records.**

of contacts among timber company workers. The attorney said, "Mr. Brown, who was down the other day representing the Lumbermen's Association, seemed very strongly in favor of having the work carried out and that you should do it."

Records do not detail what they agreed to, but one result appeared on July 16. On that day, a Miss May Clowers signed an affidavit concerning a sawmill fire near Chehalis. That document placed the blame for the arson on her father, Davis Lee "Barney" Clowers, who was estranged from the family. The affidavit and other evidence induced Clowers to confess. At the end of September, *The Oregonian* reported, "D. L. (Barney) Clowers, confessed incendiary, was Tuesday sentenced to five to seven years in Walla Walla penitentiary."[19]

A couple weeks later, May received a letter about the case from the manager of a fire insurance consortium. It said, in part, "I . . . want to congratulate you upon the very satisfactory manner, not alone in which the case terminated, but in which it was conducted."[20]

For all of 1920, Revelare logged nearly seventy cases, including eight death cases with nine victims (the Scott-Cady case being a double murder). Some missing chickens sparked the final death case for the year. Peter "Pete" Colagino was sure birds were being stolen from his coop by one of neighbor Alex McGibbon's kids. When Pete went to the police, Alex headed for Colagino's place to talk about it. In the subsequent confrontation, Pete fired a pistol three times, one slug striking McGibbon with deadly effect. When he was arraigned on a first-degree murder charge, Colagino claimed self-defense.

A month later, May issued a report on his assessment of Colagino's revolver, the fatal bullet, and three spent cartridges. He noted that the weapon was a very cheap, low-quality model, and the chambers in the revolver's cylinder did not line up properly with the barrel. When the gun was fired, the exposed edge of the barrel scored one side of the bullet. The misalignment also caused an unusual, very clear-cut pattern in the grooves on the bullets. And, finally, a major groove width matched perfectly between test and death slugs. These distinctive features allowed May to conclude, "This revolver fired the bullet taken from McGibbon's body."[21] Colagino was found guilty and sentenced to life in prison. In reporting on the case, the *Seattle Times* said, "The trial, one of the most speedy murder cases in the history of the court, lasted exactly two days."[22]

Of course, murder cases were only a small part of the Revelare workload. Also, some that looked like they involved a murder didn't go anywhere. In the spring, May received a letter from the district attorney of Union County, Oregon, in La Grande. The attorney noted that he had collected "very satisfactory testimonials as to your methods of running down crimes and criminals."[23] He wondered if May could indeed match "a certain bullet" to "a given pistol." The attorney closed with, "You doubtless recognize that the most serious handicap with which county officials have to contend, in securing services such as you offer, is the lack of funds."

May also received a letter from the Union County sheriff dated the same day. The note said, "Although we are unable to tell whether or not the same will come to trial, we would like to satisfy ourselves as to the gun and bullet."[24] The sheriff wanted to know how much a test would cost and how long it would take.

The criminologist replied with a list of rates. Although he says nothing in the letter, the amounts quoted seem to be rock bottom, compared to the normal Revelare charges. May gave careful instructions on how to package the exhibits so a proper chain of custody would be maintained. In closing, he said that if they could get the exhibit to him right away, "I should be able to give you a report within 24 hours after it is received."[25] County officials apparently found the Revelare rates acceptable. A week later, they sent him a .38-caliber Colt automatic pistol (No. 1786), a spent shell, and a soft nose bullet. (Neither the victim nor the suspect were identified.)

May sent back a long, detailed report. He found several features of the pistol that distinguished it "from those usually found in 38 automatics" and left unique imprints on the spent shells.[26] He wrote, "A microscopic examination of markings left by the extractor and ejector on the bottom of the base and on the inside edge of the rim . . . are identical in the shell submitted to me for examination with those fired for test purposes." Based on these peculiar traits he concluded, "I am satisfied that the empty cartridge case submitted for examination was fired in and ejected from Colt Automatic Pistol 38 Caliber No. 1786."

May noted that the pistol's barrel had slightly shallower grooves and narrower lands (the higher areas between the grooves) than were typical of that make and model. These conformed exactly to the rifling signs found on the evidence bullet, making it highly likely that it had been fired from the weapon submitted. However, he also observed some slightly different marks compared to his test bullets. These had probably been caused by debris that had been removed from the barrel before he received the pistol. May then returned the exhibits to the sheriff. Unfortunately, no further correspondence appeared in the case file. Usually, when a case seemed to go no further from this point, it was because officials could not firmly tie possession of the weapon to a particular suspect.

Luke May's chain-of-custody advice for the sheriff showed another aspect of his character. Over the years, he would prove to have the instincts of a dedicated teacher. He didn't want to just practice scientific detection; he had an urge to explain it to the world. Another customer contacted Revelare to have them examine a signature on a will that was up for probate. However, the document could not be released for direct examination, so a photograph had to be made. May sent the lawyer detailed instructions on how the image should be recorded. That included the specific type of film to be used. In addition to absolutely sharp focus, he wrote, "The light should be diffused evenly over the whole document and the long exposure then made using the smallest stop on the lens."[27]

By now, Luke and Clara May had been living in Seattle for some time. They had settled in the Franklin Apartments in the Belltown District, about a mile from downtown. Streetcars provided easy transport to the Revelare offices in the Lyon Building. Those offices were located less than a block from the King County Courthouse.

None of May's early 1921 cases generated much interest outside the Pacific Northwest. However, summer brought one that made headlines all over the country. It involved Kate (Keeler) Mooers, wealthy Seattle real estate owner. Everyone who knew her agreed that she was strange. Her road to affluence had begun with a string of boardinghouses in Montana. Acquaintances figured she'd been married at least three times in her sixty-five or so years. At forty-five, she had reportedly married a nineteen-year-old boy, but they were soon divorced.

Figure 5.2.   Franklin Apartments in Seattle. *Source*: May-Reid Records.

Her most recent husband had been physician Charles E. Mooers, who was seven or eight years younger than Kate. He filed for divorce when she insisted he hire only male assistants and tell her whenever he treated a female patient. Told how she sometimes fired a revolver out the window just for show, the court readily granted the divorce. After the separation, Kate's real estate holdings and other assets were estimated to be worth more than $200,000. (That would be about $2.6 million today.)

Kate loved to show off her expensive jewelry and drove a fancy car. Yet in other matters, neighbors and business people knew her to be downright stingy. Thus, news reports generally described Kate as eccentric. Her latest eccentricity was to marry ex-convict James Edward Mahoney. Aged about thirty-six, James was the son of a woman who ran a small downtown hotel that belonged to Kate. He had been paroled after serving three years of a five- to eight-year prison sentence for robbery. James and Kate were married in February 1921.

In April, the couple announced that they were headed east to St. Paul, Minnesota. Their belated honeymoon would probably last about a month, they said. To finance the trip, Kate purchased a batch of travelers' checks, signing them with her new married name. Soon, Kate's two nieces began receiving postcards, ostensibly from their aunt.

But near the end of the month, James Mahoney returned, alone, to Seattle. He claimed that Kate had decided to extend the trip to Havana, Cuba, and then to New York. However, Mahoney's parole limited the amount of time he could spend out of state. He would have to wait until that restriction was lifted in June. A letter purportedly signed by Kate gave James access to her safety-deposit box. He also had a notarized power-of-attorney allowing him to control her other business affairs.

One of Kate's nieces lived in Vancouver, British Columbia, another in Wenatchee, Washington. They compared notes and agreed that the postcards did not quite look like Kate's handwriting and just didn't sound right. They voiced their suspicions to Captain Charles Tennant, top detective for the Seattle police. Tennant had spent six years as a beat patrolman before being made a detective in 1903. After two years of that, he was promoted to the post he held for the rest of his life. His approach was strictly old school. Talk to enough people, apply the right pressure, and someone would eventually talk.

He had no trouble believing something was fishy. A fairly young, spry ex-con married a rich old dame? Mahoney was obviously up to no good. Old-fashioned detective work soon convinced Tennant that Mahoney had murdered his wife. He suspected that James had disposed of the body in Lake Union, located about a mile north of downtown Seattle. Police picked up Mahoney for questioning, but they needed something to hold him. Luke May now entered the case as a handwriting expert. He determined that the signature on the safety-deposit box letter was not that of Kate Mahoney. Two days after James was brought in, he was booked on a charge of forgery.

At the same time, police watercraft began dragging Lake Union. That set off a media frenzy. The *Seattle Times* blared the headline "Drag Lake Union for Body!"[28] Pressed by reporters, Tennant told them they were searching for a trunk that might contain a body "believed to be Mrs. Kate M. Mahoney. . . ." Newspapers everywhere latched onto that information, thereafter referring to the episode as the "Trunk Murder."

Meanwhile, May examined more writing samples and found more forgeries. His report concluded, "In the instances of the travelers checks and the power of attorney . . . the difference in the writing is clearly apparent."[29] A follow-up on the power-of-attorney struck pay dirt. The woman who had signed the document as Mrs. Mahoney was not Kate. Prosecutors now had several forgery charges to keep Mahoney in jail while police searched for the body.

Through June and July, the police continued to drag the lake. They even brought in deep-sea divers to look. Finally, in early August, a trunk broke free from the concrete block that had anchored it. An autopsy of the body inside showed that Kate had been drugged with a strong dose of morphine, then killed by blows that crushed her skull.

Aside from all the forgeries, a solid chain of evidence linked James to the murder. Mahoney's defense attorney claimed that it was all a frame-up by Tennant and the Seattle police. They wanted to "get" an ex-convict. Grasping for any shadow of doubt, the lawyer even went after May. A *Seattle Times* subhead for September 27 said, "Pen Expert Grilled."[30] The attorney tried to tempt him into an off-the-cuff signature assessment. The *Times* said, "The witness promptly replied he would not attempt an answer without a chance to compare it with a known signature of Mrs. Mahoney, which would require some time for study."

Foiled, the lawyer abandoned that try. On redirect, "May said he would not consider the alleged forgeries on the bottom of the travelers' checks 'clever,' but that some of them are 'good.' As to the alleged forgery of the writing of Kate Mahoney on the power of attorney, he would say it was 'poor.'"[31] A few days later, after less than five hours deliberation, the jury found Mahoney guilty of murder in the first degree. They also voted for the death penalty. After fourteen months of failed appeals, James Mahoney died on the gallows.

Nothing May had done before received the heavy publicity of the Centralia and Mahoney deaths. Nor did he receive much personal notice in the news media for those cases. They would be recalled, however, when he was associated with another sensational case a few months later.

Even so, it's worth repeating that the bulk of Revelare's work took place behind the scenes. For example, during the summer, one agent described how easy it was to obtain liquor in downtown Seattle. He was out on assignment when, shortly before noon, a friend invited him up to his room. There, the man "sent for the bell boy and asked for a quart of whiskey. The bell boy left and returned shortly with a quart of Johnnie Dewar Scotch Whiskey for which my friend paid him $15."[32]

In mid-afternoon, the agent left the friend to sleep it off and walked to another hotel nearby. "Here," he wrote, "I found George Von Reuten, a bootlegger. I bought a round of drinks to get him to talk." George was well connected and could provide a lot of information about the Seattle underworld, "but it is necessary to get him half drunk first."[33]

Evidently, the agent knew how to nurse his drinks. After two hours there, he asked George where he could get some beer. At the suggested bar, the agent ordered a near beer. He soon discovered that the place to be was down a flight of stairs. The agent walked in and found the bartender about to pour a drink for a customer. "They both were surprised and angry at my sudden and unexpected appearance, but before they had a chance to recover, I started kidding them and told the bartender he might just as well pour out a drink for me as long as he had the bottle out."[34]

Another agent reported a similar experience. One morning about eleven o'clock he ran into a sailor who had been drinking. The sailor was evidently tired of boozing alone and invited the agent up to his room. He had about a quarter bottle, and they quickly drank that up. The sailor hurried out to get some more. He was gone no more than ten to fifteen minutes. He had clearly found it pretty easy to acquire a fresh bottle.

Another of May's summer cases stayed undercover until the real work was done. On August 1, employees of the Great Northern Lumber Company in Leavenworth found a bomb behind the company's dam. (Leavenworth is located almost eighty miles directly east from Seattle, deep in the Cascade Mountains.) A few days later, a manager for the firm asked May to examine the bomb for fingerprints.

The company asserted that the bomb was "of sufficient size to have blown up the biggest portion of the town."[35] Whether or not that was accurate, blasting the dam would have certainly released a flood and caused major damage in Leavenworth as well as several small towns further downstream. May judged it to be a "very well made bomb, enclosed in a five gallon jug which was full of loose dynamite or T. N. T. that had been taken from the original package, weight about 73 pounds all together."[36]

In a follow-up letter, May said his agent in Leavenworth had heard locals assert that "the bomb was placed there by the Great Northern Lumber Company themselves, to . . . aid them in litigation."[37] He closed with, "This, of course, was only rumor, but shows the frame of mind of some parties there."

A bit over a week later, *The Oregonian* said, "Five government agents have arrived in Leavenworth to investigate an attempt to blow up the dam of the Great Northern Lumber Company here. . . . The discovery was kept secret until today."[38]

The Leavenworth bomb was one of five sabotage cases May logged for the year 1921. All told, the agency recorded around ninety cases, up nearly 30 percent from the previous year. As a possible harbinger of the future, a third of the cases involved questioned document examinations. Eleven cases involved death investigations, with eleven victims. As we'll see shortly, May logged the last two of those death cases between Christmas and New Year's.

Two years of solid work had made Luke May well known to law enforcement and legal people in the northwest. For example, a prosecuting attorney in Chehalis sent him a letter to thank him for his help: "I especially compliment you for the valuable assistance you have rendered Lewis County and the State of Washington in bringing to justice the I.W.W.'s who are seeking to bring about a reign of terror in Western Washington."[39]

Along the way, newspaper coverage of the Centralia and Mahoney cases had introduced Luke S. May, Seattle criminologist to readers. During the two or three years to follow, that phrase would become widely recognized by the public at large. That would start with a case as well publicized as the Mahoney trunk murder.

· 6 ·

Education, Innovation, and More National Renown

$\mathcal{M}$ay's next sensational case began with the *Seattle Times* headline "Bachelor Murdered, Woman Missing."[1] The dead man was Ferdinand Hochbrunn, age seventy-two, who owned considerable real estate in Seattle. The elusive female was Clara Skarin, who was about twenty-eight years old. The relationship between Skarin and Hochbrunn was complex and somewhat odd. Years earlier, Skarin's widowed mother had been Hochbrunn's housekeeper. Informally adopting the daughter, Ferdinand paid for her clothing and a business school education. Clara and her mother then went out on their own.

But Clara got involved with a married man, Robert Winborn. Bitterly angry, Winborn's wife shot and wounded Clara, killed Clara's mother, and then committed suicide. From her hospital bed, Clara claimed there was nothing between her and Robert. She declared, "I am only 18; Mr. Winborn is close to 50."[2] She was, in fact, then closer to twenty-five years old. When Clara recovered, she took a job as a telephone operator using an assumed name. Then Winborn, in ill health, moved to Michigan to be near family. Clara promptly quit her job and followed him there. After he died, Clara claimed she had married him on his deathbed, although no marriage license was ever found. She even used her purported married name for a while.

Clara told contradictory stories about her return to Seattle and what happened during the summer and fall of 1921. Hochbrunn paid her fare back, and she definitely lived at his flat for several months. Then, in September, she went to stay with an older female cousin. How long Clara had been at Hochbrunn's without telling her family was unclear, and she gave several versions of why she finally moved.

Finally, in mid-October, Hochbrunn unexpectedly failed to appear at a job site where he was helping repair one of his properties. Yet Skarin continued to visit Hochbrunn's apartment. Late in the month, she told attorney Edward von Tobel, Hochbrunn's longtime friend and business manager, that Ferdinand was in Portland. After a while, von Tobel sent a note to the Portland address and asked for instructions on his friend's business affairs. When no response came, the attorney quietly engaged a private detective. In late November, he mentioned the inquiry to Skarin. She left Seattle a day or two later.

Not quite a month after that, freezing temperatures in Seattle caused a pipe to burst in Hochbrunn's apartment. Searchers tracing the leak found the old man's body. The coroner declared that Hochbrunn had been dead at least two months. Suspicion naturally fell on Skarin. May logged the case six days after the body was discovered. He received an evidence package that included "One deformed lead bullet taken from the head of F. Hochbrunn, for the purpose of examination."[3]

He sent in his report about ten days later. Because the slug was so badly deformed, he wrote, "it would be practically impossible to positively identify the gun firing this bullet."[4] By now, May had studied hundreds of bullets, fired by many different firearms. Thus, key features of the slug provided solid evidence for the type of weapon that fired it. "Although I am unable to give a positive opinion due to the deformity of the bullet," May wrote, "I am satisfied it came from a 32 [caliber] Smith and Wesson revolver."

Gun makers usually produce many models of firearms. The core components are a barrel, firing chamber, and the "action." The action links the trigger to the firing mechanism and, for an automatic, inserts cartridges and then ejects empties. But each model has varied features due to the gun's design and the manufacturing processes. For rifled guns, bullets fired by the weapon show specific traits.

These so-called class characteristics are common to a particular make and model. Two that are relatively easy to measure are the diameter (caliber) and weight of the bullets the weapon fires. Even today, guns sold as ".32 caliber" take ammunition that can vary from 0.312- to 0.321-inch in diameter, depending upon the model. That may not sound like much, but one can, with reasonable care, measure a difference of 0.001-inch with a hand tool. Bullet weights vary by much more than that and offer more data about the type of gun.

The rifling defines a full set of class characteristics. These grooves, cut along the inside of the barrel, impart spin to the bullet. The number of grooves for different models typically range from two to eight, but some have as many as twelve or sixteen. The width and depth of the grooves provide two more key properties. Of course, the wider the grooves, the narrower the lands between each, all other things being equal. The grooves can be cut to spin the bullet in a right (clockwise) or left direction, called the "twist." The twist rate adds yet another dimension. The twist rate is the length of barrel that would be required to take the grooves through a full turn. (The actual barrel length is often less than the twist rate.)

At the same time as the Hochbrunn work, May also had a death case in Aberdeen. A stevedore named Karl Magi had been shot and killed. Police sent May the fatal bullet and a suspected murder weapon, also a .32 caliber. The gun was an unusual model, a Warner Arms automatic pistol called "The Infallible." May's report to the police chief stated that they had most likely sent him the right gun. However, he wrote, "Before going into court and testifying, it would be necessary to confirm it with a number of Warner automatic pistols to show and corroborate my opinion."[5] That proved difficult because no dealers in the region carried the line. May even advertised in the newspapers, offering "Infallible" owners a fee if they would loan him their guns for a day.

But unlike the Warner, Smith & Wesson handguns were ubiquitous, and May was quite familiar with their class characteristics. Police never found the actual weapon that killed Hochbrunn. However, they did locate a pawn-shop owner who sold a .32-caliber Smith & Wesson revolver to a woman he identified as Clara Skarin. Authorities also found the police officer who issued her a gun permit. Clara was a very attractive young woman, with thick auburn hair and large, expressive blue eyes. That gave her away, despite the phony name and address she used.

Headlines about the death and the search for Skarin appeared all over the country. Ironically, her striking appearance again betrayed her, as an informant in Oakland, California, recognized her on the street. In September,

Figure 6.1.   Magi Death Weapon, "The Infallible." *Source*: May-Reid Records.

a *Seattle Times* headline shouted, "Clara Skarin Held in Murder Case!"[6] A few days after the arrest, Clara confessed that she had indeed shot Hochbrunn but claimed it was self-defense. She had bought the gun three weeks before using it because, she said, "I have a sixth sense which warns me of danger."[7]

She claimed that on the night of October 12 or 13 (she couldn't quite remember which) the old man had made "improper advances" to her. When she flashed the revolver, he took it away from her, but she managed to regain it. "Then," she said, "He started to run and I pulled the trigger. He was hit in the small of the back. I left him there and got out of Seattle as soon as possible."[8]

In reality, Hochbrunn had been shot in the back of the head. And afterwards, she stole $700 off the old man's body and remained in Seattle for almost seven weeks. Later, Skarin revised her story to say they had wrestled over the gun. She claimed that she had finally managed to hold it against Hochbrunn's head and press the trigger with her thumb.

When the trial began, Skarin's lead defense attorney, John F. Dore, had answers for the inconsistencies. Skarin wanted to surrender to police right after the shooting. However, von Tobel, Hochbrunn's old friend and attorney, had talked her out of it. *He* had told her what to say so he could gain control of Hochbrunn's rental income. Not one shred of evidence supported these accusations, and they were totally discredited in court. Even so, the defense pulled out all the emotional stops about their orphaned, homeless client with a tragic past. Reportedly, one juror sobbed openly, and another had tears when one of Skarin's attorneys dramatically related the awful events of her life.

And, in the end, the evidence seems to have meant little. On one side the jury had an elderly, not particularly sympathetic victim. Skarin was young, pretty, and had those big, "innocent-looking" blue eyes. Friends had always remarked on her soft, sincere voice and open face. She had, after all, managed to convince neighbors that Hochbrunn was out of town when she knew full well he was long dead. Those same features served her well on the witness stand.

Although a few jurors first voted for conviction, the jury acquitted Skarin after less than two and a half hours. They did not even suggest she might be guilty of a lesser charge—involuntary manslaughter, or some such. In his writings, May seldom commented on trial results, and this case was no exception. One rather suspects he might have been dismayed and disheartened by how the panel ignored what seemed like a clear pattern of evasion and deceit. Of course, jury verdicts that seem contrary to the weight of evidence were, and still are, not unheard of.

Not long after May submitted his first report for the Hochbrunn case, the *Seattle Times* published a long article about scientific crime detection. The item featured "Luke S. May, the criminologist," and noted that he was the program chairman for a gathering of Pacific Northwest law officers to be held in Bellingham. Organizers expected at least two hundred people to attend the meeting. The newspaper said the conclave was "the first gathering of its kind in the history of the Northwest."[9]

The reporter then described what it was that a criminologist did. "His role is to find the scientific facts, without prejudice or bias, neither for nor against one side or the other from either a personal or professional standpoint." The writer discussed evidence in the form of fingerprints, blood, and more. What was even more interesting, he said, was what the criminologist could do with a pattern of bloodstains. "From these stains, no matter how few or how small, he is then able to determine the manner in which the crime was committed and perfect a complete mental pictorial version of its enactment."[10]

But even then, the detective's job was not done. "The stiffest task of all remains," the writer declared. "And that is the difficult ordeal he must go through in making the jury assimilate his ideas and scientific facts and hypothesis."[11]

This is another area where the depiction of May as Sherlock Holmes breaks down, by the way. In the authentic Holmes stories, the detective never appeared on the witness stand in court. The reporter closed his article about May and the conference on a related note. If the expert is not in command of the situation, he wrote, "The lawyers will controvert his evidence . . . before he ever leaves the stand."[12]

On the first day of the conference in late January, attendees formalized the Northwest Association of Sheriffs and Police. They elected private detective May as their first president. That oddity arose because, as noted in chapter 1, he would hold deputy sheriff status in many, many counties during his career. The association started out with a bang. In April, they announced plans for a clearinghouse for crimes and criminals, with a first focus on moonshine and narcotics. May told the Associated Press, "Lists of all narcotic addicts and peddlers will be compiled by the clearing house and distributed to all law enforcement officials."[13]

A couple months later, crime-fighting pioneer August Vollmer also presided over a law enforcement conference. He was then president of the International Association of Chiefs of Police. Officers from all over North America gathered in San Francisco to discuss a wide range of problems. Most ambitiously, they advocated a criminal identification system at the national level. One of their many other topics was the use of radio in police work. At the time, radio was the coming thing among professionals as well as amateurs.

No evidence exists to indicate that May and Vollmer corresponded regularly. Still, both headed large police associations, and they had the same goals.

Living on the Pacific Coast, they almost certainly compared notes. In the fall, the Northwest Association followed up on the radio idea. The *Bellingham Herald* reported, "Luke S. May, of Seattle, president of the Northwest Association of Sheriffs and Police has arranged with the *Seattle Post-Intelligencer*, a newspaper that maintains a broadcasting station, to send out the latest information of crimes, with directions to officers."[14]

While the advantages of a police radio system seemed clear, few cities had worked out such agreements. In part, that was because of regulations imposed by a precursor to the Federal Communications Commission. At first, their rules severely restricted the hours that a given station could operate. The federal interpretation of other rules led to an oddity. Every police broadcast had to be intermixed with some form of entertainment. Thus, we are told that Detroit police broadcasts, which began in 1923, were always preceded by the playing of "Yankee Doodle."

The Seattle station handled the rule partly by having the police band play. But the *Post-Intelligencer* unit shut down early the following year. Luckily, the police made arrangements with another station to do the broadcasts. Awkward as this early approach was, it still proved to be a valuable advance. Officials continued to piece together service for five or six years, until they obtained a shortwave radio system dedicated to police business.

However, the Association faced many other problems. Perhaps worst of all were the crippling jealousies and turf disputes. A writer for *The Oregonian* noted that, not only did officers not cooperate for their mutual benefit, sometimes they actually worked against each other. "Instances have been known in some cities where one group of officers has tipped off a [liquor] raid just so a rival group would not get the credit of making arrests."[15]

At its first big meeting, the Association had also proposed the creation of a school to teach applied criminology. They asked May to head the school and devise a complete, practical curriculum. The school was first called the Northwest College of Criminology. Later, it would be renamed the Institute of Scientific Criminology. The founding of the school was featured in the nationally distributed *Police Journal*. Items about it also appeared in newspapers all across the country. The *Springfield Republican* in Massachusetts observed that "the universities have not been very attentive to this important branch of social science."[16] The school started classes in the fall of the following year.

Naturally, May's normal work did not go away while he led the Northwest Association. In fact, the Revelare caseload rose even more during this year. However, except for the Skarin trial, those cases made hardly a ripple in the news outside the Pacific Northwest. Conversely, May's invention of the "Revelaroscope" hit newspapers all across the country. In July 1922, the *Seattle Times* headlined it as the "Mastodon of the Microscope Family."[17]

Figure 6.2.   May Describing His "Revelaroscope." *Source*: May-Reid Records.

The optical chamber of the giant microscope looked roughly like an extra-tall metal beer keg. That barrel was firmly anchored to a steel post that came to about May's shoulder. The *Times* said, "So powerful is the instrument that the tiniest strand of human hair is made to resemble a section of the trunk of a giant spruce tree."

Its large view screen eased the eyestrain normally felt after hours of staring through a conventional optical lens. In fact, early that year, May had to tell a customer that his final report on a bullet examination would be delayed. He wrote, "My eyes have played out on me having used the microscope too much in the last few days."[18] Such episodes surely must have spurred work on the Revelaroscope. A local company fabricated most of the parts for the device. May then assembled and fine-tuned the scope in his lab. Most of May's early uses seemed to be in document examination.

In fact, publicity about the Revelaroscope had one fascinating result. Albert S. Osborn was described in an earlier chapter as the preeminent questioned documents examiner in the United States, and perhaps the world. In 1922, Osborn published *The Problem of Proof,* which dealt with the best ways to present evidence in court. Naturally, May soon obtained a copy to study for himself. In July 1922, Osborn sent a letter to May. In it, he wrote, "In a newspaper clipping I see the reference to your enormous microscope for the examination of handwriting, and I am much interested in the matter."[19]

He then mentioned his text, *Questioned Documents.* There, Osborn said, he had discussed various instruments used to examine handwriting. He found the Revelaroscope "very interesting" and wanted to know more about it. Over the years, May distributed hundreds, if not thousands of brochures and fact sheets. He surely sent Osborn the information he had asked for. However, the Revelaroscope did not attract much interest after the initial burst.

Of course, the scope was useful for examining many kinds of evidence, obviously including bullets and shell casings. Late the previous year, May had handled a suicide in Tacoma. The victim was the wife of a prominent businessman, so the *Seattle Star* identified the couple involved only as "Mr. and Mrs. John Doe Smith."[20] One feature of the case was the identification of a specific revolver as the death weapon. After his long interview with May, the reporter wrote, "No two guns shoot exactly alike. Barrels rifled in the same factory by the same machinery, operated by the same workmen, have microscopic differences, which . . . mark and brand that bullet as unmistakably the bullet fired from that particular gun."

These differences allowed May to go beyond the class characteristics he used to determine a weapon's make and model, as he had done in the Hochbrunn case. In France, Victor Balthazard addressed that issue in a paper published three months after May's Tacoma case. The professor wrote,

"When the accused weapons are of the same type and the same caliber, it is not enough any more to examine only the rifling marks, and one must resort to the study of the fine scratches caused by the defects of the guns."[21]

That is, as May told the reporter, the repetition in the factory is never perfect and the tools themselves wear over time. A particular barrel might have an extra scratch, a ripple in an edge, or whatever. Over time, wear and corrosion change the bore a little bit more. So, when that gun is fired, these imperfections put unique markings on the bullet. These so-called individual characteristics will show up under a microscope in the slugs fired by that gun, and no other. Over the coming years, this would be verified by thousands upon thousands of test firings.

As a matter of fact, 1922 saw a number of important advances in firearms identification. Emile Chamot, a professor of chemical microscopy at Cornell, issued a monograph titled *The Microscopy of Small Arms Primers.* A primer is the chemical-filled capsule on the back of a cartridge that explodes when hit by the firing pin. That, in turn, sets off the powder. Chamot's main tool was a comparison microscope assembled by the Bausch & Lomb Optical Company in Rochester, New York. His goal was to check primers for defects, but other uses were clearly possible. In Missouri, a court allowed expert testimony to describe how an empty shell casing could be traced to a specific firearm. In Arizona, bullet and shell comparisons helped convict a murderer. Defense attorneys then challenged the admissibility of the firearms evidence and the competence of the expert who presented it. The Arizona Supreme Court ruled against the appeal, confirming a legal precedent for the use of such evidence.

Meanwhile, May's firm continued its heavy workload, logging more than ten cases each month. Naturally, the ones that made the news involved killings. One incident occurred in the hills on the Washington side of the Columbia River, midway between Portland and The Dalles.

A mile and a half from the river, the four men paused at the edge of a slight depression in the hillside. Their guide pointed the way ahead and then turned back down the rough trail. A local, he could not risk being identified as an informer. Heavy brush clogged the slope rising to the left of the low spot. Any number of ambushers could lurk there. The breeze blowing up the river canyon swirled through the underbrush but gave little relief from the hot early-afternoon sun.

Federal Prohibition Agent John Pickett led the way along the lower edge of the slope. Deputy Sheriff Wilfred Rorison followed a few yards behind. Prohibition Agent James Morgan brought up the rear a few more yards back. They had not gone far when muffled voices rumbled from behind and above them. Morgan and Rorison heard the sound first and stopped, so Pickett widened his separation before he too halted. The officers turned back along the trail, now with Morgan leading. Agent Pickett trailed by ten to twelve yards.

Moments later, they saw a man standing up the slope near a spring. He held a 30-30 lever-action carbine at the balance point, with the muzzle pointed down. Morgan was already past the man's location, while Rorison was directly downhill from him. Agent Morgan shouted, "Drop that gun, we are federal officers!"[22]

The suspect, later identified as moonshiner Paul Hickey, didn't hesitate. He snapped his carbine up and fired at Morgan. The slug blasted the officer's weapon from his grasp, then ripped his right arm. Weaponless, he began a staggering run toward the shelter of a tree. A burst of gunfire rang out behind him. Morgan never recalled how many shots were fired. But one of the slugs clipped his skull, and he blacked out. The near miss may well have saved his life because Hickey saw Morgan fall and assumed he was out of action. The moonshiner also hit Rorison, but the officer got off one shot before he went down. The deputy's one round hit Hickey in the groin.

Agent Pickett could not see clearly who was firing. When the other two officers fell, he knew he might be outnumbered and outgunned. He started to run for help from the town of Stevenson, about two miles distant. But when he saw no sign of pursuit, he turned back up the trail. Meanwhile, Morgan had come to and crawled over to check Rorison, dead from a bullet in the chest. Stumbling down the trail, he met Pickett coming back. The two of them made it into Stevenson, where the sheriff quickly organized a posse. The posse found Hickey sprawled near his still, about fifty feet from the spring. The moonshiner barely had time to tell his story before he died from loss of blood.

A week or so after the shootings, May received as evidence the bullets removed from Morgan's arm and Rorison's chest. Along with those, the prosecutor sent him some shells taken from Hickey's pocket. Authorities needed to know if any other weapon had been used during the firefight. The damage to the Morgan bullet hampered the analysis, of course. Still, within those limits, both slugs had probably come from the same gun. This case involved crossed jurisdictions, with a county prosecutor handling a murder where federal officers had been in charge. Thus, not for the last time, almost a year passed before May was paid for his work.

Most of May's other death cases during the year were homicides, but none generated as much interest as the Hochbrunn-Skarin matter. Newspapers across the country reported the death of Rorison and the moonshiner, but there was no follow-up. In fact, months would pass after the Skarin indictment before Revelare had another really big murder case. In the meantime, May made some changes in the business and his home life.

In November 1922, the *Idaho Statesman* Society page announced the marriage and transfer of J. Clark Sellers. On October 25, he married "Miss Jeanette Daniels, daughter of Mr. and Mrs. David Daniels," of Pocatello.[23] Recall that, after the Centralia Wobblies trial, Sellers had returned to Pocatello to take charge of the Revelare office there. Now, the item stated, Sellers was being transferred to Seattle. The *Statesman* went on, "Mr. and Mrs. Sellers are leaving for an extended trip which will include points in British Columbia, before going to their new home."

As noted earlier, Luke and his wife, Clara, lived in the Franklin Apartments in the Belltown District after they first moved to Seattle. While the location was convenient to a streetcar line, the units there were fairly small. The construction was considered of high quality, but amenities in the apartments were rather limited. Nor did the building have an elevator. But in late 1922, the Fionia Apartments opened in the Queen Anne Hill District. Located near the south edge of the district, the five-story structure is more than a mile and a quarter from downtown. Fortunately, several trolley lines passed within a half block of the Fionia. As with most taller structures built after about 1910, the building did have a small elevator.

The newspaper description said the west side apartments had "A panoramic view of the Olympics and Puget Sound from the East Waterway to Smiths Cove."[24] For those on the other side, the owners planned to have a roof platform where everyone could go to enjoy the view. In addition to the latest fixtures, all the units had inlaid hardwood floors and bathrooms finished in white tile. The structure contained apartments with two, three, or four bedrooms. The floor plans all placed the living rooms and galley-style kitchens on the outer wall to take advantage of natural light. The Mays took up residence at the Fionia soon after the building opened. They would have had fine views from their third-floor flat. And the nearby trolley made it easy for Luke to commute to the offices and labs in the Lyon Building.

During 1922, Revelare logged 127 cases, up another 43 percent over the previous year. More than a third of the cases involved questioned documents examination. The log included eleven death cases, with fourteen victims. Aside from the ongoing Skarin trial, the next year began rather quietly. But on March 9, 1923, newspapers all over the country reported a horrific crime. The *Evening Times* in Trenton, New Jersey, had a typical headline: "11-Year Old Girl is Brutally Murdered."[25] The little girl's name was Anna Nosko, and she had been murdered in Battle Ground, Washington, about ten miles north of Vancouver. Her almost nude body had been found just hours after she disappeared on her way home from school. Her throat had been cut, and the assumption was that she had been raped.

Clark County Sheriff William Thompson soon focused his attention on twenty-year-old George Edward "Eddie" Whitfield. Eddie lived close by and had been seen that afternoon near where Nosko's body was found. Moreover, he had an "unsavory" reputation in the area. By a lucky chance, the sheriff had attended May's lectures on criminology. May devoted a short chapter in *Crime's Nemesis* to this case. He wrote, "Sheriff Thompson stripped the suspect and when he found a few bits of foreign substance on his genitals, he carefully wrapped them in cigarette papers."[26]

Crucially, one of the bits was the needle from a fir tree. Whitfield also had blood on his underclothes. He claimed that was from a butchered chicken and vehemently denied having anything to do with Anna's death. Officials called on May to help, and he arrived in time to assist with the autopsy. May and Dr. Robert L. Benson, University of Oregon pathologist in charge, first confirmed that the little girl had been sexually assaulted. They also found that a blow to Anna's head had driven a piece of skull bone into the brain. That, and the resulting large blood clot would have killed her, even without the throat slash.

May's ten-plus years of experience provided a new perspective. The doctor had apparently done little, if any, criminal work. After their initial scrutiny, May felt they must have missed something. Unfortunately, more than sixty years would pass before DNA analysis became a usable tool for the criminologist. Still, the examiners repeated their study, now aided by a powerful magnifying glass. Using the somewhat sanitized wording of his day, May reported, "At the mouth of the little womb we found what appeared to be a speck of dirt. At least it was foreign matter."[27]

The speck turned out to be the tip of a fir needle. Within hours, May told newspaper reporters that they had found "highly damaging evidence" against their suspect.[28] The details would not come out until the trial, he said, but he was convinced of Whitfield's guilt. And they had plenty of other evidence, including eye-witness testimony as to his presence near the murder site. Tests also confirmed that the stains on Whitfield's underwear were human blood. Officers had also linked a knife stained with human blood to him.

Prosecutors were, however, taking no chances. Jury selection began a couple months later. They then asked prospective jurors if they "objected to a verdict of guilty of first degree murder if the state's case was based almost solely upon circumstantial evidence."[29] The defense did its best. They even challenged, unsuccessfully, the tests that proved that the stains on the knife and Whitfield's clothes were human blood. *The Oregonian* declared, "Dr. Benson's testimony and that of Luke S. May of Seattle, criminologist, form probably the strongest links in the chain of testimony so far introduced by the state."[30]

May also provided what might have been the final nail in the coffin. He produced a magnified comparison of the fir needle tip recovered from Anna's body to the needle found on Whitfield's genitals. The broken ends matched perfectly, like "the edges of two pieces of torn paper when fitted together."[31] The technique, now known as "end matching" or sometimes "fracture matching," had been part of document examination for quite some time. But May's use in a criminal case might well have been a first.

The jury found Whitfield guilty and recommended the death penalty. After the usual appeals, Eddie Whitfield died on the gallows just over fifteen months after he raped and murdered little Anna Nosko. The trial did not get as much coverage as the original furor, perhaps because the state's case was so strong. Still, the events did give May more national exposure.

During the period when the Nosko investigation occupied May's time, the company made another change. In April, Revelare moved from the Lyon Building address to the Arctic Building. The Arctic Building is just one block away from the Lyon and still near the King County Courthouse.

Of course, as suggested before, not every murder garnered big headlines like the Nosko and Friedman cases. And few non-death cases received much coverage, if any. Still, special circumstances might attract some attention. The case against Mary K. Griffin, owner of a women's clothing firm in Seattle, was one example. She had bilked several business owners out of varying amounts of money, around $30,000 in total (more than a million dollars in today's consumer values). An attractive female swindler gave the story a newsworthy twist, so her arrest, release on bail, and subsequent disappearance made the papers.

May entered the case in the spring. Using his nationwide contacts, he traced an alias she used to a mail drop in New York City and then to a post office in Baltimore, Maryland. A local detective agency found her and turned the case over to the police. Her arrest there in late summer was the only time the case was mentioned on the front page of a Seattle newspaper. Turns out, however, Griffin was married to John "Jack" Bagley, grandson of a former Michigan governor and an heir to a tobacco fortune. On a legal pretext, the Maryland governor denied an extradition request. She was released and immediately left town.

It took May two years to track her down again, in Detroit. But politics intruded once more, as the Michigan governor also denied an extradition request. A grand jury indictment against her was the last (small) coverage in the news. In the end, perhaps, the Bagley family made restitution so the case went away. While it had only a small impact in the news, this case showed May's ability to reach across the country in pursuit of a suspect.

The end of July brought an interesting case that the papers also covered to some extent. May's part remained behind the scenes. The *Bellingham Herald* for July 28 published a report from Seattle with the headline, "Steamer *Rainier* is Rammed in Straits."[32]

It had been hit by the Japanese freighter *Mandasan Maru*, inbound from Asia, San Francisco, and Portland. The *Maru* radioed the port of Seattle that the two ships had collided about two o'clock in the morning. Heavy fog clogged the Straits of Juan de Fuca, and the *Rainier* mishap was one of a rash of collisions and groundings. Most of the crew had been taken off by the *Mandasan Maru* and were landed in Seattle a day after the crash. After drifting for a while, the *Rainier* was towed to safety. Her bow was down in the water almost to the foredeck when she docked. Newspapers eventually reported that the owners planned to dismantle the ship. They would keep the boilers and other machinery for use in another vessel. But even before the *Rainier* reached port, the owners had filed a suit against the Japanese vessel. The *Seattle Times* reported "last night [it] was in the custody of the United States marshal."[33]

Three days after the collision, May received "the Engineer's Deck Log and two Apprentices Logs" from the *Mandasan Maru*.[34] Frank A. Huffer, attorney for the *Mandasan's* owners, delivered the logs. May's specific task was to "determine whether or not an erasure had been made of the numerals '52.'" The acquisition note went on, "No fee was quoted Mr. Huffer, who represents a great number of Japanese shipping interests." May clearly felt that doing this small job free of charge was good business. The case file did not explain the meaning of the narrow assignment.

Less than two weeks after the mishap, the *Mandasan's* owners filed a counterpetition to limit their liability in the matter. The status of the vessel itself was not mentioned in the news item. However, just over three weeks later, the *Mandasan Maru* was allowed to sail with relief supplies after a massive earthquake and tsunami devastated Yokohama and Tokyo. There are no records that the ship ever returned to this country.

As noted earlier, the first classes for the criminology college were scheduled for the fall of 1923. The college prospectus said, "Open only to reliable persons of good character, the courses have been especially outlined to give a practical working knowledge of the science of modern criminology."[35] Some of the curriculum topics included "fundamental study of crime and criminal psychology"; "finger print forgeries, methods and systems for their detection"; "criminal law, evidence and procedure"; and "modern methods of crime prevention."

So, at the end of the summer, May was finishing some low profile cases and preparing for classes to start at the Northwest College of Criminology.

All that proved to be the calm before a storm soon to blow up about twenty miles south of Coos Bay on the Oregon coast. The furor centered on a man named Arthur Covell.

Covell had big plans, plans that could make him rich. The family had moved to the coast about fifteen years back. Arthur became head of the household when his father died a few years later. The household included his nephew, Alton, who was somewhat retarded mentally. Arthur had cultivated a strong mental hold over the boy.

All was well until an accident on the dairy farm broke Arthur's back and left him an invalid. Then his mother died. At that point, brother Fred and his wife, Ebba, moved to the farm from Bandon, about five miles to the north. Fred had a chiropractic practice in town. Two more of Fred's children were now part of the household, including Lucille, who was about two years younger than Alton. She followed the boy's lead and also fell under Arthur's spell.

Bedridden, Arthur pursued an interest in astrology. Soon, his client list for mail-order horoscopes had names from all across the country. Some of them were well-known stars in Hollywood and on Broadway. Yet even with those glamorous customers, the work did not pay all that well. Arthur felt he was only hitting the penny-ante stuff. "The stars" would point him toward more lucrative targets among local people. But Ebba seemed more and more suspicious of his schemes and could ruin everything. Arthur wasn't up to putting her out of the way, so fifteen-year-old Alton would have to do the job.

On September 3, 1923, Arthur waited in his room after Fred left for work. He had told Alton that his astrological calculations gave eleven o'clock in the morning as the ideal moment to act. Finally, Arthur's anxious vigil ended when the boy entered his room and told him what had happened. Right on time, he had crept up behind his stepmother. He pinned her arms, but she thrashed about, and Alton could barely hold her. Luckily the smothering cloth Arthur had specified did its job and she soon went limp. Arthur had the boy help him to the telephone. When his brother came on the line, he said, "Come home right away. Something terrible has happened to Ebba!"[36]

By the time the sheriff arrived to investigate the unexplained death, little evidence besides the corpse remained. Alton told officers he had been herding a cow into the barn and found the body when he returned to the house. The other children could tell them nothing. Fred seemed oddly indifferent. He had already begun making arrangements with an undertaker. Ebba was, after all, his fourth wife.

Early on, officials noted that Ebba's body was covered with random bruises. But they also jumped to the conclusion that she had died from a broken neck. Doctors made a cursory scan and then agreed with the assertion of a coroner's jury. Newspapers would report that an assailant had beaten up Mrs.

Covell and then killed her by breaking her neck. Three days after the killing, *The Oregonian* reported, "Alton Covell and his father Dr. Fred Covell are in the county jail at Coquille, each suspected of the murder of Mrs. Covell."[37]

Officials thought they had a cause of death and two prime suspects. Yet their investigation stalled. They apparently decided that Alton lacked the strength to physically overpower an adult woman. A chiropractor might be strong enough, but Fred's alibi proved solid. Finally, the Coos County district attorney invested in a long-distance call to Luke May.

"The notes taken at the coroner's inquest were very meager," May quickly found after he arrived at the county seat.[38] He also learned that while the examiners were competent physicians, "they were not familiar with medico-legal autopsies." May examined the crime scene closely, then he and the deputies searched Fred's office. They found nothing suspicious there. Arthur's diary, sprinkled with astrological signs, offered only cryptic items. His other notes seemed to be written in code.

May also began to doubt the stated cause of death. At his urging, authorities exhumed Ebba's body for another examination. They recruited a doctor who had had previous experience with a coroner's office in Pennsylvania. May wrote, "This second examination revealed that the neck had not even been dislocated, let alone broken. However, we did find a dark, livid discoloration on the deceased woman's face."[39]

Somehow, they did manage to keep reporters from learning about the exhumation. Still, at the end of the month, *The Oregonian* had discovered that Luke S. May, "professional criminologist of Seattle, had been working on the case for the last two weeks."[40] Reporters assumed May "had not found evidence of any importance." They derided the prosecutor's claim of (unspecified) "additional evidence." That was just "sparring for time and hoping that something would turn up."

Actually May and county officials now knew a lot. Analysis had shown that ammonia had caused the facial stain. The pattern on the skin suggested that she had been smothered by a cloth saturated with the chemical. Further investigation showed that Alton had purchased strong ammonia about a month before the murder.

May had also deciphered many of Arthur's coded notes. These revealed an amazing, twisted array of plots. Ebba's name was just the first on a list of more than two dozen men and women in the region. For each, Covell had divined the ideal astrological time for action. Some were candidates for death threats and extortion. Others would die by carefully planned accidents, with faked wills bequeathing their estates to Arthur Covell. The schemes seemed too fantastic.

Indeed, when confronted, Arthur claimed they were just that. Trapped in his body, he had whiled away the time with idle fantasies. Yet Ebba had been killed, and at the time specified. May had also interviewed Alton and Lucille. "Uncle Artie" clearly had some power over them. They surely knew more about the death than they let on. Finally, May and the prosecutor's office released the story to the newspapers. They billed the information as a "confession." The result appeared in *The Oregonian* under the headline "Cripple Plots Crimes."[41]

One local paper agreed to use the headline "Crippled Astrologer Plans Murder—Arthur Covell Confesses to Planning Murders."[42] With this newspaper in hand, May again interviewed Alton. "I let him read the headlines; that was all," May said. "I didn't care to let him know just what his uncle had confessed." Finally, the boy admitted that he had smothered his stepmother with ammonia. When Arthur saw Alton's written confession, he immediately penned a statement taking full blame. In his confession, he said, "Both Alton and Lucille were at all times under control of my mind and will. . . . My influence over both was so complete they seemed incapable to resist or think independently beyond my wish."[43]

Covell asserted that they should not punish the boy. Then, when both he and Alton were tried for first-degree murder, he repudiated the confession. However, after a sensational trial, the jury took only about two hours to return a guilty verdict. Even with appeals of his conviction, Arthur was hanged less than two years after Ebba Covell was murdered. Alton received a life sentence but spent only about ten years in prison.

In many ways, the Covell circus became Luke May's "coming-out party," literally around the world. His biggest earlier cases had been brief sensations but offered no special story lines. Conversely, newspapers across the country and overseas could not resist the "murder-by-the-stars" narrative. They loved the mad plots, with a flavor of the occult. The *Evening Star,* in Washington, DC, carried an article that featured "Luke S. May, the Seattle criminologist, who tracked him down and unraveled the diabolical schemes."[44]

The case also earned May a new nickname, which the *Portland News* in Oregon put in a headline: "Luke May of Seattle—Real Craig Kennedy."[45] The item observed that scientific criminology had finally left the realm of literary imagination. American writer Arthur B. Reeves created fictional detective Craig Kennedy, who first appeared in *Cosmopolitan* magazine in 1910. The character became immensely popular. Over the next twenty years, Reeves featured Kennedy in more than a hundred short stories. The fictional detective also starred in more than two dozen novels. Linking May's name to the ubiquitous character served to further enhance the real-life detective's mystique. And, the writer said, "Sherlock Holmes and Craig Kennedy are characters of fiction, but Luke May is real."

With all the furor, regional demand for Luke May as a speaker blossomed. Until now, May had spoken only to law enforcement groups. Less than a month after news reports linked May's name to the case, he was invited to speak to a businessmen's club in Seattle. The following month, about two weeks after Covell was convicted, he spoke to a church group. Less than a week after that, he gave a talk at a trade association convention in Seattle. His main topic seemed to be "dealing with the criminal," but he could obviously publicize his agency while indulging his innate urge to teach.

In fact, May would be in demand as a speaker around the region for the next forty years. And his name would remain in the *national* spotlight, with few lulls, for almost two decades. The run would begin with the busiest year he was ever to have, in terms of case numbers.

· 7 ·

Fame Grows, at Some Cost

*R*ight after Thanksgiving in 1923, May set out to solve a "murder" that was thought up by the *Seattle Star* newspaper. A reporter named Seaburn Brown played the victim of "a theoretical crime, constructed by the *Star* to permit Luke S. May, criminologist, to show *Star* readers how modern-day science convicts criminals."[1]

Details of the scheme were probably known only to three people: the official of the paper who set it up, the "murderer," and the "victim." May presumably explained how they should arrange to fire a shot through a dummy before the victim sprawled where he was to be found. He left the rest to the participants. The *Star* said, "May entered enthusiastically into the idea of the manhunt—and so the search . . . is on."[2]

Over the next week, May explained the evidence he had found and how it was assessed in his laboratory. Clues included fingerprints, a spent bullet, a mysterious handgun, and more. Naturally, he made many photos of the crime scene. The reporter tracking the case then wrote up May's explanation of how the tests worked and what the results meant.

To obscure the trail, the paper arranged for May to find three weapons, including a Colt revolver near the death scene. May immediately deduced that weapon was probably a plant, since he had also found an empty shell casing on the floor. A revolver does not obligingly leave a shell behind, unless the shooter stops to reload. Examination of the "fatal" bullet showed that it was from an automatic pistol manufactured by the Savage Arms Company. May next searched the desks and home quarters of every potential suspect. During those searches, he found two Savage Arms automatics of the same make, model, and caliber. This was exactly the scenario described in the previous chapter, where the class characteristics were the same.

Not a problem, the *Star* assured its readers. "You see," May said, "It is possible, with the aid of a microscope, to tell either from a bullet or from the ejected shell not only what kind of gun it was fired from but also to select the one particular gun used from any number of the same make and caliber."[3]

He was, of course, assuming favorable conditions. Still, he did indeed identify the specific weapon that had been used. The series was a big hit, generating many interested letters to the paper. Finally, after a week, May successfully identified the "killer." The pseudo-perpetrator, another *Star* reporter, said, "I've watched Mr. May on my track for a week, and the realism of the thing . . . set me to shivering."[4]

May and Revelare hardly needed the extra publicity generated by this stunt. They logged an average of three new cases every week for the year. The final total of 155 cases, including nine death cases, was more than any year before. The episode was surely another example of Luke's urge to teach people about scientific criminology.

Corporate records show that the company processed a considerable cash flow during the year. May felt financially comfortable enough to plan for moving out of the Fionia apartment. He made a down payment on a two-story residence in the North Beacon Hill neighborhood, a couple of miles south of downtown. However, it was ominous that Clara S. May no longer appeared as an officer of the firm. The only names were those of Luke, John L. Harris, and J. Clark Sellers.

The pace of business continued at a high level into the first half of the following year. That included an increase in death cases. In February, May made his first report on the death of Dr. Albert F. Mattice a couple months earlier. Mattice had spent a year as an eye specialist at a base hospital in France during the World War. While there, he was apparently hit by the infamous "Spanish" flu pandemic of 1918. Mattice was lucky; he survived. Around the world, at least thirty million died (and possibly many more). The estimated loss in the United States was around 675,000 deaths.

After the war, Mattice returned to his successful practice in Seattle. Thirty-eight years old in 1923, Mattice belonged to several prominent social clubs and was engaged to be married. But reoccurrences of the flu and perhaps memories from the war induced bouts of depression. The fall capped a period when he had reportedly been drinking a lot. A fine clarinet player, he often found solace in music. He had also dabbled in spiritualism, attending several seances.

Mattice had awakened to a dreary Thanksgiving morning. A moderate breeze off the Sound coated the windows with spray from the ongoing showers. Weakness from a two-week relapse of the flu lingered. He would not be able to make the seventy-mile trip north to Sedro Wooley, where his parents were hosting a family reunion.

Later, Mattice went to Dr. Fenton Whiting's home in north Seattle. His fiancee, Whiting's stepdaughter, lived there, and several guests had assembled for a musicale. Alfred played several tunes as part of a trio. Then, shortly before three o'clock Dr. Whiting and another guest played a lyrical but rather melancholy tune called "The Sweetest Story Ever Told." As the final strains faded away, Mattice walked into a nearby alcove. There, he picked up a .45-caliber revolver and shot himself in the head.

His stunned companions eventually recovered enough to call the police. Officers found nothing mysterious about the situation. The revolver belonged to Dr. Whiting, who carried it when he had to make house calls at night. He had removed it from his bag to get at some sheet music and set it on the windowsill. No one noticed the weapon further until the tragedy.

About two months later, a life insurance company hired May to verify the coroner's verdict of death by suicide. Mattice had several life insurance policies. All contained suicide exclusions. May received the autopsy report as well as photographs of the death scene. His report said, "I find that the wound is inflicted in the favorite suicidal spot, having entered the right temple and the gun must have been held in almost immediate contact with the skin."[5]

The bullet had traversed the doctor's temples on a level track. From there, the missile punched a hole in a window facing out onto the street. The trajectory, May concluded, "precludes the possibility of accidental discharge." He also said, "I am quite satisfied that this can be shown to the satisfaction of a jury when my examination and study of the case has been completed."[6]

His confidence proved to be misplaced. The amount of insurance totaled about $155,000. Some policies included double indemnity clauses for accidental death. Naturally, the beneficiaries fought the suicide assertion in court. The case dragged on for more than a year. They found experts who, with special pleading, claimed to show how Mattice could have shot himself by accident. On the other side, the *Seattle Times* reported, "Luke S. May, criminologist, appeared for the defendant insurance company and explained his theory as to how the revolver was fired."[7]

In the end, sympathy for the survivors overrode what seemed to be clear evidence. The jury officially declared that "Dr. Albert F. Mattice, Seattle oculist, who died from a revolver wound on Thanksgiving Day, 1923, came to his death by accident."[8] Naturally, the company immediately began the appeal process. Within a few months, the *Times* noted that the various claims had all been settled out of court.

Including the Mattice "accident," Revelare had accepted four death cases by the end of the first quarter. All told, they had logged thirty-six cases, putting them on a pace to approach the load for the previous year. The types of cases ran the full gamut, from fingerprints to murder. One case was interesting because May's evidence led to dismissal of a liquor charge against a Seattle druggist. He described this as a detectiphone investigation, a term for what is today called a "wire" or "bug." He probably had an agent try to buy some liquor and recorded the conversation when the druggist refused the request. Such a sting operation was not without cause. As one historian of that period in Seattle said, "Booze was banned but could be easily purchased from your neighborhood bootlegger or the corner druggist."⁹

Recall that, three years earlier, May's agents had no trouble finding liquor in downtown Seattle. At that time, the United States had been in a postwar downturn. But by 1924, the Roaring Twenties were at full throttle. In Seattle and around the country, the recession had given way to boom times (except in the farm sector, which still suffered, and drove many into the cities in search of work). People indulged in mass-produced consumer goods, movie productions grew more lavish, and barnstormers gave air shows everywhere.

But the era was perhaps most visible at the friendly neighborhood speakeasy. Except for those in the working class, the presence of women in saloons had not been all that common. That changed drastically in the Twenties. Now, women mingled at the speakeasy with male laborers, lawyers, salesmen, and anyone else who wanted to knock back a few. And this so-called new woman had bobbed her hair and abandoned her corset and long gown for a straight, loose-fitting dress whose hemline approached the knees. Up top, the bodice was looser and more revealing than would have once been considered quite proper.

This "flapper" style is often seen as the enduring image of the Roaring Twenties. Show her dancing a hot number, the Charleston being perhaps quintessential, and you've completed the picture. Many men followed with a variety of tighter, or much looser, attire . . . and brighter, even garish color schemes. And, dancing or just listening, lively couples flocked to where black bands played jazz and ragtime. (Seattle had a particularly vibrant jazz scene.)

Luke May took no part in all that frivolity. Except on his now-infrequent hunting and fishing trips, he always wore a conservative three-piece business suit. Photos taken in his laboratory show him with his coat off, but with a vest and formal long-sleeve shirt. Reporters who interviewed him commented on his serious mien. Yet he could surprise them with an expressive smile and his dry humor.

Unfortunately, after the huge year in 1923, the continued business boom for the firm backfired. According to family memories, May chose to first plow profits back into the company. That is, he spent any lucrative windfall from a case on new equipment, not bonuses for himself or his people. Thus, some-

Figure 7.1.   May "Dressed" for the Lab. *Source*: May-Reid Records.

time early in the year, J. Clark Sellers decided he could do better on his own. He left Revelare and opened an office in Los Angeles, California. Later correspondence shows that May and Sellers parted as friends. Although Sellers started out as a general criminologist, he eventually specialized in questioned documents examination. There is some indication that John L. Harris also began to consider leaving the company at this time.

In Utah and Idaho, May had been an avid hunter and fisherman. One photograph shows him with two huge trout and the fly-fishing rig he used to land them. But apparently he no longer found much time for all that after he moved to Seattle. The heavy influx of cases could have only made that worse. Such stress undoubtedly contributed to a separation from his wife, suggested earlier by her nonappearance in the company documents. Again, we have no personal papers to tell us how May felt about the departure of Sellers and his estrangement from Clara.

May probably focused even more on work. Along those lines, he would have surely been interested in an article that appeared near the end of spring. To learn more about crime from the source, police pioneer August Vollmer had sponsored a special lunch for the prisoners at a Los Angeles jail. Some months earlier, Vollmer had taken a leave of absence from Berkeley to serve as the chief of the Los Angeles Police Department (LAPD). For years, citizens there had complained that the LAPD was inefficient and corrupt. The uproar finally persuaded the mayor to bring Vollmer in to clean house. The chief did have some successes. He established a municipal police lab, the first in this country, and set up a system to manage crime records. Vollmer also implemented professional hiring standards and a couple of special crime units. These well-publicized reforms muted the worst criticisms.

Newspapers all over the country published the results of Vollmer's jail luncheon. As might be expected, he got an earful. Some officials would do anything to get a conviction. Courts were inconsistent and unfair. And on and on. But Vollmer had little time to use what he had learned in Los Angeles. His reforms had stirred up a lot of opposition inside and outside the department. Although there was some talk of extending his leave, the Los Angeles experiment ended after the year was up.

May would have been equally interested in news from Washington, DC. About a month after the Vollmer luncheon, newspapers reported that the director of the U.S. Bureau of Investigation (the future FBI) had resigned. Assistant Director J. Edgar Hoover was expected to run the bureau until a replacement could be found. Toward the end of the year, Hoover was confirmed as director and held that position for almost a half century.

During this same time frame, May played a role in a death case with a strong federal link. Six years earlier, U.S. Army Major Alexander Cronkhite had died from a gunshot wound at Camp Lewis, Washington. A board of inquiry concluded that Cronkhite shot himself accidentally while engaged in some informal target practice.

But the major's mother rejected that verdict. She insisted that he must have been murdered. Alexander's father, himself a major general in the army, helped to get the case reopened. Two prime suspects were identified, but then the case dragged along for more than five years. The trial of one man finally began in Tacoma at the end of September 1924. By then, federal prosecutor Thomas Revelle had already told higher-ups, "We have indicted a man on the charge of first degree murder without a single fact to substantiate the charge."[10]

But the defense took no chances. A few weeks before the trial, they hired May to look over all the evidence. The autopsy showed that the bullet had entered Cronkhite's torso on the upper right side, ripped his aorta, and ended up in the left shoulder muscle. Another observation proved to be key: there were no powder burns on Cronkhite's uniform or skin. May's report said, "In all cases of self-inflicted wounds, powder burns are an important factor."[11]

The death weapon, a Colt .45-caliber revolver loaded with a rimless cartridge, would leave obvious powder burns, but only out to about six inches. Standard military training for one-handed pistol firing called for the shooter to stand sideways with his gun arm extended roughly in line with his shoulders. The major, who was then recovering from the flu, had probably lost his grip on the weapon and then clutched it to regain control. But the revolver had rotated around his trigger finger and his hurried grasp fired a shot.

The scenario seemed implausible, but May showed how it could happen and would have inflicted the exact damage done to Cronkhite. The defense then put a U.S. Army captain on the stand to present the gun evidence in court. The jury took less than two hours and just one ballot to declare the defendant "not guilty." The case against the other suspect was immediately dropped.

May did not appear on the stand in the Cronkhite matter. However, a case where he did testify bore one eerie similarity to the major's death. In March, a family member found Virginia Clarke shot to death in the family's summer cabin in The Highlands, an upscale country development about ten miles north of downtown Seattle. About twenty-six years old, Virginia was the wife of banker Casper W. Clarke and the mother of two young, healthy daughters. The body was sprawled on a bed with a .45-caliber automatic pistol nearby. The weapon belonged to her husband. She had been carrying it because there had been prowlers in the neighborhood.

Neither family nor friends knew any reason she would commit suicide. They thought an intruder had somehow grabbed the gun and shot her with it. May first verified that the automatic was the death weapon. The bullet had hit the woman in the chest near the heart and passed through her torso at a sharp angle. From there, it had lodged in the wall about four feet above the floor.

By tracking the path through the wounds and into the wall, May concluded that the victim had been leaning over far enough to look under the bed when hit. The weapon had perhaps slipped out of her hand or fallen out of a pocket. Like Cronkhite, she might have tried to grab the weapon and it went off. Or the automatic might have fired when it hit the floor, something May knew from experience could happen. There were no unknown fingerprints on the pistol. A coroner's jury accepted May's assessment and issued a verdict of death by accidental shooting.

Aside from the Rosenbluth trial, most of May's death cases in early 1924 created only local and generally short-lived interest in the newspapers. His next sensational case surfaced in the summer. From Pierce County, the *Seattle Times* reported, "County officials and private investigators have been working . . . to solve the strange disappearance of Mrs. Pearl R. Conner."[12]

Her husband, Richard, told police she had him drop her off about a half mile from her parent's country home. That was on a Monday afternoon. When he went to get Pearl on Thursday, her parents said they'd never seen her. It was a matter of record that the Conners had had a divorce dispute some weeks before she disappeared. Pearl had accused Richard of hanky-panky with another woman. But the two had supposedly reconciled since then. Now, Richard claimed to have seen a Chevrolet sedan parked not far from where he had left Pearl. Perhaps, he hinted, his wife had run off with another man.

These insinuations outraged Pearl's family and friends. *Richard* was the one with the roving eye. He tried to convince one of his wife's female friends that some of Pearl's clothes were missing. She, however, noticed that Pearl's most personal possessions—makeup, nightgown, and so on—remained at home.

Suspicious, prosecuting attorney James W. Selden hired Luke May to dig for some background. An agent quickly tracked down the other woman suggested by the short-lived divorce action. A recent divorcee, Mrs. Frances McArthur worked for the same grocery store where Conner drove a delivery truck. She freely admitted that she was having an affair with Conner. In fact, they had had a tryst the very night that Pearl had disappeared. She had no reason to disbelieve Richard's story that his wife had gone off with another man.

A search of the Conner home in south Tacoma confirmed the friend's observations about Pearl's personal belongings. They also discovered a Luger automatic pistol. But they needed to find the *corpus delicti* to make a murder charge stick. As May said, "Regardless of how impressive the circumstantial evidence in the case may be, the missing body of the victim thwarts every effort to build up a case for conviction."[13]

Ione Holt, a friend of prosecutor Selden's, offered to help. She was also a longtime friend of the Conners. Evidence suggests that Richard considered himself "God's gift to women." Ione felt she could gain his confidence by pretending she found him attractive. She proved to be an excellent judge of character. Conner welcomed her notion of telling the police she had seen Pearl after the day she had supposedly disappeared. Then Conner overreached. May recorded his bright idea in *Crime's Nemesis*. Conner said, "Why don't you write a letter to me, supposedly coming from my wife, telling me that she has run away with a man, and is now in California."[14]

They must have then refined the idea, because the letter ended up being sent to Pearl's parents. Shortly after the note was delivered, Selden had Conner arrested. Still, he wanted to bolster the suspect's confidence in Holt, his undercover agent. Selden told reporters, "I don't believe in this letter any more than I do in the affidavit signed by Mrs. Ione Holt of Ashford that she saw Mrs. Conner on the road near Ashford [on] May 21."[15]

The fact that Conner had encouraged the letter ploy provided strong circumstantial evidence against him. But there was still the problem of the body. So, Selden sent Holt to visit Conner again. Officials had put hordes of searchers out, she said. Perhaps she could plant some false evidence, possibly something to point to the mysterious stranger in the Chevrolet. Incredibly, Conner swallowed this fantasy, and then tried to improve on it. He claimed that Pearl had tried to shoot *him* and killed herself when she missed. Sure that no one would believe him, he said, he had hidden her corpse and cooked up the story about the other man.

Conner described the abandoned well where she should leave fake clues. Searchers quickly recovered the body. Nearby, they found the spent shell from a 7.65 mm Luger automatic pistol. May then verified that the shell had been ejected from the Luger found at the Conner home. Later, Conner's defense would assert that police had reclaimed a shell from his backyard practice range and planted it at the crime scene.

As it happened, the abandoned well where searchers found the body was located on the Camp Lewis military reservation. That meant the crime fell under federal jurisdiction, just like the Cronkhite case. Federal attorney Thomas P. Revelle took over the prosecution. Thus, ironically, May found himself on the same side with Revelle.

When the trial finally started, months later, the defense faced a huge uphill battle. Frances McArthur, much against her preference, set the negative tenor with a clear motive. Conner, she testified, "was greatly concerned when his wife applied for a divorce because of the fear he would lose all of his property."[16]

Next, the papers reported, "Luke S. May, Seattle criminologist, gave thrilling and important testimony for the government late yesterday. Producing Mrs. Conner's skull, with two bullet holes in it, Mr. May testified that scientific examination proved that the fatal bullets were fired by Conner's Luger pistol."[17]

After his conviction, Conner's attorneys exploited every potential legal slip-up in their appeals. Even so, the courts sustained his life sentence at the McNeil Island Federal Penitentiary. Later, Thomas Revelle sent May a letter to express his "high appreciation of the assistance which I have received from you during my term of office as United States Attorney."[18] The letter went on, "It was my privilege to have you associated with me in the famous Conner murder case, tried by me at Tacoma. . . . The service you rendered the Government at that time connecting up the shell found near the dead body of Mrs. Conner, with the wound in the deceased's skull, impressed me with the great advantage of having expert testimony in such matters."

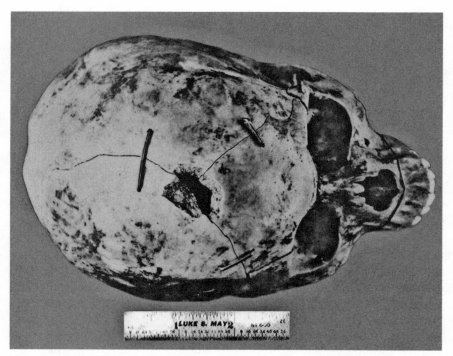

Figure 7.2.   Fatal Wound in Pearl Conner's Skull. *Source*: May-Reid Records.

Revelle concluded, "It will always be my pleasure to recommend you to anyone who is looking for a real expert in handwriting and firearms."

Unfortunately, May's personal life was not so favorable during this period. Thus, on September 10, 1924, Luke filed for divorce from Clara on the grounds of cruelty and alienation of affection. Clara did not contest the action, which became final after six months. The decree showed no division of property, nor did Luke have any alimony to pay. Records show that Clara still occupied the Fionia Apartments unit at this point. She probably stayed until a lease ran out and then left Seattle. Luke had moved to the property purchased earlier in the North Beacon Hill neighborhood.

Along with that negative, Revelare's total workload was down drastically for 1924, from 155 to 117 cases. And that decline would continue, especially after John L. Harris left the firm. Harris resigned during the fall and set up his own detective agency in Seattle. Oddly enough, the number of death cases increased to a total of fourteen, with sixteen victims. Despite that, the following year began rather quietly. May didn't log his first death case until the middle of February. Before that, however, a discovery in downtown Seattle gave people a thrill.

A raw southerly wind whipped bursts of rain along King Street. That and temperatures in the forties made for a nasty morning. Federal agents Walter Patterson and Irving Brown could hope the foul weather would divert attention. This was the heart of Seattle's Chinatown, where most walkers were Chinese or Filipino. The agents wore casual flat caps and nondescript working clothes, yet their presence could not have gone unnoticed.

They entered the dingy four-story Kong Yick Building just east of Canton Alley. Brightly painted signs with exotic Chinese characters did little to counter the blocky, utilitarian style of the structure. The top floors held a grid of small rooms that provided cheap rental housing for workingmen. On the fourth floor, Patterson and Brown positioned themselves to watch a room fitted out as a Chinese shrine.

Several hours passed as visitors called at the shrine room, then left. Finally, about noon, their two key suspects came out and walked down the hall. The agents burst from hiding and placed the Chinese men under arrest. A quick search uncovered several packets of opium hidden in their clothing. The agents also found a key to the shrine room. After packing the drug dealers off to jail, Patterson and Brown searched their room. Besides several incense burners, the agents found what the newspapers called a "heathen idol." Hidden among niches that held drug paraphernalia they uncovered about $1,000 worth of opium. But inside one compartment, the agents discovered something far more ominous.

The *Seattle Times* for January 22, 1925, briefly reported the raid under the headline, "Opium and Bolos Are Found in Joss House."[19] A more detailed *Post-Intelligencer* article said the agents had found "ten wicked looking bolo knives."[20] Then the scary part: "On the blade of the most rapier-like of these was what appeared to be a blood clot, in which were imbedded several hairy strands."

Authorities feared they might have evidence of a brutal murder. They immediately contacted Luke May. Microscopic examination confirmed that the clot probably was blood. The *Post-Intelligencer* item said, "One of May's chemists made [the] snap judgment that the blood and hair are both from a human." May, of course, quashed that unsubstantiated assertion. Further tests drove home the point. The blood came from a chicken, and what looked like hairs were actually threads of wool and silk. Subsequent inquiry established that the traces had been part of the initiation ceremony into a local secret society of Chinese men, a "tong."

About two weeks after this false alarm, May logged an actual death case. A woman named Anna Case had been shot to death during a robbery attempt on the Tacoma waterfront. Police found a man's cap beside the woman's body, and May identified Negroid hair strands on it. A few days later, officers arrested a black sailor as a suspect.

Investigators had found an Iver Johnson revolver in the man's room. They passed it along to May, who noted a "distinguishing nick" on bullets fired from the weapon.[21] However, the fatal slug was too distorted for a full analysis, plus the fine lines on the bullet were very faint. He could not definitely say that it had been fired from the suspect's weapon. And—in those days long before DNA analysis—he could not trace the hairs to a particular person. Authorities spent another five weeks looking for more evidence and then released their suspect. The murder was never solved.

May's next death case involved a murder that took place long before there was a break in the case in the spring of 1925. Four years earlier, an unknown assailant gunned down Harry E. Hallen in Tacoma. Hallen was an assistant superintendent at the Griffin Wheel Works. Investigators found empty shells from a .45-caliber automatic at the scene.

A month or so before the Hallen murder, someone had twice taken multiple shots at a Griffin Wheel Works foreman. Noting the job connection, police had May compare shells found at the scene with the Hallen shells. He replied, "I find them to be fired by the same gun, making distinctive identifying marks on the body of the shells as well as distinctive marks on the base caused by the breech block."[22]

In an automatic weapon, the breechblock is a movable plug that seals the back of the breech, the chamber where a cartridge is inserted. When the weapon is fired, the breechblock keeps the shell in place while the bullet traverses the barrel. The powder explosion slams the brass cartridge case against the steel breechblock with tremendous force. That impact stamps a mirror image of the breechblock's distinctive features into the base of the shell. "Breech prints" are generally invisible to the naked eye, but readily apparent under a microscope.

The breechblock is just one part of a weapon's action. Another key component is the firing pin, which sets off the cartridge primer. And, depending upon the design, the action may have other components that can leave distinctive marks on the shell. These markings are yet another way, besides the bullets themselves, that the firearms expert can tie a particular weapon to a crime scene. In the Hallen case, May found not only the base impressions but also individual marks on the body of the shell. That showed that the death weapon had a defect in the breech itself.

Meanwhile, police had turned up one Gino Spadoni as a prime suspect. Spadoni had been laid off from a job at Griffin. Sources in the Italian community said he blamed the foreman and Hallen. But Spadoni had disappeared from the Northwest right after Hallen was murdered. Informants said he might have fled to Chicago, or even overseas.

Then, about three years later, one of those odd events that could only happen in real life . . . happened. A brush fire in a vacant lot touched off rounds from a discarded .45-caliber automatic pistol. The lot was about three blocks from where Hallen was murdered, so the police made the connection to the shooting. But with no suspect in custody, assessing the pistol seemed not worth the effort and cost. The break came from San Francisco, where Spadoni had finally ended up. A girl he fancied married another man, so he began to set nuisance fires and inflict other vandalism at the couple's home. Police probes led to his arrest in late March 1925, quickly followed by an extradition request from the state of Washington.

Five days after the arrest, May wrote in a case file, "Received of Robert B. Abel, Deputy Prosecuting Attorney, Pierce County, Tacoma, Washington, one .45 Colts Automatic Pistol, Model 1911 U.S. Army, Number 487215, in a rusty condition."[23] This was the weapon discovered in the burned-over lot. May was not at all sure they could learn anything from the artifact. There could be no surviving fingerprints, and corrosion would surely invalidate any bullet comparison. And that assumed he could recondition the pistol for test firing.

It took May "seven days of careful treatment with oil and gentle forcing" to ready the gun for a test.[24] In the process, he discovered an incredible happenstance. Despite those years exposed to the weather, the pistol's breechblock had survived in a clean condition. A cartridge in the chamber had protected the breechblock from muck oozing down the barrel. And tight construction and gun oil had stopped corrosive penetration through the automatic's action. This changed everything.

May carefully explained all of this in his report. He knew that scientific firearms evidence of this type was not then common knowledge, even among law enforcement personnel. He concluded, "I am positive that all of these four shells were fired in .45 Colts Automatic Pistol #487215."[25] So the Tacoma police knew they had the murder weapon. A difficult and time-consuming search finally put the automatic in Spadoni's possession at the time of the murder. For obvious reasons, that conclusion was based on informant testimony, not actual documentation.

Even with the firearms evidence, the trial proved difficult. Some of the key witnesses were Italian immigrants. Many of them spoke only rudimentary English, so translators had to mediate the interrogation on the stand. That led to arguments about the accuracy and nuance of the translations. Still, in June 1925, a jury found Spadoni guilty. The evidence was all circumstantial— no one had seen him do the shooting or heard him admit to it later. Thus, the jury did not impose the death penalty.

Spadoni's lawyers appealed his life sentence. Again, the dependence upon translated questions and answers created problems. Finally, after almost a year, the Washington Supreme Court cited various technical issues and granted Spadoni the right to a new trial. By then, key witnesses had left the state or were no longer willing to testify, at least one having received death threats. With that, the prosecution's case fell apart. They agreed to a directed verdict for acquittal.

"Murder by the stars" had splashed May's name across the country. Then the Conner and Hallen cases kept it there. Over the next twelve months, he would handle a steady stream of cases that at least sparked interest in the Pacific Northwest. That relative lull would end when another lurid murder put May back in the national spotlight.

· *8* ·

Notoriety Follows a Lull

The Hallen murder was just one of a flood of cases that Revelare handled to start 1925. In fact, by the time May received the Hallen murder weapon, they had logged an average of two cases every week. Although that was under the rate for the previous year, by midyear they would have more than fifty cases, including seven deaths. Yet even the deaths gained little newspaper coverage, and most of the others less so. Still, near the end of March, a *Seattle Times* headline read, "Embezzler Easy Oil Stock Victim."[1]

The item noted that The Highlands, Inc.—which managed the exclusive residential community mentioned in the previous chapter—had hired May to look into a suspicious financial situation. After a few weeks, Luke had police arrest accountant L. Stewart Brockway for embezzlement. May does not reveal exactly how he fingered the accountant. However, he told the *Times* that Brockway was "a wizard with figures, perhaps as good an accountant and bookkeeper as you will find."[2]

Sadly, he also had an expensive sideline. All the money he diverted, around $47,000 from various clients, had been lost on phony oil and mining schemes. After looking over the sales pitches, May could understand how someone with Brockway's addiction might be taken in. May commented, "Some of these are masterpieces of their kind."[3] Despite an unbroken record of failure, Brockway still hoped to finally hit it big. He had even kept a private set of books so he could pay everyone back. The court imposed a five- to fifteen-year prison sentence.

While May was busy with these early cases, his personal life changed again. Luke's parents, William and Mary, had stayed in Salt Lake City when he moved to Pocatello. William was now about sixty-six and Mary around sixty-four. Available records indicate that none of their close family members were particularly well off, and they had lost touch with the rest. Thus, in April 1925, William and Mary moved to Seattle. They took up residence at the large North Beacon Hill property where Luke had gone after his separation from Clara. Luke moved out of the house before the year was out. His parents, however, lived there until their deaths in the 1940s.

From 1922, when he unveiled the Revelaroscope, through the spring of 1925, May handled almost forty death cases. For nearly three quarters of those, a rifled firearm caused the death or deaths. Yet through that period, May had surprisingly few cases where he might have obtained results using the fine details, the "individual characteristics" described earlier. For suicides, accidents, and a few other cases, the identity of the gun was usually not a crucial question. May handled about a dozen such investigations where he simply verified the make and model of the death weapon.

For another ten or so murder cases, officials never found the weapon. Of course, police often *thought* they had the right gun, so May tested and eliminated a lot of exhibits for those cases. In four other cases, including the Anna Case death described in the previous chapter, the bullets were deformed or the distinctive markings were too faint. Thus, the Conner murder was the first big case where May could really use the technique. For that, he gave positive results for both the death bullet and for the empty shell discovered near the crime scene.

The Hallen case provided the next chance. That gave conclusive results for the shells, but he made no bullet comparisons due to corrosion of the barrel. One can begin to understand why May never took the time to write up his

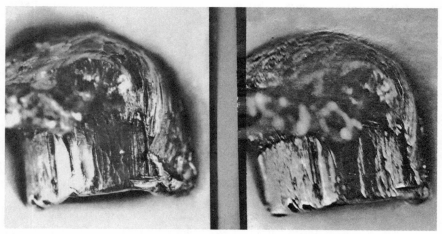

Figure 8.1.   Early (Deformed) Bullet Comparison. *Source:* **May-Reid Records.**

work for a wider audience. The honor of publicizing methods for systematic firearms identification rightfully belongs to the Bureau of Forensic Ballistics in New York City. During the spring of 1925, Major (later Colonel) Calvin H. Goddard helped launch the bureau as a going concern. This became a notable milestone in the history of firearms identification.

The bureau was the brainchild of Charles H. Waite, who had worked for the New York State attorney general's office. He entered the field in 1917 when he saved an innocent man who had almost been executed through grossly inept firearms assessment. Appalled at what might have happened, Waite accumulated a huge inventory of guns, ammunition, and related firearms data. Around 1923, he began to put together an informal team to exploit and extend all that material. One of the experts he consulted was Philip O. Gravelle, known as an expert photographer and microscopist. Gravelle designed a new comparison microscope specifically for bullet and shell tests. Waite had John H. Fisher, a physicist, develop the "helixometer." The helixometer combines a light source with optics to examine the rifling of gun barrels.

Waite also corresponded with gun expert Edward C. Crossman, last mentioned in 1922, when he retired from the army. Since then, Crossman had increased his writing efforts even more. Thus, in 1923, he published the book *Gun and Rifle Facts,* which discussed big-game rifles, shotguns, pistol ballistics, and much more. Goddard visited Crossman in the West a year or so after the bureau began operations.

Born in Baltimore, Goddard completed a medical degree in 1915 and joined the army as a surgeon. A gun enthusiast, he proved to be the catalyst the Bureau of Forensic Ballistics needed. (When Waite died in 1926, Goddard assumed leadership of the bureau.) During the summer, the *Saturday Evening Post* published a feature about what the team could do—"Fingerprinting Bullets: The Expert Witness."[4] The article said, "No two revolvers or pistols ever leave precisely the same marks upon a bullet, and . . . it now is possible and practicable to link the bullet to the weapon in virtually every instance."

Later in the year, Goddard published a paper about their equipment and methods in the *Army Ordnance Journal.* May probably obtained a copy of the *Ordnance* paper, and we know he did see the article in the *Saturday Evening Post.*

On May's side of the country, Edward Heinrich made an important advance. In December, a disgruntled worker shot and killed the foreman who had sacked him. Police soon captured a prime suspect and found a .38-caliber revolver on his person, with one fired cartridge. The murder trial started a few months later. Like Goddard and May, Heinrich had followed developments in matching fatal bullets with test missiles from a suspected murder weapon. But Heinrich did more, guided by a practice commonly used in handwriting tests. He prepared highly enlarged photographs with the fatal bullet alongside a test bullet, showing the matched microscopic marks. His display caused a sensation in court and eventually became the normal way to present firearms evidence.

Meanwhile, as publicity for the Bureau of Forensic Ballistics spread, at least three optical companies began offering comparison microscopes. Like Chamot's earlier device, the basic design depended upon an optical bridge that connected two microscopes, one for each item to be viewed. An arrangement of prisms brought the images together so they could be viewed side-by-side through a central eyepiece. May eventually obtained a comparison microscope of this design. However, he had spent too many hours squinting through narrow oculars. He preferred his own approach, where the objects could be viewed on a full-size screen. So, May continued to improve his custom instrument.

May's next case of note was a questioned documents examination. Unlike most such cases, it briefly made the news. In May, a *Seattle Times* headline blared, "Sues Son for Forgery."[5] The account said that Winston Sisco "was sued in Superior Court yesterday by his widowed mother, Mrs. S. Ellen Hanna." The mother had been married and widowed three times. She and her son played a prominent role in Seattle real estate development, either individually or as partners. Among other projects, they had jointly formed a company to erect buildings to serve the Seattle Public Market, now the famous Pike Place Public Market.

Less than a week after the news item, May received a warranty deed that purported to transfer a piece of valuable Union Street property from her to him. The signature she claimed was a forgery turned out to be genuine. However, using a strong photographic light, May discovered that the ink of some crucial wording had not aged along with the original document. He wrote, "It is my opinion that the words 'of Seattle' and 'Winston West Sisco,' written in a bluish-colored ink, have been written within the last two months."[6] The conflict dropped out of sight after May issued his report, so the two must have reached some settlement out of court.

Despite his substantial caseload, May found time to continue his participation in the Northwest Association of Sheriffs and Police. In July, the group unanimously reelected May as the association president.

Also during the summer, one of May's death cases led him into unusual territory. In late July, he was called upon to investigate the disappearance of John Woodard, a well-to-do cattleman and small-town banker. He had vanished while on a trip to Seattle. When police made no progress on a missing-persons complaint, the family turned to May for help. Woodard had last been seen at a card room located about three blocks from his hotel. The search was hampered because the family had no clear, recent photographs of Woodard, who was in his early sixties. Thus, the *Seattle Times* reported, May "adopted a plan heretofore unused on the Pacific Coast and but rarely employed by the police of larger eastern cities."[7]

First, he collected all the useful photographs of Woodard the family could find. He gave these to a portrait artist. With successive input from people who knew Woodward, the artist produced an image of how he looked as an older man. Flyers with the very best likeness were then distributed to contacts all across North America. Some weeks later, May received a reply from provincial police in the Peace River area of far northern Alberta, Canada. In mid-August, a man answering the description had checked in at a local lodging house. He gave his name as F. M. Wright and claimed to be investigating possible oil and gas properties.

Unfortunately, Mr. Wright had hiked off along the Loon River and had not been seen since. Indian trackers lost his trail in the rocks near some wild rapids. In September, the *Seattle Times* reported, "Although descriptions of Wright tally exactly with those of Mr. Woodard, the identification is based principally on samples of Wright's handwriting now in Mr. May's hands."[8] Less than a week after that item appeared, the provincial police reported that the body of Wright/Woodard had been recovered from the river.

Also in September, May made an important change in his personal life. On September 17, 1925, he married Helen Ione Klog. Miss Klog had joined Revelare as a stenographer sometime in the spring or summer of 1922. Now she married the boss, eight months after his divorce from Clara was final.

For some reason, they had the marriage ceremony performed by a Baptist minister in Shelton. Both of them listed their current residences as Thurston County, whose county seat is Olympia. (Shelton is about sixteen miles northwest of Olympia.) Actually, they then lived in Seattle (King County). Family memories do not explain these anomalies. Certainly, it was not an elopement. Helen's mother, Johanna "Josie" Klog, was one of the witnesses. Luke's new mother-in-law was unlikely to protest the somewhat odd proceedings. Johanna Kaspersen had run away from home in Denmark at the age of sixteen because her wealthy family had arranged her future marriage to "a young man she despised."[9] She ended up in San Francisco, staying with an aunt and uncle. At some point, she met Thomas Klog, a native of Iceland. They married in 1893. Her family then disowned her, but Johanna considered that amusing rather than distressing.

In due time, Thomas and Josie had a son, Leslie. A few years later, Thomas followed the gold rush into Yukon Territory. Later, he brought his wife and son north and, in September 1900, Helen was born. Through the years that followed, Helen never lost her love and longing for the simplicity and beauty of those early years. But in 1918, her parents decided she needed to go to the States for more education and wider opportunities. Her mother made the trip with her and, by 1920, the family had reunited in Seattle.

Helen first landed a job as a clerk. She then took a course in stenography and went to work in that field. However, she found her duties for her first employer routine and dull. Criminology seemed like a much more interesting line of work. There's no evidence that May interacted much, if at all, with his in-laws from his first two marriages. From this third marriage, Luke gained a *compadre* in his new brother-in-law, Leslie, along with a new wife. Thus, this hitch would last the rest of his life. Helen also shared Luke's love of animals, so the family was never without a pet dog.

John L. Harris had left the firm by this time. In fact, he had opened an office in the Dexter Horton Building, right across the street from where May had his offices. Despite that, Revelare still logged more than one hundred cases for the year. More than 40 percent were document examinations, but there were also thirteen death cases.

Most of the death cases were fairly routine and received little newspaper coverage. Still, an interesting point was raised by a murder that took place about twenty miles southeast of Bellingham. Elderly farm wife Nellie O'Neil was beaten to death by her husband. He, however, was so drunk on moonshine he never remembered any of it. But as evidence of the violence of the attack, police found what appeared to be blood spattered liberally on his clothes. The county prosecutor hired May to prove that the spots were indeed human blood. The blood verification and spatter pattern analysis were quite straightforward. The husband was convicted and apparently died in prison.

But in requesting May's help before the trial, the prosecutor wondered "if there is any way that the blood on the garments could be traced to be the same as the party who was killed."[10] Unfortunately, the attorney's desires far outran reality. Recall that Karl Landsteiner had discovered the A-B-O blood groups back in 1901. But after that, the field largely languished. Not until 1922 did University of Turin Professor Leone Lattes publish *The Individuality of Blood*, the first text to discuss blood grouping in terms that could be applied to crime scene investigation.

Unfortunately, blood groups are not very specific. In fact, they can really only *eliminate* people. If a stain is type A, then that excludes people having other blood types. Other than that, analysts had no way to narrow the range of possibilities. May replied, "At the present writing, courts have not accepted testimony as to the blood coming from a particular individual."[11]

It is worth noting that, during this period, some Revelare cases still required an agent to visit a crime scene to develop latent fingerprints. Many small jurisdictions had no one trained in that narrow but vital skill. Some years earlier, May had developed his own improved fingerprint powder. During his studies, he also found several ways that fingerprints could be counterfeited at a crime scene.

Of course, smaller law enforcement units needed even more help when the stakes were high. A week or so into 1926, May received a letter from the Shoshone County prosecutor in Wallace, Idaho. Wealthy rancher James Montgomery had been murdered. Officials had the death bullet and the weapon they thought had killed him. The prosecutor said they needed "some expert advice on this point and several different parties have referred me to you."[12]

May's subsequent report outlined the analyses performed, continuing his education program for law enforcement people. He noted that the "comparison is made under a microscope especially constructed for the comparison of bullets."[13] He applied the clincher in a follow-up letter: "In the hundreds of experiments which I have conducted, I have never found two guns marking bullets exactly the same in relation to the fine microscopic marks."[14]

The jury took little time to convict Lee Foyte, a casual laborer from North Dakota, of murder and to recommend the death penalty. He eventually received a sentence of twenty-five years to life. In a follow-up letter, Prosecutor Horning told May, "I am very glad to tell you that you made a very good impression before the jury (as almost the entire jury have told me since the trial) and that no one who heard your testimony was left with any doubt as to the gun from which the fatal shot was fired. Opposing counsel made a feeble and ill-advised attempt to ridicule you in his final argument but got nowhere."[15]

As noted many times before, cases like the Foyte murder inquiry grabbed most of the headlines, along with the occasional big-money dispute like the Hanna-Sisco documents case. But an unusual case occurred in Hoquiam, Washington, a bit under fifty miles west of Olympia. It began as an *ad hoc* car race about six months before Revelare logged the case.

Bill Eubanks pressed hard on the gas pedal of his Buick roadster, trying to close up on Wade. His brother, in a rental car, had really stepped on it. They'd all spent the night drinking at the roadhouse. The sky was bright to the east; the sun would be up any time now. Should be a nice day. The road got a little tricky at the approach to the Little Hoquiam River. The temporary bridge didn't really line up properly. As Wade's car roared onto the span, it seemed like he overcorrected. The rental swooped to the right, rode along the handrail, and then crashed through.

As Wade's taillights disappeared over the side, Bill eased off on the gas. Then he stomped hard on the brakes. The bridge itself was collapsing! Incredibly, the roadster shrieked through a neat 180-degree turn and slid backwards. There was a thump as the rear wheels fell off the broken end of the bridge, but the car stopped just short of going over into the water. Bill and his passenger hurriedly scrambled out. The other man slid down the steep riverbank and swam out to help Wade and his three passengers out of the river. Badly shaken, they otherwise escaped with only bumps and bruises. Newspapers around the region published photos of Bill's roadster hanging precariously off the end of the bridge. The center span was nothing but a jumble of timbers and planks in the water.

Not much happened for months after the crash, then the city contacted Revelare on January 16, 1926. Five days later, a *Seattle Times* headline read, "Autoists Sue Hoquiam for Bridge Collapse."[16] Bill, Wade, and the rental company had all filed suits against the city. They charged that the city had been negligent "in allowing parts of the bridge to become rotten and unsafe." The total of the claims in the three suits was more than $6,000.

City authorities had a preliminary assessment that the bridge was sound and prepared to defend that position. May sent an agent to some of the local hot spots to learn more. There, the operative lubricated a few tongues to the tune of more than $76, a considerable sum for 1926 even at bootleg liquor prices.

Figure 8.2.   Near Miss on Hoquiam Bridge. *Source:* **May-Reid Records.**

At one session, with several customers present, Bill Eubanks commented that "they had all been drinking the night of the accident."[17] He also confirmed that they had been speeding and might have even been racing at times.

The city engineer reported that the bridge "was well constructed of sound timber, with the ends and all joints creosoted."[18] It was, in fact, in "excellent condition." Scrapes and "rim marks" showed where Wade's car hit the guard rail with enough force to crush it. From there, the vehicle "headed directly for the end post" of the bridge truss and knocked it loose. "The end post is a vital member of the truss," the engineer declared. "Without it in place, the truss would collapse by progressive failure at the panel points both top and bottom."

Together, these reports showed that, contrary to the lawsuit claims, reckless driving had caused the bridge to collapse. When he submitted an expense report, May wrote that he was "hoping that you will prove success-ful in resisting the fraudulent claims."[19] Several weeks later, the Hoquiam finance officer sent May a letter praising the Revelare investigation. A check for services rendered and all expenses would follow in a few days, he added.

Alongside the normal cases, May also had the criminology school in full swing. But even with all that, May found opportunities to educate other people about scientific detection and related topics. As the bridge case was winding down, he was invited to speak to the Seattle Soroptimists Club. Over the previous year, he had also talked to a joint Kiwanis-Rotary club luncheon and then lectured on forgeries and other bank-related crimes to first a county and then a regional bankers' association.

Later in that year, May addressed a Federation of Women's Clubs gathering in Seattle. He urged their support for a new home for the feeble-minded in western Washington. The existing home in the eastern side of the state was already overcrowded, he pointed out. And such individuals had special needs that a reform school could not handle. (Sadly, fourteen years would pass before the state built such an institution.)

Early in 1926, he spoke to the Seattle YMCA and gave a series of il-lustrated lectures on criminology to the Women's University Club. His talk to the Soroptimists came four days after the last of those lectures. The *Seattle Times* said that May had "pointed out to Seattle Soroptimists . . . what a dominant force business and professional women, by reason of their experi-ence in the outside world, might become in stirring up public resentment against crime and in bringing about the needed legislation to curb it."[20] May also said, "Every university in the United States should embody in its cur-ricula possibilities for [the] study of criminology in all its phases, a plan that has been a part of European institutions of learning for generations."

May's urge to teach dovetailed with people's craving for novelty and excitement during the Roaring Twenties. A couple weeks before May's Soroptimist talk, a major *Seattle Times* advertisement appeared for the documentary "The Amundsen Polar Flight."[21] The account of Roald Amundsen's attempt to fly over the North Pole was billed as "more thrilling than a thousand dramas." Amundsen's two seaplanes were forced down onto the ice 150 miles short of the pole, and one had to be abandoned. After Herculean efforts, the two crews boarded the surviving plane and roared down a path laboriously chipped and stamped into the snowpack and ice. Flying low to conserve fuel, the aircraft had to dodge icebergs for mile after mile. But, eventually, they returned to safety and a well-deserved heroes' welcome.

That same entertainment page also listed a dozen feature films along with numerous vaudeville acts. Nearly all the movies catered to that thirst for the new and were soon forgotten. In fact, most of the performers in those silent movies would fall by the wayside when the industry switched to talkies a few years later. A movie that starred one who survived the transition happened to be playing in Seattle at that time. *Sally of the Sawdust* was the first feature film for vaudeville comedian W. C. Fields.

With his busy schedule, it's unlikely that May would have been able to view the feature films. However, he might well have made time to see the Amundsen three-reeler, which ran a total of thirty-six minutes. May had hunted fugitives in the Rocky Mountain wilderness in all kinds of weather. He could appreciate, better than most, the ordeals endured by Amundsen and his men.

May also spoke later in the year at a conference of the Northwest Association of Sheriffs and Police. In his main address, he blamed an increase in crime on "improper political influence in granting pardons and paroles."[22] But he also pointed a finger at "lack of reform and rehabilitation in prisons, and lack of scientific training for criminal investigators."

Revelare continued to average more than one firearms case per month, most of them deaths. In fact, except for some luck, all the gun cases might have been deaths. A month after the Foyte case, two Wenatchee police officers waited at the Columbia River bridge. It was about four o'clock in the morning and still very dark. They had information that a certain car would be returning from East Wenatchee with a load of liquor. Finally, as a vehicle approached, they stepped onto the pavement and tried to wave it down with their flashlights.

However, taxi driver Ray Hungate did not recognize the two as police officers in the glare of his headlights. He figured the pair were trying to rob him and floored the gas pedal. The officers leaped aside, drew their service revolvers and tried to shoot out his tires. Hungate then grabbed his own gun and fired back. Events got a little confused after that. Patrolman Harvey El- liott had been hit in the leg, but the officers finally straightened matters out. Hungate ended up in jail on a first-degree assault charge, unable to post a $10,000 bail. He languished there quite a long time.

May issued a preliminary report in early March, nearly two weeks after the incident. He had received a bullet and several bullet fragments, along with "Smith & Wesson 32-20 revolver #127346."[23] May sent a technician to a remote location south of Seattle near Puget Sound. He had the tech con- duct a series of experiments in which the proper type of .32-caliber bullet hit bone. In each test, hunks of beef were wrapped around cattle bones and tied in place. A pile of magazines and a boulder formed a backstop.

Results varied depending upon the angle at which the bullet traversed the flesh and struck the bone. Some slugs simply shattered when they hit the bone squarely. In one such case, a fragment "lodged in the bone to the depth of about ¼"."[24] Still, the tester retrieved several bullets that could be compared to the slug extracted from the policeman's leg.

"The fragments of the bullet submitted are . . . from a .32-caliber re- volver," May said in his preliminary report.[25] However, neither the bullet nor the fragments could be shown to have been fired from the pistol submitted. After several days passed, the prosecutor's office sent him two more revolvers. One was a Colt and the other was a Smith & Wesson, designated #50296. And not until two weeks after that did the prosecutor call to ask about results. The attorney thought the defense might try to prove one officer had shot the other and "wanted to know your opinion as to whether or not this could have been possible."[26]

In his report, May declared that the bullet that hit the officer had *not* been fired by "the Colt, or the first Smith and Wesson which was submitted."[27] He went on, "It is my opinion that the bullet was fired from the old Smith and Wesson revolver #50296." Then came the trump card: "In the event that this gun belongs to either of the officers it would be impossible to convict anyone else of the shooting."

Three days later, the *Wenatchee World* reported, "Motion for dismissal of the criminal action against Ray Hungate, taxi driver, charged with first degree assault, was filed today in the Chelan county clerk's office by Sam R. Sumner, prosecuting attorney."[28] The next day, a *Wenatchee Sun* op-ed columnist briefly mentioned the dismissal motion. He also grumped that the independent testing had "resulted in the report from Detective May that the bullet had been fired from the gun of Officer Minton. Luke set the local folks back $125.00 for the information."[29]

For the year following the end of the Spadoni trial, May had logged about a dozen death cases. While a few had points of interest, none made a big national splash. That changed on June 17, 1926, when a huge front-page block-letter headline in the *Seattle Times* screamed, "W. A. Gaines Niece Slain!"[30]

The victim was twenty-two-year-old Sylvia H. Gaines, a recent graduate of Smith College, the elite women's school in Massachusetts. The perpetrator had beaten her on the head with a rock and then strangled her to death. Searchers found her on the shore of Green Lake, a pond about five miles north of downtown. The body was nearly nude, but she had not been raped.

Her uncle, William A. Gaines, was well known in city-county government. Sylvia had been visiting her father, Wallace "Bob" Gaines. Her parents divorced when she was four or five years old, so she had lived with her mother in Massachusetts. Meanwhile, Gaines remarried. After graduation, Sylvia traveled west to meet the father she barely knew. Newspapers in Massachusetts gave the story a lot of play, and it also made news around the country. The morning edition of the *Miami Herald*, for example, had the front-page headline "Woman Killed in Grove Near Seattle Lake."[31]

At first, authorities assumed she had been attacked by a drifter. Then, guarded remarks began to surface that pointed to her father, Bob Gaines, as a suspect. William Gaines angrily told the newspapers that his political enemies were behind those malicious rumors. His brother, a World War veteran who suffered from a mild case of what was then called "shell shock," had loved his newfound daughter. He'd never do anything to hurt her.

Detective Captain Charles Tennant also rejected the barely veiled accusations. As noted before, Tennant was an old-school cop. He firmly believed that common sense and persistence were the keys to good police work (something that Luke May did not disagree with, by the way). Experience and intuition convinced Tennant that Sylvia had been the victim of a transient sexual predator. Prosecuting Attorney Ewing D. Colvin went so far as to call a press conference to squelch the talk. A reporter asked, "Will the aid of a criminal investigator, Luke S. May, for example, be requested?"[32]

"Right now I have no such intention," Colvin replied. Four days later, as a coroner's jury convened, the prosecutor changed his tune. New facts had piled up fast. But Chief Tennant was fixated on a shadowy suspect who he thought might have already left town. Concerning this other evidence, he declared, "I refuse to be stampeded into doing something I know is useless."

But on June 25, the *Bellingham Herald* reported, "Luke S. May, a Seattle criminologist, whose name has figured in [the] solution of many Pacific Northwest murders, was tonight asked by Prosecutor Colvin to come here from an international crime conference in Spokane, Wash."[33]

Four days afterwards, sheriff's deputies arrested Bob Gaines. Lurid testimony from the trial that began six weeks later made headlines all across the country. More than just the fact of murder held readers' attention. Testimony from multiple witnesses showed that Gaines had had an "unnatural relationship" with his daughter. Their intimate behavior was so blatant that Bob's wife had tried to commit suicide. However, in the days before Sylvia's death, they had quarreled about something. Word filtered out that she planned to leave Seattle soon. Fear of exposure provided an obvious motive.

Besides having agents confirm some of the most damning witness statements, May also presented lab evidence for human blood spattered on Gaines's clothing. However, testimony from hotelkeepers and others about incestuous trysts grabbed the most attention. Still, the headline in one Connecticut newspaper was fairly restrained: "Gaines is Charged With Paying Undue Attention to Girl."[34] It took the jury a bit over three hours to bring in a guilty verdict. Wallace Gaines was hanged about two years and two months after Sylvia was found dead.

May's reputation received another boost in the September 1926 issue of the *American Magazine*. This national publication claimed around 2.2 million readers. Magner White, a Pulitzer Prize-winning writer for the *San Diego Sun* newspaper, interviewed May at his office suite. White titled the article "May Hunts Criminals With a Microscope."[35] White first outlined some of May's earlier career and cases. Then he wrote, "May isn't at all the story-book type of detective. He doesn't wear a slouch hat down over his eyes; and his eyes aren't sharp and ruthless. Instead, they are mild and rather mystic. He dresses immaculately and in general appearance reminds you of a college professor."

May's giant microscope greatly impressed the writer. White did not discuss the College of Criminology but did say that May gave guest lectures on "Physical Evidence in Criminal Cases" to students at the University of Washington. May told White that he "always charges a flat fee—usually one hundred dollars a day where court attendance is required." The "flat fee" approach was rather like Luke May's fictional model, Sherlock Holmes. He also said, "The cost of investigating a homicide where the assailant has been able to hide his identity usually runs from $1,000 to $3,000."[36]

By the fall, May had consolidated his office, laboratory, and home. He moved everything to a structure near today's Seattle University Park. Reporters often considered his location part of the affluent Capitol Hill neighborhood, but it's now south of the official boundary. From this time until World War II, May would operate all aspects of his business from his home. Even the Institute of Scientific Criminology (when he renamed it) had its headquarters at that address.

With his casework, self-study, and teaching, May had likely decided he needed a more efficient arrangement. He perhaps also needed more room for his collections. May kept a large inventory of different firearms for testing, racks and racks of test-fired bullets, and a considerable library. Those were directly related to his work and study, of course. But beyond that he collected stamps, coins, mineral samples, and more. Granddaughter Mindi Reid particularly recalled a huge chunk of iron pyrite (fool's gold).

Sometime during this period, May also acquired a boat and ventured onto the waters of Puget Sound for recreation. His new brother-in-law was an avid big-fish fisherman. Moreover, his new father-in-law, a skilled carpenter and cabinetmaker, had once built a forty-five-foot vessel to carry supplies up the Fortymile River in Alaska and the Canadian Yukon. They and Helen almost certainly influenced Luke's choice of leisure activities.

Luke took to boating in a big way. Over the next twenty years or so, he and Helen would own a succession of boats, join the Seattle Yacht Club, and enjoy many excursions on the water. Luke and Helen might have rented a boat initially, but they eventually acquired a craft they called the *Cheerio*. Sales and registration papers described the vessel as an auxiliary yawl. Records suggest that the boat was around thirty-five feet in length and did not have an especially powerful motor.

Meanwhile, with Clark Sellers and John L. Harris both gone, the 1926 Revelare caseload declined about a third, to just seventy-three. However, death cases remained high, with a total of twelve, involving fourteen victims. Those, of course, included the ones discussed earlier in the chapter. None of the others received much national newspaper coverage. Even so, one of May's death cases for the year—the murder of Charles R. Harris—holds a curious place in scientific criminology. It also pairs logically with one that is historically and legally significant. Both will be discussed in chapter 10.

Beyond that, the Harris murder received very little national newspaper coverage, although it was heavily reported in the region. That, in fact, was true of most of May's death cases and some of his other prominent investigations, where the events only received scattered mentions nationally. However, that "kept his name alive" for when the periodic blockbuster came along . . . like the sensational Gaines murder. That pattern would continue until just before World War II.

• 9 •

Work and Play

May's early death cases for the following year generally fit the regional-interest pattern. Little is known about the first for the year, which might have been an accident or suicide. The second was a murder in Sultan, a village located twenty-five to thirty miles northeast of Seattle. The victim was Town Marshal Percy Brewster. The killer was Edward Sickles, a career criminal with a string of convictions for small-time offenses. He was also an escape artist, having broken out of jail on several occasions. In this case, he was out on bail from a robbery charge.

Marshal Brewster became suspicious of a car parked behind a Sultan bank. Inside he saw two rifles and a stock of ammunition. When Sickles approached the vehicle, Brewster detained him for questioning about some earlier break-ins. But the criminal, determined to avoid jail, pulled a hidden gun, shot the marshal, and fled. Brewster lived long enough to give a description of Sickles, and he was soon captured. Pacific Northwest newspapers covered these events extensively, but they made no impression elsewhere.

The subsequent trial was interesting for what did not happen. Damning facts piled up and then reached the point where Luke May was to describe the firearms evidence. The *Seattle Times* reported, "Admission of the defense linking the bullet taken from Brewster as one fired from the pistol found on Sickles came after the state had called Luke S. May, Seattle criminologist, to the stand."[1] The wording indicates that May did not actually testify. Sickles's attorneys must have feared that May's detailed analysis would make too big an impression on the jury. But in the end, the panel took little time to convict Sickles and to recommend the death penalty.

A week after the verdict, he broke out of jail. That escape did make the national news with the typical headline, "Man Escapes, Was to Hang."[2] After

117

that, Sickles hid out, using a mountain cabin about fifteen miles northeast of Everett as a base. From there, he made jaunts into every major Washington city using cars he stole. Then, about three months after his escape, a spurned girlfriend betrayed his hideaway to police. Determined not to hang, Sickles shot it out with the posse sent to arrest him. Ripped by bullets and shotgun blasts, he died in an Everett hospital three hours later.

Having his testimony cut short in the Sickles trial was probably just fine with May. He was very busy during the early months of the year, with at least four other active death cases. May also continued his educational efforts. In February, he presented a number of lectures at the University of Oregon in Eugene. His subjects included crime-scene protocols and "Preparation of a Criminal Case for Trial."[3] For those who could spend a couple more days, he gave a series of four lectures on "Criminal Types."

The following month, May spoke to the King County Democratic Club. As usual, he advocated the greater use of scientific methods in crime prevention and detection. May declared it a "disgrace" that Washington did so little to collect statewide data on crime and criminals. He also said, "All expert witnesses in criminal cases should be employed by the court and not by the prosecution or defense."[4]

May was all too aware that questions could be raised about the objectivity of experts being paid by one side or the other. Many documents—articles as well as letters to and from outsiders—affirm May's total dedication to the unbiased assessment of evidence. If that ruined the client's case, so be it. But he also saw, firsthand, that not everyone shared his level of commitment. And May's proposal seems odd only in the context of the adversarial legal process used in this country. In countries with different legal approaches, court-appointed experts are actually the norm. They are usually drawn from a pool of pre-certified professionals.

In the spring of 1927, May had reason to be pleased about his educational program. Some eighteen months earlier, Nathan A. Baker had been sales manager for a Seattle candy company. But after training at May's criminology school, he was identified as an assistant on a few important cases, including the Sylvia Gaines murder. Then, on May 1, 1927, the *Seattle Times* reported that "for the first time in the history of King County the sheriff's office would have a special bureau of criminal investigation with a criminologist in the service of the county."[5] The item also said that "N. A. Baker, formerly assistant to Luke S. May, has been selected to take charge of the new branch."

Crimes like the Gaines murder grabbed the headlines, but more and more of May's work involved questioned documents. In fact, for the first time, QD work made up more than half the cases logged during the year. And one case that involved handwriting analysis and other investigative techniques did make national headlines. It began late the previous year, when wealthy eccentric Sarah Smith Scollard made an urgent radio call to her attorneys in Seattle. Her new husband, George Scollard, had tried to strand her in Buenos Aires, Argentina. Fortunately, she had become suspicious that there was another woman in her husband's life and had hired a local detective to watch him.

Then George and Sarah had both boarded a morning train leaving Buenos Aires, supposedly for an excursion into western Argentina. But George hopped off just before the departure. A few hours later, he and a lady friend left the city on a steamer headed to New York City. Sarah did not get back to the city until late that evening and several days passed before she could arrange transport out of Buenos Aires. Sarah first boarded a steamship whose route led north and then through the Panama Canal to Los Angeles. That trip would take about eight weeks, while George would reach New York in little more than three. With so much of a lead, George might then use his position as her husband to make away with her considerable fortune.

That was no small matter since Sarah was worth at least $2 million, and perhaps as much as $15 million. (She seemed purposely vague about how much she was really worth.) She had inherited a substantial fortune from an earlier husband and then built it even larger investing in Chicago real estate.

At Montevideo, Uruguay, Sarah switched to the SS *Southern Cross,* which was headed directly for New York. By the time Sarah arrived in Seattle, her husband was in hiding somewhere. And George had indeed moved some assets to places of his own choosing. A warrant was issued for George's arrest. Sarah's lawyers also hired several detective agencies to find him and to locate the cash and securities he'd hidden. George was arrested in Vancouver, British Columbia, about a week after her return. However, he had none of the missing assets with him.

After another week of searching, May's agents found a Vancouver hotel where employees thought they recognized George as a man who had registered as "George Stacy." May quickly confirmed from the handwriting that he had indeed been George Scollard. That finding led agents into the financial district, where they discovered that George had leased several safety-deposit boxes under phony names. Again, May was able to verify that "Frank Evans," at the Canadian Bank of Commerce, was George. At the Royal Bank of Canada, he had signed as "Frank Martin." Based on witness identifications and the handwriting evidence, a Canadian court quickly issued orders to open the boxes. The Royal Bank box contained $69,000 worth of Sarah's securities and other assets. The Commerce box held more than $250,000 worth of bonds. Scollard stories made headlines for many months afterwards.

Figure 9.1.   Steamship *Southern Cross* (as Navy Troop Ship). *Source*: U.S. Navy, NH 102894.

During the summer after the main Scollard hoopla, the Northwest Association of Sheriffs and Police held its annual meeting in Nelson, British Columbia, a town about 125 miles north of Spokane. One of the attendees was Harry Caldwell of the Oakland police and leading founder of the International Association for Identification. Although he had retired as president of the IAI in 1921, he was still very active in the organization. Northwest Association delegates selected Boise as the location for the next annual meeting and again elected May as president.

Luke's reelection enlivened his contact with another West Coast pioneer, Edward Crossman. Since his retirement from the army, Crossman had often appeared in court as an expert witness on firearms. But he still made his living as a writer and, early in the year, *Scientific American* magazine published his article about firearms identification. Crossman felt that far too many so-called experts lacked a thorough knowledge of the weapons they might encounter on a case. As a result, he asserted, they just "go into court and bluff the matter through."[6]

In his view, only Goddard in the East and May and Heinrich in the West were professional enough to get it right. Shortly after the issue came out, May wrote to Crossman to introduce himself. Although they had never met, May said, he felt like he was "talking to an old friend."[7] He thanked the writer for his kind words and said, "I have been an admirer of your articles for a great number of years." Then came the clincher. "We both know that any man who has monkeyed with the identification of guns as long as we have, must have some-thing wrong with him, so that there certainly must be a bond of mutual interest."

In his reply, Crossman agreed that they had a lot in common. He felt that hands-on experience with guns and ammunition was vital to be-ing a competent firearms expert. Recently, Crossman asserted, one of their contemporaries had suffered because he did not have that background. The supposed firearms expert had been tied in knots on the witness stand by the defense. The result—admittedly not just because of the expert's stumble—had been a hung jury. Prosecutors had then hired Crossman and Clark Sellers as gun experts for a new trial. Crossman concluded, "Risky business, this idea that a good microscope training and a couple of Winchester catalogues makes a bird a firearms expert."[8]

May and Crossman exchanged more letters, mostly devoted to their lat-est technical developments. Then, after the association meeting, May wrote to Crossman to say that he had a trip scheduled to Washington, DC, in September. While he was in the East, he also planned to visit arms factories to collect information about their latest products. He asked Crossman about specific places he should tour and people he should try to meet. May also said that Sellers was "as capable an investigator as we have in the West, his first primary prerequisite being an honesty and integrity that cannot be bought. With this, I am sorry to say, I believe some individuals known to both of us are not endowed."[9]

Crossman replied with many suggestions, including the names of several personal contacts. "Use my name with any of these people."[10] He agreed that Sellers was "a fine square shooter" who was handily outclassing the local tal-ent "in the hand-writing line." Crossman did think that Sellers was "naturally weak on firearms technicalities, not being an old shooter." Then, rather sar-donically, he observed, "But as long as defense attorneys are as dumb as they are, he will have no trouble."

Crossman also offered congratulations on May's reelection as president of the association. (May would continue to be reelected for another eight years.) Crossman said, "It is most unusual for a man in [a] private line of work to be constantly elected to office over peace officers with the usual jealousy that prevails among such men."[11]

About the time of these letters, May was involved in an interesting and unusual case. It was rare because May was hired by the defense, and he faced off against a former student. In mid-June, Lulu Gruber shot and killed her estranged husband, Charles. She said they had been living separately for some time when Charles came to her house and started an argument. Then, she claimed, he had threatened her with a gun. But Lulu somehow managed to wrestle the gun away and shoot him with it . . . five times.

She claimed self-defense, but prosecutor Colvin filed a first-degree murder charge about ten days later. The *Seattle Times* said, "Colvin is expected to rely upon the testimony of Deputy Sheriff N. A. Baker, criminologist, who has charted the course of each of the five bullets found in Charles A. Gruber's body."[12]

So, having its own criminologist available, the prosecution had no need to contract for May's services. But the defense basically got double value by hiring him. Obviously, they had his expertise as a consultant. But they also kept him away from the prosecution in case the inexperienced Baker faltered on the stand. Ultimately, both sides got part of what they wanted. The jury felt that the prosecutor's evidence did not support a first-degree murder charge. But five bullets, some at longer range, seemed a bit more than simple self-defense. They convicted Lulu of second-degree murder. The parole board released her after she served just under seven years of her ten-year sentence.

Overall, May's 1927 caseload dropped slightly compared to the previous year. The number of death cases declined even more, to just eight, including the Sickles and Gruber cases. Several non-death cases kept May busy toward the end of the year. Still, the lower total workload allowed him more time for family and recreation. In December, Luke and Helen sold the *Cheerio* and purchased an auxiliary sloop, which they named *It*. The *It* might have been only slightly longer than the *Cheerio*, but the vessel apparently had a much bigger engine.

May's workload increased slightly in the new year. Death cases returned to a more normal load of about one a month. However, none of the early cases—not even the murders—generated much newspaper interest outside the region. Ironically, one documents case again brought him into contact with ex-assistant Nathan Baker.

The sequence began when King County Sheriff Claude Bannick charged three "South End constables" with extortion.[13] The men would show up at a suspected illegal liquor site with a search warrant signed by a local justice of the peace, William Wilson. Then, for a suitable consideration, say $65 to $150, they promised to just go away. Deputy Sheriff Baker collected a good deal of evidence against the men. He also found that Wilson, who owned and operated a grocery store, often pre-signed a batch of forms so the constables could move quickly on a hot tip. This was a fairly common practice.

Then prosecutors asked Wilson to cross-check his records against county reports of improper or unlawful raids by the constables. Soon after, Wilson told them that two of the three officers had searched a property using a warrant with a phony signature. So, authorities added forgery to the counts against the men. May logged his part in the case in early January, and the trial began later that month. The extortion charges were to be prosecuted first.

However, Justice Wilson created a stir when he retracted his forgery claim. He testified that he had made the statement "only because he was threatened with 'embarrassment' by Deputy Sheriff N. A. Baker."[14]

Naturally, Baker denied making any such threats. And it was more likely that Wilson had come across a raid that was so egregiously illegal, he wanted to disavow *any* involvement in the event. So, he declared that even his signature was a forgery. According to those who worked in the field, this is not uncommon. But if May disproved the forgery, as he most likely would, Wilson might face a perjury charge. He repudiated his earlier statement, and the forgery charge was eventually dropped. Two of the three men were convicted on the extortion charges. They received prison sentences of eighteen months to three years. The other suspect was acquitted.

A month or so after the extortion decision, Revelare received a request from the prosecuting attorney for Spokane County. Rancher Leslie Bagwell claimed to have come home from some evening errands to find his wife Elsie dead. He said she had been tied onto a bed, with a gag in her mouth and her hands tightly bound. A cloth around her neck suggested that she had been strangled.

However, when the sheriff arrived at the home, he and his deputies immediately began to doubt the husband's account. There were no signs of a struggle, and the couple's two children—aged nine and eleven—had been sleeping in the very next room. The strips supposedly used to bind her were piled neatly on a chair. They showed no sign of having ever been stretched, and some would have been nearly impossible to untie had they been tightly knotted.

Last but not least, the gag was not wet. It had either never actually been tied in place, or she was long dead when it was. As the sheriff told reporters, "There are so many impossible things in his story."[15] An autopsy showed that she had not died of strangulation and detected no other obvious cause of death. Prosecutors contacted May a couple days after the coroner completed the autopsy. They had access to a local medical laboratory but apparently wanted someone trained in criminal work as a backup.

The local lab issued its report five days after May logged in the case. They stated that they had tested samples from "the stomach contents, stomach, liver, kidneys and brain."[16] Their tests gave negative results for arsenic, strychnine, and a whole shopping list of other poisons. They did find more than half a gram of oxalic acid, another poison, in the contents of her stomach. The analyst, a medical doctor, opined, "The amount of oxalic acid present is apparently too small to have caused death, yet the amount is too large to have been derived from the vegetable matter in her diet." The report then rambled into a couple of "well, maybe" notions but ultimately failed to identify any cause of death. Incautiously, as it turned out, the County Coroner endorsed the report below the pathologist's sign-off.

May took his time in assessing the lab report, consulting numerous toxicology references. His response began with the flat statement that the results showed a "sufficient amount of oxalic acid, in my opinion, to place the cause of death as oxalic acid."[17] However, he had spotted a problem in the documents for the case. The official autopsy report filed with the court by the coroner "shows that no internal examination was made of the head." May had therefore directly queried the coroner, who "was certain that the brain had not been removed."

Either the coroner's report and memory were faulty or the lab was mistaken about having analyzed samples from the brain. May then delivered the crusher: "This variance, needless to say, would be fatal in any prosecution based on the finding of oxalic acid . . . unless it could be conclusively shown that . . . the coroner was wrong, and that the brain was examined."[18] May offered no further comment on the case, so we do not know what happened behind the scenes. However, a little over a month later, the court in Spokane honored a motion from the county prosecutor to dismiss the first-degree murder charge against Bagwell.

Despite the high workload, May still made time for his new hobby. The *Seattle Times* for March 18, 1928, reported, "The increasing preference for the Ford marine engine conversions was demonstrated in a cruise in a 38-foot converted fishing boat owned by Luke S. May, Seattle's famous criminologist, last week."[19]

May took the reporter and the engine builder for a cruise on Lake Union. The reporter told readers, "Mr. May plans an extended cruise this summer and at present is having another engine built which he will carry as ballast."[20] It appears that the summer excursion did not go as well as the Mays had hoped. They sold the *It* and, at the end of August, bought a powerful twin-engine vessel they called the *Lady Luck*.

As summer ended, May handled two death cases that were interesting but unusual because they did not involve firearms. The first was the death of Thurlow Hudlow. Born in Missouri, Thurlow worked for several years at his brother's ranch in north-central Washington, a few miles from the Canadian border. He was just under forty years old, not married, and happened to be in Tacoma on the early evening of September 5. The driver of the speeding car may have not even have seen him when he stepped off the curb. The car's bumper slammed into Thurlow, and his head hit the fender hard enough to make a dent that broke through the metal. He was killed instantly. The body flew aside, and the auto barely slowed its hurtling flight.

Fortunately, a police officer got a good look at the make and model, although he could not read the license number. Less than an hour later, police found a car of the right type a few blocks away. The vehicle showed clear signs of recent damage to a fender. Subsequent inquiries verified that the driver had probably been drunk.

May discovered several strands of hair clinging to the broken edge of a big dent in the fender. Fresh bits of flesh on the ends showed that the strands had been forcibly torn from a living body. Microscopic examination proved that it was human hair. Moreover, the color and structure closely matched the hair on Thurlow's head. Yet even that might not have clinched the case against the driver. However, May also found dust and skin flakes on Thurlow's scalp and hair that exactly matched material on the hairs taken from the car. Nothing else on the car was anything like it. At the trial, May's presentation of this evidence sealed the driver's fate. He was convicted of manslaughter.

The other case, a murder near Spokane, made the news across the country. Two prune pickers found the body of Mrs. Katherine Clark in a field near Spokane. She had been killed by multiple blows to the head with a shingler's hatchet, which was found beside the body. Suspicion quickly fell on a millworker named Archibald "Archie" Moock. Neighbors knew that Clark, a divorcee from Boston, Massachusetts, had been staying at the Moock home.

When the police questioned Archie, he told a bizarre story. He was, he said, only a go-between for a man named "James Murphy." He knew Murphy from having worked with him at a mill a couple years earlier. Murphy and Clark had met through a matrimonial bureau and were to be married. The evening before her body was found, Archie had driven her to meet Murphy. Moock claimed that Murphy had then handed around some moonshine to celebrate. The libation was either extra strong, or drugged, because Archie soon fell asleep. When he awoke, Murphy and Mrs. Clark were gone.

Officers found Moock's story unlikely in the extreme. Archie couldn't seem to recall how Murphy had arrived at the rendezvous site. How had Murphy and his prospective bride gone away, leaving Archie asleep? Authorities became even more suspicious after they checked with people in Boston who knew Clark. The woman had carried something like $1,400 with her to Spokane. Moock was locked up as a material witness, pending other possible charges.

May probably arrived in Spokane within a day or two after the murder. At that point, he would have been tasked with examining the murder weapon and looking for other blood evidence. The weapon was linked to the car Moock had been driving, but traces of blood on his shoes were too minute to test whether they were human blood. Meanwhile, police searched the Moock property for other clues. The results hit newspapers all across the country and particularly in Katherine's hometown. The *Boston Herald* reported, "Archie F. Much [*sic*] tonight was formally charged with having decoyed Mrs. Katherine Clark of Boston, to Spokane under promise of marriage and with slaying her with a hatchet for her money."[21]

Searchers had dug up a sheaf of money wrapped in newspaper. Total amount: About $1,390. In another hole, they found a bundle of what they called "love letters," signed by "James Murphy." May took little time to declare that, in his expert opinion, Archie Moock had written the letters.

Moock steadily maintained his innocence throughout the subsequent trial. It was all Murphy's doing, his attorneys insisted. Murphy had slain the woman—for some unknown reason—and planted the money and letters in Archie's yard. But no amount of searching, by the defense and by the police, turned up any trace of Mr. Murphy. Company files at the mill contained no one named "James" or "Jim" Murphy. A jury found Moock guilty of first-degree murder and recommended the death penalty. Just short of two years after Katherine Clark was brutally murdered, Archie was hanged at the state penitentiary in Walla Walla.

The fall saw May busy preparing for the Moock trial as well as two other death cases. The agency also had a flurry of questioned documents cases. Even so, Luke managed to get out in the *Lady Luck* with Helen and Leslie. He even took time to record his thoughts about a couple of early excursions. On a trip in October 1928, they got more than they bargained for.

The *Lady Luck* motored quietly out of Lake Union toward the locks. Luke remarked that the afternoon was "quite stormy looking. Lake Union kicked up in choppy white caps."[22] The forecast for Saturday said Puget Sound would have rain showers and fresh southerly winds. But a bit of rain shouldn't bother the fish. They passed through the locks around 3:30. Soon after, they exited the canal and turned north. The Sound was fairly smooth, with very little swell. Finally, they cut down to one motor and trolled off Meadow Point. Salmon were jumping all around the boat, but they had no luck.

After a while, they cranked up the engines and arrowed north. They arrived at Possession Point, at the southern tip of Whitbey Island, as the sun sank low in the west. Again, they went to trolling. After more of that, Helen—"Little Skipper" in Luke's affectionate phrase—seated her rod in a holder and casually picked up Luke's. She said disgustedly, "There are no fish." Just then the reel on Luke's rod began to sing. Little Skipper pushed the pole toward Luke and urged him to take it. "Quick, quick, quick!" she cried. "It's a big one and he will get away."[23]

Figure 9.2.   Boat Owned by Luke and Helen May, *Source*: **May-Reid Records.**

Leslie disengaged the propellers while Luke took the pole and played the hefty salmon to the net. As Leslie brought it aboard, he said, "Gee, it is a nice one." Little Skipper excitedly said she had finally caught a big one. Without cracking a smile, but surely with a twinkling eye, Luke said, "You don't catch a fish unless you bring it to the net. You can't give the pole to someone else to land your fish."

Helen was not pleased and refused to accept his reasoning. On the next two trolling passes, she caught a couple of nice trout. Still, dusk was moving in fast now, and she wondered if they shouldn't anchor for the night. Then Little Skipper's reel shrilled "like a hoist down a shaft broke loose." She wailed, "Oh here, here, I got another big one. Take the pole, quick."

Luke refused: "You land your own fish."

She begged Leslie to take the pole instead. The big salmon made another run and distracted her. Luke winked at Leslie and said, "No, you land him alone or you lose him."

"That's what we're fishing for," Leslie chimed in. "For the sport of it."

After that, the two settled down to offering cheerfully helpful advice. The line stayed taut, then went slack, then snapped out again with a "sickening crack." But all the while Helen was slowly gaining ground. Under the boat, then out. Finally over the net, but away again. At last, the fine fish was brought aboard. At the end, Luke observed, "Little Skipper . . . masterfully landed a he-man salmon."

They anchored in a supposedly protected lee for the night. Morning came with waves pounding against the hull and whitecaps turning their anchorage ugly. Luke said, "Clouds and weather foreboding."

They tried to fish for a while before breakfast, without any luck. Perhaps they could do better in the calmer water on the mainland side near Edmonds. No bites there either. Luke said, "Weather is kicking up right smart out in the Sound." Off Point Edwards, south of Edmonds, Luke observed, "Water is too rough for good trolling, and small boat fishermen are going in."

They decided to head home and began pounding their way south through steadily rising wind and chop. After about two miles, Luke wondered if they should take shelter behind Point Wells. He looked to the south of the point and said, "Wind is starting up in [a] real blow. Waves running high and choppy." But the little headland didn't really offer much cover, so they plunged ahead. That led to a major pounding. "Crash, bang, wham! Cups down, cooking utensils scatter, drawers come out. Little Skipper stows them and goes to stern."

The *Lady Luck* hammered through. "Once or twice she is half out of water, coming down with a slap and a boom," Luke said. "If she takes this punishment without taking much water, she is some boat." At times, they made almost no headway, but finally they reached the ship canal and headed for the locks. "Great crowd of people at the locks, with many anxious faces," Luke remarked. "Junior yacht races had been caught by the blow, and many boats disabled." The *Lady* arrived at its home dock shortly before four o'clock. Luke's final summation: "After all, a wonderful trip."[24]

Not so grand for some others, however. Across the Sound from Seattle, waves swept a sailboat crewman, a professor at the University of Washington, overboard. It does not appear that his body was ever found. The *Bellingham Herald* reported, "Three other men were rescued from imminent death and a dredge was blown ashore at Alki Point, while small boats suffered broken masts, lost canvas and other damage during the storm, said to have been the heaviest blow on Puget Sound in three years."[25]

May did not leave any memoirs for trips later in the year. However, they were obviously pleased by the performance of the *Lady Luck*. They kept the vessel for many years.

One of May's more interesting non-death cases for the year sent him and an agent to Ryegate, Montana, a tiny town about fifty miles northwest of Billings. The area had been plagued by a series of bombings. No one had yet been hurt, but everyone feared that the episodes would get worse. Tracing the bomb materials and other clues, May and his agent quickly collected overwhelming evidence against a local youth.

The county prosecuting attorney was surprised. In a letter to May, he wrote, "As you know, all along, I never was able to reconcile myself as to the guilt of the defendant, until after your work was in, and your evidence so assembled that I had to admit there was no other conclusion to be reached."[26] The day after being arrested, the youth saw the evidence against him and confessed. The attorney said he spoke for himself, the sheriff, and "the people of this county" in expressing "our appreciation of your effort" in closing the case.

May's total work rate for 1928 remained about the same—seventy-three cases—but returned to a more normal load of thirteen death cases. Three of those were the Bagwell, Hudlow, and Moock cases. In December, he also logged a noteworthy rape case in tiny Roy, Washington.[27] That case would have lasting importance and, like the Charles Harris murder mentioned earlier, those events will be covered in the next chapter.

Sometime during the year, May had discontinued the Revelare name. After this, the *City Directory* associated him with the "Institute of Scientific Criminology" and the "Scientific Detective Laboratory." He started the new year with a rush, logging five death cases in less than two months. Later, that rate slackened somewhat to an average of just over one death case per month. Still, despite the high workload, he somehow found time to submit a patent application for his "Comparison Magnascope." This was the name he now used for the improved version of the Revelaroscope. Using a standard design was, he wrote, "extremely tedious and wearing, and straining upon the eyes."[28] With his new design "such inspections and comparisons can be made with the normal vision of the two eyes."

The device was still huge and would have been expensive to mass-produce. So far as is known, May's prototype was the only one ever built. We do know that May also acquired a conventional comparison microscope, so it seems even he knew the magnascope design was not the best tool for the job. Still, he surely had hopes for further improvement, and the big machine had great publicity value.

Naturally, firearms assessments were the most glamorous use for a comparison microscope, whatever its design. But the application also said, "It may similarly be used for comparison of two specimens of typing, or of writing."[29] But high magnification is not useful for questioned documents examinations, so May would have presumably substituted a less powerful lens.

A week after Luke filed for his patent, a Tacoma attorney retained him to authenticate some documents associated with the John McAleer estate. McAleer had immigrated to the United States from Ireland sometime after 1882. He became very successful, first as a dairyman and then as a real estate investor. By 1920, McAleer had retired to the life of a gentleman farmer. He leased out most of his considerable acreage and came to depend upon a Japanese man and the man's son to handle the home ranch. McAleer had married late in life, to a woman almost thirty years his junior. But they had no children, and she passed away in the spring of 1927, a year before him.

McAleer's total estate was valued at $150,000–$200,000. His will, written about seven weeks before he died, gave 140 acres of land to the Japanese helper. He must have received good advice, because the property was to be passed on to the son after ten years. Under law, the father, who was not a citizen, could not permanently hold the land. But the son had been born in the United States and could. McAleer's relatives, a brother and sister still in Ireland, tried to get the provision thrown out. But the documents May assessed reinforced McAleer's intention to reward the man and his son. According to a special report to the *Post-Intelligencer* in Seattle, the judge "denounced several of the witnesses who testified" in support of the attempt to break the will.[30]

"Some of the complainants were honest in their belief that McAleer was not in his right mind when he signed his will," the judge said.[31] But he branded several other witnesses as "roisterers" who had sponged off the old man, or racists "with an antipathy" toward the caretakers. But he reserved his greatest scorn for the housekeeper. She was "in a class by herself" as a perjurer and oath breaker. With that, the judge approved a court order ruling that the caretaker was rightfully entitled to the bequest.

While May worked on the McAleer case, Albert Osborn published a major revision of his book, *Questioned Documents*. This edition contained twice as much material as the original. A reviewer in the *Marquette Law Review* wrote, "Not only should this book be in the library of every bank and financial institution, but no lawyer with a document case should be without it from the beginning of his investigation until the argument on appeal."[32]

On top of the McAleer case, the various deaths and the patent application, May was also involved in the notable rape case mentioned earlier. In early March, a judge passed sentence on the convicted rapist. As suggested above, this case has historical and legal significance. The story of that case and the 1926 Charles Harris murder are told in the next chapter.

· *10* ·

Tool Marks Are the Key

The science of tool marks forged the link between the Harris murder and the rape case in Roy. "Tool marks" are just what they sound like: marks left on an object by a tool applied to it. There are two types: impressions and striations.

Impressions are the marks left when a sledgehammer smashes a safe door, or a screwdriver forces open a cash drawer. The principle is the same as the marks left by a steel breechblock on a brass cartridge case, as described in chapter 7. But with handheld tools, the object would need to be soft enough to take the impression, yet strong enough to stay intact. As a rule, impressions will have class characteristics, but individual ones are less likely.

Striations are more or less parallel grooves that a tool cuts or scrapes into a surface. Class characteristics can tell the observer that the mark was made by a certain kind of tool, perhaps a chisel, screwdriver, or adze. However, the individual marks needed to identify a specific tool almost always require magnification.

Actually, tool mark comparisons and firearms identification are really two aspects of the same process. Breechblock impressions are one clear parallel. The other similarity arises from the fact the distinctive marks on a bullet are carved there by the imperfections of a rifle bore. By 1926, May had processed scores of firearms cases and made comparisons for hundreds of bullets. Those studies supplemented his experience with regular tool mark work.

May logged the first of the special cases on November 14, 1926. But the events that led up to that moment began more than two years earlier. A band of crooks accosted four Bon Marche couriers just outside the store in downtown Seattle. They stole $14,000 in cash and $8,000 in checks. The heist was well planned in one way—police never recovered the loot. But

131

several bandits were soon identified, caught, and convicted. Edward Lee "Eddie" Fasick and his wife, Esther, were among them. Eddie was sentenced to a term of twenty-five to fifty years in prison. This was "the heaviest sentence ever imposed after a robbery conviction in King County." Esther received a seven- to fifteen-year sentence.[1]

Originally from Kansas, Eddie had moved to Seattle around 1909, when he was about eighteen years old. Fasick was working as a watchman for a shipping company when he registered for the draft in 1917. Prohibition, however, changed his life. Eddie opened a soft drinks emporium. Such establishments were then a well-known cover for liquor joints. Such appeared to be true for the Fasick soda counter.

Yet the profits from that enterprise were somehow not enough. Seattle police had some evidence to connect Eddie with at least a half dozen other armed robberies. These possible crimes might have been pursued but seemed not worth the cost. Luke May, meanwhile, was tied up by three active death cases and much other work.

Eddie and Esther remained free on bond while their attorneys launched a drawn-out appeal process. They continued to pal around with their friend and business partner, Charles R. Harris. Harris was a boarder at the Fasick apartment, along with another probable partner in crime. Harris, actually Carl Schwuchow, was from Kenosha, Wisconsin. As Schwuchow, he had enlisted in the U.S. Navy for World War I and then gone into the merchant marine afterwards. Appearing in Seattle as Harris, he not only smuggled liquor but may have also helped run an illegal still. Eddie Fasick quite possibly bankrolled those activities.

In the spring of 1926, Charles went back to Wisconsin to visit family and friends. Harris and the Fasicks kept a wad of cash in a shared safety-deposit box. When he got back in July, Harris complained about how much Eddie had spent of their common pot. The squabble seemed to pass, but Charles commented to a friend, Richard McCoy, that the relationship had cooled.

Then the Supreme Court confirmed the sentences imposed on the Fasicks for "The Bon" robbery. But the court gave the two quite a lot of time to wrap up their affairs. On September 29, McCoy spoke with the Fasicks as they drove off with Harris in their car. That was the last time any outsider saw Harris alive.

When the Fasicks returned about three hours later, they told their other boarder that Harris had gone east again. They asked him to find new quarters for them all and move their belongings to it. Their current lease ran out at the end of the month, and they had to go east for a while. The Fasicks left the next day. Soon—he could not remember exactly when—McCoy found a note from Eddie telling him that Harris had gone east. The Fasicks returned a few days before they were due in prison. They reportedly left Seattle for Walla Walla on November 3.

Eight days later, someone walking in the forest happened upon the body of an unidentified man. It was located a mile and a half into Snohomish County, about fifty yards off the road to Edmonds. (Edmonds is about twelve miles north of Seattle.) The corpse had been dumped behind a log and covered by a shield of cut branches and saplings. The coroner estimated that the man had been dead for five or six weeks.

Four days after the body was found, area newspapers reported that the police had identified him as Charles R. Harris. They speculated that he had been killed by fellow bootleggers, or by someone who had hijacked a Harris load. The *Bellingham Herald* reported, "Luke S. May, of Seattle, criminologist, found that Harris had been shot to death, one bullet penetrating the skull and another grazing the chest."[2]

In fact, the fatal bullet had passed completely through the head. From the nature of the wound, May gave a preliminary opinion that Harris had been shot with a .38- or .45-caliber firearm. Further search uncovered the spot where the shooting had actually taken place. Searchers must have found the fatal bullet, because May thereafter identified the murder weapon as a .45-caliber Colt revolver.

Meanwhile, the police had focused their attention on Eddie and Esther Fasick. The Fasicks had been the last to see Harris alive. Moreover, "Snohomish County officers said Fasick was known to possess" a .45-caliber revolver at one time.[3] He had probably sold it or given it away before going off to prison. Sources in the underworld provided a motive in addition to the disputes over money. Eddie was said to be afraid that Harris would start blabbing too much while Eddie and Esther were in prison.

The trial began January 17, 1927. Two days of testimony provided the means, motive, and opportunity. Motive was easy: money and fear of exposure. The means criteria was weakened by the inability of the police to find the murder weapon. Still, police records on firearms gave prosecutors enough evidence to work around that. However, investigators had found no witnesses to place the suspects at the crime scene. That hurt the opportunity leg of the prosecution's case. That possible hole was closed on the third day of the trial, in a most dramatic and unprecedented fashion. The *Bellingham Herald* reported on "the sensational testimony offered today by Luke S. May, Seattle criminologist."[4]

May's testimony keyed off a knife found on a bureau where Eddie and Esther had been living after the murder. With that knife, May asserted, someone had "cut the fir boughs that covered the body of Charles R. Harris."[5] However, when May began to explain his tool mark work, defense attorneys objected vehemently. Sending the jury out, the judge considered the proposed evidence. Among other points, the judge noted that the prosecution had not firmly linked the knife to the Fasicks. With that and his doubts about May's premise, the judge at first sustained the defense's objection.

Then, with other testimony, prosecutors did place that specific knife in the hands of Eddie and Esther Fasick. Next, they established the fact that May had used that same knife to cut test branches of the same type of wood. At this point, the judge allowed May's photomicrographs of the cut faces to be placed in evidence. The images showed that flaws or a worn spot in the blade had left a unique pattern in the surface of the wood. Those marks matched the pattern of grooves in the branches found at the crime scene. This, the newspaper noted, "was probably the first time that such evidence ever had been introduced at a murder trial."[6]

In the end, the jury found Eddie Fasick guilty of second-degree murder. The circumstantial nature of the evidence made them unwilling to sustain a first-degree murder charge. Esther Fasick was judged not guilty. Three days after the verdicts were announced, a deputy prosecuting attorney sent a letter to May. In it, he wrote, "I want you to know that the verdict of guilty of murder in that case was due, in my opinion, largely to your testimony. . . . Except for your enlarged photographs and expert testimony, we had no other evidence to bring the defendant closer than fourteen miles to the scene of the murder."[7]

About three weeks after the verdict, a judge pronounced sentence: twenty-five to thirty-five years in the state penitentiary. Fasick remained in prison serving his robbery term while lawyers appealed his conviction for murder. More than eighteen months passed before the Washington Supreme Court handed down a decision (*State v. Fasik*, 1928). Oddly enough, the justices began with a concession. They wrote, "We think there was sufficient circumstantial evidence to take the case to the jury as to who killed Harris, when he was killed, and where he was killed."[8]

In retrospect, that statement seems peculiar. They were about to negate the only evidence that placed the appellant (Fasick) at the scene of the crime. Recall that the defense objected strongly to May's testimony, and they were sustained by the judge, at first. At that point, the judge essentially questioned the use of science in the courtroom. He huffed, "Here is an ordinary knife, so far as anybody can see, and my personal opinion is that I couldn't tell in a thousand years whether those two pieces were cut by the same knife."[9]

Still, the judge must have had second thoughts as the prosecution managed to work in more evidence about the knife. With that, "the court overruled the objections and let in the knife, the two cut boughs and [the] photomicrographs." The Supreme Court decision then said, "In this we think the court committed error. Harris had not been killed with a knife. It was important only in connection with the cut surfaces on the boughs found over the body."[10]

In a sense, the justices were chastising the defense attorneys for not challenging *all* references to the knife. The court had already said that the knife cuts showed nothing, so all the evidence linked to those marks was irrelevant to the trial. That is, by the "rules of the game," none of the evidence involving the knife or cut branches should have been admissible. Plus, it must be stated, the prosecution's assertion that *only* the Fasicks would have had access to the knife was somewhat shaky.

In that context, the justices were surely predisposed to discount the photomicrographs anyway. And, in truth, the images did not make the prosecution's case as well as they might have. In the end, the court disparaged any use of such evidence. Their opinion said, "It will not do to compare this kind of evidence with the shoe tracks of a person or a horse, nor with finger prints, because in those cases the thing making the impression comes to rest in making the impression."[11] They then offered reasoning that seems curious, given how the court finally ruled. They said:

> It is common knowledge that a knife with a faulty edge used in the right hand, one side of the blade being down, often makes a different impression on wood than if used in the left hand with the other side of the blade down. Again, such a knife used in the hand will oftener than otherwise make a different impression upon wood cut by it whether tested by the microscope or not, according to whether it is forced through wood at right angles, with the point forward or with the point following and according to the angle of the slant of the knife with respect to the wood cut. There was no attempt in the evidence in this case to overcome these things.[12]

Put another way, they were saying that how a knife is handled will more often than not make the resulting cuts look different. That is surely true, under some conditions. But that also makes the point that cuts made by different knives have even less chance of looking the same. So how does one decide in a situation where the striations *do* match up, even if they're not absolutely perfect? Science favors the simplest explanation. The marks were most likely made by the same knife, applied in a way that was close enough to the original use. Random chance with two different knives has essentially zero probability.

That was not how the majority on the court saw it. The knife and branch evidence, they wrote, "fell far short in our opinion of being admissible. It was in our opinion reversible error to admit these articles in evidence. Reversed, and remanded to the Superior Court with directions to grant a new trial."[13]

Oddly enough, the chief justice disagreed. He had served on the court for nearly thirty years, ten years longer than any of the other justices. One would expect him to take the most conservative approach to this new kind of evidence. Instead, he wrote, "In my opinion, the articles the majority find objectionable were admissible as evidence. I therefore dissent from the conclusions reached here."[14]

With their most crucial evidence ruled inadmissible, prosecutors chose not to bear the expense of a new trial. The Washington governor paroled Esther Fasick from her robbery sentence in the summer of 1929. Eddie spent ten more years in prison before being released. The Supreme Court handed down their decision on September 6, 1928. May surely found their process strange, since they seemed to reason one way but decided the other. As we will see, he focused on the statement that he had not done enough to answer questions about the blade angle and the force applied.

Three months after that decision, a shocking crime in Roy, Washington, gave May another chance. Roy is a tiny town located about fourteen miles east of Olympia. It had once been an important stop on the Prairie Line of the Northern Pacific Railway. However, by the late 1920s, trains called at Roy only when dispatchers reported enough freight to make it worthwhile.

On December 6, fourteen-year-old "Jane Doe" started walking home from school. The time was about four o'clock in the afternoon. The cloudless day and bright sun had done little to ease the cold snap of the past few days. Now the sun was low on the horizon, and the already cool temperature was dropping fast. We do not know who "Jane" was, but Roy was a small place, with fewer than ten girls in the right age group. A composite suggests that she had almost certainly been born in the state of Washington. Her father was a sawmill worker or logger, probably in his mid-forties and originally from Michigan. Her mother was around forty-one and most likely from Minnesota. Jane was probably the oldest child still living at home, with three younger siblings.

She followed a familiar path, one she had used many times before. In places, brush and fir trees grew near the trail. But, as May observed, "With Christmas only a few days away she was probably day-dreaming of Santa Claus."[15]

Out of nowhere, someone knocked her down, threw a cloth over her face and then tied it tight. The mask muffled her cries as he picked her up and moved away from the path. The cloth itself was permeated with something that gave it a sickening odor that took her breath away. Finally, the man dumped her on the ground and brutally raped her. Throughout the ordeal, the rapist talked to her, but she remembered nothing that he said. At last, the man let her up, removed the cloth, and shoved her toward the path. Jane was still woozy, but she remembered brown high-top shoes, dark overalls, slightly rolled up, and a dark coat and cap. He wore a mask of white cloth over his face.

Jane stumbled to the path and rushed home to sob out the awful story to her mother. By the time Pierce County Sheriff Tom Desmond arrived, the sun had set. His interview with Jane gave them very little to go on. Irish-born Thomas Desmond had come to this country as a teenager and was living in Tacoma by 1890. Despite having little formal education, Tom first served as a deputy sheriff in 1914. After a period with the county auditor's office, he again became a deputy sheriff. He was elected county sheriff in 1922.

Tom and his deputies visited the crime scene as soon as possible. (The low light of dusk made it hard to see, so they would return at least twice more in the daytime.) But the attacker had been very careful and, at first, seemed to have left nothing incriminating behind. However, during the inspection, a deputy pushed aside what he thought was a sapling and it fell over. It was actually a cut-off branch that had been stuck in the ground. Officers quickly found more sprigs, which formed a blind near the path where Jane was attacked. Jane had not mentioned anything like this. But its presence could explain how the attacker had taken her by surprise. Showing what May later called "exceedingly good judgment," Desmond and his officers made careful notes on where each branch had been positioned.[16]

The sheriff also observed that their perpetrator was probably someone the girl might recognize. Why else would he have worn a mask? Also, he knew the path she took and the best place to put his hideaway. Then Desmond engaged further in what we would today call "profiling." He theorized that the rapist was most likely a sex-starved bachelor, who had given in to his baser instincts.

Dramatic fictional accounts notwithstanding, small towns do not keep many secrets for very long. The officers and their local advisers asked themselves: Who around here might conceivably fit that description? According to May, they came up with a list of nine men. By a process of elimination, they focused on one of them, twenty-four-year-old Franklyn Clark. Originally from Kentucky, Clark lived by himself in a Roy hotel and had been around long enough to be known in town. He apparently made an adequate living from odd jobs around the area.

On little more than that, Desmond and his deputies approached Clark at his hotel room. After a round of questions, they arrested him on suspicion and searched his belongings. They found a knife with three blades, one of which was smeared with pitch. Clark said that was from three cedar branches he had cut for decoration at the hotel.

Later that evening, Jane listened to Clark talk and asserted that he had the same voice as her assailant. She also said his height and build seemed about right. His clothes also matched, but that was very common working apparel. Deputies also found an odorous cloth among Clark's belongings that Jane said smelled like what the rapist had used.

Over the next few days, officials sought more evidence. Several people had encountered him near the rape site three days before the attack. In retrospect, the reasons he gave for being there seemed unlikely. Other witnesses placed him in the area just before and just after the time of the crime. At least one remembered his high-top shoes and partly rolled-up overalls.

May filed the log sheet for the case five days after the attack. The client listed was the Pierce County prosecuting attorney. One wonders exactly what May said to the prosecutors to persuade them to try using tool mark evidence. In any case, May had devised a way to address the issue of how the knife was handled. He assembled a system of rods, levers, and gears to mimic the structure and actions of a person's arm. Mechanically driven, the device could hold the knife at various angles and make cuts with different slicing motions. (Sadly, May did not leave a photo of this contrivance.)

May then tinkered with the settings until he had cut marks that exactly matched those on the branches of the rapist's blind, as well as on the cedar boughs. He then prepared enlarged photographs of the cut ends and created a kind of collage, where strips showing various cuts could be matched along their edges. May also produced a clincher. He assembled a set that showed a strip from one of his test cuts, then from a cut on one of the fir branches used for the blind, and then from a cedar bough cut for hotel decoration. The tool mark lines clearly tracked across the image from one strip to the next to the next, offering dramatic proof that all three had been cut with the same knife.

A jury rather quickly found Franklyn Clark guilty, and the judge sentenced him to twenty to thirty years in prison. The *Bellingham Herald* reported, "The sentence . . . is the most severe ever imposed in Pierce County for a statutory offense."[17] Naturally, Clark's lawyers appealed. They identified three technicalities to challenge but spent the most effort on the admissibility of the tool mark evidence. The Supreme Court countered that they found the evidence not only admissible but compelling. They then offered a much-quoted assertion:

> Courts are no longer skeptical that by the aid of scientific appliances, the identity of a person may be established by fingerprints. There is no difference in principle in the utilization of the photomicrograph to determine that the same tool that made one impression is the same instrument that made another impression. The edge on one blade differs as greatly from the edge on another blade as do the lines on one human hand differ from the lines on another. This is a progressive age. The scientific means afforded should be used to apprehend the Criminal.[18]

The judges then offered reasons why this case was different from the Fasick case. First, they wrote, "In the Fasick case, there was only one mark on the two pictures admitted in evidence which compared one with the other. In the case at bar, there are more than fifty marks appearing on the pictures of the cut surfaces of the fir boughs which can be identified as appearing on the cut surfaces of the cedar boughs."

Secondly, "In the Fasick case it does not appear that the knife was the property of the appellant. In the case at bar, the ownership of the knife was admitted as was the cutting of the cedar boughs, the surface cuts of which were used for comparison with the surface cuts of the fir saplings." Result: "Finding no error justifying reversal, the judgment is affirmed."[19] As a matter of interest, two of the judges who had voted for reversal of the Fasick decision were still on the court for this affirmation.

Despite the judge's words, the news media acted as though the court had totally changed its mind about tool mark evidence. For example, the *Bellingham Herald* said, "The decision reverses a previous holding of the supreme court which granted a new trial to Eddie Fasick, of Seattle, because the state attempted to convict him of murder with the aid of markings made by a knife. In both cases crucial evidence of the prosecution was [photo enlargements of the marks] . . . left by knives used in cutting branches off of trees."[20]

However, as the court tried to make clear, they had simply ruled on the "sufficiency" of the evidence presented in the two cases. In the Fasick case, the testimony linking Eddie to the knife was barely enough to make the case. (In fact, that weak link alone might have been enough to reverse the decision, even if the court had accepted the knife marks.) Clark's knife was in his possession at the time of his arrest, and he admitted to its ownership.

Figure 10.1.   Tool Mark Matches for Clark Case. *Source*: May-Reid Records.

On the key matter of the knife marks, the court recognized only one good match in the Fasick case. Moreover, May would have had to admit that he had trouble reproducing test cuts that matched well. That, in the court's view, was insufficient to prove the point. But for the Clark case, the court counted fifty matching features. Also, with his improved method, May could make as many matching cuts as anyone wanted. Thus, the court did not reverse itself on tool marks. They simply ruled the evidence for the first case to be insufficient, but sufficient in the second.

The final decision, *State of Washington vs. Clark* (1930), became a legal precedent for the later use of tool marks in court. It is perhaps less often understood that the affirmation was not a blanket approval for the admissibility of all such evidence. The expert must be prepared to show that the tool mark evidence is sufficient to prove the point. Luke May left relatively few statements of his personal feelings. But he later wrote that the acceptance of his tool mark breakthrough was "gratifying to the writer."[21]

And even before the final ruling, he received a letter from fellow criminologist Edward Heinrich. The note began, "Recently while riding on a train I was reading a copy of the Tacoma *News-Tribune*."[22] He went on, "My attention was at once attracted to a report of the conviction of Franklyn G. Clark." The article described, with photos, how May had explained the tool mark evidence to the jury. Heinrich then said he felt "unrestrained admiration" for May's "exceptionally clear" presentation. "I want to congratulate you on the success of your effort."

This praise from a fellow criminologist must have also been gratifying for May. Heinrich's closing implies that the two did occasionally exchange ideas and thoughts about crime detection. He wrote, "Under separate cover I am sending to you a copy of *The California Monthly* which contains a recent article from my pen."[23]

The tool mark precedent would be a factor in a case that played out five years later in the glare of international publicity. But long before that, May's expertise would be urgently called upon in the aftermath of one of the most horrific crimes of the gangster era.

· 11 ·

Chicago Calls

$\mathcal{S}$ix weeks after the Clark rape decision, a faraway event initiated another milestone in the history of criminology. A panel reviewing the St. Valentine's Day Massacre in Chicago heard testimony from firearms expert Major Calvin Goddard. The group had been convened two months after rival gangsters gunned down five members and two associates of the North Side Gang on February 14, 1929. Two of the killers had been dressed in police uniforms, so many people thought "the cops" had been in on the crime.

Police had collected seventy empty .45-caliber cartridge cases from the crime scene, along with two empty shotgun shells. Goddard examined this evidence and concluded that one shotgun had been used, along with two Thompson submachine guns. Goddard also test-fired a host of weapons submitted by police precincts around the city. None of the guns in those arsenals were involved.

The inquest panel included a number of prominent Chicago businessmen. Goddard impressed these men with his clear, incisive approach. Why, they wondered, did Chicago not have anyone like this? And surely there had to be a better way to handle crime investigations than what the police had shown. What they needed was something like Goddard's independent forensics bureau, an agency free from police politics and likely corruption. Their wondering soon led them to John Henry Wigmore, dean of the Northwestern University School of Law. A legal scholar of towering repute, Wigmore had joined the Northwestern law faculty in 1893. He had been dean of the school since 1901. During World War I, he served with the judge advocate general's staff.

Figure 11.1.   Dean Wigmore in Uniform, World War I.
Source: **Library of Congress, LC-USZ62-88065.**

May first heard about the Chicago effort from a friend in the Bureau of Investigation (later to be the FBI). James S. Egan, a Nebraska native like May, had joined the bureau in 1922. Self-effacing almost to a fault, Egan was a trusted adviser to Director J. Edgar Hoover. Egan had met May through attendance at the annual meeting of the Northwest Association of Sheriffs and Police. He might have attended the conference two years earlier, in British Columbia. He definitely attended the two following years, first in Boise, Idaho, and then in Missoula, Montana.

On May 19, Egan wrote to tell Luke about his meeting with Wigmore in Chicago. Egan said, "He brought up the subject of crime and its detection etc."[1] Wigmore presumably explained some of their tentative plans. Egan went on, "I told him that he should not make any selections until he got in touch with you, . . . informing him of how far advanced you were and of the equipment you have."

Having attended a number of different crime-fighter conferences in the West, Egan surely knew of August Vollmer and Edward Heinrich. Yet his recommendation was for Wigmore to contact Luke May. Egan told Luke he had gone so far as to try "to get you a Seat at the Uni." He then said, "I get a pain when they tell about this and that and something else and they don't know what it is all about. My reason for doing this was to in some way try and return the many past favors I have received at your hands."[2]

Then Egan showed he understood how the wind really blew. In closing, he wrote, "Please treat this letter as confidential."[3] He even added a post-script: "Let me hear from you from time to time. But address your letters to me care of the Arlington Hotel, Washington, D.C." Even then, insiders seem to have understood Hoover's quirks. The director was unlikely to react well if he heard a top aide was getting advice from a private detective.

Shortly after that, May received a letter from Wigmore. It began, "On the recommendation of Inspector Egan, . . . I am writing you to ask if you would be willing to give us your opinion as to the best method to establish a crime detection bureau here."[4] Wigmore outlined some of their plans. He then went on, "I am told that you have organized the only really scientific Police Laboratory in the United States, certainly the only one on the Pacific Coast."

Less than a week later, Seattle newspapers lamented the possible loss of Luke May to Chicago. Articles discussed what people in that city were trying to do in the way of a scientific detection laboratory. Meanwhile, May spent more than a week in Chicago talking to civic leaders and university representatives.

Seattleites were highly relieved when May returned, with no suggestion that he might leave. Actually, with his lack of academic credentials, May probably had little chance to be offered a responsible position at the new crime lab. Yet rumors persisted. In mid-June, Heinrich added a postscript to a postcard he sent to Luke: "Hear you are removing to Chicago. Any truth in it?"[5]

Later in the month, Northwestern University officials announced their plans for the laboratory. Major Goddard had been lured away from New York to head the new organization. The Bureau of Forensic Ballistics had struggled financially throughout its life, so he was probably not hard to persuade. By the end of the year, Goddard had most likely dissolved the bureau and moved at least some of its equipment to the university. In early July, Wigmore sent May a letter to show their "progress in the arrangements for the Scientific Crime Detection Laboratory here."[6] He then said, "You have been the pioneer in this field. Your advice has been most valuable to us."

During all this, May's regular casework went on. As noted in chapter 9, he started the year with a rush of five death cases logged in less than two months. That high rate continued and could have actually been worse. Shortly before May left for Chicago, a near miss occurred on the outskirts of Spokane. The fact that it was not a double murder was not for lack of trying by the perpetrator. Young William Johnson wanted to show off his new car to a girl he was dating, Hazel Huller. He drove to the edge of the city on the main highway and then decided to head back to town.

As he turned around, a man described as having "dark snappy eyes" approached and stuck a gun in Johnson's face.[7] Neither of the two were carrying much money, so they were confused when the robber gagged them and began to tie them up. Confused and frightened, Johnson made a break but was felled by a hail of bullets. The report in the *Bellingham Herald* said that one bullet lodged in his jaw. Another missile "barely missed the large artery in his neck."[8]

The young man passed out at that point, then the bandit dumped him in the front seat of the car. When Johnson came to, "Miss Huller and the unknown assailant were in the back seat of the car together." At that point, the odor of chloroform "was very noticeable in the closed tonneau."[9] The attacker may well have drugged the woman and raped her, but reports never talked about that. The news item did say she was "suffering terribly from shock and nervous strain," although supposedly not harmed.

But it is perhaps significant that, two days after the attack, she told police that "as far as I am concerned" they could drop the case. "I can't see any use of investigating."[10] In any event, the attacker next drained gasoline from the car, set it on fire, and ran off into the woods. Despite loss of blood and his tied hands, Johnson kicked his way out of the car. Huller managed to open the back door, so both staggered away before flames engulfed the vehicle. Huller eventually stumbled to a farmhouse, while Johnson was picked up by a bus on the main road. A posse tried to track the attacker, but the fire had obliterated any trace of his passage.

Three months went by before police caught a suspect named Joseph W. Cress. Cress had spent time in prison for second-degree murder and for first-degree burglary. On his person, officers found a pistol, which they passed along to May. Later, the *Olympian* reported, "Luke S. May, Seattle criminologist, testified yesterday that a bullet extracted from the jaw of William Johnson . . . was fired from the same gun taken from Cress when he was arrested."[11]

Cress was convicted on several counts. Then, under Washington's habitual criminal law, he was sentenced to life in prison. A few weeks after the conviction, the Spokane County sheriff wrote a letter of appreciation to May. He said, "Your identification of the bullet as having been fired from the identical gun taken from the defendant upon his subsequent arrest, was the culminating proof of the facts that made a conclusive case against the defendant. We talked with jurors afterwards, who stated that your explanation of the means of identification of the bullet removed the last vestige of doubt."[12]

Summer brought another close call. Nineteen-year-old Cameron McIntosh mooned after the woman of his dreams, pretty Charlotte Reed. Two years older and more interested in dating mature men, she hardly knew he existed. One evening, McIntosh tried to intrude in a conversation between Reed and her older male friend, George Oakes. Rebuffed, he pulled out a .22-caliber revolver, sprayed the two with bullets, and fled. Reed was hit twice in the arm, while Oates barely survived two wounds in the chest. Quickly caught and linked to the near-death weapon, McIntosh claimed he didn't remember anything about the evening. After some delay for psychiatric examinations, he was sentenced to "at least three years at the State Reformatory at Monroe."[13]

May handled more than one death case per month for the year, but without some luck in the attacks just described, he could have easily added two more, with four victims. Most of May's death cases involved firearms. However, a murder in early November called May's blood spatter expertise into play. The investigation began when a wife called the police in Wenatchee to report that her husband had been hurt. In fact, former wheat farmer Walter Woodall had been bludgeoned to death.

The wife claimed that, early that morning, she had asked her husband to bring in some firewood. When he did not return after a while, she sent her son to find him. Woodall's body was sprawled near the woodpile. Police briefly considered the notion that Woodall had caught a transient stealing from the property. A thick soup bone lay nearby, which soon caught their attention. (It also led many newspapers to refer to the killing as the "soup-bone murder.") The day after the killing, newspapers reported that officials had "sought the services of a criminologist from Seattle to assist them."[14] That crime expert was, of course, Luke May.

Even before he arrived, police learned from the Woodall children that the parents had quarreled about something the evening before the murder. Finally, the wife admitted that she had killed her husband. She was afraid he would find out she had been unfaithful to him. She had hit him with a car jack first and then made sure with a hatchet. Knowing she might disavow her confession, authorities urged May to go ahead with a thorough analysis.

May did find human blood on the jack and hatchet but not on the soup bone. Although the wife had washed her clothes, he also found traces on her dress and on a blouse she had worn over it. The pattern of drops showed these had spattered as she first stood near and then leaned over her victim. May also detected "blood on the inside of the right shoe."[15] However, her hosiery showed no signs of blood. Subsequent questioning revealed that she had burned the stockings she had worn during the assault.

Mrs. Woodall was convicted and sentenced to life in prison. About a week after the sentencing, the prosecuting attorney sent Luke a letter of appreciation. He wrote, "As usual, your tie-up of the blood stains, on the clothing particularly, constituted the connecting link which made our case an air tight case."[16]

Overall, May logged fifteen death cases in 1929, the most the firm had ever had for a year. The year also featured several milestones and notable events in the field of criminology. Clearly, one key event was the formation of the Chicago crime lab, which involved both May and fellow pioneer Calvin Goddard. Another event added to the Western theme for criminology pioneers. In 1929, UC-Berkeley promoted Dr. Paul L. Kirk to a position as instructor in microchemistry. With degrees from Ohio State University and the University of Pittsburgh, and a Ph.D. from Berkeley, Kirk would soon turn his microscope and chemical knowledge to problems in criminology.

Besides Kirk, UC-Berkeley had also graduated another criminology pioneer, Dr. John A. Larson. A Canadian, Larson had received his Ph.D. from Berkeley early in the decade. After graduation, he applied his degree in physiology to a job with the Berkeley police department. Shortly thereafter, encouraged by Chief Vollmer, he combined several physiological tests so they could be administered and recorded simultaneously. (Hence the name polygraph.) His device is considered the first workable lie detector. By 1929, Larson had moved to the University of Iowa as a professor of psychiatry, where he demonstrated the machine at conferences in the region. But even then, he was concerned by the intrusion of poorly trained examiners trying to make a fast buck in the field.

Luke May himself began using such a device some time during the latter years of the decade. He too stressed the need for well-trained operators. May told the *Seattle Times* that an experienced examiner with "a properly designed apparatus" found the technique useful "not only in pointing to guilt but in establishing innocence."[17]

Also in Berkeley, Chief Vollmer initiated the use of shortwave radio to communicate with receivers installed in police cars. This was a first on the Pacific Coast.

Meanwhile, for the first time in a decade, the International Association for Identification held its annual convention next door in Oakland. Among their stated objectives was "to pay homage to Harry H. Caldwell," founder of the organization.[18] Edward Heinrich and Clark Sellers both gave talks at the meeting.

The year also featured the "Wineville Chicken Coop Murders," a sensational case that received massive newspaper coverage.[19] The killings took place west of Riverside, California, and Sellers and Edward Crossman testified against serial killer Gordon Stewart Northcott. A jury convicted Northcott for one specific death, but he was suspected to have sexually molested and then murdered perhaps twenty boys. Two weeks after Northcott was hung, Wineville officials announced they were changing their town's name to "Mira Loma," in part because of the "unsavory notoriety given the vicinity by the Northcott murders."[20]

Activities for the other pioneer criminologists were not quite so spectacular. John L. Harris handled a case that led to the disbarment of a lawyer for jury tampering. A milestone for Albert S. Osborn was the publication of the revised edition of his *Questioned Documents* book, described in chapter 9. Of course, May also had a major milestone with his precedent-setting tool mark case in 1929, although that wasn't finally settled until the following year.

May would continue a high number of death cases in 1930, the second in a run of four years where they would average more than eighteen death cases per year. But he actually started the year with a lull in new death log-ins. That did not mean he was not busy, however. Most importantly, in Idaho he had the McClurg death case, which required one of his most complex crime reconstructions.

Freezeout Hill, located about twenty miles northwest of Boise, near Emmett, has been notorious since wagons first crossed the region in the mid-nineteenth century. From the brow of the hill, the slope drops more than four hundred feet in less than a third of a mile. The route was still no picnic even after a tortuous switchback road was hacked into the face.

In December, a somewhat disheveled John McClurg appeared at his brother's home in Emmett. A local farmer had helped him get there after a terrible "accident" on Freezeout Hill. He claimed his Ford coupe had gone off the road high on the hill. He escaped, but the crash had killed his young wife. Seemed plausible enough, yet this did not look like any ordinary mishap. The car showed no evidence that it had rolled over, yet it was badly burned. And the wife's charred body lay beside the vehicle, not inside it. High on the hill, the sheriff found a seat cushion, stained with what looked like fresh blood.

Officials became even more suspicious when they learned that McClurg had recently taken out a life insurance policy on his wife. Further investigation revealed that McClurg, aged thirty-seven, had had run-ins with the law about bad checks, bootlegging, white slavery, and auto theft. The *Idaho Statesman*, in Boise, reported, "It was learned that payment on a $10,000 insurance policy . . . had been stopped Wednesday pending results of the investigation now under way."[21]

May began with the autopsy results. The back of her skull had been thoroughly crushed, and dried blood showed that a huge clot had formed. There were no other signs of severe trauma, but the head wound could perhaps be explained by a freak blow during the purported accident. However, they had also found that the upper part of the seat cushion was absolutely saturated with blood. Yet the cushion would have sailed out of the car only seconds after it left the road.

With that and other evidence, May was able to reconstruct the crime. At some point, probably in a secluded spot, the husband had bashed his wife on the back of the head. Not yet dead, she had slumped back against the seat, bleeding heavily, while McClurg drove to where he staged the run-off. At that point, random chance upset his plan. McClurg surely expected the car to roll over and bounce crazily. Anyone seeing the steep slope would agree. Instead, the car slithered through the brush all the way to the bottom of the hill without turning over. As May said, "Explain it if you will!"[22]

So there the Ford sat, upright, with relatively superficial damage. Inside was his wife, perhaps dead by now, perhaps not. May declared that what happened next was somewhat "a matter of conjecture,"[23] based on the position of the wife's body and the burn pattern. But McClurg almost certainly started the fire himself after splattering gasoline around. He had pulled his wife's body from the car hoping to make sure the fire destroyed evidence of her wounds.

The subsequent trial in Emmett was a local sensation, with spectators jammed into a makeshift courtroom. The *Idaho Statesman* in Boise reported, "As the trial progressed the crowd increased, the biggest day being Friday, when the state put Luke S. May, criminologist, on the stand."[24] McClurg was convicted and sentenced to death, which gave the case its only national coverage. The headline in the *Miami Herald* was fairly typical—"Murderer of Wife Sentenced to Hang."[25]

But the governor noted that the evidence against McClurg was only circumstantial. He referred the case to the Board of Pardons, which commuted the sentence to life in prison. Ten years later, the board freed him altogether. At the time of his release, he was said to be "a hopeless invalid . . . paralyzed from the waist down."[26] No such disability was noted on his Draft Registration Form two years later, however.

Besides his casework, May made time to further his goal to educate people about scientific criminology (and, obviously, to publicize his consulting service). Before the McClurg trial began, he spoke about scientific criminology to the Seattle Municipal League and the Women's Century Club. Then, in early January, he spoke on "medical jurisdiction and criminology" to a nurse's association in Seattle.[27]

Later in the month, *The Oregonian* announced a Police School short course at Willamette University in Salem, Oregon.[28] Assembled by the dean of the university's School of Law, the course would span six days. The faculty included several law enforcement officials plus professors from Willamette University, the University of Oregon, and Oregon State. A lecture series would be presented by the deputy attorney general for the state of Oregon. The article also said, "The recognition, preservation and presentation of criminal evidence will be another series by Luke S. May, Seattle criminologist."

The sessions ended in the second week of February, so it was back to work on various existing and new cases for May. One was a questioned documents examination that appeared in the newspapers. The story began with the death of Frederick "Fred" Zimmerli, age seventy-three, in a Seattle hospital. A native of Switzerland, Zimmerli came to the United States in 1887. Moderately successful in the tailoring business, Zimmerli married twice, but divorced the first and outlived the second. He had one daughter, Edna, by his first wife. His relationship with Edna blew hot and cold, apparently depending upon how Fred felt toward Edna's husband.

Thus, while an earlier will gave her half the estate, the one in force at Zimmerli's death left her only one-eighth. The value of the estate was about $35,000. For context, that was what a ritzy Seattle boys' school thought their new physical education building, with full gymnasium, would cost. When the will went to probate, Edna made a startling assertion. She had examined some of Fred's clothes and claimed to have "found a second will in an inner-vest pocket bequeathing her the entire estate with the exception of $500."[29] Her attorneys hired "two so-called handwriting experts" (Luke's words) to vouch for the signature on the new will.[30]

May, however, found clear differences from known Zimmerli sign-offs. He did concede that the document "was one of the cleverest forgeries I have ever seen."[31] Of course, he knew the issue could go either way in court when experts disagreed. So, he looked for further evidence. It happened that the earlier will had been prepared using a standard form where the legal verbiage—the boilerplate—was preprinted. Turned out, the new will had been entered onto what seemed to be another sheet of the same preprinted form. As May said, "The forger had been very adroit in this respect."[32]

But May noticed subtle differences—typeface wear marks and line spacing—in the copies delivered by the commercial print shop. Further investigation revealed that the shop had not started the print run of the sheets used for the new will until a week after it was supposedly prepared and signed. The fake will was thrown out.

Earlier in the year, Dean Wigmore in Chicago had written again to May about the Scientific Detection Laboratory, "for which we received such useful advice from you last June."[33] Little progress had been made since then because lab director Goddard had been traveling in Europe. "So," Wigmore wrote, "though a place has been leased, the equipment is not yet installed and things go slowly."

He had mainly written to tell May about a new journal they were starting. "I had intended to ask you to become one of the Associate Editors," he said. But they had heard that May was supposedly in the process of starting a journal himself, so they had gone elsewhere. Then Wigmore went on, "But will you not prepare an article recounting some of your experience? Or describing your laboratory and experience? It's all for the good of the cause."[34]

When Goddard returned, he became the managing editor of the *American Journal of Police Science*. During the summer, they published May's article, "The Identification of Knives, Tools and Instruments, A Positive Science."[35] The main highlight of his paper was the Franklyn Clark case and the strongly worded affirmation by the state Supreme Court. But he also discussed the staged Keyser burglary in Salt Lake City and a case where he identified tools used to force open the money boxes in a number of telephone booths.

That same summer, May was reelected as president of the Northwest Association of Sheriffs and Police for the eleventh straight term. During his president's message to the convention held in Vancouver, British Columbia, he celebrated what he saw as a better spirit of cooperation among the various law enforcement organizations. But he also said, "There must be an awakening of the people that with increased population and increased crime laws, we must have an increased number of men who are to do the law enforcement work."[36]

He also spread the word in other ways. A couple weeks after the convention in Vancouver, May spoke to a conference of attorneys in Walla Walla. And that fall, he addressed the Seattle Women's City Club. Over the years, he seldom passed up a chance to advocate for scientific law enforcement.

As noted earlier, May began 1930 with a lull in death cases. But he more than made up for lost time by logging six in April and May. The case that grabbed the most headlines involved a man known to the newspapers as Everett Frank Lindsay. But that name was just the last in a long line of aliases, so many he could not remember them all. Born in Australia, in 1921 he married Audrey Reid in Seattle, under the name Lindsay. By then, he had deserted from two armies (Australian and U.S.), fathered two sons, and abandoned them and three or perhaps four wives. On several occasions he had become intimately involved with underage girls but was never charged.

By 1930, Everett and Audrey had adopted a daughter, Pearl, and were considering the adoption of another, Helen. The girls were around ten or eleven years old. In late February, the couple had a huge row. A few days later, Everett told friends that Audrey had gone to Canada. About two months after that, Lindsay dropped Helen off with her birth mother and left the state with Pearl. Shortly after Helen talked to her mother, police issued a warrant for Lindsay's arrest.

May entered the case when police had him verify that Lindsay had forged his wife's signature on the contract for a second mortgage. Fortunately, he also joined the police search of the Lindsay home. Officers thought the house looked clean. May said, "To the casual observer, the room in which the murder was committed had been placed in perfect order."[37] Yet with close scrutiny, he found numerous almost-invisible blood spatters in one bedroom. The pattern of stains showed that a violent assault had been committed.

That made a relatively fresh patch of disturbed soil in the backyard more significant. The hole contained a mix of trash over a length of sewer pipe. Lindsay probably hoped to divert attention away from any foul odor. But further digging unearthed Audrey's body. She had been beaten to death with savage brutality. Right away, newspapers along the West Coast reported on the murder and the search for the fugitive. Four days later, authorities found Pearl in California. She had been abandoned in an Oakland boardinghouse.

Lindsay remained on the loose for more than a year, with the manhunt ending via an interesting sequence. The key actor was Hollis B. Fultz. Born in Indiana, Fultz moved to Washington before 1920. By 1930, he had taken up freelance writing and was a contributor to at least one popular "true crime" magazine. The Lindsay case, with child molestation and a murdered wife, was a prime candidate for a sensational story. The break came from a Los Angeles restaurant manager who was a fan of the magazine. The photos that accompanied the article looked a lot like a man who had worked for him under another name. By mid-November 1931, Lindsay was under arrest and back in Seattle.

The following month, the *Seattle Times* reported, "In an eerie scene in the criminological laboratory of Luke S. May . . . a shuddery drama was being reenacted—Mrs. Lindsay's slaying, as the authorities reconstruct it."[38] Under May's direction, workmen had dismantled the corner of the bedroom where Audrey Lindsay had been murdered. May said, "As the killer swung his heavy instrument, the adhering blood had taken flight ceiling-ward with each upward stroke, had formed a trajectory arc and had struck the wall and picture on its descent."[39]

A few days later, the setup was moved into the courtroom. There, May repeated his reenactment for the judge and jury. Lindsay had confessed to the killing, but claimed that his wife had nagged him unmercifully for years and that he had finally snapped. Thus, his attorneys focused on getting the first-degree murder charge reduced so he would not face the death penalty. Testimony hinted at his roving eye for other women, but his attentions to underage girls was never allowed to come to light. The jury found Lindsay guilty of second-degree murder. He received a sentence of sixty to seventy-five years in prison.

May's overall workload declined in 1930. He logged only fifty cases, twenty-two of which were questioned documents examinations. However, as mentioned earlier, death cases remained high. Including the Lindsay investigation, he logged fourteen death cases, with fifteen victims. One was the Simmons suicide case, described in chapter 1.

Figure 11.2.   Where Simmons's Car Was Found. *Source*: **May-Reid Records.**

Another sad but interesting case was the hit-and-run death of four-year-old Gene Roberson in Seattle. Police quickly spread the word about a gray Chevrolet sedan that fled the scene. An alert garage mechanic called them when a customer brought in a car of that make and color. The vehicle was missing its headlights and had what the mechanic thought were suspicious stains and hairs on the fender. The driver was arrested, but May's analysis found only some touch-up paint and what were probably brush fibers. The car owner was released and the case was never solved.

Along with his cases, May's outreach efforts led to his election, late in the year, as president of the Seattle Kiwanis Club. Some weeks later, the *Seattle Times* published a tongue-in-cheek photo of Luke. The caption read, "Luke S. May, criminologist, couldn't resist examining the gavel for finger prints of past presidents when he was installed as president of the Seattle Kiwanians."[40]

One wonders how May made time for all this. We know he worked incredibly long hours, visiting crime scenes, working in the lab, and testifying. On top of all that, travel time made up a significant part of his schedule. May spent hours on trains to testify at trials away from Seattle. As his name became better known, he also traveled to meet with other detectives and law enforcement officers around the country.

Yet Luke and Helen still owned a good-sized boat. Also, some time earlier, they had purchased a small island inside a bay on Bainbridge Island. About an acre and a half in size, the islet was roughly twelve cruising miles from the dock where they kept their boat. When they bought the property, it was called Dead Man's Island, for the cemetery that had been there. But the graves had been moved long before the turn of the century. They changed the name to Treasure Island, as it is still known today. There were no buildings on the land, and it's not clear how much work Luke had to do on the dock. Luke's papers do not say a lot about the island or their excursions to and from it. Perhaps none were eventful enough for him to write about them, like he did the fishing trip in 1928.

In any event, Luke May's fame clearly rested on more than just cases that made sensational headlines. Other crime fighters exchanged ideas with him, and the Chicago crime lab obviously benefited from his expertise. The new decade would offer more opportunities for him to handle big cases, consult with fellow pioneers, and improve public law enforcement.

• *12* •

Spreading the Word

In mid-January of 1931, May sent a letter to "Friend Crossman."[1] He did not offer any idle chit-chat, but plunged directly into remarks about "marks left on bullets (before being fired) by loading machines." After that technical discussion, he brought up some "interesting experiments with the expanding metal" he'd mention in an earlier letter. The material "becomes fluid at about the boiling point of water."

Although he does not name it, May here described "Rose's Metal," a material known since the eighteenth century. The alloy of bismuth with lead and tin is most often used to solder electronics or piping. It could also anchor metal railings into rock cavities. May had devised a new and unique application. He put a cork stopper partly along the barrel of a handgun, poured the molten alloy into the barrel and breech, and then allowed it to cool and solidify. Then he carefully tapped it out. From this, May said, "You have the prettiest cast of the breech or the inside of the barrel that you have ever looked at, showing all of the minute imperfections and microscopic machine marks."[2]

Less than a week later, a prosecutor called on his firearms expertise for the first death case of the year. A few days after that, the *Seattle Times* published an item about "Seattle's world-famous criminologist." It began, "Under the powerful lens of the scientist's all-seeing eye, the traces left by the wrongdoer become an eloquent record which he cannot escape."[3]

The writer had visited May at his work-home setup. Luke and Helen lived on the second floor. The ground floor housed company offices and work rooms. "In the basement," the reporter said, "are his laboratories, photographic shop, darkrooms and other departments."[4] He discussed some of May's equipment and then wrote, "In a giant steel safe he keeps records of cases that are strictly private. No mention of them ever gets into the press." For at least two cases, the interviewer asked May about the specific verdicts. "It is not my job to determine whether or not a man is guilty," May replied. "I merely present evidence. The jury decides guilt or innocence."[5]

The writer noted that courts of law had become more accepting of scientific evidence. May probably cringed at another statement, however. The reporter wrote, "The man of science . . . is now assured a hearing and his testimony is accepted as absolute fact."[6] May always stressed that his work dealt in probabilities. Of course, it can still prove facts "beyond a reasonable doubt," as required by law.

May began the year with a normal load of death cases, logging two by the end of February. In mid-March, he returned to Willamette University. There, he again delivered his lectures for the police short course. Enrollment was reported to be "nearly double the number in attendance a year ago."[7]

May logged his third death case a day after the conference ended and another a week later. Both were car accidents. Wealthy Seattle businessman Samuel B. Asia had crashed through a guardrail near downtown and plunged into Elliott Bay. Companies holding more than $150,000 in life insurance tried to have it ruled a suicide, thereby canceling some policies and avoiding double indemnity on others. May and his agents found that Asia was such a terrible driver that some of his friends refused to ride with him. It took almost a year, but the heirs finally received a bit more than 80 percent of the insurance amount.

The second case was a fatal car crash at what was then Seattle's northern city limit. The weather had been gloomy, with temperatures below 50° and occasional showers all day. Not long after ten o'clock in the evening, yacht salesman Russell Mooney was headed north. He thought he was on an arterial street, so he did not slow for the next intersection. With the poor visibility, the Buick that entered from the right caught him totally by surprise. Both men in the Buick were thrown from the car, and the driver, Clarence Kelly, died later in the hospital. His passenger was injured but survived. One passenger in the car Mooney was driving was injured while three others were shaken but not hurt.

Officers at the scene assigned no specific blame to Mooney and made particular note that he had not been drinking. Even so, Mooney hired May's firm six days after the collision. Agents interviewed several people who had seen the crash or were on the scene early. Their statements helped clarify exactly where the cars collided and what happened. One witness said, "The Buick did not slow down and cut the corner and the two cars came together." Another "described how it [the Buick] was just simply hurled out of the street into the vacant lot."[8]

Figure 12.1. Damaged Packard Driven by Mooney. *Source*: May-Reid Records.

From these accounts and the damage to the two vehicles, May could reconstruct how the accident unrolled. A few days later, an inquest ruled that both drivers "were driving too fast through an intersection and neither used proper precautions."[9] Mooney, however, did not have the right-of-way so his culpability was considered greater. He was convicted of manslaughter. However, he received a governor's pardon before serving any of his one- to two-year sentence.

A couple weeks after the Mooney trial, May was in Ketchikan, Alaska, along with Helen. Luke was there to testify in the trial of Bert McDonald for the murder of a fish buyer. He declared that the death bullet had indeed been fired from a gun belonging to McDonald. The jury convicted McDonald, and he was sentenced to life imprisonment at hard labor.

The list of witnesses for the trial apparently caught the eye of the staff at the *Daily Tribune* in Ketchikan. They seem to have arranged an interview in advance, since May had brought along summary sheets for many of his cases. Luke greeted the newsman warmly. The writer said, "He has a startling habit of unexpectedly flashing his white teeth and crinkling up the corners of his thoughtful brown eyes in a smile that completely changes the expression of his usually serious face."[10]

But Luke's cordiality and good humor came with a catch. The paper must agree to publish nothing more than a brief item about him until after the jury returned a verdict. May had made this a rule because "you newspaper boys are inclined to play up some of my more spectacular cases."[11] That, May felt, had "a tendency to invest me with a reputation for infallibility." And that, in turn, might unduly influence the jury.

Thus, the long article came out a week after the trial ended. Early on, the writer said, "Mr. May was accompanied on this initial trip into the Territory by the charming Mrs. May, who can truly claim to be a real daughter of the northland, since her birthplace was Dawson City, in the hectic days of the Yukon gold rush."[12] Luke loaned the packet of case summaries to the writer, who described the Covell case in great detail. Also, the Simmons suicide allowed May to reiterate the point that his findings sometimes freed suspects who were innocent.

The article reinforced that point using a store holdup in which a Tacoma grocer had been shot and killed. The fatal slug was .38 caliber and, nearby, police caught a young man who carried a recently fired weapon of that caliber. Officers were sure they had the right man. May, however, proved that the killer had used "an automatic of a foreign make," while the young man's gun was a Colt. The writer then said, "Only two other men in North America— Colonel Goddard of Chicago and Captain Crossman of Los Angeles—can take equal rank with Luke May as an expert on ballistics."[13]

May clearly charmed the reporter. The article concluded, "Luke May remains a modest, unassuming, delightfully human person, who likes to put a fly for cut-throat trout and who might, in appearance, very well be a professor of English literature."[14] Even back then, Ketchikan was known as a great jumping-off point for fishing trips to regional lakes and streams.

The McDonald trial was just one of eight death cases May handled in April and May. That put him far ahead of the pace for a normal year. Along with the rush of death cases, May also found himself spending time in Portland and Salem, Oregon. Earlier in the year, the Oregon legislature had authorized the creation of a state police. The chairman of the committee was the state adjutant general and one member was a general in the Oregon National Guard. The other Oregon members were a Portland attorney, and the dean of the Willamette University Law School (the police short-course organizer). The other member was Luke May.

The committee met first in late spring and then several times during the summer. The governor appointed a state police superintendent in early July.

Per the legislature's directive, the force went into official operation on August 1. However, few of its ninety-five officers were trained to a level that satisfied May and the other committee members. The state soon started a police academy to address that problem. But eight years would pass before Oregon had a statewide crime lab.

While May was in Oregon on the state police consultation, he also logged a death case there. Early in May, night patrolman James Iverson had been shot to death in Silverton, a small town about twelve miles northeast of Salem. Police floundered until they hired May about three weeks after the murder. A later look back at the case noted, "Questions concerning the make and caliber of the gun firing the fatal shot were answered ably . . . by Luke S. May, famous Seattle criminologist."[15]

News reports said only that the murder weapon was a .25-35 rifle, and material retrieved from the Luke May Papers does not specifically identify the make. However, the .25-35 cartridge itself was (and is) relatively unusual. Introduced by Winchester in 1895, only three other gun makers followed their lead, with rather limited production runs. In any case, tracing the uncommon rifle helped lead investigators to the three crooks. One turned state's evidence and was paroled after less than five years in prison. Of the other two, one died in prison, while the last was released after thirty-one years.

With the state police consultation and so many death cases, May was surely doing well financially. Thus, at some point during the year, Luke and Helen had two log cabins built on Treasure Island. The structures were made from the madrona trees growing on the island. (Madrona is an evergreen with hard close-grained wood.) The main cabin housed a living room, bedroom, and kitchen. The second structure was a smaller guesthouse. Both displayed superb workmanship. Many years later, a local historian said, "The guy who built [the cabins] for May was the Stradivarius of log-cabin builders."[16] Over time, Luke himself built furniture for the cabins, also from the trees on the island. His daughter considered the pieces both "rustic and artistic."[17]

In late June, May presided over a meeting of the Northwest Association of Sheriffs and Police in Seattle. Besides May, one of the conference speakers was his friend James S. Egan of the Bureau. Meeting organizers set up an unusual teletype show. The two main press agencies had been using teletypewriters for more than fifteen years. Yet only five states had police networks working or authorized. The oldest, in Connecticut, had been in use for just four years. Moreover, only one interstate system was in use, connecting New Jersey, New York, and Pennsylvania.

The association's setup linked sixteen cities to Seattle. Sites ranged from Vancouver, British Columbia, to San Diego, and as far east as New York. It was, the *Bellingham Herald* said, "probably the largest police teletypewriter

Figure 12.2.   Luke May at Treasure Island Cabin. *Source*: May-Reid Records.

hook-up in history."[18] The demonstration was a rousing success. Replies were "noted by flashing lights on a large map in colors in the convention hall."

The Seattle meeting ended on Wednesday. The very next afternoon, many of the same delegates moved on to Bellingham. There, the Washington State Sheriffs' and Peace Officers' Association was holding its annual meeting. Both May and Egan gave talks at the conference. Part of May's speech recalled another back in 1922. At that time, he had called for better teamwork among law enforcement departments. Sadly, almost a decade later, he was still calling for "a more serious attempt at co-operation."[19]

Meanwhile, the unprecedented surge in death cases continued. By the end of September, May had logged a total of nineteen. One of the September cases was interesting because it appeared to be an *accidental* suicide. Aberdeen police had found Filipino Dalmacio Bolong shot to death, with a gun nearby. They called upon May to confirm that the weapon was indeed the one that killed him. Of equal importance, however, was a somewhat garbled note to the man's brother. It might have been a suicide note, yet the wording made that uncertain. May did verify the gun and that the note was written by the victim.

However, the message itself seemed to read at cross-purposes. The man may have intended to shoot himself, but then changed his mind. Or perhaps he was still planning to kill himself but decided to stall by cleaning the gun. Then, when he went to do that, he accidentally inflicted the fatal wound. The message might have started as a suicide note, then switched in midstream to say he had shot himself as he was cleaning the gun.

By early December, May had logged two dozen death cases. He and his agents must have been incredibly busy, especially since the Lindsay murder trial was then in progress. Thus, he opened a mid-December letter with, "I wish to apologize for the delay in sending you the information requested relative to establishing a Crime Detection Laboratory in connection with your force."[20]

The long letter was addressed to Major Henry M. Newson, in Ottawa, Canada. Newson was then director of the criminal investigation branch of the Royal Canadian Mounted Police. The story behind this letter shows how small and tight-knit the law enforcement community was during May's peak years. And personal relationships meant a lot.

It began with a request from RCMP Commissioner James H. Mac-Brien. Shortly after he took office in 1931, he sent out a form letter asking for advice in creating a scientific Crime Detection Laboratory. Transmittals went to many recipients. Those included Scotland Yard and the U.S. Bureau of Investigation but not Luke May. Major Newson, however, had worked in British Columbia before his move to Ottawa. He knew of May and had met him briefly when the law officers' association convened in Vancouver.

Newson sent a letter to the top RCMP inspector in Vancouver. He said he was anxious to learn more about May's operation. He wrote, "I would like you to write him for me, as I think you know him better than I do."[21] The Inspector knew May's reputation very well, of course. However, he too had only met Luke briefly. But a good friend of his, a former police chief in Lethbridge, also lived in Vancouver and knew May personally.

The inspector asked his friend for a letter of introduction, which was sent. May replied that he would "be delighted to furnish Major Newson such information as he desires."[22] Along with that, he wrote directly to the major. He suggested that, if he knew why the major was asking, "I think I can then advise you intelligently."[23] May also mentioned his work in helping organize the Oregon State Police. He wrote, "In the formation of that force, I tried to inject much of the tradition of the R.C.M.P."

May's lengthy December letter covered a wide range of topics. He talked about bloodstains, firearms, crime scene preservation, microscopy, and much more. But time and again, May stressed the importance of the attitude and training of the lab personnel. "The ideal examiner of physical evidence," he said, "is a man who primarily has an investigation background, who is above all a successful detective and investigator."[24]

Such a person could then acquire "the technical knowledge and skill to make such examinations as are submitted to him." Starting the other way rarely worked, May contended. With regard to bloodstain assessment, he wrote, "My experience has taught me that doctors and chemists . . . without a criminal investigation background, are unsuited to this class of work."[25]

As another example, he noted, "The photography of physical evidence is vastly different from commercial photography." Law enforcement photography included not only mug shots and crime scene images, but also close examination of evidence items. All were crucial. So, with training, "a competent photographer with investigative experience can be made a very valuable man and an asset to any laboratory."[26]

May then addressed the issue of that training. He wrote, "The method to be used in such instruction must be a practical one." While one might start with lectures, the techniques must be *shown*, via clear demonstrations. That was the only way to convince your students, he said, "because many of them are old officers who have fixed ideas and methods."[27]

May then spent most of a page describing the optical and chemical equipment they should have. Sadly, the Great Depression had hit Canada hard. So, the RCMP moved slowly, acquiring lab facilities and personnel piecemeal over a period of years. They mark 1937 as the year of the official founding of their Crime Detection Laboratories. A history written for their fiftieth anniversary said, "The one reply that carried [the] most weight was written by Lucas [*sic*] S. May, President of the Northwest Association of Sheriffs and Police."[28] The history then quotes several important passages from Luke's letter.

May's attention to the RCMP request shows his commitment to spreading the word even in the midst of a deluge of work. The firm had logged eighty cases, the most they'd had since Sellers and Harris left. They also handled twenty-four death cases, double the number for a normal year. Still, they did experience an eventual lull in death cases, with just one logged in December and none in January of 1932.

Meanwhile, one Saturday morning in late January, readers opened their issues of the *Olympian* to find the headline, "Olympia Bank Closes Doors Friday."[29] Directors of the bank blamed the closure on "heavy withdrawals occasioned by a whispering campaign and ill-founded rumors as to the solvency of the bank." Soon after the closure, May received a letter from Hollis Fultz, the crime story author noted in the previous chapter. Fultz began, "On last Wednesday, I deposited in the Olympia National Bank the check for the Cavanagh story; Thursday I wrote you a check for $150 and put it in the mailbox; it was still there Friday morning and Friday morning the darn bank failed to open."[30]

It is not clear when Fultz began checking May's cases for true crime story ideas. But it was at least sometime in 1931. Luke's article "How I Solved the Strange Kelso Killing" appeared in the January 1932 issue of *True Detective Mysteries* magazine.[31] Since the byline was "Luke S. May," he apparently wrote the item himself, perhaps with revisions by Fultz. Magazines devoted to detective stories had become very popular even before World War I. Afterwards, they began a "golden age" among the "pulps"—magazines printed on cheap wood-pulp paper. *True Detective Mysteries* was credited with starting the true crime genre in 1924. Their detective stories were not made up, they were based on real cases.

In fact, the "Kelso Killing" was not May's first mention in the publication. In November 1925, the magazine offered "Talking Needles," an account of the rape and murder of Anna Nosko.[32] The byline was that of a prolific pulp writer, but the point of view made it seem like he had personally witnessed every key moment. In one scene, the narrator said, "I saw Luke S. May, a dignified gentleman with the face of a thinker, take the stand." After more description, the story continued, "The jury sat tensed in their chairs. Their faces showed that the testimony of Luke S. May and his enlarged fir needle photographs had broken down their last doubt as to the guilt of the prisoner at the bar."[33]

At the time, professional journals in North America largely ignored studies related to crime science. In 1932, the periodical where May had published his tool mark article was combined into the *Journal of Criminal Law, Criminology and Police Science*. It and the handful of other publications that dealt with the study of crime and criminals leaned toward tracts on legalistic and academic topics. They did not seek articles from the "trenches" on practical subjects or the use of standard methods. May's urge to teach the world about scientific criminology therefore found an outlet in *True Detective Mysteries*. He disliked the sensational flavor of the magazine but felt that it was the best medium to reach an interested general audience.

True Detective Mysteries published the "Cavanagh" case in the April issue, with Fultz alone on the byline. He based the article on the murder of Thomas Cavanaugh, one of May's 1917 cases. Perhaps wanting a catchy title, he called it "Smiling Sam Hanna's Sinister Secret."[34] That was a takeoff on newspaper coverage that referred to the actual killer as "Smiling Dan" Ruth. Such name changes were not unusual in the genre. It's not clear how much the magazine paid for the piece. In his letter, Fultz said, "I will have to make the $150 up to you out of some of our subsequent stories."[35] (No small matter. At the time, you could buy a used Chevrolet Landau sedan for $145.)

The magazine published articles based on eleven of May's cases during 1932, most of them with the Fultz byline. The two had also drafted manuscripts or shared ideas about several other cases during the year. Some of these would be published later. Fortunately, May had some time to pursue this writing venture. Most of his serious cases from the previous year were winding down, and he received only two new death cases in the first two months of the new year.

Then he gained a sideline, of sorts. On March 1, 1932, the infant son of Charles and Anne Lindbergh vanished from their home in New Jersey. Newspapers in the Pacific Northwest seemed to expect Luke May to know all about the case. And he was the preferred recipient for offers of help in Seattle and the Pacific Northwest. May told reporters he had received many tips, "chiefly from clairvoyants and psychics."[36] As for himself, he said, "I would not presume to advance any theories because I have no facts . . . from which to form an opinion." So far as we know, May played no direct role in the case. Yet his work *would* affect the outcome.

While the search went on, May's fame got another boost in the April issue of *Popular Science* magazine. The article, titled "Blackmailers and Forgers Betrayed by Their Pens," discussed the various ways that scientific detectives could track down such criminals.[37] The authors said, "If a vote were taken among handwriting sleuths as to the most valuable recent aid to their work, the ultra-violet ray would stand at the top of the list."

May had, in fact, made himself an expert in the use of so-called black light, for questioned documents examination. The article noted that, "Luke S. May proved a typewritten contract had been altered by showing that the '9' in $49,000 responded differently under the bombardment of filtered ultra-violet rays from the other figures in the number."[38] Today, of course, ultraviolet light sources are a common tool for criminal investigation.

Meanwhile, after the slow start, May logged enough new death cases to have six by early May. None of these received more than passing national interest. One, however, was interesting because it revisited the issue of getting paid when the federal government was involved. A young American Indian named David Carden had apparently been stabbed and thrown into a river on the Colville Reservation. Officials had little hard evidence to go on, so this information perhaps came from an anonymous informant.

They packed up what little physical evidence they had and sent it to Laboratory—Washington State Board of Health in Seattle.[39] Could they please check for the presence of human blood? The Board had no crime lab capability, so they passed the items along to Luke May. He made a thorough examination and found no traces of blood, of any kind. May reported these results to the Colville subagent and asked him to please send the proper forms so he could officially submit his bill for $50. Five days later, he received a reply from the agency superintendent. That official wrote that his request would need to be "referred to the Office of Indian Affairs, Washington, D.C."[40] There is no evidence in the case file that May was ever paid for his tests.

The day after the agency letter was sent, a giant headline in the *Seattle Times* announced that the Lindbergh baby had been found dead. (Six weeks later, Congress passed the "Lindbergh Law," making interstate kidnapping a federal offense.) Coincidently, that same issue announced the death from natural causes of Caroline McGilvra Burke. She was the widow of Judge Thomas Burke. Besides serving for a time as chief justice of the Washington Supreme Court, Thomas fostered many civic projects in Seattle. His lucrative law practice and real estate dealings allowed him to leave a considerable estate to Caroline when he died in 1925. Now the combined estate came up for probate.

That led to one of May's most complex cases with the Seattle Trust Company, the executor of the estate, as his client.[41] The extensive real estate holdings surely required detailed property histories to guide the appraisers. They might have also branched into more involved title searches, since some of the holdings traced back into Territorial days. Beyond that, there would have been a need to locate and verify the identities of a number of individuals who were to receive small bequests.

The estate also held large amounts of potentially valuable personal property. One headline in the *Times* noted that the estate was searching for a specialist to appraise Mrs. Burke's antique and modern jewelry.[42] The same would have held true for an extensive list of antique furniture, Oriental rugs, and other artifacts. May surely helped track down the necessary specialists.

Besides the smaller bequests and the personal property, Caroline left a major portion of the estate to be used to establish a suitable memorial to her late husband. Many years later, that bequest helped build a permanent home for the Washington State Museum at the University of Washington. Today, the institution operates under the descriptive title Burke Museum of Natural History and Culture.

May's summer must have been extremely busy. Besides several ongoing cases, he attended two "crime" conferences. One was an International Police Convention, held in Portland. Among others, he shared the speaking program with James Egan. According to *The Oregonian,* the agent "presented [the] views of J. Edgar Hoover, director of the bureau, in urging that enforcement officials transmit fingerprint records of persons in custody to the Identification Division of the Bureau of Investigation."[43] A month after that, May attended the annual meeting of the Northwest Association of Sheriffs and Police Officers. There, he was again elected president, continuing his long service.

One of the death cases May handled during the summer went to trial about ten days after the Northwest Association meeting. The shooting of

Japanese grocer George Ikeda made headlines in the region and along the Pacific Coast but got little coverage around the country. Ikeda's store was located about a mile northeast of downtown Seattle. A hardened criminal going by the name of Ted Bradley had already robbed the grocer four times. Two policemen were there interviewing witnesses when, incredibly, Bradley came back for a fifth heist.

The grocer was killed in the resulting gun battle, and Bradley was wounded, along with one of the officers. He escaped but was soon caught. Bradley proved to be a surly patient at the hospital, frightening the nurses and other staff. After a day or so, officials doubled the armed guard kept at his room. During the trial, Bradley's attorney tried to suggest that the grocer had been killed by a stray police bullet. But the fatal slug was .32 caliber, while the officers were armed with standard .38-caliber weapons. Moreover, May found that Bradley's gun created very clear striations that matched the evidence bullets. During the trial, he said, "The evidence was never more conclusive in any case I have investigated."[44] The convicted killer went to the gallows just over twenty-six months after he murdered George Ikeda.

During the same period, work began on a crime laboratory in Washington, DC, for the Bureau of Investigation. Charles A. Appel, another of Hoover's "Big Five" agents, led the effort. Appel did not visit Luke May, nor did he invite him to Washington. However, James Egan's face-to-face meetings with May as well as their correspondence could have provided answers to specific questions that Appel might have had. In fact, in an earlier letter, Egan had sought May's advice on the purchase of a dictaphone for the bureau. He also wrote, "We are going to start a large library here on Criminology, and . . . I would like to buy the books you could recommend."[45]

Thus, it is more likely than not that May played a behind-the-scenes role in the creation of the bureau's technical laboratory. Yet there is no formal record that he played any role in the founding of the lab. Given what we know of Hoover's quirks, that was to be expected. (Recall that Egan took pains to conceal his earlier correspondence with Luke.) The bureau selected late fall for the official opening of the lab.

That same fall, May had another case that showed the power of his reputation. It had begun the previous summer, when a Seattle savings and loan association was forced into receivership. Three weeks later, Ahira Pierce, the former operating officer, was arrested for embezzlement, forgery, and grand larceny. But Pierce's chronic illness repeatedly delayed the case.

A trial on the grand larceny charge finally began in early November. Almost immediately, the *Bellingham Herald* reported, "The services of Luke May, criminologist, were excused yesterday by Prosecutor Robert M. Burgunder."[46] May was scheduled to testify that Pierce had forged several signatures to withdraw money from the association. But now, his lawyers "had agreed to admit in court that Pierce had 'simulated' the signatures." Pierce was convicted and sentenced to twenty to sixty-five years in the state penitentiary.

May's caseload for 1932 dropped back to a more common level of fifty-eight, but death cases remained high, with a total of twenty. This completed a two-year span where he logged a total of forty-four death cases, three-quarters of which were murders. It is perhaps significant that these two years and the one to follow were the worst of the Great Depression. Unemployment jumped to an unprecedented level in 1931, with one in six of the usual workforces being jobless. That was almost triple any normal expectation. The rate rose to nearly one in four unemployed in 1932. One cannot escape the notion that the associated fear and frustration were partly to blame for the spike in death cases.

The following year began with a typical level of death cases, with a new one in January and another in February. That went along with continuing work on four death cases carried over from the previous year. Besides the usual mix of questioned document assessments and other cases, in February May took on a bombing investigation in Havre, Montana. A bomb had gone off in the front yard of Arthur Lamey, a prominent local attorney. Another device had been recovered from under a foot bridge in the area. The only other piece of evidence was a pair of overalls, discarded nearby. The county attorney had sent these overalls, fragments from the explosion, and the unexploded bomb to May.

May found that the two devices had been of the same design, with dynamite as the explosive. He also confirmed that the overalls showed traces of the same kind of fuse used for both bombs. Then he wrote, "The owner of the overalls had worked in the harvesting field, harvesting wheat and . . . in all probability, in a coal mine, or at any rate worked around soft coal."[47]

May added some general clues about the wearer's age and habits. In a second letter, May pointed out that a bomb exploded in an open yard could not have been expected to cause much real damage. It was almost certainly meant to frighten the target. The county attorney agreed and attributed the attack to bad feelings from a recent political dispute. He said, "I believe . . . that if the party who threw the bomb is not in the county, that at least those who hired him to do it are."[48] More correspondence followed. It concluded with the attorney asking May how much he might charge to travel to Havre and investigate personally. The county evidently decided they couldn't afford May's services because nothing else appears in the file.

May's pace of general work continued at a high level. Then, on April 4, 1933, the main front-page headline of the *Seattle Star* blared, "Storm Hurls

Akron into Ocean."[49] A violent thunderstorm off the coast of New Jersey had wrecked the U.S. Navy's rigid airship, the USS *Akron*. The newspaper had several articles dealing with the disaster and the history of the *Akron*. May no doubt read news of the calamity with some concern (all but three of the seventy-six men aboard were killed).

But another item, high on the page, was also of considerable interest. The headline read, "Famous Criminologist Now is Proud Father."[50] Such was his fame that the birth of the Mays' daughter, Patricia Helen, made front-page news. As could be expected for a man in his forties, Luke adored this new addition to the family. She, in turn, worshipped her father. Far ahead of his time, Luke took an enlightened approach to child rearing. Reason and understanding were the key, he felt. In her memoir, she could only recall one specific occasion when that failed, and he resorted to spanking. She clearly felt the lesson was deserved and freely pardoned him.

Patricia was too young to have extensive memories of the house she lived in first. She did remember that Luke installed a folding safety door at the head of the stairs that led up to their second-floor living area. It's unclear how much domestic help the Mays employed up to this point. After Patricia was born, the staff usually included a nursemaid-housekeeper, a houseboy to fetch and carry, a part-time yardman, and someone to assist on wash day.

The little girl's maternal grandmother lived not too far away, so she was also there to help out. Sadly, Luke's father-in-law, Thomas Klog, never got to see his only grandchild. He died two months before Patricia was born. She remembered excursions with Nanny to Volunteer Park. And, at the Seattle Art Museum, Patricia "would delightedly ride the giant stone camels,"[51] sculptures that frame the museum entrance. Luke's parents lived further away, still at the North Beacon Hill property. Patricia only recalled meeting them at family dinners.

Beyond all the individual cases during this period, May's other activities surely had the greatest impact. His advice to the Oregon State Police, the RCMP, and behind the scenes to the Bureau of Investigation had results that still echo down to the present day. And his popular articles both entertained and educated at least a portion of the general public. He would add to those legacies in the following years. But fate was about to add something else new to May's life.

• 13 •

Chief of Detectives and Criminologist

"$\mathcal{T}$ennant's Death is Mourned by All Seattle" read a front-page headline in the *Seattle Times* for April 18, 1933.[1] Chief of Detectives Charles Tennant had suffered a severe stroke the previous afternoon and died that same evening. Highly respected, Tennant had never wavered from his old-school ways. In fact, he once told a reporter—"not talking for publication"—that, as far as he was concerned, "There's a lot of hooey to criminologists."[2]

But Seattle Mayor John F. Dore felt a new approach was needed. A week after Tennant's death, he appointed Luke May as chief of detectives. May was to be classed as a special patrolman. That ploy avoided certain technicalities of the city Civil Service regulations. Dore said May would be given a free hand to reorganize the detective department any way he saw fit.

The choice was not without controversy. Dore even received a death threat, surreptitiously hand-delivered to his home. Some Council members condemned the trick that dodged the Civil Service rules. But the *Seattle Times* also said, "Others saw humor in the mayor's selection of May, his old-time courtroom enemy. They recalled the scorn with which the attorney-mayor disparaged May's scientific criminology abilities to . . . juries when May has been a witness against Dore's clients."[3]

May agreed to assume the role, but said, "I take this responsibility dubious of my ability to accomplish as much as people may expect."[4] He was also aware that the experience might not end well. May said he realized "that communities have short memories and that little thanks await me for my efforts." May made a quick survey and found many problems, which he immediately took steps to fix. Men who did not measure up were sent back to patrol duty. May planned to replace them with "uniformed men who have

169

demonstrated their ability or show unusual promise."[5] May soon reworked the bunco squad and created specialized homicide and bomb units.

A bit over a week after he began, May sent a letter to Bureau Director J. Edgar Hoover. He needed to be the contact point for the monthly bulletin on wanted fugitives. In his reply, Hoover began with, "My congratulations upon your appointment to the position of Chief of Detectives of the Seattle Police Department."[6] He was having two copies of the current bulletin sent right away. Also, May's name had been added to the mailing list. Hoover closed with, "I have conveyed your regards to Inspector Egan and he has asked me to reciprocate the same."

The effect of May's changes were soon visible. Looking back a few months later, the head of Seattle's Junior Chamber of Commerce wrote, "Our organization has noticed a decided increase in the efficiency of the Detective Division of the City Police Department since May 1, 1933."[7]

Meanwhile, May's private work continued, although at a reduced level. He produced a pocket-sized manual called *Scientific Murder Investigation*. His advertisement in *Popular Science* magazine said readers could purchase a copy for a dollar. He identified himself as "Luke S. May, internationally known

Figure 13.1.   FBI Director J. Edgar Hoover. *Source:* **Library of Congress, LC-DIG-hec-21053.**

criminologist and scientific detective."[8] In the introduction, May assured buyers that the advice was based on years of experience. He wrote, "The reader, therefore, may study this manual with confidence that it is decidedly practical in its application to the investigation of mysterious homicides."[9]

Then, in just over ninety pages of succinct text, May took the reader from building the case through his or her final report to authorities. He also cross-referenced his other publication, *Detective Science: Field Manual of Criminology*. That manual, priced at two dollars, gave "detailed technical instructions in the many field tests and methods of procedure for the detection and preservation of physical evidence."[10] Some of the most important advice, he said, described what "detectives or criminologists *should not do* at the scene of the crime" [May's emphasis].

Naturally, both of May's publications advertised the Institute of Scientific Criminology. The institute now offered three years of instruction and hands-on experience. During this year, the Institute gave May a protégé who became more than just a colleague. The student's name was Edward C. Newell. The 1926 article about May in the *American Magazine* had excited Newell about the field of scientific criminology. He was then fifteen years old. Son of a country doctor in New Hampshire, Edward finished a college education at Dartmouth and then headed west. He began studying with May in early 1933.

Bright and hard-working, Newell soon became a trusted deputy to May and almost a part of the family. Newell later said, Luke "had a habit of taking work from his labs . . . getting on his power yacht and going to 'the island' to work on Wednesday afternoon."[11] Newell often went along, and "the first order of business" when they arrived was to dig a bucket of clams. Back then, they could fill a pail with mature, wild geoducks in ten to fifteen minutes. (The geoduck is the largest burrowing clam in the world.) During his three years with May, Newell would assist on several of Luke's most difficult cases.

Between the chief's job and his private caseload, May was surely a busy man. Yet another thread entered his life in late summer. On August 7, the *Seattle Times* said that May would address the local reserve officers' association. Less than two months later, May was himself commissioned a lieutenant commander in the naval reserve. The import of that role will be discussed in chapter 16.

In October, Chief May began a program to seize machine guns and submachine guns. Earlier in the year, the legislature had made it a felony to own such weapons, or even the parts to repair them. Late in the month the *Seattle Times* reported, "Detective Chief Luke S. May this afternoon revealed that thirty-two machine guns had been seized and impounded in Seattle in a campaign to prevent any outbreak of Eastern gangsterism here."[12]

With his new position as a vantage point, May also chaired a commission to study the feasibility of creating a statewide shortwave radio system for law enforcement. The contents of the commission's final report were not made public. Unfortunately, state finances during the Depression allowed only piecemeal progress. Nearly a decade would pass before the Washington State Patrol installed a full communications center in Olympia.

The same financial pressures also caused problems in Seattle itself. City tax revenues had fallen far short of expectations. The police force found itself doing more and more, with fewer officers. As a result, there was a noticeable rise in street crime. In the fall, May submitted a report to the mayor outlining what he thought needed to be done to improve the police force. That report was never released. Then, in late November, May made a statement that no politically savvy official would ever consider. He advised prosperous looking citizens to stay off the streets at night. They were too likely to be slugged and robbed. Asked to elaborate, he declared, "I never go on the streets alone at night and I tell my friends not to do so."[13]

Naturally, his blunt declarations caused an uproar. The chief of police declared that there was no crime wave, as May had suggested. The *Seattle Times* professed to be outraged and wondered, in a front-page editorial, if someone should declare martial law. The mayor, who returned the following day from a trip, said basically that the statement was "unfortunate." He had no plans, however, to censure May or to ask him to resign. Countering the indignation, a number of groups in the area wrote the mayor to support May and the job he was doing. At least, with the passage of the Twenty-First Amendment on December 5, 1933, the police no longer had to enforce Prohibition.

Through all this, May and his private agents continued their regular detective work. Thus, the firm logged fifty-eight cases during the year. That included a more normal load of thirteen death cases. The number of victims, seventeen, was high because of a probable arson south of Tacoma that killed a family of four. May found some evidence that pointed to the landlord, but the flames had destroyed too much. Part way through the trial, the judge called a halt and ordered a directed verdict of not guilty. The accused was certainly "a cowardly drunken scoundrel," he said, but the state's evidence was not sufficient for a conviction.[14]

Meanwhile, in January 1934, even publications in Portland—the *Northwest Police Journal* and *The Oregonian* newspaper—extolled the fine job May was doing as chief of detectives. The force had vastly improved its success rate, particularly on burglaries and cases of fraud. Morale was said to be at an all-time high. Reporters now knew that May was an officer in the Naval Reserve. Some felt a certain naval *esprit de corps* had rubbed off on the detective division.

In late January, May began a series of Friday afternoon lectures and demonstrations designed especially for the division. He clearly hoped to leave some legacy of expertise behind. May also took every opportunity to speak about crime prevention to civic groups around the area.

Meanwhile, there had been another change in his personal life. Luke's brother Vincent and his wife, Laura, had moved from San Diego to Seattle. They joined Luke and Vincent's parents at the large Beacon Hill structure where the two had been living for about eight years. Neither the 1934 *City Directory* nor the 1940 U.S. census listed any business or occupation for Vincent. It's likely that he and Laura took care of Luke's property and the older couple, who were in their seventies.

As detective chief, May processed a number of King County death cases that were not logged with his private work. Meanwhile, he and his company continued to handle a wide variety of cases. None of the death cases early in the year received any national newspaper coverage, but one was of some technical interest.

On the night of February 16, musician Cecil Montgomery had gathered an orchestral group at his cabin in Bend, Oregon. Not long after midnight, they were about to break up when a man began bellowing curses and threats through the front door. Montgomery cracked the door open and told the shouter, who was clearly drunk, that he had the wrong house. When he stepped out to calm the intruder, he was shot to death. Montgomery was just twenty-four years old.

None of the young man's companions had seen the shooter. Investigators soon found the fatal bullet, which had passed through the victim's chest and buried itself in an inside wall. As could be expected, the slug was somewhat distorted. Deputies looked for possible witnesses in the area. They had one neighbor who lived within a few blocks whom they were sure would cooperate. Thomas Baughn was an ex-convict, being on parole from a "life" sentence for murder in Oklahoma. Baughn indeed seemed anxious to help. He even handed over a rifle of the right caliber for them to check. There were actually several rifles in the house. Baughn, a self-taught gunsmith, was repairing them for friends.

Within a few days, officials sent both the rifle and the fatal bullet to May. But Luke's assessment was hampered by the damage to the slug and what he called "peculiar circumstances"[15] associated with the suspect rifle. Still, after much careful work, he found "many similarities" between test slugs and the fatal bullet. By then authorities knew a great deal about Baughn's movements on the night of the murder. May's guarded statement provided the capper, because officers immediately arrested the ex-con.

Four days after being locked up, Baughn confessed to the murder, to avoid a trial and possible death sentence. Two threads perhaps converged to drive his admission. Baughn's brother was in the Oregon State Prison on a manslaughter conviction. If Thomas didn't already know May's reputation, his brother, tipped off by the prison grapevine, could have given him reason to worry.

Beyond that, the arrest allowed May to enter Baughn's shop where he worked on guns. If Baughn had tried to rework the barrel of the rifle, May would have soon found marks that matched a tool in the killer's shop. In fact, a couple of weeks after Baughn was taken off to prison, May told the sheriff that they "were finally able to definitely identify this gun" as the death weapon.[16] And, given the odd circumstances, "We are very desirous to keep it in the Scientific Detective Laboratories if it is possible for us to do so." It's unclear whether they were able to work out some sort of agreement.

Besides the follow-up on the Montgomery shooting, May handled three new murder cases in March. The most important of these came at the end of the month and horrified people everywhere. It began simply, with some barking dogs.

The sun was lowering, but the clouds overhead still glowed with light as Tom Sanders made his way through the trees. The Douglas firs near the Flieder place had grown tall enough so the grove was fairly open. But he had to be careful treading on the carpet of needles, even where there was a path. The weather had been rainy off and on for the past several days. That and daytime temperatures in the fifties had kept the soil very soft.

Frank and Anna Flieder were good neighbors. Frank had retired comfortably from a grocery business after he married Anna, a wealthy widow. They had frequent parties at their fine ten-room home, three to four miles north of Bremerton. But there were seldom a lot of people, and the festivities never got loud or rowdy.

Thus, the barking was an oddity to be checked. Seemed like the dogs had been yelping forever, certainly a couple of days or so. As Tom drew closer to the house, he realized that the cries were coming from inside a Packard parked near the garage. The Flieders' Buick was still inside, so they hadn't gone off somewhere in that. When Tom looked into the car, three small white poodles began leaping wildly at the windows, and their barks grew even more frantic. The pooches had clearly been inside a long time. The Flieders were nice people; surely they'd never willingly let that happen.

He banged on the outside door that led into the kitchen, but no one answered. Now even more puzzled, he tried to see inside. To the left of the kitchen, Tom noticed that a window blind was up an inch or so. Peering through the crack, he saw a worrisome sight. A man and a woman were slumped into what seemed like unnatural positions. Thwarted, Tom hurried along a narrow path to the cabin that belonged to Magnus Jordan. A retired navy man, Jordan lived on a small pension and income from caring for several of the nearby summer homes. Jordan's place was open, and the lights were on, but he wasn't there. Nor did Magnus have a telephone.

As Tom rushed back by the Flieder place, he confirmed a suspicion that had grown on him. The man he could see inside was probably Jordan. Captain Knute Erland lived off the other way; he had a phone. Erland first called one of Frank's brothers. Then Sanders and Erland hastened back to the Flieder place, while the brother called the county sheriff's office. The Packard wasn't locked, so the two men could free the dogs and give them eagerly consumed water and food.

The county undersheriff enlisted a State Patrol officer as well as the county prosecuting attorney and headed north. They arrived at the scene about twenty minutes later. By now, it was dark, and a light rain was falling. That only added to the somber atmosphere. Tomorrow would be Easter Sunday, April 1, 1934. What officials found when they forced their way inside shocked the world. The Flieders and four party guests were all dead, murdered in a brutal and bloody fashion. All of them had been tightly bound, and some were blindfolded.

The killer had beaten Frank Flieder to death with a hammer. Anna Flieder had been stabbed with a thin knife that had a staghorn handle. The victims Tom had seen first had both been shot with a .32-caliber handgun. One was indeed Magnus Jordan, while the other was Margaret Chenevert. Eugene Chenevert, her husband, was found dead in another room. A big, burly man, he had burst his bonds and put up a terrific fight before the killer could beat him to death with the hammer. The Cheneverts, under the stage names Bert and Peggy Vincent, had been regulars on the vaudeville circuit. The killer also used a hammer to murder the sixth victim, Fred Bolcom, a local bartender.

Late that evening, the Kitsap County sheriff called May. After describing the scene, he said, "It's terrible, Luke, terrible!"[17] By now, May had handled more than two hundred death cases, quite a few involving multiple victims. He sympathized, but, like people in the medical profession, he had learned to cope. It was too late to catch a ferry, so May went to bed. He later said, "The boat the next morning was crowded with newspaper reporters, most of whom I knew."

The sheriff drove him to the scene. May would "act as consultant, preserve physical evidence, and, if possible, reconstruct the crime as it was carried out."[18] Meanwhile, deputies interviewed all the neighbors as well as many merchants in and around Bremerton. Several thought they had seen one or more of the victims some time on Thursday, March 29. A storekeeper and a bartender even said they had sold them goods on that day. Neither had any firm records, like a dated receipt, but both were sure that's when it was. Officials concluded that the murders had taken place Thursday evening, and that view was widely reported in the news.

By now, May had been in the detective business for a quarter century. His first rule was to never jump to conclusions. He also did his best to avoid a dependence upon eyewitness testimony and unverified human memory. Even when two witnesses agreed, he remained skeptical unless physical evidence supported their story. May knew from his first look at the crime scene that the case would be especially difficult. He said, "I was gazing at the handiwork of the most deliberate slaughterer, or slaughterers, I had ever been called upon to investigate."[19]

May and Ed Newell spent most of three days in the house and accumulated three trunks full of evidence. Their task was complicated by the fact that, despite May's clear instructions, officers had not totally sequestered the crime scene. Newell took many of the crime scene photographs. He later said, "There had been three tours of 11 people and officers taken through the entire house before we got there."[20] So their examination had to sort out usable evidence from what the sightseers might have altered. As we have seen in the past, May was quite willing to tell police and prosecutors when they had no case. And, on occasion, he had even told them when they had irreparably ruined a case through their actions, or inaction. Fortunately, he was able to salvage many key items of evidence.

Careful study led May to a result that was crucially different from that of the sheriff. He and Ed found Wednesday editions of all three Seattle daily newspapers. Not one Thursday edition was on the premises. The Wednesday mail had been collected, but not that for Thursday. Milk delivered on Thursday morning was still on the porch the next time the milkman came by. And, finally, autopsies revealed that the victims' stomachs contained none of the food supposedly planned for meals on Thursday. From these and other clues, May concluded that the victims had been killed on Wednesday, March 28, probably in the evening.

May's analysis also produced three other conclusions. First, at least two perpetrators had been involved. With so many victims, one crook would have had to hold the group at gunpoint while the other bound their hands. Second, one of the victims had probably recognized at least one of the invaders. The crime seemed well planned as a robbery. Murder was necessary only to keep someone from talking. And, finally, one of the perpetrators was probably a woman. Searchers had found the heel of a woman's shoe, freshly torn off. It could not be accounted for by any shoe found in the house.

Eighteen months passed, filled with dead-end leads, false accusations, and irrelevant red herrings. These would be too tedious to describe here and were ultimately fruitless. Oddly enough, authorities already had two keys to the mystery in hand. During their routine interviews, they heard from two men who had a home in Bremerton and tended bar at a lounge there. They recalled an early-morning visit by a young woman they knew as Letha Hurt. She was exhausted, her clothes were soaked, and she'd lost the heel of one shoe. Letha claimed she'd gone for a ride with a sailor but jumped out and ran away when he got fresh. The bartenders built a warm fire and let her dry out her clothes. Later, they dropped her off at the ferry to Seattle.

The other event took place on the Seattle ferry. Police interviewed ship-yard worker Cecil Long. Riding an early-morning ferry from Bremerton to Seattle, he met a man he knew casually from a previous yard job. The other rider had a bad gash on his head and several cuts around the face. When asked what happened, the man said he'd been in a bar fight. This encounter, like the Letha Hurt visit, had taken place Thursday morning.

At the time, officials were convinced that the murders had happened Thursday evening. Thus, those accounts were buried in the files and forgotten in a flurry of other reports. They were not shared with May and surfaced only after there was a break in the case. May himself said, "I had long since given up hope that the fiend or fiends would ever be trailed through a clue which had been left in the house." He had not *totally* given up hope, however: "That still did not eliminate Fate and Providence."[21]

The break came from a two-time loser named Larry Paulos. He faced a third felony conviction that could earn him a mandatory lifetime prison sentence as a habitual criminal. Paulos proposed a deal. He'd give them a hot tip on the unsolved murder of an Oregon special investigator if officials would back off on the life sentence. Negotiations closed the deal, and Paulos fingered the contract killer as one Leo Hall. Hall was well known in the Pacific Northwest underworld and feared by many.

And then Fate or Providence truly rewarded May's patience. About five months after the massacre, Larry had married barmaid Peggy Peterson, aka Letha Hurt Peterson. Paulos offered prosecutors a bonus. His wife knew something terrible about Hall, he said, and was deathly afraid of him. She'd sometimes rouse Larry with half-awake cries of, "Leo, don't kill me!"[22] When confronted, Peggy Paulos at first said she had no idea what her husband was talking about. Later, she realized that Larry was indeed going back to prison, even if not for life. Faced with the prospect of no husband around for protection, her fear of Hall exploded. Leo had, in fact, coerced her into helping with the robbery that turned into the Bremerton Massacre.

She had warned him that the Flieders might recognize her, even though they both wore bandanna masks. Not only had she attended parties there, but Anna had given her old but nice clothes she could tailor for herself. Leo started his murder spree when Anna did recognize her. Peggy fled in terror when she realized he had already killed Anna and one other victim and planned to kill the rest. He had even taken a wild shot at her as she ran. After signing a written confession, Peggy walked May and the prosecutor through the house describing what had happened before she fled. She did not, of course, know what evidence May and Newell had collected. But her story dovetailed nicely with their clues. Those signs included crucial bloodstains (photographed, but since cleaned up), mislocated furnishings, the spent bullet from Hall's shot at her, and her lost heel.

Her flight had surely been the distraction that allowed Eugene Chenevert to free himself and go after Hall. Chenevert's desperate fight tied in with the shipyard worker's story. The worker later testified that it was Leo Hall whom he had seen, cut and battered, on the Thursday morning ferry.

Prosecutors charged both Hall and Peggy Paulos with first degree murder. Hall's attorneys made as much as they could of the lack of direct physical evidence to link him to the crime scene. They also tried to impeach the Paulos story, but those efforts seriously backfired. On the stand, her intense fear of Hall was palpable. He had forced her to tie up the victims, using adhesive tape until that ran out and she switched to torn sheets.

In her confession, Peggy said Hall had given her a pair of woman's gloves to wear. (He too wore gloves so they would not leave any fingerprints.) Hall's lawyer confidently handed her a pair of gloves and challenged her to bind his hands with adhesive tape. He had perhaps tried it himself and found it impossible to tie the sticky strip into a knot. She quickly secured his hands behind his back and finished with a firm knot. The lawyer struggled, but finally had to ask to be cut loose.

Close inspection showed that she had folded the tape lengthwise at the ends so the adhesive stuck to itself. This was exactly what May had found at the crime scene and was one of many points where his testimony verified every key detail of what she said happened in the Flieder home. After a sensational trial, the jury found Hall guilty and recommended the death penalty. They declared Peggy Paulos not guilty. Hall's appeal went to the Washington Supreme Court, but he died on the gallows in September 1936.

Long before that, Mayor Dore had lost a bid for reelection. Thus, at the end of June 1934, Luke May resigned as chief of detectives for the Seattle police. A University of Washington professor was commissioned to assess the performance of the detective division during May's tenure. The *Post-Intelligencer* reported the dramatic results. It said, "The records since then show that the force has become twice as efficient in solving bad check cases, three times as efficient in robberies, eleven times better in fraud cases and fourteen times better in clearing up burglaries."[23]

Through all that, May's business had moved along. In September, the U.S. Patent Office approved a patent on the latest version of the magnascope. As noted earlier, however, no one besides May ever expressed any serious interest in the custom-built image magnifier.

Including the Montgomery shooting and Bremerton Massacre, May logged thirteen death cases in 1934, with eighteen victims. Well over half the year's fifty cases involved questioned documents, and none of those made the newspapers. The company also handled a "near-death" firearms case. In that episode, the criminal was actually the target. Three men held up a grocery store about a mile and a half northeast of downtown Seattle. The grocer made no resistance as the three took $25 from him. However, this was the sixth time he'd been robbed at that store. So now he grabbed a .45-caliber revolver, ran out onto the sidewalk and fired a shot at the robber's car as it drove away. The car wobbled and almost stopped, but then continued on.

The three were soon captured, mainly because one of them had been shot in the head. A reporter told the grocer the bandit might die and asked him how he felt about that. His reply: "I'm fed up with being held up by these birds. The more of them I can kill the better."[24] Actually, the wounded man did survive. He and the other two pleaded not guilty to robbery charges. But May testified that the bullet taken from the one bandit's head had indeed been fired from the grocer's weapon. The three spent five to ten years in prison.

All but one of the eleven other death cases involved firearms. The exception took place in Idaho, where a store owner who dealt in furs died from a blow to the head. In an unusual turn, a deputy hand-delivered the victim's felt hat, a hammer, and a hatchet to Seattle. May had to proceed on the basis of a description of the head wounds, plus blood, and a cut mark in the hat. The shape of the cut strongly suggested that the hatchet was the murder weapon. That was confirmed when he found traces of blood on the hatchet but not on the hammer.

The prosecutor did not welcome that news. He wrote, "I had almost convinced myself that the hammer was the weapon used."[25] Turned out, they could clearly trace the hammer to their prime suspect but not the hatchet. Obviously, there's no way to know what clues the officers might have missed because of their preoccupation with the hammer. In any case, their suspect was found not guilty when the case came to trial.

During the second week of December, May traveled to Washington, DC, to attend a crime prevention conference. In many ways, the year had been good for national law enforcement. In May, law officers from Texas and Louisiana had tracked down and killed gangsters Clyde Barrow and Bonnie Parker in rural Louisiana. Two months later, in Chicago, celebrity bank robber John Dillinger died trying to escape a stakeout by Bureau of Investigation agents. Late in the year, the bureau got Charles "Pretty Boy" Floyd. A month after that, in an all-out gun battle in a Chicago suburb, agents shot and killed Baby Face Nelson. However, they lost two men in that fight.

Despite those flashy successes, officials in Washington knew that bandit gangs like Dillinger's were only a small part of the crime problem. President Franklin D. Roosevelt's attorney general therefore organized the conference to pool ideas. The president himself gave the opening address. The phrase "war on crime" had been around since early in the century but had taken on more urgency during Prohibition. Still, some historians assert that Roosevelt was the first president to take it as a major theme of his policies. He did not put the phrase in his speech but used the metaphor when he advocated a "major offensive" against crime.

The conference ended with a host of recommendations and resolutions. They included a "continuing crime organization and establishment of a national training school for police officers."[26] Conferees also called for better cooperation and coordination among local law enforcement units. These ideas matched what May had been trying to push for more than a decade through the Northwest Association of Sheriffs and Police. Now they would be given national attention. Thus, May could rightly say that the message about systematic and scientific crime detection was getting across as the Thirties rolled along.

Less than three weeks after the conference ended, the *Seattle Times* featured the extra-bold headline "Lindbergh and Wife Tell Jury of Baby's Kidnaping."[27] That banner marked the big sensation of the new year, the trial of Bruno Hauptmann for the abduction and murder of the Lindbergh baby. He had been tracked down when banknotes from the ransom money began to show up in New York City. During more than six weeks of testimony, every issue of the *Times* had something about the trial on its front page. In fact, with perhaps a half dozen exceptions, the trial was always the *featured* front-page story. Only a few events managed to eclipse the hoopla. One was Amelia Earhart's solo flight from Honolulu, Hawaii, to Oakland, California. That story pushed the trial down a notch for a couple of days.

As noted in the previous chapter, Luke May had no personal involvement in the case. However, he did have a pair of indirect links to it. Those connections had to do with two kinds of crucial physical evidence. One type was the many ransom notes sent to the Lindberghs. Eight handwriting experts agreed that Hauptmann had written all the notes. One of the experts was J. Clark Sellers, May's former partner and student. His clear and confident testimony was widely praised in accounts of the Hauptmann trial. At one point he said the features in the notes were so distinctive that "Hauptmann might just as well have signed each and every one of them."[28]

A second key piece of evidence was a handmade wooden ladder. The intruder had used it to enter and leave the second-story window of the nursery. With little to go on, officers turned to Arthur J. Koehler, wood expert at the USDA Forest Products Lab in Madison, Wisconsin. Koehler's investigation followed the same process Luke used for his own tool mark work. Class characteristics identified the make and model of industrial planer that prepared the yellow pine board used for one ladder upright. Individual characteristics fingered the specific mill that produced the plank. Koehler then laboriously traced a shipment of that lumber to a yard in the Bronx.

When Hauptmann was arrested on the banknote evidence, officers quickly established his probable link to the pine board. Then Koehler used tool marks to show that the plank had been further worked with a hand plane known to belong to Hauptmann. Moreover, the surface had marks from a chisel that probably belonged to a set owned by the accused.

The defense strongly challenged all the evidence offered by the prosecution. They did not, however, contest the *admissibility* of the tool mark evidence. An article in the *Seattle Times* noted the connection between Koehler's analysis and the precedent set by May's "State vs Clark" case in Washington. Of course, prosecutors had a lot of other evidence. The jury found Hauptmann guilty, and he died in the electric chair just over four years after little Charles Jr. disappeared.

During the Hauptmann deliberations, the *Seattle Times* reported that the "newly-formed Seattle Crime Prevention Council" had selected a leader.[29] The council would be meeting soon to appoint more committees to address various crime-prevention issues. The article also said, "Luke S. May . . . has been chosen *ex-officio* member of all committees which may be appointed." Warren G. Magnuson, then King County prosecuting attorney, chaired the legislative committee, which was to suggest needed changes in criminal law. Later, Magnuson became a highly influential member of the U.S. Congress, where he served the state for forty-four years.

Over the next few months, May would carry the message of crime prevention around the area. That included a lecture on that topic to a Seattle American Legion post. For a meeting of Presbyterian ministers, his topic was "The Crime Problem—Who Are These Criminals? and What Made Them What They Are?"[30] He also spoke on "handwriting, typewriting, ballistics and allied matters" to a statewide crime conference in Portland, Oregon.[31]

And May continued to spread the word at a more personal level. Some months earlier, May had investigated a murder case in Bozeman, Montana. In February, he received a letter from Edmund Burke, the county attorney he had worked with there. Burke told Luke that in local detective repute, "you occupy the 'King-Fish' position."[32] He then asked for a copy of Luke's new

Figure 13.2. U.S. Senator Warren G. Magnuson.
Source: Library of Congress, LC-USZ62-110242.

detective's manual. May sent him a copy of his *Scientific Murder Investigation* at no charge. Burke also asked for some of May's fingerprint powder because "the powder which we now have is not satisfactory."

Also, during the spring, Hollis Fultz interviewed May for a long personal profile in *True Detective Mysteries* magazine. Fultz briefly described May's many advanced items of equipment along with several key cases. While Fultz was in the lab, May received a revolver to examine. It was wrapped in a handkerchief. May branded that a mistake . . . the cloth might smudge any fingerprints on the weapon. May said, "Someday we will have suitable protective holders for all these things so that the police may preserve them for the criminologist in their original state."[33]

Toward the end of the feature, Fultz said that May was preparing "a series of highly scientific articles" which were to appear in the magazine. As it happened, May and the magazine devised an even better way for him to share his expertise. The results appeared shortly after Fultz's profile article. But before that, May logged his most notorious case for 1935.

· *14* ·

Riding the Crest

$\mathcal{F}$riday, May 24, 1935, had been a fine, clear day in Seattle, with light breezes and temperatures in the low sixties. Luke May and Ed Newell left the building on Capitol Hill around five o'clock. May said he planned to look for a new car at Buick and Hudson dealers during the evening. Newell headed to his boardinghouse about a mile and a quarter to the north.

Though lowering, the sun was still bright when Ed and the other boarders were called to dinner. Dessert had just been served when the phone rang; it was a bit before seven o'clock. Moments later, the landlord said the call was for Newell. When Ed picked up the phone, the voice on the other end identified himself as the chief criminal deputy of Pierce County. They needed to reach Luke May right away, and no one at the office knew where he was. Their problem: "We have a $200,000 kidnapping case."[1]

The nine-year-old son of John Weyerhaeuser, wealthy lumber magnate, had disappeared during the day, and the family had just received a ransom demand via special delivery. They needed May to test for fingerprints and see what else he could learn from the message. Newell said he thought he could find May but that it might take some time. The deputy urged him to "come as quickly as you can get here. . . . Fly if you have to."[2]

Newell advised the caller to contact the Bureau of Investigation. Strictly speaking, the Lindbergh Law applied only to interstate kidnapping. However, Director J. Edgar Hoover had shown a willingness to involve his agents in high-profile abduction cases. Ed gave the deputy the number in Portland where he could reach Northwest Agent-in-Charge Cleo Spears.

Newell hurried out and found May with his second try. Newell explained the situation as they rushed back to the office. By the time they had gathered their working kits and left, the sun had set although twilight still glowed bright to the west. Newell said, "We went thirty miles in twenty-one minutes."[3]

Police and county officers had cordoned off the Weyerhaeuser home overlooking Tacoma's Commencement Bay. As soon as he and Newell arrived, May began his analysis of the ransom note. So many people had handled the package that he found no usable fingerprints. The message had been prepared on a Corona portable typewriter, a model very popular with travelers. The paper was heavy linen, a type commonly used by women for their personal letters. The kidnappers included more than twenty demands and instructions in the text.

Within hours after May and Newell arrived in Tacoma, Bureau of Investigation agents were in the city. The message had warned against letting the word get out. Yet a morning paper in Olympia informed readers about the kidnapping, the ransom note, and the fact that bureau agents had been seen arriving at the Tacoma airport. Later in the day, the *Seattle Times* told readers that Luke S. May was on the case.

The story quickly spread across the country. The *Boston Herald*, for example, displayed a subhead that said Hoover's "G-Men" had been called in.[4] As it happened, the fact that the ransom note arrived via the U.S. Postal Service was a violation of federal laws on extortion. That gave bureau agents all the justification they needed.

Coincidentally, the action-packed movie *G Men*, starring James Cagney, was then nearing the end of its run in Seattle. The show was the first big production to glamorize the role of Hoover's men in fighting crime. In the movie, Cagney played a new G-Man who undergoes the rigorous training required for every agent. The association between the movie and the Weyerhaeuser headlines should have pleased the director.

However, Cagney played his role with a cocky, wisecracking brashness that was the polar opposite of the image Hoover wanted for his agents. It was perhaps no accident that Hoover issued a firm declaration a few weeks later. Henceforth, the preferred term for his organization was the Federal Bureau of Investigation. His investigators were to be called FBI agents. Newspapers reported that Hoover considered the term "G-men" to be "undignified."[5]

Meanwhile, with no fingerprint clues, May began assessing the content of the ransom note. That proved to be quite revealing in the way certain words and phrases were used. Newell said that on "the second or third day,"[6] Luke made three prescient assertions. First, he declared, the leader of the kidnappers was an ex-convict. Key usage of underworld and prison jargon suggested that he had been in for bank robbery. Second, a couple was involved in the plot, probably a man and wife. And finally, May deduced that the conspirators had some connection with Salt Lake City. With that guidance, what we today would call "profiling," he and bureau agents soon developed a list of potential suspects.

Happily, the boy was released in the early morning hours of June 1. With him safe, officers began an intense hunt for the kidnappers. Federal agents had recorded the serial numbers of every bill in the ransom payment. Right away, small amounts began appearing in eastern Oregon and in Spokane. One purchase was a train ticket to Salt Lake City. Just over two weeks after the abduction, agents in Salt Lake City arrested Harmon Waley and his wife, Margaret. The husband was a convicted burglar and robber. He had met and married Margaret Thulin in Salt Lake City about eighteen months earlier. Caught with thousands of dollars of the ransom money, the couple soon confessed to their part in the kidnapping.

But the mastermind of the crime was one William Dainard. As May predicted, Dainard had served prison time for bank robbery. Police just missed catching Dainard in Ogden and then in Butte, Montana. He stayed free for another eleven months. While Dainard remained on the run, Harmon Waley pled guilty to federal kidnapping charges and was sentenced to forty-five years in prison. Margaret's defense attorney had her go on trial, claiming her role was coerced. She was found guilty of kidnapping and sentenced to twenty years in prison. (Both wanted to avoid being charged under a Washington State kidnapping law. That statute called for the death penalty unless the jury specifically voted for a lesser punishment.)

Federal agents finally tracked Dainard down in San Francisco. He pleaded guilty to a federal kidnapping charge and received a sixty-year prison sentence. Margaret spent thirteen years in prison, then divorced Harmon as soon as she was released. Harmon was paroled after twenty-eight years in prison. According to Newell, May tried very hard to keep his name out of the news on this case. But, by now, he was far too well known for that to succeed.

About the time a judge in Tacoma was deciding on a sentence for Margaret Whaley, May was at a meeting of the Northwest association of Sheriffs and Police in Seattle. He again was able to meet with his friend, FBI Inspector James Egan. During the meeting, for the first time, the association selected a new president. Luke May became president emeritus and chairman of the executive committee. May surely felt he needed to focus more on other commitments. That included his naval reserve duties and a new sideline.

Early in the year, *True Detective Mysteries* magazine had offered May space for a regular column. There, he would answer questions from readers about crime fighting. "Luke May's Department" proved immensely popular, and May found himself swamped with letters. Many asked the same, or similar questions, but Luke found a wide enough variety to offer a fascinating range of answers.

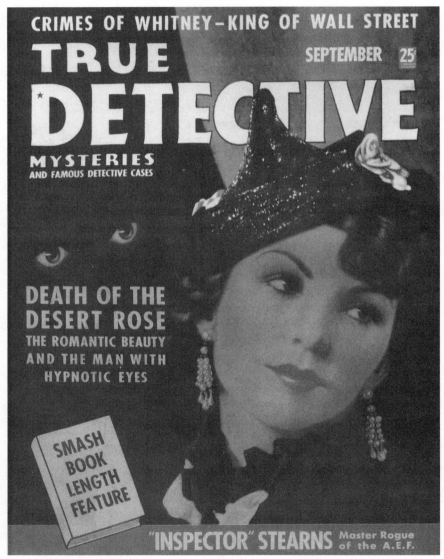

Figure 14.1. *True Detective Mysteries* Cover. *Source*: Author.

One reader asked about so-called truth serum. May answered that the term generally referred to certain inhibition-releasing drugs such as scopolamine. He noted that the method had been "fully developed by my friend, Dr. House of Ferris, Texas."[7] This referred to Dr. Robert E. House, a physician who had first proposed the idea in a paper presented in 1922. He noticed that his patients often spoke without inhibitions when influenced by such drugs. Such candor does not necessarily mean "true," of course. Rather the statements are what the speaker believes is true or thinks the interviewer wants to hear. In fact, House did not use the term "truth serum" at first. He began doing so only after newspaper writers popularized it.

Each month, May provided many answers:

"There is a decided variation in a person's signature over a period of time."[8]

"Many extravagant claims have been made relative to phrenology, but such claims have not been based on scientific fact."

"In the hands of one properly qualified to operate it, the lie detector is an invaluable aid to modern crime detection."

He usually provided additional background information and sometimes described cases where he himself had used a technique. May and the *True Detective* editor became friends, and they met face-to-face at least once during 1935. Somehow, the subject of turning some of May's cases into movie shorts came up. The editor said he had had "a long talk . . . with Norman H. Moray, who is head of the Shorts Department of Warner Brothers."[9] Unfortunately, he found that "the market was never worse than it is right now due, chiefly, to the universal practice of running, now, two full-length features at almost all the theaters." The editor suggested that May contact people in Hollywood directly. "Everything presented in New York has to be referred to their California offices anyhow." Luke did just that within a few months.

Along with his magazine column and association work, May logged fifty-seven cases for the year, including twelve death cases, with thirteen victims. A few death cases received heavy regional coverage, but only the Weyerhaeuser kidnapping made much news nationally. But even without the publicity, many of May's cases carried over into the following year and kept him busy in court.

Yet he also took time to help other law enforcement people. In early January, he received a letter from Inspector Forbes Cruickshank, a divisional commander for the Provincial Police in Vancouver, British Columbia. A medical doctor who did "considerable work for our Department"[10] wanted to visit May's facility to improve his background in crime science. As a personal favor, Cruickshank asked Luke to show him around. May agreed. The commander knew that May sometimes got called out of town with little or no notice. He said he had warned the doctor to phone ahead when he was ready to come.

A few weeks after that visit, the MacMillan publishing company released May's book, *Crime's Nemesis*. May said, "It is the purpose of this volume to reveal the so-called mysteries of criminology."[11] He used his own cases as examples. However, he went on, "I have tried to avoid burdensome details that would interest only the professional technician. In other words, it is not a technical treatise in which laboratory findings are allowed to overshadow the human story . . . that is the warp and woof of every crime."

Reviewers all across the country praised the book. A review in the *Daily Republican* in Springfield, Massachusetts, set the general tone. It assured readers that May's actual cases "rival in interest and suspense the imaginary adventures of the immortal Holmes."[12] The review concluded, "The book affords a clear description of the potent weapons used by scientific criminologists to combat lawlessness."

May soon began using the book in his talks to business and social clubs. He surely must have also mentioned it at the law enforcement meeting held in Portland that summer. The Northwest Association of Sheriffs and Police voted to change its name to one that more closely matched its scope. The organization became the "Pacific Coast International Association of Law Enforcement Officers," with members from Canada and Mexico.[13] May continued as president emeritus and served on the committee to plan the next association meeting.

Inspector Egan was also at the conference. He said that changes in federal law had, in his opinion, really started to curb the worst crime. Egan particularly liked legislation on bank robbery and the Lindbergh Law. A year earlier, Congress had made it a federal crime to rob a nationally chartered bank or a state bank that was part of the Federal Reserve system. That had greatly cut those offenses. In connection with the Lindbergh Law, he said, "The last big kidnaping we have had to deal with was the Weyerhaeuser case."[14]

In an interview with a reporter for *The Oregonian*, May agreed that the attention afforded by the federal kidnapping law had made a big difference. "Law enforcement is now receiving more support from the public than ever before," he said.[15] That's because, he went on, "No home was safe from this type of criminal." The reporter noted that, along with his president emeritus status, May was president of the Institute of Scientific Criminology. The institute, May's book, and his articles all served to educate the public as well as people in law enforcement. In fact, the curriculum offered by the institute was one of the few correspondence courses in crime science approved by Canadian Departments of Education.

At about this time, the field had finally received some notice from higher education in the state. The University of Washington had been teaching a few summer courses in criminology for four or five years. Now, they planned to have a full four-year police school. To kick off the plan, the university asked August Vollmer to speak. In his remarks, the Berkeley police chief said, "Within a few years there is no reason why the Seattle Police Department should not have 600 Luke S. Mays . . . and 600 J. Edgar Hoovers."[16]

Later in the year, Washington State College (now University) also spelled out plans to teach courses in criminology. Within a year or so, both schools had classes scheduled. Five years down the road, Washington State would create a Department of Police Science and Administration. Graduates trained by these programs would do much to make publicly funded crime labs a reality in the region.

It was perhaps no coincidence that two men May had trained left Seattle during this period. John L. Harris seems to have been the first to go. Recall that he had started his own detective service in late 1924, with offices right across the street from where May was at that time. During the spring of 1936, the *Seattle Times* reported that members of the Montlake Community Club had given a farewell party for Harris and his family, who had just moved to Los Angeles. The Montlake District was, and is, an upscale residential area located south of the University of Washington campus. The Harrises were longtime residents, and John L. had served as president of the Montlake Community Club.

Edward Newell probably left Seattle not long after that. On the first of July, he sent Luke a letter from his hometown in New Hampshire. Newell had returned there after visiting crime labs from Washington, DC, north to Boston. He had also talked to and observed some of the technical experts in the region. Newell wrote, "Most of the experts . . . are not very good witnesses and do not seem to have any resourcefulness when they lose out on a point."[17]

He had tried to visit James Egan at the FBI, but the agent was away on a case. Newell did meet with Wilmer T. Souder at the National Bureau of Standards (now the National Institute of Standards and Technology). Souder was one of the eight experts who testified that Hauptmann had written the Lindbergh ransom notes. Newell said, "I . . . find that he is going over to Europe on the 16th of July."[18] Souder told Newell that Colonel Goddard was also in Europe, "collecting data for a new book." Newell himself traveled to Europe later in the month. He visited police schools and labs in Edinburgh, London, Brussels, Berlin, and Vienna. In each case, Newell's association with Luke S. May gave him entrée, because, Ed said, "he was recognized everywhere."[19]

Newell's statement was confirmed later the same year. May received a letter from the director of the Scientific Academy of the Supreme Police of "Jugo Slavia" in Belgrade. The director's English was somewhat labored but deeply sincere. He expressed the academy's "true hearted appreciation" for May's help in setting up a rigorous curriculum in crime science. It was, he wrote, "worthy of your reputation as a world famous educator."[20]

Newell had intended to stay in Europe until the following spring. However, it was not a good time to be on the continent. A few months earlier, Germany had reoccupied the Rhineland. Then, about the time Ed sailed, the Spanish Civil War broke out. By the end of summer, tensions were high all over Europe, and experts worried that some incident might escalate out of control. Newell returned to New York from Southampton, England, in mid-October.

A few weeks after Newell's return, May's most prominent death case for the year went to court. The previous fall, police officers Trent Sickles and Theodore Stevens had responded to a reported burglary at a tavern in northern Seattle. Thinking the crooks had already fled, they entered the building and walked into an ambush. Sickles died on the spot from two shotgun blasts in the back of the head and neck. Stevens, hit in the belly by a .38-caliber slug, died on the operating table that afternoon.

Aside from a set of burglar's tools, investigators had little to go on. The .38-caliber Colt revolver that killed Stevens had been stolen from behind the bar and was found in the street just around the corner. The sawed-off 12-gauge shotgun used to kill Sickles was found next to the body. Police and May strongly suspected a professional job. And, indeed, underworld connections led them to three suspects. They were members of a gang that stole slot machines for resale to area taverns and nightclubs. (The devices were illegal under city and state gambling laws, but no one paid much attention to that.)

May's verification of the murder weapons was, by now, routine. His agents and the police then tried to link the shotgun and the burglar's tools to the accused men. That proved difficult, but, fortunately, the felon who shot Stevens was overcome by remorse and turned state's evidence to implicate the other two. He received a life sentence but served only thirteen years. The man who fired the shotgun died on the gallows a few days less than three years after the officers were murdered. The third man died in prison.

Newspapers in the West extensively covered the Sickles-Stevens murders and subsequent trial, but the case was largely ignored in the rest of the country. And in 1936, May logged the smallest number of cases—and the fewest death cases—he had had since he began keeping records in 1920. Including the Sickles-Stevens murders, they handled just seven deaths, with eight victims. Still, along with his cases, May continued to write monthly columns for *True Detective Mysteries* magazine. One letter asked about a system that could "classify eyes in the same manner as fingerprints."[21] That referred to the "Retinascope," May replied. The device had been created by

Drs. Carleton Simon and Isadore Goldstein. "On my last trip to New York, I spent an evening with Dr. Simon. I am convinced that his method provides a positive means of identification."[22]

Carleton Simon was a psychiatrist who had studied in Vienna and Paris and later went into criminology. Isadore Goldstein was a practicing ophthalmologist. In 1935, the two devised a way to identify people by the pattern of blood vessels in their eyes. They then built a system to record the patterns for photo matching. Today, the retinal scanner is a common part of biometric identification.

Other readers asked about bulletproof vests, a matchlock pistol, powder burns, and detecting altered brands on cattle and horses. One reader said he was a professional knife thrower. Did May know "of any one ever having been killed with a thrown knife?"[23] Luke answered, "There are . . . countless incidents of record in the provincial constabularies where death has been caused by the throwing of knives in African tribes." He also assured the reader that he knew personally of people in the United States who had been injured by thrown knifes. May then provided a little background. For some Africans, such knives were "regular implements of warfare." Some even had flat multi-pointed blades that were "thrown with a spinning motion."

Besides the regular column, the magazine also published articles about two of May's cases. One was the five-part story about the Bremerton Massacre. May's column and the publication of *Crime's Nemesis* sparked another opportunity to publicize scientific crime detection.

The story began about the time of the Weyerhaeuser kidnapping and the release of the movie *G-Men,* both discussed above. Radio producer Phillips H. Lord had been looking for a new program concept. Lord saw what a hit the movie had become, so he created his own weekly radio version, also called *G-Men.* With the support of the U.S. attorney general, he based his scripts on FBI case files. But J. Edgar Hoover was less than thrilled and edited the material with a heavy hand. Lord then decided that there would not be enough acceptable FBI cases to sustain a weekly program for the long term. He gave it up after just thirteen episodes.

But listener response showed that the "true-crime" concept was sound. Lord unveiled a new program, *Gang Busters,* in early 1936. Each show opened with blaring sirens, machine guns firing, racing automobiles, and more. (Hence the phrase, "came on like gangbusters.") Scripts were now based on law enforcement cases from all across the country. The show was wildly popular; it would stay on the air for more than twenty years.

After a few months, when success seemed assured, Lord cast around for other ideas that exploited the popularity of true-crime drama. One notion was the crime lab itself. Lord's staff quickly came up with "Dr. Luke May" as one of the "outstanding crime laboratory experts in the country."[24] He arranged a meeting with May at the Waldorf Astoria Hotel in New York City. They talked for about two hours. In a later court appearance on another matter, Lord claimed that May offered to move his lab to New York to support the show. That seems highly unlikely, but May perhaps did offer to open an alternate lab in the East.

Lord said he would test the concept on the air and get back to May. Far too much ahead of its time, no such crime lab series made it onto radio. Still, four *Gang Busters* episodes definitely contained material associated with May, including the Weyerhaeuser kidnapping and the Bremerton Massacre. At least two others probably benefited from his contributions. However, the show focused on the lawmen who chased criminals and made the actual arrests, so May's work would have been in the background.

May also explored the *True Detective* editor's suggestion about having some of his cases turned into movie shorts. As it happened, May had an in-law in the business. Folmar Blangsted (Pedersen), who then worked at Columbia Pictures, was cousin to Luke's wife, Helen. (Entering the United States in 1924, he dropped the "Pedersen" on his naturalization papers.) Blangsted had most likely visited the Mays in Seattle. In any case, in October, Luke wrote a letter making Blangsted his agent to the movie industry. Blangsted was to be his "sole representative with relation to the matter of producing a series of scientific detective scenarios based on plots" developed from May's cases.[25]

But in early December, Folmar sent May a letter that said, "Since your last visit to Los Angeles I have been promoted to full directorship."[26] Thus, due to the time demands of his "first solo production," Blangsted would not be able to do anything on May's project for a while. He closed with, "Please give my kindest regards to Aunt Josie, Cousin Helen and your little girl."

May replied that he was "very much elated on learning that you had received this well deserved promotion."[27] Blangsted directed two films for Columbia, both low-budget Westerns. After World War II, he worked for Warner Bros. as a film editor. May, of course, got involved in war-related matters. The two would not reopen business correspondence until many years later.

In early 1937, May's activities did receive some publicity from the popular broadcast media of the day. John Nesbitt, a top radio personality, featured Luke and his work for one of the earliest episodes of *The Passing Parade*. The *Parade* focused on bizarre-but-true events or interesting individuals. His approach was somewhat similar to the more familiar *Ripley's Believe It or Not!* The newspaper item about the upcoming show quoted May: "You can't walk into a room and out of it again without leaving some trace behind that may identify you."[28]

By the spring of 1937, May was heavily involved in his naval reserve duties. That work was largely behind the scenes, but his naval affiliation sometimes appeared in the news. Thus, a *Seattle Times* item noted that "Lieu-tenant Commander and Mrs. Luke S. May" were among the guests of honor at a banquet and reception hosted by the Lafayette Lodge of the Masonic Order.[29] A retired navy admiral and several captains from the navy and coast guard were among the other guests of honor. The newspaper did not mention any specific reason for the festivities.

Another event during the spring made a much bigger splash, largely due to Luke May's fame. In late March, a photograph of the Mays' new home on Summit Avenue dominated the real estate page of the *Seattle Times*. The article about the purchase described the property as "one of the well-known homes on Capitol Hill."[30] With timbered ceilings, solid oak paneling, and mahogany trim, the four-level house could rightfully be called a small man-sion. The formal dining room was even blessed with a spectacular chandelier. The home is perched on the escarpment so the rear overlooks the south end of Lake Union. Daughter Patricia remembered the views as being "simply breathtaking."[31]

The lowest level contained the usual house service areas. However, most of that level was taken up by offices, laboratories (including a darkroom), a tool room, and other work areas. The largest single area was a room equipped with individualized worktables. Patricia described that space as Luke's crimi-nology classroom.

Figure 14.2. May Home on Summit Avenue. *Source*: **May-Reid Records.**

Besides buying the fancy home, the Mays went upscale in another way. Records show that Luke joined the Seattle Yacht Club sometime during the year. His listing in the club yearbook included the note that the Mays owned a boat called the *Bonnie Doon*. It's not clear when they had sold the *Lady Luck* and bought the new boat. The *Doon* was a substantial vessel of some forty-six feet, powerful enough for ocean cruising, with a full galley just aft of the pilothouse. Bunks in the forward area provided sleeping space for several people, with quarters for four more behind the galley.

Throughout this period, Luke May's department flourished. One reader asked, "How in the world could someone empty a pistol and miss everything?" That is, "without shooting a man full of holes only a few feet distant?"[32] May replied, "This is a question that is often propounded to me." In his experience, all but the best-trained shooters could go awry in the "stress of excitement." May described one case where a man fired seven shots at a distance of "not more than six feet" and only punched holes in his intended victim's clothing. May himself was a skilled and experienced shooter with both rifle and handgun. He won many awards in competitive shooting, including the once-in-a-lifetime Members Medal from the National Rifle Association.

An investigator in New York City asked a real-world question. He had had a coded message from one of his own cases deciphered. Everything was clear enough, except a block of three letters that seemed to be "g-o-w." He had been unable to find the word in any dictionary. Did that mean anything, or was the deciphering at fault? In reply, May wondered if the message related "to smuggling activities or illicit dealing in narcotics."[33] In underworld slang, "gow" referred to "opium." The term was probably based on the name of a river in China.

In other columns, May discussed truth serum again, the lie detector, cobra venom, and silencers for pistols. One reader wondered if a person could be identified by his or her voice, and if such evidence would be accepted in court. May replied that the issue had been dealt with on a case-by-case basis. As a general rule, voice recognition was considered unreliable and chancy. But some courts had admitted such evidence, leaving it up to the jury to decide.

Another reader wondered if anyone made an automatic pistol that ejected the empty shells out the left side. May told his readers that a line of automatics made by Walther, a German arms company, all ejected to the left. He then related a hold-up case where one eyewitness said the bandit's weapon ejected to the left. Police then discounted what that witness had to say because they "knew" the person was wrong about the gun. Of course, when May got the shells and bullets from the crime scene, he quickly saw that the witness had been totally correct.

May's ability to provide such details from his own cases was surely a big reason for the popularity of his column. After the lull in the previous year, May logged a more normal caseload in 1937. His total of fifty-three included fourteen death cases with nineteen victims.

In August, May logged a most interesting death case that was probably unique in his career. Some months earlier, furniture business owner William O. Azling had died suddenly in Portland, Oregon. Azling was only fifty-two years old and seemed in good health, yet little was done initially to explain his death. Family members finally contracted with May to study the case, wondering if Azling might have been poisoned. Luke learned that Azling, beset by the usual Depression-era worries, often used the sleep aid Veronal. But people who take the drug regularly build up a tolerance for it, so they have to take larger and larger amounts. May concluded that the victim had probably died from an accidental overdose. His report said, "Many of the cases of poisoning reported have resulted from taking, at too-short intervals, two or more doses."[34]

That same month, May was called to investigate the bizarre death of William Arnold in Mason County. Five deer hunters were following a heavily overgrown trail through rough country about twenty miles north of Olympia. Suddenly one man's weapon went off, and the bullet drilled Arnold through the chest and wounded another man ahead of him. May closely interviewed the hunters, who all agreed that the lever action rifle that fired was in the proper safety position. May performed a number of tests and discovered that a thin branch could indeed thwart the mechanism and cause the gun to fire. The incident was ruled a tragic accident, and no charges were filed.

May had another interesting case two months later that, unfortunately, did not reach closure. Nineteen-year-old Ivan Jensen was walking his milk delivery route in North Seattle when a speeding car struck and fatally injured him. The auto also hit Jensen's dog, but the animal was less seriously hurt. Fresh headlight debris left at the scene marked the vehicle type as one of two Chevrolet models, which set off an intensive search all over the region. Eventually, the car, a 1931 Chevy sedan, was found abandoned on a mountain road southwest of Wenatchee. Sadly, no evidence remained to link the car, which had been stolen in Kittitas County, with any suspect.

Handling these and other cases prolonged a busy, successful run for Luke May. Newspaper reports had kept his name before the public. Articles about his cases in *True Detective Mysteries* magazine helped him reach a wider audience. His column and *Crime's Nemesis* were educating the public about scientific crime detection. Although the Hollywood connection fell through, it truly seemed that May's career was riding the crest of a wave.

But the wave was breaking. Academic institutions had entered the field in a big way. Plus, more and more publicly supported crime labs were being established. That meant that May's main clients might no longer need his services. In fact, May would never again log as many as fifty cases in a single year.

Worse yet, war was engulfing the world. The previous July, Japanese troops had staged a pretext to attack northeastern China, penetrating the Great Wall. By the end of November, Chinese forces had been expelled from Shanghai. The Japanese then began moving up the Yangtze River toward Nanking. The U.S. Navy gunboat *Panay* had been protecting American interests along the Yangtze for around a decade. Despite a large American flag painted on the top of the main cabin and an actual flag flying, Japanese aircraft attacked and sank the gunboat. Japanese officials claimed it was all a mistake and paid a substantial reparation.

A few days after the bombing, newspapers reported information that had probably been leaked to gauge public opinion. France and Great Britain planned to make key concessions to ease tensions in Europe. Since they viewed the *Anschluss*—German annexation of Austria—as inevitable, they would not raise a serious protest when it happened. They would also officially recognize the Italian conquest of Ethiopia. Of course, such appeasement only fueled the appetites of Hitler and Mussolini. But the moves seemed necessary at the time. With European tensions eased, "France and Britain could do something about Japanese aggression in the Far East."[35]

But with all that, knowledgeable observers felt that a major outbreak of war, somewhere, was inevitable. Some thought it would come in no more than two or three years. May was very likely among those of that opinion. In the next chapter, we will see that he began to cut his private work drastically as war drew closer.

$$\cdot\ 15\ \cdot$$

War Clouds Gather

*P*rivate criminologist May had plenty to worry about going into 1938. He had seven case files open, three of them deaths. However, *Lieutenant Commander* May had equally grave, if not worse, concerns. As will be discussed in the next chapter, he was serving as the assistant to the district intelligence officer of the Thirteenth Naval District, based in Seattle. He would have had access to confidential reports that said the attack on the USS *Panay* was deliberate. The continued Japanese bombing in and around Canton (Guangzhou) would have sharpened his sense of foreboding. Each step in this undeclared war heightened the chance of a larger conflict.

In any case, May still had to make a living, since he was not, technically, on active duty with the navy. By now, around half his cases involved questioned documents. One such case spent years in litigation, even before May entered the process. The key event took place nearly three years before the court drama came to a head in the spring of 1938. The steamship *Denali* had carried freight and passengers from Seattle to various Alaskan ports. But one night, just before three o'clock in the morning, the *Denali* ran aground on a known reef in a channel between islands about sixty miles from Ketchikan, Alaska. No one was hurt, but the ship and its payload were a total loss.

Two-and-a-half years later, the *Denali*'s owners asked a federal court in Seattle to void around $375,000 in claims for the lost cargo. The reef did appear on channel charts, but currents between the islands and around the obstacle were known to be tricky and dangerous. The owners blamed poor navigation—that is, pilot error—for the accident. Under their interpretation of maritime law, the captain and crew were responsible because the company had passed control over to them.

May was hired by attorneys for the major claimant shortly after the owners filed their request in federal court. His specific task was to examine the SS *Denali* logbook. May's study of the ship's log apparently did not find any untoward incidents recorded until the crisis itself. However, he did discover two key points about the voyage.

First, during the days *en route* before the incident, only two mates had been responsible for navigating the vessel. That violated U.S. maritime law, which required that three certified navigators share that duty for each day. The shortage of trained and experienced navigators led to the second problem. The intent of the law was that each officer should average no more than eight hours in a given day. But May's assessment showed that the *Denali* navigators had averaged twelve hours per day for several days in succession. Still, the first judge to hear the case felt these laws were open to interpretation. At the very least, those apparent violations seemed to be the responsibility of the captain and crew. In April 1938, the judge supported the company's position, that they were not liable for the cost of the lost cargo.

Naturally, the losers appealed. During that process, testimony showed that company "established practice" dictated the illegal schedule. The appeals court frankly wondered "how long the [ship's officers] . . . would have held their jobs if they failed 'customarily' and 'voluntarily' to violate the provisions of this safety statute and . . . serve over its required time."[1] The appeals court reversed the original decision about a year later. A year after that, a federal court rejected a counter-appeal. So, more than five years after the incident, the company and the claimants finally had to negotiate some sort of settlement. Those results never made the newspapers or May's files.

May recorded his first 1938 death case in the early spring. Twenty-three-year-old Clara (Compton) Richardson had been rushed from a Seattle hotel to Harborview Hospital. She died a few days later from scalding burns on much of her body. Her husband claimed she'd gotten hysterical after being denied a sleeping pill and had thrown herself into the tub. But an autopsy showed that Clara had also sustained multiple bruises, a black eye, and a fractured wrist. Those injuries plus evidence from the hotel room allowed May to reconstruct the beating she had taken before being thrown into a tub of scalding water.

Further investigation revealed that the dead woman may have only *thought* she was married to the man. The ceremony had been performed in Mexico and documentation was lacking. It eventually came out that, in Portland, he and his sister had a stable of four young women who may have been forced or tricked into prostitution. Police suspected, but could not prove, that they had killed his young wife when she refused to be part of a comparable Seattle operation.

The case went to court with a catchy newspaper title of the "bathtub murder" and racy stories of "white slavery."[2] Yet despite all that, only papers on the Pacific Coast made much of it. Reporters speculated that the couple's defense attorneys focused more on avoiding the death penalty than on proving them innocent. In that, they succeeded. Both the husband and sister received life sentences.

Through all of this, May continued to work on questioned documents cases. In fact, the company logged a dozen such cases by early spring. In that regard, May would surely have been interested in a new book from documents guru Albert S. Osborn. The book, titled *The Mind of the Juror as Judge of the Facts*, was not strictly about document examination. Instead, Osborn assessed the entire jury trial system, based on his years of experience as an expert witness.

Too often, Osborn felt, lawyers and witnesses considered only the bare facts of the evidence and not how the testimony would affect "the mind of the juror."[3] To provide context, Osborn turned a spotlight on the entire process, from jury selection to the judge's final instructions. He found strengths and weaknesses at every step and illustrated key points with anecdotes from his own cases. Law school journals across the country reviewed Osborn's book. All recommended it to practicing attorneys and to students. May had himself spent many hours in the witness box. He no doubt found another point of view interesting and informative.

As a matter of fact, criminology and its pioneers experienced quite a few key events during 1938. The Crime Detection Laboratory at Northwestern University had struggled financially from the start. It was finally sold to the city of Chicago after protracted negotiations during the year. Calvin Goddard had himself left the lab three years earlier, having received a Guggenheim fellowship. A year after leaving the lab, he published *A History of Firearm Identification*. Besides his consulting and research on another book, Goddard also presented lectures around the country. In late May 1938, he gave a talk to the Ohio Gun Collectors Association.

That same spring, John A. Larson was giving lectures about the polygraph. By 1938, he had become vocal in his rejection of the term "lie detector." At a talk in Detroit, he declared, "It is essential to realize that this testing does not detect lies."[4] Rather, the grilling uncovers "painful complexes" in the subject's psyche, which may have little or no link to the matter being investigated. That was why Larson strongly opposed any notion of using the results in court.

Another pioneer in the West, Harry Caldwell, was also doing a lot of lecturing. He had retired from the Oakland police and opened a private practice. Besides talks to civic and business groups, Caldwell was on the program the 1938 annual meeting of the California Division, International Association for Identification. Caldwell was identified as the dean emeritus of the division.

August Vollmer had also retired. He and his wife took a world tour and then he published three books on police work and organization. In 1938 he returned to teach a summer course on police organization and administration at UC-Berkeley. Three years after that, he founded what became first the Society for the Advancement of Criminology and then the American Society of Criminology. In keeping with Vollmer's primary interests, the society emphasized practical, hands-on education and training for police officers.

As Vollmer reduced his activities, Berkeley pioneer Paul L. Kirk came to the forefront. Kirk had begun criminological work a few years after he became an instructor at UC-Berkeley. In 1938, he developed crucial evidence in a brutal murder case. By then, Dr. Kirk was the acknowledged leader of the criminology program at the university. Kirk would contribute significantly to making the field a respected academic and scientific discipline. In fact, he initiated the use of the term "criminalistics" to described what practitioners studied. That is now the preferred term for the collection, analysis, and presentation of crime scene evidence.

Figure 15.1.   Chief August Vollmer, Berkeley. *Source:* **Library of Congress, LC-USZ62-69954.**

May's other western contemporaries—Harris, Cross, Sellers, and Heinrich—all had newsworthy cases during 1938. Harris traced a libelous pamphlet distributed during a bare-knuckles political campaign in Orange County, California. But the document more or less backfired on the originators so nothing much came of the brouhaha.[5] In late 1938, Edward Crossman testified in the shooting death of a sailor in San Diego. His match of the fatal bullet to a weapon carried by a suspect helped convict the shooter.

Clark Sellers and Edward Heinrich worked a case together. Early in the year, a bomb severely injured a private detective investigating links between Los Angeles officials and widespread vice. Sellers and Heinrich quickly found evidence that pointed to two members of a secret "spy squad" within the LAPD. Conviction of the two, along with other evidence, led to a recall election that installed a new reform mayor for the city.

Investigators like May, Osborn, Sellers, and Heinrich were well known and had little trouble finding cases. As a newcomer, Ed Newell found the situation quite different. Newell did contribute to discussions about the formation of a state police force for New Hampshire. The blueprint he published in a Manchester newspaper clearly drew from May's work with the Oregon State Police. By 1938, the force was in full operation.

Newell asked May about doing cases for insurance companies. May replied bluntly. In his opinion, insurance companies were "the biggest chiselers in obtaining investigation data that there are in existence."[6] He also said, "Do not be misled by promises unless they are backed up by something more concrete in a material way."

Thus, in the summer of 1938, Newell told Luke that he was probably going to look for work away from general criminology. In that regard, he felt his training on the West Coast actually counted against him, even though he was from New England. Some years later, he commented about "provincial attitudes" among Easterners at that time.[7] That snobbery kept them from "deigning to call upon a Westerner for any skill." In fact, in the 1938 letter to May he also wrote, "I am impressed with the need of a formal degree."[8] He went on, "It is merely the fact of a degree, rather than what may be behind it that seems so important."

He asked for suggestions from May and then commented, "Patricia must be very grown-up by now. Bring along a picture the next time you come East."[9] With May's help and contacts, Newell pieced together enough consulting work to get by until the United States entered World War II. He spent the war as a combat photographer in North Africa and then Europe. After the war, he became an inventor and management consultant. Through all that, he remained a close friend of Luke and his family.

May continued to process about one death case each month. Also, during that summer, he gave a talk at the annual meeting of the Pacific Coast International Association of Law Enforcement Officers. More than a thousand delegates attended the conference, which was held in Vancouver, British Columbia.

Besides that, Luke May's department still drew an amazing mix of questions to *True Detective Mysteries* magazine. One reader in St. Louis wondered if May had any advice on protecting a car against professional auto thieves. May replied that they considered it "inadvisable to set out here the different techniques used by car thieves."[10] That meant he could not be very specific. However, he went on, "I personally know that the police department in your city is well equipped to furnish you with first-hand information relative to auto theft prevention."

Many readers asked about reading character from the head (phrenology, again), handwriting, or the palm of the hand. May discounted all such unscientific methods. Certainly, May averred, "Criminals do not have a particular type of palm pattern."[11] Another reader had seen a passing reference in May's column to "the Atcherly [*sic*] method of crime detection." He wondered what that was. May said that referred to "a system of identifying criminals by the peculiar method in which their crimes are committed. It is now in general use and is called the M.O., or *Modus Operandi* system."

Figure 15.2.   Lead-in to "Luke May's Department." *Source*: May-Reid Records.

The method of operation approach to crime fighting came into use in the first decade of the twentieth century. Sir Llewelyn W. Atcherley devised the first system while he was chief constable in Yorkshire, England. He based it on the fact that, by and large, professional thieves tended to fall into habits. Around 1913, Atcherley issued a pamphlet describing his approach. He divided the facts about a theft into ten categories. One was the entry route—by way of window, door, vent, or whatever. That usually went along with the means of entry, such as a lock pick, crowbar, and so on. And criminals often had a preferred target—house, apartment, or business. The system proved amazingly effective and soon spread around the world.

Another reader asked him about the poison curare. Where might it be obtained, and how did one detect its use? Naturally, May only wrote broadly about South American sources where it was prepared by "a secret formula known only to the natives." The resulting chemical makeup differed from place to place, although the active agent was always some form of the toxin "curarine." May said, "There are very definite chemical methods of detecting curarine."[12]

Actually, poisons were seldom a factor in May's investigations since more than three-quarters of his death cases involved firearms. That made 1938 an anomaly because fully half the death cases did *not* involve firearms. Among those were the "bathtub murder" and one that had a tragic connection to great events of the world. On a Saturday night in late November, an unidentified Asian asked to see Kimigi Ichikawa, the owner of a Japanese restaurant in Walla Walla. When the owner stepped outside, the stranger stabbed him to death and then fled. A few days later, Chinese immigrant Lee Yuen was found hanging in his home. May was called to verify a suicide note that said he had killed the Japanese man in "revenge for my family. Revenge for my country."[13]

By that time, Japan and China had been at war for well over a year. Two sons of the Chinese man had been killed in the failed defense of Canton, and other members of his family in China were starving. Just a week before the Walla Walla murder, newspapers had reported heavy bombing of civilian targets in several Chinese cities. It had all proven too much for the father. The article that reported the "revenge" note concluded, "A city in Eastern Washington counts two deaths in the Sino-Japanese war."[14]

Although the number of death cases May handled stayed high for the year, his total number of cases dropped off to just forty-one. That caseload would fall by another third in 1939, death cases even more drastically. In fact, May would not record his first death case until mid-spring. Before then, he had logged a half dozen questioned documents cases. He was also called to testify at an opium-smuggling trial, bringing to the fore yet another analytical technique. Three crewmen of the steamship *Don Jose*, based in the Philippines, had been arrested in Portland. A team of U.S. customs agents discovered about 130 pounds of pipe opium hidden in the ship's coal bunker. Valued at $70,000 to $80,000 (roughly $2 million today), the find was reported to be the "second largest opium seizure here in forty years."[15]

The opium had been divided into one-tael packets. (A tael weighs about one and one-third ounces.) Packed into a number of tin cans, the stash had come aboard in a large suitcase. May not only verified that the packets were indeed opium, he also found that some of the powder had leaked into the suitcase.

The crewmen actually had customers in the Philippines but had been unable to sneak their shipment ashore when the *Don Jose* last made port in Manila. They had planned to try again on their next call there, but the drug bust by customs found their cache. At no point while they were in the United States did the men try to get the opium off the *Don Jose*, which sailed under a foreign flag. Once these facts were clearly set, a federal judge ordered a directed verdict of acquittal on the smuggling charge.

Almost two months passed after this trial before May logged his first death case. The victims were Benjamin "Ben" Sutton, aged forty-seven, and his wife, Willia, a year younger. Their badly burned bodies had been found in the remnants of a tent in a rustic area about six miles north of Redmond. Their new home, a log cabin, was under construction nearby. The Suttons had lived in the area less than a year. They were comfortably well off, so authorities suspected robbery as a motive. But the deputy sheriff who handled the case fixated on the notion that the event had been a murder-suicide. He lost control of the crime scene, and intruders made off with a motorcycle, two bicycles, and several other items.

By the time the county coroner's office brought May into the case, it was more likely than not that crucial clues had been lost. An autopsy showed that both victims had been shot in the back of the head with a .22-caliber rifle found at the scene. But lung damage suggested that Ben had been still breathing when the fire started. Only special pleading could sustain a murder-suicide scenario. The case made a brief flare across the country but then dropped from sight. Papers in the Puget Sound area covered the case longer but tended to focus on the jurisdictional disputes among county authorities.

May's name now appeared in the newspapers more than ever before in items not involving his cases or talks. Early in the year, the *Seattle Times* noted that May had introduced a guest speaker to a meeting at the Washington Athletic Club. The speaker was director of the Baltimore Crime Commission. During the course of his talk, the director took a moment to commend May for his work in scientific crime detection.

Besides such business-related news, Luke and Helen also appeared in the society pages. Luke showed up as one of the organizers of a benefit circus performance sponsored by the Shriners. Later, he and Helen were identified among the crowd at a school festival where daughter Patricia appeared as part of the cast. A month after that, they attended a graduation event at the school. Luke was also the toastmaster at an awards banquet for the National Sojourners. The Sojourners are an organization for Masons who are serving, or have served, in the U.S. armed forces.

In her memoir, Patricia recalled that Luke and Helen also entertained with "smaller very elegant catered dinner parties."[16] Most of these were connected to May's work as an officer in the naval reserve and were not publicized in the newspapers. "Mother never really enjoyed all this," Patricia said. Since Helen had to deal with bouts of depression all her life, that was probably an understatement. Still, Patricia went on, she "carried it off with seeming aplomb." Luke himself brought a considerable *savoir-faire* to these occasions, especially as a mixologist. Patricia admired his flair in taking care of his guests with their preferred beverages. "Margaritas, in particular," were a specialty, she said.

Sometimes, the Mays were invited to events sponsored by other navy personnel. Patricia recalled attending a fancy luncheon aboard the battleship USS *Tennessee* while it was docked in Seattle. That would have been in July 1939, when she was six years old. The battleship's skipper, Captain Damon E. Cummings, was a friend of Luke and Helen, and the families even exchanged Christmas gifts. Patricia's attendance would have been quite a treat for her. In keeping with the times, she was normally introduced to guests and then whisked off to bed or some supervised activity.

Except for the naval reserve connection, it's not clear why the Mays joined the social whirl at a time when Luke was reducing his caseload. Still, even with all that, his regular work did continue. That, of course, included his ongoing self-education. In early summer, Professor Balthazard, last mentioned in chapter 6, and his research group presented a crucial paper at the Congress of Forensic Medicine in Paris. They had completed a long study of bloodstain patterns, extending and refining the work Piotrowski had done decades earlier. Their experiments tried to better relate the shape of a stain to the size of the drop, how fast it was traveling, and the angle at which it hit a surface. They also tried to determine how different surfaces—wood, cloth, and so forth—affected how a drop spread out when it hit. All of this would have been of great interest to May.

Oddly enough, May addressed a question about bloodstain patterns in a summer issue of *True Detective Mysteries*. That had to be a coincidence since he would have written the "Department" column at least a month or two before Balthazard's paper came out. The questioner had read "in a scientific journal of a method purportedly invented by you" called "pinning and threading."[17] The method, May explained, used pins placed at the ends of several elongated bloodstains. Threads tied to the pins were then stretched backwards along the axes. The point where the threads converged showed roughly where the drops had originated. The method took much time and care because overlaid stain patterns might have come from different blows.

A reader in San Francisco found himself connected with a case where opium was involved. He wondered how much material one needed to actually "prove it to be opium." May described the *Don Jose* smuggling case, including the discovery of a tiny amount of powder in the suitcase lining. Thus, May concluded, "The presence of opium may be detected from microscopic particles."[18]

While May usually answered serious questions like these, his column was not without a leavening of humor. Sometimes this came in answers to novel and short story writers, who asked about some exotic clue. In an earlier column, a would-be crime author wanted to know about blood evidence. Could he somehow have it point to a certain individual? Perhaps there was some "slow tropical fever" that marked the blood. Of course, in those days long before DNA evidence, none of that was possible. May remarked, "I have often wanted to do in some of my real cases what you are trying to do in fiction."[19]

Dry humor aside, the fall of 1939 was an ominous time for the world at large. The Sino-Japanese conflict seemed to be in a lull, but new flare-ups could be expected at any time. In Europe, Germany and the Soviet Union had completed the partition of Poland. France and Great Britain had declared war on Germany, but there was essentially no military activity on land in the west. Britain had imposed a blockade on Germany, and that did lead to clashes at sea. And on November 5, newspapers across the country reported that Congress planned to authorize a massive naval building program. The chairman of the naval affairs committee said, "We are determined to keep war away from our shores."[20]

During the week that followed, one of Luke May's most unusual questioned documents cases got under way. The first odd point was that it went into court at all. The second oddity was how long and involved the court proceedings turned out to be. Events began with the death in Seattle of Russell Fisk in early 1938. He was just thirty-nine years old. Planning on a medical career, Fisk served in the ambulance corps during World War I. Poor health dogged him after the war, but he married and fathered a son in 1922. Then, the increasing onset of multiple sclerosis made it difficult for Fisk to hold a regular job. His wife divorced him, apparently in the mid-1920s. After a period of training, he tried to sell real estate, even opening his own agency.

For a while, he lived with his mother. (His parents had divorced when Russell was a child.) But they parted around 1928.

About a year later, an old high-school friend, Miss Viola Goehring, invited him to move into the small house where she and her brother lived. She was a vocational education teacher, but the demands of taking care of Fisk eventually forced her to quit. In 1934, Russell's father, a wealthy Utah physician, died. After some litigation, Russell received a bequest of nearly $450,000. That amount had been reduced to about $200,000 by the time of Fisk's death. In his will, Fisk left that money to Goehring, with token amounts to his mother, ex-wife, and son. His son had received a trust fund from the estate of Russell's father.

Both his mother and his ex-wife contested the will. Goehring's attorney contracted with May to examine and authenticate both the will and a host of supporting documents. The will was indeed valid, and the other items supported Russell's intention to reward Goehring. In mid-January, the *Seattle Times* reported, "A total of 679 exhibits have been entered in the case, which has been on trial for nine weeks and is expected to continue an additional two weeks."[21]

That total later rose to 871 exhibits. Finally, after not two but *eleven* weeks of further litigation, the judge upheld the bequest to Goehring. Remarking on the many years of devoted care she had provided, the judge said, "It is hardly necessary to add that a service so loyal as well as intelligent can hardly be procured by money alone."[22]

May logged just twenty-six cases in 1939, by far the smallest number since 1920. Only four of those, including the Sutton murders, were death cases. And, as noted above, publicity about the Sutton case quickly died down. But May's next death case had both national and international ramifications. On the night of January 5, 1940, a young mother, Laura Law, was found dead in the living room of her Aberdeen home. She had been bludgeoned on the head and then stabbed in the chest with what appeared to have been a narrow-bladed knife.

Two factors made this death more than a sad domestic tragedy. First, Laura was married to Richard "Dick" Law, a leader in the militant arm of the labor union movement. Second, she had been born in Finland. Her parents—both Finnish—had lived in the United States for a number of years and got married in Aberdeen. But the mother had returned to Finland to give birth to Laura. When police arrived at the scene, they found that the main rooms had been ransacked. However, the intruder had not awakened the Laws' infant son, who was sleeping in another room. By this time, Luke May was heavily involved with his naval intelligence work. Even so, he agreed to serve as a consultant and to analyze what physical evidence officers found.

Right away, Law declared that one of his many enemies had murdered his wife to get back at him. When he named names, police sent officers to question them. And, indeed, Richard Law did have many enemies. He was involved in a maelstrom of conflicts: trade unions versus business, Communists versus anti-Communists, and even ethnic separations. Worse yet, each of those factions had fractured into splinter groups.

Law was on the executive board of the International Woodworkers of America (IWA). The IWA sided with the more militant elements of the labor movement. Some IWA members and many of its leaders were Communists, including Law, according to police records. However, many IWA members were strongly anti-Communist. Thus, Law had enemies in his own organization as well as in the less-militant union groups. Naturally, he could also count on enemies in the business community, whether they were anti-union or anti-Communist (or both).

Still, the husband is almost always the prime suspect in such cases. Investigators soon found a possible other woman, who worked at union headquarters in Seattle. However, a relationship was never confirmed by independent evidence, like a motel receipt or some such. Thus, we will simply identify the woman as "Rachel." Two of her childhood friends testified at the inquest that she and Dick had been carrying on an affair. They also asserted that there was an understanding that the two would marry if Laura would give Dick a divorce.

Rachel, however, denied those stories and accused the authorities of character assassination. According to other witnesses, Dick and Laura got along fine. They only argued—apparently in a friendly manner—about the finer points of their mutual left-wing views. And finally, Law's union colleagues gave him a solid alibi for the night of the murder. May and the police found what might have been the blunt weapon, but it could never be firmly linked to the crime. They also found fingerprints that could not be identified as any of the family or regular visitors. But at this point, the normal police aspects of the investigation blew up into a *cause célèbre*.

Many of the competing groups noted above tried to use the case to further their own agendas. That raised so many red herrings and side issues, it was hard to sort out the relevant evidence. Naturally, this furor made headlines all across the country. On top of everything else, some five weeks before Laura's murder, the Soviet Union had invaded Finland.

That split the Finnish-American community. "Red" Finns, not necessarily pro-Communist, supported the move. They saw it as a necessary measure to protect Leningrad (St. Petersburg) against a likely German attack. "White" Finns, some of whom were themselves Communists, protested the capture of sovereign Finnish territory. Laura was apparently in the latter group. It was unclear whether she was a Communist Party member. However, she was at least a fellow traveler, someone who supported the party's aims without being a member. For years, she had worked closely with Dick on a wide range of Communist-inspired union programs. But whatever the details, evidence suggests that Laura turned against those programs because of the invasion.

Thus, for years after her death, rumors surfaced that she had written a long letter telling how the Communists had infiltrated the labor union movement. She was supposedly deciding what to do next when she was murdered. Indeed, a decade later, an ex-Communist informant claimed that she had been assassinated by a party operative for that very reason. Evidence for such a scenario was, however, very weak. Barring a sensational disclosure from old records, we will never know who murdered Laura Law.

Although May now accepted few new cases, he did continue his column for *True Detective Mysteries*. One reader asked him about small radio-telephones. Were any available that could be "carried on the person by detectives in the field . . . or by police when walking their beats?"[23] May assured the questioner that they did exist and were in use by police officers, firemen, and forest rangers. However, except for short-range work, most such devices were "too bulky to be concealed on the person."

A concerned reader asked May to settle an argument. Could the movies really turn children bad? The writer contended that with proper upbringing "the movies won't do any harm."[24] His friend "claims that children learn all their bad habits at the movies." May agreed that some movies were "too dramatic to be seen by children." From his own work, he went on, "I have received confessions from a number of youthful criminals who stated they were using the methods which they had learned in the movies."

Another reader wondered if it was "possible to distinguish between two different inks by photographic means only." May replied, "I have had a number of cases where the ink seemed to be the same color, and through the use of special films, [and] ultra-violet and infra-red light, I have been able to differentiate between the two inks used."[25]

May also continued his outreach by accepting invitations to speak to various business and social organizations. In one instance, he shared a weekly billing with "Mlle. Eve Curie, the brilliant daughter of the renowned scientist."[26] Luke would speak to the Washington Athletic Club on Wednesday evening, Curie on the evening that followed.

May's growing commitment to his naval duties brought other changes. As noted above, he and Helen seemed to be more in view around the Seattle social scene. They also continued their membership in the Seattle Yacht Club. But they sold the forty-six-foot *Bonnie Doon* in the spring of 1940. Almost immediately, they bought a speedy twenty-six-foot Garwood family cruiser, which was much easier to maintain. In a letter to a navy friend, Luke wrote, "I can go to my island from the locks in eleven minutes—if I get a chance to go."[27]

That same spring saw the war in Europe explode. German forces struck south and conquered France and the Low Countries in little over a month. During the summer, the famous Battle of Britain began, as Hitler's air force tried to soften up England for a planned invasion. At sea, German U-boats tried to choke off shipments into the British Isles. Informed observers were sure it was only a matter of time before the United States was drawn into the conflict.

As we shall see, May had long been involved in preparing for that inevitable day. Then, after years of technically inactive volunteer status, he was assigned to active duty in the navy in the fall of 1940. Probably in anticipation of that change, May logged only twenty cases during the year. Most of them were documents examinations, and the Laura Law investigation was the only death case.

That meant May's income from his private practice during the year was down drastically. And placing him on active-duty status would not help since a lieutenant commander's salary could not come close to making up the difference. Thus, they began selling off real estate assets in an attempt to maintain the home-office-lab facility on Summit Avenue. The following spring, he liquidated a piece of Utah property the family had held for more than twenty years. At some point, they also sold Treasure Island, but the exact date is uncertain. It's possible that both the Mays and the new owners used the property during a time-payment period. Luke and Helen managed to keep the Summit place for a couple of years. However, it became difficult to obtain domestic help, so they finally sold it. They then moved to a smaller home in the Laurelhurst District, a mile or so east of the University of Washington campus.

May continued to participate in high-level law enforcement activities. He still held a position on the executive committee of the Pacific Coast International Association of Law Enforcement Officials. In February, he attended a committee meeting in Portland, where he could again interact with James Egan of the FBI. Then, during the summer, he attended the association meeting in the same city. At that conclave, he and Egan became members of a permanent committee on international police relations. Also, in mid-November, newspapers around Puget Sound carried an item that said, "Lieutenant Commander Luke S. May, Seattle criminologist, now on active duty in the Navy, has been promoted to Commander."[28]

On a morning three weeks later, the May family quietly prepared for a Sunday outing. The early fog was burning off, and the forecast was for a slight easing of the cold and wet of the past few days. Then the phone rang.

Patricia vividly recalled Luke's reaction when he answered. "I still remember the extremely grave expression on his face when he received the call and its shocking information."[29] The Thirteenth Naval District had very powerful radio monitoring facilities. Just minutes after the first bombs fell, they would have picked up an urgent all-stations message: "AIR RAID ON PEARL HARBOR X THIS IS NOT [A] DRILL."[30]

May left immediately. For security reasons, and because no one knew much at that point, he told the family little about what was going on. But around 11:30 that same morning, national networks broadcast news of the attack. Details were still scant, but the reports painted a stark and horrifying picture. Patricia said, "That whole day seemed so dark and foreboding . . . knowing that we are now a country at war!"[31]

· *16* ·

Naval Intelligence Duty

$\mathcal{A}$ distant prelude to the Pearl Harbor attack sounded almost nine years earlier, in February 1933. At the time, Luke May was extremely busy, coming off the stretch where he logged forty-four death cases in two years. In fact, he had five death case files open at that time, along with seven other investigations, including the Burke estate in Seattle and the Lamey bombing in Montana (chapter 12). But he could not have missed the large block-letter front-page headline in the *Seattle Times* for February 24, 1933: "Japan, Rebuked, Bolts League."[1] The League of Nations had endorsed the so-called Lytton Report, which branded Japan an unlawful aggressor in its takeover of Manchuria. Japanese delegates staged a showy walkout to express their displeasure. Then, a few weeks later, they confirmed their country's official withdrawal from the league.

The history behind the Japanese breakaway goes back into the previous decade, and the details are not crucial to May's story. But the event caused much concern among U.S. policy makers. Any counter to Japanese aggression would fall heavily on the navy, which was severely undermanned. During their so-called Fleet Problems—large war games—some of the smaller ships operated with half crews. Still, there was little turnover among the officers or enlisted men, so all were well trained. But they had some key blindspots. One of those oversights would make Luke May's role vital to preparations for war.

The problem began at the U.S. Naval Academy. The academy trained graduates to fill slots in the deepwater fleet. Engineering, seamanship, practical math, and so on mattered. History, government, and other such subjects got lesser amounts of time. Midshipmen received little or no training in the broader field of intelligence. Many years later, a navy commander observed, "In the early years of Navy Intelligence and up to World War II, education and training in Intelligence procedures was gained largely through experience and self-study, and rarely through institutional instruction."[2]

Yet the navy *had* addressed the issue of strategic intelligence. In 1882, the department created the Office of Naval Intelligence (ONI). The ONI's mission was basically to tell naval commanders what they faced, given a particular foreign power. What warships did they have and how were they armed? What strategic and tactical doctrines did they follow? How did they supply the fleet? Directives specified other ONI missions, but those were crucial ones.

The mandate for the ONI was weak on how data was to be collected. Those duties were generally assigned to young officers, either explicitly or by default. Thus, men sent to foreign embassies as naval aides were expected to "keep their eyes open." Those with extra interest might collect more aggressively. But they had to be careful. Too much focus on one job could hurt an officer's chances for promotion.

That was not just intelligence. Concentrating on a specialty could hold back any officer. Thus, during peacetime, officers took on many roles. Sea duty would be mixed with shore postings such as supply officer, Congressional aide, or even intelligence analyst. These assignments typically lasted a year or two. Slowly, the officer's rank and responsibilities increased. Nirvana was to be skipper of a battleship. It was almost a given that one could not be promoted to flag rank—rear admiral and up—without a stint as captain of a battleship. By the 1930s, every active-duty flag officer was an academy graduate and had gone through this sequence. Most knew little about intelligence in its broader sense.

This fact had not gone unrecognized. In 1925, Congress created the Naval Intelligence Volunteer Service to address that gap. Officers were classed as Intelligence Volunteer (Specialized), I-V(S). The hope was that civilians with the proper skills could be called up in a national emergency. But little else was done, and the program never received proper funding.

As their delegation staged its show at the league, the Japanese army was busy occupying Chinese territory north of the Great Wall. At first, newspapers gave extensive coverage to the undeclared war. However, in early March, the Lindbergh kidnapping took over the front page. Some months earlier, Saito Makoto, an ex-naval officer, had become Japanese prime minister. Western strategists deduced that Japan was now eying the oil-rich East Indies. That moved naval matters even more to the forefront. Thus, in 1933, the chief of naval operations raised the quota of authorized I-V(S) positions. The various naval districts stepped up their search for suitable candidates. Meanwhile, during the spring, Mayor Dore appointed May to be chief of detectives for the Seattle police department.

Available records for the following two or three months do not show any contact between naval authorities and May. However, on August 5, a King County Superior Court judge wrote one of three letters of recommendation for May for his "appointment as an officer in the Naval Reserve Corps."[3] A complete package was ready by the end of the month. May was commissioned a lieutenant commander, I-V(S), on September 23, 1933.

Given the Navy's needs, his recruitment made sense. The rank assigned, however, suggests that more was involved. Keep in mind that May lacked normal academic credentials. Nor had he had any kind of naval training, although he did own and operate a private vessel. Yet they jumped him four levels in the commissioned ranks. Someone clearly understood how much they needed his expertise. May's navy date of service is listed as about two weeks after his commission. That was probably when intelligence officers in Seattle, headquarters of the Thirteenth Naval District, were able to brief him at a secure location.

May must have been disturbed at how little the navy knew about Japanese intelligence activities. The Puget Sound area, with its important seaports, would surely be a prime target for espionage. Also, the navy shipyard at Bremerton was vital for shipbuilding, renovation, and repair. Sabotage seemed like a real danger. Working as an unpaid volunteer, over the next two months May prepared a confidential "situation report" that was sent to the Office of Naval Intelligence. In an unclassified version, he identified the prime adversary as "Black," by which he meant Japan. Early on, he wrote, "There is reason to suppose that they receive confidential Intelligence information from this country. It is desired to learn what, if any, agents they have in Seattle for this purpose."[4]

That task would be more difficult because "there are numerous Black nationals living in and around Seattle." Worse yet, poor practices in the past had almost certainly "given local Black observers considerable knowledge of our organization." Among other problems, he wrote, "Meetings have been held in public places." Also, "other branches of the Reserve have known of our identity and have been indiscreet."[5]

May's report quickly reached the director of naval intelligence in Washington, DC. The director commended May's initiative and asked him to suggest how to ease the problems outlined. May's replies were most likely all classified and copies are not now available. However, in late October of 1934, a curt telegram acknowledged their existence. The message said, in part, "Bu considers Cdt 13th ND let re investn of Japanese activities on WC of great importance & regrets that no funds are avail for paym of LTCDR May."[6]

Figure 16.1.   Carriers Docked in Bremerton, circa 1930. *Source*: U.S. Navy, photo NH 95037.

Headquarters did direct the commandant of the Thirteen Naval District to place one "Lt jg Madden" on active duty to carry out the West Coast investigations. May perhaps aided that effort with his own agents because enough was learned for him to define further steps that needed to be taken.

That December, May traveled to Washington, DC, to attend the crime conference mentioned in an earlier chapter. May was also able to meet with the director of naval intelligence. He later wrote, "I was directed by that office to visit New York, N.Y., and indoctrinate certain personnel in the Third Naval District in the plan which I had developed."[7] May had clearly broadened his advice to cover general counterintelligence rather than just in the Pacific Northwest. He carried several letters of introduction to contacts in New York City signed by an intelligence officer in the Thirteenth Naval District.

One contact was business executive Walker Buckner, whose link with naval intelligence was left unclear. However, the writer noted that May was an "internationally famous scientific criminologist."[8] He then said, "If Mr. May is presented to Mrs. Buckner be sure to tip her off to ask him to tell her a detective story. If you can once get him started the evening will be replete with thrills of the most hair raising, yet authentic, stories."

Another world event that heightened the tension in naval circles happened at the end of that month. Japan announced that it would no longer be a part of the Five-Power Naval Limitation Treaty. That treaty, negotiated in 1922, set upper limits on the number of large warships each power—the United States, Britain, Japan, France, and Italy—could have. It headed off an all-out arms race after World War I, but now its provisions interfered with Japan's building plans.

In early June 1935, May became the assistant to the district intelligence officer (DIO), although he was still not on active duty. (He was heavily involved with the Weyerhaeuser kidnapping at that time.) The DIO slot was normally filled by a captain who had been rotated to shore duty. The officers May served under were all academy graduates. They often had additional titles and duties. Also, as suggested above, they seldom had much expertise in intelligence.

By placing May in an official position, the commandant made it possible for him to give orders to lower-ranking naval personnel. But, being still on volunteer status, he did not receive navy pay. Nor were there many intelligence personnel he could give orders to. The historical review, *A Century of U.S. Naval Intelligence,* highlighted the problem: "In all naval districts, the organizations for collecting information vital to security were being impeded by a lack of personnel."[9]

May worked to educate himself for his new duties. The naval personnel bureau acknowledged his successful completion of courses on naval intelligence and on naval regulations and customs. The second acknowledgment said, "The Chief of Bureau wishes to congratulate you on this evidence of your initiative and interest in increasing your efficiency as an officer of the Naval Reserve."[10]

With this new background, May further refined his plans. He also addressed the poor integration among district intelligence organizations. The *Century* document said, "There was no active unit in ONI charged with general administration and coordination of the DIO activities."[11] Thus, in 1936, the ONI had May brief personnel in several other naval districts, with visits to offices in San Francisco, San Diego, Chicago, and New York. At each stop, he discussed counterintelligence, personnel recruitment, and data exchange. The communication protocols he devised became part of the standard naval intelligence manual, ONI-19.

In October, U.S. Customs appointed May as an agent of the service. For this, he received "compensation of $1.00 per annum."[12] The designation provided a plausible cover for him to join in inspections of foreign merchant ships.

Two months later, May was installed as president of the local chapter of the National Sojourners. As noted in the previous chapter, the Sojourners are made up of military and naval personnel who are also members of the Masonic Order. In February 1937, May added another item to his résumé in the form of a course in international law. The following month, he purchased the mansion on Summit Avenue, previously described in chapter 14. And that was just one way that May raised the level of his lifestyle.

Yet he was coming off a year when he logged by far the fewest cases and therefore the least income, in more than fifteen years. May was also about to enter a stretch of years where his caseload would fall by almost two-thirds. Could he see war coming? He was certainly in a position to know the state of the world better than most. The *Century* history provided a possible clue. It said, "Intelligence Reserves in the 13th Naval District . . . were influenced to a great extent by LCdr. (later Cdr.) Luke May, a private detective with an international reputation in scientific crime detection and an expert in the development of informant networks."[13]

May was one of only two intelligence reserve officers *Century* identified by name in the years before and during World War II. The paragraph went on, "Meetings were held in Cdr. May's home or in the Washington Athletic Club in downtown Seattle."

As a matter of interest, May bought the Summit mansion just five days after ONI sent out a letter telling every naval district to step up efforts to identify personnel to fill vacancies in naval intelligence. They especially needed young officers for overseas naval attaché positions. As suggested above, few of these men would have had any training in intelligence collection.

Did naval intelligence secretly subsidize May's purchase of a home that had space for a larger classroom? Possible, but rather unlikely, since their budget remained flat or declined during this period. However, the navy *could* pay tuition for officers sent to the Institute of Scientific Criminology. Neither the Luke May Papers, nor his service records, preserved any class lists. However, the *Century* document says he taught a crime detection and surveillance curriculum. It is reasonable to infer that he supplemented the standard course with special sessions for naval intelligence personnel.

In May 1937, May acquired a new naval boss, Captain Damon E. Cummings. The captain was not only the district intelligence officer, he was also director of naval reserves. As noted in the previous chapter, Cummings and his wife became very good friends of Luke and Helen. Cummings was appointed commander of the USS *Tennessee* after about eighteen months as DIO.

Late that year, Japanese aircraft sank the USS *Panay*. As implied at the end of the previous chapter, the Thirteenth Naval District played a significant role in signals intelligence—radio direction finding and traffic monitoring. Officials there would have been privy to intercepted messages that directed Japanese naval aircraft to attack the gunboat. President Roosevelt and his advisers had that same intelligence, but it was kept closely guarded. They were afraid it would further inflame public opinion, and the navy did not want to reveal their intercept capabilities.

The attack surely increased the pressure on the intelligence service. During the summer of 1938, the ONI planning officer assessed the readiness of the naval intelligence reserves. He identified many problems with the system. These meant that the reserves were "not ready, and that the organization was ineffective."[14] In general, the planner wrote, "Commandants of the naval districts did not appreciate the importance of district intelligence or of intelligence reservists."

The commandant of the Thirteenth Naval District, Rear Admiral Edward B. Fenner, might have been an exception. Either that, or Captain Cummings was able to convince him of the importance of May's work. As a lieutenant, Fenner had been an assistant instructor at the Naval Academy while Cummings was a midshipman there. In November 1938, Fenner signed a letter that noted May's "extremely beneficial" work for the navy. The text concluded, "It is highly recommended that the record of Lieutenant Commander May be allowed to be considered by the Selection Board" for promotion to commander.[15] However, no such promotion was forthcoming at that time.

The ONI planning officer's report did spark some improvements in the intelligence reserves program. Also, the *Century* history noted, "In June 1939, the need for expanded investigative resources was suddenly recognized."[16] The general references behind that statement left it unclear how much of a role May played in this realization. This was, however, the time when Luke and Helen were hosting those "elegant catered dinner parties" for naval personnel.

By now, Poland had been conquered, and France and Great Britain had declared war on Germany. Meanwhile, Japanese diplomats sought to soften U.S. export restrictions. In the early fall, Chinese forces had repelled a Japanese probe north of Hong Kong. A lull in the fighting ensued. However, on November 15, newspapers reported that Japanese troops had opened a new invasion. The *Daily Olympian* headline was typical: "Japanese Launching South China Drive."[17]

Two days after that news report, Commandant Fenner again recommended that May be promoted to commander. At this point, the DIO was Captain William J. Giles. The academy connection continued, since Fenner and Giles had been midshipmen together. Still, after two months in the system, this request was also denied.

At the end of August 1940, Rear Admiral Charles S. Freeman took over as commandant of the Thirteenth Naval District. It must have felt like old home week. Freeman had also been a midshipman when Fenner and Giles were at the academy. Less than three weeks after Freeman took command, he called attention to a problem regarding May in a letter to the navy's bureau of personnel. The letter said, in part, "Due to the expansion of the District Intelligence Organization, which has necessitated calling to active duty several I-V(S) officers, the present duties performed by Lt-Comdr May presents an awkward situation wherein a reserve officer not on active duty . . . instructs and directs officers that are on active duty."[18]

He therefore recommended that May be called up. The navy took less than a month on this decision, calling May to active duty on October 15, 1940. May's naval duties did not change. Even before being made active, he had drastically cut back on his private work. The company would average only about thirteen cases during each of the coming war years.

About three months after he got May put on active duty, Admiral Freeman once again recommended Luke for promotion to full commander. Three months later, when no action had been taken, he submitted another request. Still nothing was done. On September 19, 1941, Freeman sent a more strongly worded recommendation. In it, he wrote, "He has done the major part of the work in the indoctrination of I-V(S) officers and by his ability and unstinting efforts has achieved signal success in schooling new officers in their duties."[19]

Nearly eight weeks passed before the navy acted on the recommendation. Two interesting situations developed in the interim. The first was the entry of a new student into May's intelligence training classes. Ensign Donald McCollister "Mac" Showers was fresh out of Officer Training School at Northwestern University. Showers later said, "It really was investigating people who were put up for security clearances, and they had to investigate their background, and so forth. Went by the nickname of door-knockers, and gumshoes, and things like that."[20]

Showers completed the training but gained little or no actual experience. Instead, he used his journalism degree to wrangle a position in public relations. When he was transferred to Honolulu a few months later, his lack of investigative time got him assigned to Station Hypo. Hypo became famous for the code breaking that led to the decisive U.S. naval victory at the Battle of Midway. Showers was not himself versed in cryptography or Japanese, but he proved to have a knack for intelligence analysis and integration. He went on to a long and distinguished career in naval intelligence, attaining the rank of rear admiral. Showers was the only one of May's students known to have attained flag rank. After his retirement from the navy, Mac served as an adviser to the Central Intelligence Agency.

The second event occurred in late October 1941. The U.S. Customs Service rescinded May's designation as a customs agent. Since May was now on active duty with the navy, his cover as a customs inspector was no longer credible. Finally, in November, May was promoted to the rank of full commander. Shortly after the AlNav (All-Navy) message came out with the promotion list, Luke began receiving letters of congratulations.

One of the first was from Captain Cummings. Cummings had stayed with the *Tennessee* until the spring of 1940. Late that year, he was transferred to a shore post in the Panama Canal Zone. He sent "Hearty congratulations and our best remembrances to the family."[21] With more than thirty years of service, Cummings expected to be retired the following June. However, Pearl Harbor and the war intervened, and he did not retire until late 1946.

Another letter arrived from Lieutenant Commander Wallace "Buck" Wharton. It originated in Washington, DC, and was on Office of Public Relations stationery. He offered "Congratulations!" and chatted a bit about the promotion. Wharton closed with, "Best of regards to Captain Giles and the rest of the District gang."[22]

That last, of course, referred to the Thirteenth Naval District DIO. Wharton was not simply a public relations flack. He was head of the counter-intelligence section within the Office of Naval Intelligence. Wharton had

Figure 16.2.   Commander Luke S. May, USNR.
Source: May-Reid Records.

briefly served as an ensign in World War I. Afterwards, he resigned to work in Oregon as a newspaperman and then a state employee. During this time, he also stayed with the naval reserves. We don't know exactly how Wharton and May met, but they obviously had many opportunities. Wharton had been called to active duty in the spring of 1941.

Congratulations also came from Lieutenant Commander Eugene J. Kerrigan in San Francisco. Kerrigan had actually started out in army intelligence during World War I. He had then served as a special investigator for the U.S. Shipping Board before resigning in late 1919. He spent the next twenty years as a private investigator in the San Francisco area. Kerrigan was commissioned a lieutenant, I-V(S), in 1927. It's not clear when he was called to active duty. He and May could have met through Kerrigan's participation in law enforcement or through reserve activities. In his reply, Luke said, "I was indeed pleased to receive your very fine congratulatory letter and hope now that . . . I may have occasion to write you a similar one when they recognize your accomplishments."[23]

Three weeks after the AlNav announcement, the Japanese bombed Pearl Harbor. For a while, disaster followed disaster, with the loss of the Philippines and the Dutch East Indies. During the spring, President Roosevelt issued Executive Order 9102, which created the War Relocation Authority. That turned into the injustice of relocation camps for Japanese Americans living along the Pacific Coast. The order was fueled by racial prejudice and overblown fears that Japanese communities would become hotbeds of spying and sabotage. Certainly, the Japanese directed a substantial espionage effort at the United States. And their agents did use the Japanese communities for cover. May had acknowledged these hazards in his initial situation report.

However, he would have also known that Japanese spies succeeded mostly through payoffs to greedy native-born whites. The Nisei, born in the United States to immigrant Japanese parents, proved to be fiercely loyal to the country of their birth. May's previous cases showed that he had a solid corps of informants in the Japanese community. He must have been frustrated when the relocations disrupted those networks.

But aside from that, there was now an even greater urgency to get agents trained and out into the field. To that end, during the first half of 1942, the navy changed many of its procedures to streamline the recruitment of people for the Division of Naval Intelligence. Meanwhile, toward the end of summer, the Allies were ready to start the long road back in the Pacific. The Battle of Midway had severely crippled Japan's offensive capability. Since then, Allied forces had landed on Guadalcanal.

May was now approaching fifty. His medical records showed that he tended to work himself to the verge of exhaustion. Thus, the full week of leave he took in early September might well have been "by direction." Then May went right back to work. In November, the director of the Seattle Office of Censorship sent a letter to the DIO. He thanked the DIO for making May "available for a talk to Censorship Officers." The officer also said, "His remarks were most instructive and aroused so much interest that the conference was prolonged by numerous questions from the audience."[24]

A few days later, the *Seattle Times* headlined a change of command ceremony at the Thirteenth Naval District. Vice Admiral Frank Jack Fletcher replaced Admiral Freeman. In an interview, Fletcher conceded that leading the district was a "highly important job." However, he also said, "I feel like all Navy men. I would rather be at sea."[25] His appointment to the Thirteenth Naval District broke the "old boy" chain that had probably been helping May and his intelligence work. Fletcher had been admitted to the Naval Academy two years after Freeman graduated. They might have crossed paths during World War I, when Fletcher served on convoy duty and Freeman was commanding a series of troop ships. Aside from that, the two do not seem to have ever shared a duty station.

William Giles had overlapped somewhat with Fletcher at the Academy, but he had retired to reserve status long before Fletcher arrived in Seattle. His replacement as DIO, whose main title was chief of staff, shall remain nameless here. A very fine officer, he represented the best of the traditional "battleship navy." Besides twice commanding battleships, he had served at navy yards in New London, Connecticut, and in Boston. But he was completely out of his depth as District Intelligence Officer. He seemed little more than a figurehead as DIO until he was transferred to other duties in early December 1942. Captain Hartwell C. Davis replaced him. Davis was an experienced naval intelligence officer, but he had no personal link to the new commandant.

Davis had enrolled at Annapolis three years after Fletcher graduated. The two might possibly have crossed paths briefly during the naval operations at Vera Cruz, Mexico, in 1914. Their careers diverged widely after that. In 1920, Fletcher took an assignment in Washington, DC, with the Bureau of Navigation. Davis commanded a destroyer for a short period before moving to Japan for a three-year immersion program to learn the language and culture. Upon his return in 1923, he became one of the few intelligence specialists in the regular navy. Over the years until both were assigned to Seattle, the two never served together at the same posting.

On the anniversary of the Pearl Harbor disaster, shortly after Fletcher came to Seattle, the *Seattle Times* published war news from every important front around the world. These invited some interesting comparisons. Right after the attack, the Pacific theater was all about the Japanese surging outward. A year later, Allied forces, mostly American, were driving Japanese soldiers off Guadalcanal. When the Japanese first struck, the Axis held North Africa almost to the Egyptian border. In Western Europe, England had triumphed against the German Blitz, but their own bombing campaign had proved not very effective. On the Eastern Front, Leningrad was under siege, and only frigid weather had slowed the German assault on Moscow.

A year later, the Germans had been thrown back from Moscow. In North Africa, an Allied invasion had captured Morocco and Algeria, and troops were within twenty miles of Tunis. The *Times* overview said, "In what was described as the biggest daylight bombing operation of the war, United States Air Forces units raided the Lille locomotive works and Abbeville air field in France yesterday."[26]

May gained some interesting insights into the non-naval side of the war through letters from David Dea, a young man the family had informally adopted. A native of China, Dea worked for the Mays as a houseboy before the war. In February 1943, when he was nineteen, he joined the U.S. Army. He then sent letters to the Mays as he progressed. After the early testing, he wrote, "I had tried to be a flyer, but they did not allowed me, because of my eye sights."[27]

Dea proved to have good math skills, so he was told he would be given training as a radio repair technician in the army air force. But he was first sent to Atlantic City, New Jersey, for basic training. Dea seemed to enjoy Basic, especially rifle practice. However, in one letter he said, "Mr. May, I beg you to forgive me that I had wrinkled your 'Individual Instruction In Rifle Practice's' book cover little bit along the trip. I should learn how to take care of books better this time."[28]

From New Jersey he went to Athens, Georgia, and then to Florida. In an August letter, he said he was at Camp Murphy. "I am having radar training here. It is very interesting than plain radio. I think Mr. May knows the whole story about this."[29] Camp Murphy, near Boca Raton, was perhaps the most important air force training base for radar operators and repair technicians. Given the secrecy that then surrounded the technology and the base itself, it seems odd that censors allowed Dea's letter to go out untouched. It is perhaps significant that this was the last David Dea letter to appear among the Luke May Papers. After the war, Dea earned an engineering degree and worked in the aerospace industry.

On August 21, 1943, the *Seattle Times* published a night final extra with the huge block headline, "Kiska Isle Retaken."[30] While of minor military importance, the event was symbolic because it expelled Japanese forces from their last foothold in North America. Troops had landed six days before the announcement, but the services maintained a news blackout to deprive the

Japanese high command of information. Officials knew the Japanese monitored our radio news. They also had to assume that Japanese agents could read our newspapers and send off reports.

A few weeks later, something odd and intriguing happened. The director of naval intelligence in Washington, DC, sent a terse letter to the chief of naval personnel. Rear Admiral Harold C. Train wrote, "The Director of Naval Intelligence at this time desires to recommend the promotion of the following naval officer: Commander Luke S. May, I-V(S), USNR."[31]

The message, marked "Confidential," offered no explanation. Recall that earlier promotion requests had come from the commandant of the Thirteenth Naval District, first Fenner and then Freeman. Those had almost certainly been initiated by May's immediate superior, the DIO. Hartwell Davis had signed May's fitness report at the end of March 1943.[32] He was very impressed and emphatically checked the standard item saying he would "particularly desire to have" Luke in his command. Yet May's official navy file contains no request for promotion from either Davis or Admiral Fletcher. During the summer, May's friend Buck Wharton in counterintelligence had been promoted to captain. But he was not part of May's chain of command, and such a request would have been considered inappropriate.

Unfortunately, despite the code-breaker glory at Midway, Fletcher's wartime contact with naval intelligence had been somewhat rocky. He had had regular disagreements with his fleet intelligence officer before the Battle of Coral Sea. Later, he had complained about misleading intelligence reports sent from Pearl Harbor during the Guadalcanal invasion. Davis perhaps judged that the commandant would not be receptive to a request to promote an intelligence officer he knew little about. We can speculate that he went to Admiral Train through "back channels" to get May promoted.

Recall that his time in Japan had given Davis a solid grounding in intelligence. Train had been introduced to signals intelligence during World War I. When Davis returned from Japan, he and Train spent two to three years on duty with the Pacific Fleet. After time at other stations, in 1929 both returned to sea duty in the Pacific. Davis was specifically tasked as full-time intelligence officer with the Asiatic Fleet. Finally, from March 1932 to September 1933, both men were in Washington, DC, for assignments in naval intelligence. They then returned to sea duty. Train was at Pearl Harbor during the Japanese attack. He remained there until July 1942, when he was made director of naval intelligence. Davis was in Washington, DC, on full-time intelligence duty at the time of the attack. He thus had several months to renew his acquaintance with Admiral Train before being moved to Seattle in late 1942 or early 1943.

Obviously, there's no way to know that Davis did go around normal channels. However, *something* induced Admiral Train to send his letter recommending the promotion. Less than two weeks later, the Bureau of Personnel prepared a response. The letter to Luke May began, "The President of the United States hereby appoints you a Captain for temporary service in the Naval Reserve of the United States Navy."[33]

On September 27, the promotion document was sent as an enclosure to the commandant of the Thirteenth Naval District. The cover letter said the promotion was "to be delivered only if the appointee be found physically qualified and if his commanding officer is not aware of any circumstances indicating that promotion is not warranted."[34]

This letter may have come as a surprise to Admiral Fletcher, although we cannot know one way or another. But on October 7, he rejected May's promotion. The refusal letter listed several reasons. It began, "The necessity for the promotion of Commander to the rank of Captain is not apparent, as the duties presently assigned him can be just as well performed in his present rank."[35]

That was at least partly true, although *Captain* May's words would have carried more weight when he had to brief higher-ranked officers. The years that May spent getting naval intelligence ready for war, at no cost to the navy, meant nothing to Fletcher. His rejection letter called out May's limited *active duty* time. Then came the clincher: "He has never been to sea."[36] It provided a sop at the end. Fletcher wrote, "I wish it to be clearly understood that this letter is not in any way a reflection on either the character, ability, or performance of Commander May, who is considered an officer of excellent character."

As usual, May's papers provide no hint of how he reacted to all this. He probably shrugged and went on about his business. But the oddities continued in the spring. At the end of March 1944, paperwork came through to change May's reserve classification from I-V(S) to D-V(S). The new status placed May in the pool eligible for Deck Duty, Specialized. A few days after that, May received a letter from the chief of naval personnel. May was told to make necessary preparations and then to "regard yourself detached from duty in the Thirteenth Naval District, and report to the Chief of Naval Operations, Navy Department, for duty."[37] May reported in Washington, DC, on May 9.

Before that, Captain Davis had sent a letter to a friend in the office of the navy's judge advocate general. He led off, "It occurred to me that you would like to meet Commander Luke S. May, U.S. Naval Reserve."[38] His new duties, Hartwell said, "will not be in connection with the Office of Naval Intelligence." Davis went on, "Commander May . . . is one of the foremost in the field of investigation and a renowned criminologist. You have probably read some of his works. If not, I suggest that you do. . . . From an Intelligence standpoint his work also has been outstanding, and I regret that he has had to leave Seattle."

So, what was going on? May was in Washington, DC, the seat of power (and promotion). But he was not slated to work in intelligence. Did someone plan to give him some token sea duty, to head off objections from traditionalists when he was promoted? We can never know, because Luke May would have none of it.

The *Century* history stated that naval intelligence closed more than thirty thousand investigations from mid-1941 to when Japan surrendered. Many of these were security clearances, requiring fieldwork by what Mac Showers called "door knockers" and "gumshoes." Those somewhat dismissive nicknames are not justified, by the way. In intelligence, code breaking was often seen as the glamour field. Photo interpretation and other analytical work were not far behind. But everyone who did those "sexy" jobs had to qualify for a security clearance before they could start. Even today, the door knocker is the first line of defense for the intelligence community.

More than ten thousand investigations were completed in 1942 and probably even more than that in 1943. Agents trained by Luke May, or according to his methods, carried out many of those probes. The number of investigations plummeted in 1944, to about half the rate for the previous year. The need for May's expertise fell in greater proportion since he had already trained many agents.

Thus, on May 18, May sent a letter to the chief of naval personnel asking to be released from active duty. The first reason he gave was, "The very specialized work for which I was called into naval service has now been completed."[39] He next noted that his health had deteriorated. May then closed, "My services in a civilian capacity as a consulting criminologist will be of more value to the nation. . . . It appears that the Navy can no longer utilize to full capacity a man with my particular qualifications and training."

The navy accepted but required him to pass an "examination to determine your physical fitness for release from active duty."[40] If he did not pass, a medical officer was to propose ways to restore his health. Ironically, the doctor judged that May was not fit for *active* duty. He suffered from physical and mental exhaustion. His condition was not so severe, however, that any special care was needed. May's next orders were to "proceed to your home and upon arrival you are hereby granted three months' leave."[41]

May arrived in Seattle on June 12, 1944. During his summer on leave, May witnessed what many called the beginning of the end of the war. In western Europe, Allied forces landed in Normandy, liberated Paris, and advanced to the German border. On the Eastern Front, Soviet troops pushed deep into German-occupied Poland. In the Pacific, U.S. forces seized the

Marianas, and Allied combat units under General MacArthur drove north from New Guinea.

About the time May went back to inactive status in early September, a front-page headline in the *Daily Olympian* read, "Air, Sea Forces Heap Ruin on Japan's Inner Defense."[42] Units hit scores of targets from Indonesia to Wake Island, a span of more than four thousand miles. These attacks severely tightened the noose around Japan's defenses, although they would hang on for almost another year.

While May watched from the sidelines, men he had trained carried on. *A Century of U.S. Naval Intelligence* praised the role played by reservists like Luke May during the war. The history said their part was "of major significance."[43] It went on, "They performed very well and helped fill most of the billets in the Naval Intelligence service during World War II."

Meanwhile, as May resumed his civilian practice, he had surely already sensed that the game had changed for the private criminologist.

· 17 ·

The Game Has Changed

*W*hile he recuperated, the press paid little attention to May. He spent some of his time fixing up real estate. May's daughter knew him as "a fine, thorough craftsman."[1] He sought relaxation and fresh air working with his hands. His records show a number of property transactions during the summer and fall.

Even so, May clearly put out the word that he was ready to get back to business. He leased office space downtown but kept his lab area at home. Shortly after Thanksgiving, the King County prosecuting attorney replied to a request for help from a prominent Portland attorney. He wrote, "I suggest you contact Mr. Luke May, criminologist in the White-Henry-Stuart Building, Seattle. Mr. May has just returned from the Navy, where he held the rank of Commander. For many years, he has been a nationally recognized criminologist."[2]

On January 6, 1945, the president of a Seattle bank wrote, "I am delighted to have the announcement of your return to business. . . . The next time you are down this way I hope you will make it an occasion to drop in."[3]

May's brochures now emphasized work on questioned documents. A typical release said that in his lab "many ultra-modern instruments have been invented to assist the scientist in proving the genuineness or falsity of suspected documents."[4] May had clearly reassessed the postwar investigation landscape. He could no longer expect much work as a crime scene detective. That role had been taken over by trained police officers who now had access to publicly supported crime labs. May also noted his services as an expert with the polygraph (lie detector). Although such tests are now prohibited or highly restricted, many companies back then used them routinely. Records for that work would have been highly confidential and no longer exist. A

229

few logged cases do mention polygraph tests that were provided along with other services.

During the first quarter of the year, May recorded about ten cases. Most involved questioned documents. And, as noted several times before, such cases rarely appeared in the newspapers or went to court. The press did briefly cover one case in April. The foreman of a fish cannery sued his company management, claiming he had been shorted in a profit-sharing distribution. Press interest rose because the lead defendant, company President Lemuel Wingard, was also involved in a messy domestic quarrel. Three years earlier, the fifty-two-year-old Wingard had dumped his first wife, who was about his age. They had been married for twenty-six years. After the divorce, Lemuel married a twenty-seven-year-old divorcee. His first wife then filed an "alienation of affection" suit against the second wife.[5]

May's part concerned the profit-sharing dispute. Wingard's lawyer sent May a check and a partially used book of checks. He wrote, "If I can establish check did not come from the blanks at the back of the book that is one point; if I can establish that it did not come from the book at all that is very important. It will then develop that the stub book . . . was made up for the purpose of the trial."[6] Using edge matching, May determined that the check had come from the book, but not from the back. Wingard and the other investors won the suit against the foreman. The "alienation" suit was abandoned or settled out of court.

In the end, May logged only about thirty-five cases for 1945, none of them deaths. Nor did any of his cases receive much publicity in the newspapers. Still, as suggested above, May kept busy by dealing heavily in real estate during this period. In one deal, he sold a property on Bainbridge Island and bought another about fourteen miles northeast of downtown Seattle. His correspondence shows he had some not-uncommon landlord problems with the acquisition. First, it took an extra exchange of letters with the electric company to get them to quit billing the Mays for the old property and start with the new tract.

Also, May had allowed a renter at the new place several weeks to move out, rent-free if the house was cleaned up properly. When that failed to happen, he ended up charging rent for two full months. He also had to clean up the property himself. Then he discovered that, due to survey errors, the new lot was about 5 percent smaller than the agreement with the former owner claimed. The seller, wife of a Protestant minister, wrote, "I sold the land under the firm belief and understanding that there were the full five acres."[7] They arranged a suitable reduction in the price. In his reply, May said, "Rest assured that I have no thought that your dealings with me have been anything but the most honorable. Such mistakes may happen to any one."[8]

Early the following year, May headed east to Chicago. As noted in a previous chapter, the city of Chicago had purchased the crime lab associated with Northwestern University. They made it part of the police department and moved the facility closer to downtown Chicago. May wanted to renew his contacts in the city and to see what changes had been made in the labs. As a treat for his daughter, Luke took Patricia along. She was then twelve years old. They stayed at the Sherman Hotel, across the street from Chicago's city hall. She recalled having meals at Henrici's, a famous Chicago eatery located within a block of their hotel. But her "great fun" memory at the restaurant involved a parrot . . . a fictitious parrot, actually.[9]

Figure 17.1. Historic Hotel Sherman, Chicago. *Source*: **Library of Congress, LC-DIG-det-4a23998.**

It's worth a brief aside here to note some fascinating aspects of Luke May's character. His profession required May to hold many secrets and to speak precisely and objectively. And, obviously, humor had no place. Yet underneath that façade lurked a skillful raconteur. His guarded loquacity was coupled with a dry, wry, and gentle sense of humor. These hidden attributes came to the fore in the parrot story. Patricia recalled that Luke "jollied me along for the benefit of the couple seated next to us by pretending that he and I were traveling with a pet parrot and that it was awaiting us back in our hotel room."[10]

May recited his "colorful imaginary tale" about the bird with a straight face and total seriousness. Naturally, Patricia played along while laughing on the inside. "The couple adjacent hung on every word with obvious curiosity." Luke and Patricia applied the final touch as they rose to leave. "We saved our soup crackers for our imaginary feathered friend."[11]

Besides his cases, May continued to deal in real estate during this period. In one transaction, the Mays bought a "run down five acre ranch with house requiring remodeling" about fifteen miles north of Seattle.[12] Besides a substantial home remodel, Luke also hired a bulldozer for landscaping and put up some new fencing. They held the property for about nine months and made a profit of more than 15 percent on their investment. However, in early spring, May gave a different reason in one inquiry about an undeveloped tract about ten miles north of Seattle. He wrote, "I have a small daughter and desire to get her out where she can have the benefit of country living."[13] It does not appear that they could arrange a deal. However, the Mays later found a suitable place, where they ended up raising horses.

Sadness visited the May family at the end of the year and early in the next. First, Luke's father, William, died and then, two months later, his mother, Mary Annie. Family memories suggest that Luke's relationship with his parents was proper but not especially warm. Still, he and Helen did support them at the North Beacon Hill place for more than twenty years.

May's workload for 1946—forty-seven cases—was similar to the mid-1930s. It would never be that high again. He had only three death cases. None were particularly challenging, nor did they receive much coverage in the newspapers. Still, after more than a year back in private business, May's name again began to appear in the Seattle newspapers. Besides his various talks, the press noted his presence at other events. Early in the year, he attended a prescreening of the psychological thriller, *Dark Mirror,* starring Olivia de Havilland. The *Seattle Times* said, "May found the picture technically sound and 'fine entertainment.'"[14]

As usual, May kept up a steady schedule of public speaking engagements across the span of years after the war. Except for talks to law enforcement meetings, all these engagements were in Seattle. Not all of these events were publicized in the newspapers, but many were. Thus, he spoke about questioned documents and handwriting issues to a group of business executives, an association of safety-deposit operators, and a fraternal and service organization. Detective anecdotes and items from *Crime's Nemesis* provided interest and entertainment for the Young Men's Business Club, Kiwanis members, and the Lions Club. He also spoke at a fellowship meeting for a Methodist Church.

Also, despite a lack of spectacular cases, May's name still sparked local interest. A *Seattle Times* columnist wrote full-page articles about May and his cases for two successive Sunday editions in the spring of 1947. In the first, May said, "Some crimes remain unsolved, but not because there were no clues. They remain unsolved because nobody *saw* the clues."[15] The second article focused more on questioned documents and other handwriting cases. For that, May described one case that included both handwriting and tool marks. Someone had pinned a threatening note to the possible victim's door. He had tried to disguise his printing, but May was confident he could sort it out. He also found shavings near the door where the perpetrator had stopped to sharpen his pencil. Tools marks connected those slivers to a knife owned by the main suspect. The writer said, "With a double count against him, the criminal confessed—trapped by a few almost unnoticeable shavings peeled off the point of a broken pencil and permitted to fall to the ground."[16]

During the summer, one of May's cases ended up in court but not in the newspapers. His clients owned a filling station, and the Sunset Gas & Oil Company claimed the couple still owed them for a large delivery of gasoline. From the available records, May verified that the bill had indeed been paid. But in the end, May did not need to testify. The company finally conceded the judgment. The lawyer who sent May his payment wrote, "Your services were of great value in the case, and in my final argument I mentioned that you were in the court room."[17]

All told, May logged about forty cases during 1947. Most were document examinations. However, he did handle one case that involved nine deaths. At the end of November, a DC-4 aircraft flying for Alaska Airlines ran off the end of a runway at the Seattle-Tacoma airport. Eight of twenty-eight passengers and crew on the DC-4 were killed immediately or died later from their injuries. The plane also hit a passing car and killed a luckless woman riding in it.

At that time, the federal Civil Aeronautics Board (CAB) handled airline accident investigations. During a preliminary hearing, two CAB officials claimed they saw early problems with the landing. Yet the passengers and other witnesses said the aircraft had made a perfectly normal touchdown and that everything seemed okay on the ground at first.

Right after the accident, the pilot declared that the plane's brakes had failed utterly. In fact, he said the aircraft "rolled like it was on a bed of ball-bearings."[18] But at the hearing, a regional CAB maintenance inspector implied that they had never seen any problems with the plane's brakes. That was supported by the maintenance supervisor for the airline. Disputing that, another Alaska Airlines pilot testified that he too had had trouble with the brakes on that particular airplane.

The CAB said there would be tests and a thorough investigation. The pilot, Captain James Farris, hired May as an independent consultant less than a week after the hearing. May visited the scene and took extensive notes. There were no skid marks on the runway, even though the pilot and copilot both said they had the brake pedals all the way down.

A month or more passed before May was given access to the aircraft wreckage. What he called a "casual and superficial inspection" revealed that no one had critically examined key parts of the braking system.[19] Moreover, a few small items had been removed but not properly labeled or preserved for a detailed inspection. May sent a letter to the head of the CAB noting these problems. He also said, "It is requested that I be afforded an opportunity to examine under laboratory conditions remnant parts of the wrecked plane on behalf of the pilot and those who may be saved from future accidents of this nature due to brake failure."[20]

Many more weeks passed, but May was finally allowed to closely assess the wreckage. In early August, 1948, President David Behncke of the Airline Pilots' Association complimented May's resulting report. He wrote that it was "neatly compiled and reflects, in a clear-cut manner, the physical evidence respecting the cause of this accident."[21] Despite the poor handling of the evidence by CAB people, May's data affirmed the pilot's contention that the brakes had failed. Behncke said the CAB director "appeared, at least outwardly, to be impressed and said they would take everything into consideration."[22]

In his reply to Behncke, May explained his personal interest in airline safety. It happened that he had "just completed a survey study of various types of aircraft accidents" when Farris contacted him.[23] May found that "pilot error" was the CAB's preferred verdict for any accident. He wrote, "As the 'King can do no wrong,' an autocratic government department could *not* find itself wrong in an investigation of its own faulty inspection or certification of aircraft and attendant facilities."

May's assertion proved all too true. The following spring, the CAB issued a report that blamed a "faulty landing procedure"—that is, pilot error—for the crash.[24] They made no mention of any testimony or evidence suggesting failed brakes. Farris eventually faced two indictments for his purported negligence. Farris and the Pilots' Association vigorously challenged those charges. The case came to trial in federal court a year later. Prosecutors claimed Farris had touched down too far along the landing strip. They could not, however, offer any credible evidence to support their position. The prosecution also denied that any mechanical failures had occurred. The jury found May's evidence of specific defects far more convincing.

After deliberation, the jury declared that the pilot had not operated the DC-4 "in a reckless or careless manner."[25] They did agree that he might have landed when the cloud ceiling was a bit lower than the prescribed level. That was of such minor interest that the jury proposed just a $100 fine rather than the $1,000 demanded by the prosecution. Later, a Pilots' Association regional vice president praised May's thorough investigation. He also said, "He proved probably as fine a lay witness on the stand that it has ever been the good fortune of the Association to have."[26]

While May dealt with self-important federal bureaucrats, he also tried to improve his contacts for more local work. That included taking a position on the board of directors of the Seattle Rotary Club. And he continued to speak to various groups. In the summer, he attended the annual convention of the Pacific Coast International Association of Law Enforcement Officials. In addition to the usual business, May was an invited guest at a special luncheon honoring past presidents of the association.

This was the general period when Luke and Helen changed their recreation from boating to horses. It's not clear exactly when they sold the Garwood cruiser. However, the directory of the Seattle Yacht Club had no listing for Luke May after the 1947 edition. Daughter Patricia said they became members of the "horsey set" after they moved to the Laurelhurst area.[27]

Besides the carryover of the airline accident, May handled just one death case in 1948. It occurred in late summer at a hamlet about two miles across an inlet from Bremerton. Parents found their fourteen-year-old son—we'll call him "Andy"—dead in his bedroom. A taut strip of drapery wrapped around his neck had strangled him. Aside from the horror at his death, they also faced the bizarre fact that he was dressed in women's clothing.

The county sheriff and prosecutor chose to consider the death just a poorly done suicide. A coroner's jury disagreed. It ruled that Andy had been murdered "by person or persons unknown."[28] When county officials ignored that result, a group of concerned citizens banded together to demand an investigation. The county then said they *couldn't* do that because the budget would not cover it. As a result, the citizens took up a collection to hire Luke May.

May joined the case in mid-December. He at once called for an exhumation and a second autopsy. He told reporters that the examination had

Figure 17.2.   May Mounted on His Blooded Stallion. *Source*: **May-Reid Records.**

"uncovered new evidence," but did not say what it was.[29] By this time, Hollis Fultz was working for the state attorney general's office. Together, the two determined that a second person had probably been in the room at the time. Yet Fultz told the press, "There was complete lack of evidence of any indication of foul play."[30]

After that, the case vanished from the newspapers. A retrospective article fifty years later called the incident "an unsolved suicide," whatever that meant.[31] Yet the facts available strongly suggest an answer. The boy might have been trying "autoerotic asphyxiation" (AEA).[32] The AEA practitioner induces severe oxygen deprivation in hopes of having a strong sexual arousal. Although cases are often misidentified or even covered up, experts are convinced that several hundred people die each year trying it. (Some estimates go as high as a thousand per year just in this country, but that number is disputed.)

The vast majority of victims are male, and perhaps one in six of them are teenagers. Most often, they hang themselves in a way they think they can stop. Or, sometimes, they have a helper there to save them. For male victims it is very common for women's clothing to be involved in some way. And an autopsy generally reveals key symptoms beyond those associated with death by strangulation.

May's files were very sketchy on this case, and the reasoning above perhaps explains why. Recorded instances of AEA deaths go back at least to eighteenth-century Europe. Thus, if Andy's death was indeed an accident during an AEA episode, May would have recognized the signs. Once he explained, the family and the police would most likely have been willing to leave it as a puzzling suicide.

Overall, May recorded around forty cases in 1948, with just the one death case. As noted above, his papers contain no specific files for his polygraph work. The following year started slowly in terms of logged cases. However, in March, May tackled a case that would stretch out for years. His handwritten note on the log sheet said, "Probably run $20,000."[33] That would be equivalent to $200,000 to $300,000 in today's monetary values. He received a retainer of $2,500.

The key events took place a decade earlier. Robert Hugh ("R. H." to friends and neighbors) Phillips and his sister-in-law, Verona, got into a dispute over the estate of Verona's deceased husband. The estate included thousands of acres of wheat farmland in Adams County, about seventy-five miles southwest of Spokane. Verona became dissatisfied with the job R. H. was doing as administrator and farm operator. She finally agreed to a settlement in 1939. The agreement split the land between R. H. and Verona and her four children. There was also a lesser distribution of financial assets.

Ten years later, she became convinced that her brother-in-law had underreported the farm profits in arranging the settlement. Her lawyer hired Luke May to look for data to frame a new agreement. Three years passed before the case came to trial in Ritzville, the Adams County seat. Months later, it finally ended. An article in the Ritzville *Journal-Times* said the trial took "33 days of actual session," divided into two segments. The report also said, "[Luke] May was present throughout the trial."[34]

About three weeks later, the judge did overturn the 1939 settlement. Verona would receive two thousand acres of land granted earlier to R. H., as well as all the back profits earned on that parcel. Naturally, the attorney for R. H. appealed. Three years later, nearly six years after May was first retained, the Washington Supreme Court overturned the first court's judgment.

The Supreme Court pointedly addressed the Depression-era context of the 1939 agreement. The judge who wrote the opinion said, "In that picture, the administrator appears as one in whom creditors had confidence . . . and one who was, consequently, able to keep the estates afloat."[35] Questions raised ten years later did not, in the court's opinion, justify overturning the settlement. After that decision, the sides might have come to some further out-of-court settlement. That, of course, would not appear in any open records.

By the end of the year, May had logged only about twenty cases, with just one fairly routine death case. Fortunately, 1950 brought him back to his new normal load of about three cases each month. His one death case involved a freakish accident. In mid-July, an early-morning explosion occurred just blocks from the King County Courthouse. The *Seattle Times* reported, "The blast wrecked one three-story building, heavily damaged several others and blasted windows out of business houses and Skidroad hotels."[36]

The owner of the café on the ground floor of the building barely escaped. When he arrived to start work, he found the gas was off to his cooking equipment. Yet the basement smelled strongly of gas. He called the supplier and then left. Minutes later, the building exploded. Most likely a refrigerator motor had started up and caused a spark to set off the gas. The one victim was painter Neil Boles, who happened to be walking by at the wrong time. His body was found on a second-floor fire escape across the street from the blast zone.

Twelve days later, the owner of the building, the Buttnick Manufacturing Company, hired May to investigate the disaster. He arrived at the site in time to watch workmen clear debris and fill from over the supply pipe that ran from the main gas line across the street to the building. May observed that the pipe had a hole in it and that further along "the pipe walls were of paper thickness and friable."[37]

Some weeks later, May prepared a second report. The only defective piping had been that which lay outside the building. When he fed gas to the meter in his lab, "gas poured out of the hole which had rusted through the front of the meter." May concluded, "Either the defective gas pipe or the defective meter, or both combined, could have been the source of the leak causing the explosion as they were both under the same gas pressure and both grossly defective."[38]

A month later, the *Times* reported that "a precision-instrument concern" across the street had filed suit against Buttnick, Buttnick's insurance company, and the Seattle Gas Company.[39] The blast had blown out all their windows. Worst yet, the shock required them to recalibrate all their equipment. The papers mention no further actions, so later proceedings must have been handled out of court.

Along with his cases, May was still active in real estate. One 1950 transaction involved the North Beacon Hill property that May had owned for a quarter century. The contract wording suggests that he carried the deal as a time payment plan spread over a number of years. The sale indicates that other living arrangements had been made for Luke's brother, Vincent, and his wife, Laura. As mentioned before, the couple had joined Luke's parents at the Beacon Hill property around 1934. But Vincent had been sickly for many years. In late spring, apparently, he and Laura moved to an apartment near the King County Hospital. Vincent was admitted to the hospital in November and died there four months later.

Before that, May acquired another substantial documents case. James Thomson, a frugal Scot and a lifelong bachelor, had accumulated a million-dollar fortune in real estate, mainly hotels and apartment buildings in Vancouver, British Columbia. However, not until a year after he died in December 1948 did authorities find a will. The discovery made news briefly because the will left the estate to ordinary folks, including several hotel employees and a city fireman. The fireman, Gilbert Campbell, had been a friend of Thomson's and was to receive by far the largest amount.

About ten weeks later, May was hired to authenticate the signatures of Thomson and two witnesses, both of whom were dead. May quickly observed more than a half dozen points of difference in the Thomson signature, showing it to be a forgery. His report said that the "pictorial affect shows it to be like a drawing rather than writing when compared with the genuine signature."[40] One purported witness was Charles E. Smith, a business associate of Thomson's. That too was a forgery. The "th" had "a peculiar design that is not even closely imitated in the questioned signature." He found six major points of difference on the other witness signature. All of this played out behind the scenes until December 1950, when the *Seattle Times* posted the headline, "Beneficiary Fears B. C. Will Is Fraud."[41]

Gilbert Campbell had either been fooled himself or he'd gotten cold feet after being caught in the forgery. He had his lawyer move to have the will dismissed. However, several of the lesser beneficiaries fought to have it approved. In the end, May's testimony was supported by another expert from Vancouver, and the court threw out the fake will.

Over the next several years, Luke May averaged thirty-three cases each year. None would make the news like the Thomson will case, and none were death cases. One milestone occurred for May in February 1951. He received a letter from the chief of naval personnel that said, in part, "Having passed the statutory retirement age of sixty-four years, you were on 1 February 1951 transferred to the Honorary Retired List of the Naval Reserve with the rank of Commander but without pay or allowances."[42]

Despite his age, May never stopped educating himself. Thus, his personal library included the text *Forensic Science and Laboratory Techniques* by Ralph F. Turner. Turner was a professor of criminalistics at Michigan State University. He had been hired by Michigan State two years after the war as part of a major expansion of its School of Police Administration and Public

Safety. The school greatly broadened its curriculum to include basic crime-fighting techniques, police administration, and the criminal justice system. In keeping with that approach, Turner's book, published in 1949, was billed as the first college-level manual for training police lab technicians. In March 1951, he signed a copy with a dedication to "Luke S. May, Distinguished Pioneer in forensic science."[43] May must have been pleased to receive such recognition from a member of the latest generation of criminologists.

He would have been aware that UC-Berkeley had also formed a School of Criminology, in 1950. Dr. Paul Kirk became chairman of a new department of criminalistics. Since August Vollmer spearheaded creation of the school, the main thrust was to educate police officers. The psychology and sociology of criminals, the courts, and the penal system were generally left to the respective academic disciplines.

May experienced a personal milestone in 1952 when Patricia May got engaged to Frank Reid. The announcement in the *Seattle Times* said, "Miss May attended the University of Washington and is a member of Alpha Xi Delta. Mr. Reid is a senior at the university. His fraternity is Sigma Phi Epsilon."[44] They had a June wedding in 1953. Sadly, six months later, Helen's mother, Johanna Klog, passed away.

Another milestone could have happened in 1954. In February, Folmar Blangsted reopened business correspondence with May. Recall that, in 1936, Blangsted had considered using Luke's case files to produce a series of movie shorts. Now he wanted to "create a television series which might be entitled: *The Crime Lab of Luke S. May* or perhaps simpler, *Crime Lab.*"[45]

Blangsted said his approach would be to use May's files as the basis for episodes in a series similar to the then-popular *Dragnet*. The selling point would be the "true crime" link. However, Folmar was reluctant to draft specific sample episodes without the prospect of exclusive rights. May replied that "several Eastern parties" had also sought his material for some kind of show.[46] He judged them all to be unqualified or otherwise unsuitable. May would much prefer working with Folmar and was quite prepared to give him sole use of the case files. He looked forward to Blangsted's drafts.

The next letter came after a bit of delay. Blangsted said it would be awhile before he could have material ready. "My dear wife suffered a very serious heart attack last Thursday night so you can readily understand that I am sticking close by her."[47] May's earlier letters had been formal and business-like. This reply began, "My dear Folmar. I hope when this reaches you that your dear Anne is much better. I certainly do not wish to pressure you under the circumstances." When Blangsted felt ready, May concluded, "I will await with interest hearing from you."[48]

Blangsted's wife did recover somewhat from her attack, so Folmar could get back to work. However, five months later, Blangsted wrote, "This is a letter which I find difficult to write. You see, after many weeks of effort I must throw in the towel."[49] His two current film editing jobs—*A Star is Born* and *Strange Lady in Town*—left him no time for the crime show project. "So rather than hold you up any longer I must give up my dream of turning it into a TV series."

May's records do not indicate that he pursued the idea further. Most crime-fighter TV programs in the fifties, including *Dragnet*, featured regular law enforcement officers. Other popular shows included *Highway Patrol, State Trooper,* and *City Detective*. Private detective programs generally featured witness and suspect interviews, with lots of physical action. In both genres, technical clues—fingerprints, autopsy reports, and the like—were produced by unidentified off-camera helpers, if they appeared at all. Thus, the concept of a private crime lab did not fit the standard mold for either type of program. Blangsted's dream and May's hopes were never fulfilled.

May was still a popular speaker in Seattle, giving publicized talks to the Junior Chamber of Commerce, Lions Club, and Rotary. Also, local newspapers published the occasional feature about him. For example, in the spring of 1954, the *Post-Intelligencer* carried a three-part series. The first column gave an overview of May's early cases in Salt Lake City. The columnist ended with, "What was May's most famous case? 'Murder by the Stars' might well be, but of that tomorrow."[50] Naturally, the second column reminded readers of the Covell astrology case in 1923. The third article covered "something of the work of the criminologist of today."[51] For that, the writer summarized the Thomson will case, with some emphasis on the peculiar "th" form in the Smith signature.

However, few of May's cases made national headlines any more. In fact, in the coming years, only one would get much coverage outside the Pacific Northwest. The sole death case he handled after 1954 received only regional publicity and not much of that. Clearly, the days of the private scientific criminologist were on the wane.

· 18 ·

Playing Out the String

"*C*riminologist to Testify in Murder Trial," said a headline in the *Seattle Times* for Saturday, January 8, 1955. The item began, "Luke S. May, Seattle criminologist, probably will be called as a state's rebuttal witness in the second-degree-murder trial of Mrs. Violet Sill."[1]

The item was tucked away on page eleven and not in particularly large print. Months earlier, Violet Sill had confessed to shooting her husband with a 16-gauge shotgun. He had suffered a major death wound in the neck. She had herself been shot twice, on the left side of her stomach and near her left armpit. These were supposedly attempts to commit suicide. The *Times* article said that "sections of shotgun-riddled panels were taken from the Sill home and set up in the courtroom."[2]

This move by the defense, not long before court recessed for the weekend, caught the prosecution by surprise. They asked the judge to reconvene court on Saturday so May could examine the exhibits and give his immediate opinion. But the judge ruled that May could only testify later in the trial. On Monday, the defense continued its presentation. The *Times* headline was, "Pellet Holes in Ceiling Shown Jury."[3] News reports made no mention of Luke May being called to the stand, then or later. The jury found Sill guilty but only on the reduced charge of manslaughter. She was given a five- to twenty-year prison sentence.

But the story did not end there. Sill's attorney felt the evidence did not add up to her confession. With the help of the prison psychiatrist and a dose of sodium amytal—a so-called truth serum—the attorney brought out a new story. Of course, as discussed earlier, such drugs do not necessarily extract the truth. But they can release inhibitions on long-stifled thoughts and feelings.

Sill now said that her husband had first shot her twice. They had then wrestled with the gun before it went off and killed him. Deep-seated guilt feelings led her to confess to murder as self-punishment. An experienced firearms expert offered the opinion that her new account fit the pellet and wound evidence far better than her earlier confession did. Did May suspect something of the sort? His files are rather thin during this period. If May told the prosecution that their firearms evidence was weak, they'd have no reason to put him on the stand.

The issue became something of a *cause célèbre* as the attorney tried to get Sill pardoned. He failed, but Violet ended up serving only three years and four months. But beyond that, the Sill trial was the last time May's name was associated with a death case.

In keeping with the changed times, most of May's work involved questioned documents in civil cases. One such case that made the news involved the will of Daisy Campbell. Her husband, a lighthouse keeper and fox farmer in Alaska, had left her a considerable inheritance when he died some years earlier. When Daisy died on New Years Day 1955, she left an estate of $240,000. She had lived with a sister and her husband for the last two years of her life, and her will, dated in March 1952, left the money to them.

When the will came up for probate, one Evans Collias submitted a will purportedly signed in January 1953. Collias and Daisy had lived in the same Seattle apartment complex for a while, and the will described him as a "very good friend."[4] May, however, testified that the Collias will "contained several alterations, and that the year '1952' had been erased and '1953' written in, in ink different from that used elsewhere in the will."[5] The judge's decision to reject the doctored will was later affirmed by the Washington Supreme Court.

May also did a *pro bono* case for the U.S. Navy. In April, he received a letter of appreciation from the top legal officer at the Thirteenth Naval District. The officer wrote, "When the defense became aware of the fact that you would testify for the Government as an expert witness, it conceded that the document in question was forged, and entered into a stipulation with the prosecution to that effect."[6]

May logged about thirty investigations for the year. The year also saw the passing of two noted crime fighters. In February, Colonel Calvin Goddard died from a heart attack at the age of sixty-four. He had been living in Washington, DC, editing historical materials about the Army Medical Corps. In November 1955, long-retired chief August Vollmer shot himself. Already afflicted with Parkinson's disease, he had also developed throat cancer. An operation three years earlier had left him in increasing pain. Toward the end, he required injections of painkiller every four hours.

Vollmer's death perhaps accelerated changes in his chosen field that he would have found disturbing. He had always sought to provide better-educated police officers. But, more and more, universities and the Society for the Advancement of Criminology had begun to downplay or even eliminate police education in favor of academic studies of the psychology and sociology of criminal behavior. A couple years after Vollmer's death, new leadership pushed through a name change to the American Society of Criminology. Three years later, the Berkeley School of Criminology began a complete switch to that path. As one commentary on the field said, "There would be no undergraduate major in law enforcement at the University of California."[7]

Yet Vollmer himself felt that institutions should be prepared to pursue both. Twenty years before these changes, he had advocated more attention to the causes of crime. He also called for "new institutions and practices for handling cases now placed in the category of police problems."[8]

Luke May also felt other avenues of crime prevention should be explored. Recall that in one of his many talks to private groups, he said, "Educating the American mind in preventing rather than combatting crime is the solution."[9] At another venue, he asked, "Who are these criminals? and What made them what they are?"[10] In his experience, poverty alone was not an overriding factor in criminal behavior. Certainly, the widespread poverty during the Great Depression did not cause a major increase in crime. But May was just a private citizen with no formal connection to academia. He could only use his speaking platform to present these issues to general audiences.

Fortunately, May still logged enough dramatic cases to keep his name in the news. Thus, in early 1956, he had another notable documents case. The case started as just another disputed will. The deceased was Ethel G. Kleinlein, a retired government worker who had accumulated a $100,000 estate. Her will allocated $8,000 to her ex-husband, Arnold M. Kleinlein. He, however, sought to have the will superseded by one in which he received the entire estate.

On the afternoon of January 9, May was home in bed, feeling "rather tough" as he put it. Around 3:45, Kleinlein called him. After some brief chit-chat, Kleinlein declared, "I think we ought to have a talk."[11]

"Why?"

"It's important that you have a talk with me and my aunts."

"What about?"

"There is a hundred thousand dollars involved, and I think its important that you be on our side."

"What do you mean?"

"We should have a talk . . . its important."

"I don't want to discuss any matter with you. Don't call me again."

Right after the exchange, Luke hand-recorded his memory of what was said. May wrote that Kleinlein's tone and emphasis "conveyed the idea to me that it would be worth my while to be on their side."[12] Since Luke had already deposed in favor of the original will, he said, "I could place only one interpretation on this conversation." The bequest by Ethel Kleinlein stood as she first wrote it. The case was one of thirty-one that May logged for 1956.

One case early the following year showed that May was still a generalist. In February, a prosecuting attorney in Port Townsend sent him a sleeping bag cover as evidence. A suspected burglar had bundled his loot in the canvas sack. The bag bore the suspect's name, handwritten, but the prosecutor thought "the name of the [real] owner had been erased with some chemical."[13]

Using a magnifier, May observed some faint lines behind the suspect's name written on a bleached spot. He then worked with "micro quantities of reagents," hoping to enhance the background image. He said, "A dilute solution of Tannic acid restored the faint line a little, and fumes of ammonium sulfide accentuated this restoration."[14] Shortly after May delivered his report, the suspect changed his plea. The prosecutor told May, "I feel certain that the endorsement of your name on the list of witnesses . . . compelled the defendant to withdraw his plea of 'Not Guilty.' His attorney is no fool."[15]

In October 1957, May received a letter that linked him with a case that garnered extensive national coverage. The King County prosecutor had leveled grand larceny counts against Dave Beck Sr. and his son, Dave Jr. Beck Sr. was then president of the Teamsters Union. Back in the spring, he had been grilled by a U.S. Senate committee exploring possible union corruption. He became notorious for the number of times he invoked his Fifth Amendment right against self-incrimination. Still, weeks of testimony eventually uncovered damaging revelations that led Beck to not run for reelection as president of the Teamsters. Later, he would be convicted on a separate tax evasion charge.

The grand larceny charge against Beck Sr. arose from the fact that he had sold a well-equipped Cadillac belonging to the union and pocketed the proceeds himself. The indictment against Beck Jr. was based on his sale of *two* union-owned Cadillacs. Prosecutors needed May to verify that they had endorsed, for deposit, the cashier's checks paid for the cars. During Junior's trial, in November, Deputy Prosecutor Laurence D. Regal began the process to connect the accused to the checks. However, the *Seattle Times* reported, "After the defense stipulated as to Beck's signature, Regal said that Luke S. May, Seattle criminologist, would not be called to testify."[16]

The jury took less than an hour to find Junior guilty. Beck Sr. was also found guilty on his grand larceny count. However, appeals of that and the tax evasion conviction kept Beck Sr. out of prison for more than four years. When all appeals failed, he served about two years and six months.

May's workload for 1957 was relatively light, about thirty cases, but it would pick up the following year. Also, the summer after the Beck case, the Mays recorded another life milestone. On June 22, 1958, Patricia (May) Reid gave birth to Mindi Reid, Luke's only known granddaughter.

None of May's cases during the year generated much attention, even locally. But he still continued his confidential polygraph work. Late in the year, he sent a letter to Clarence D. Lee in San Rafael, California. Twenty years earlier, Lee, then a captain with the Berkeley Police Department, had designed the psychograph. That was Lee's name for his version of a lie detector. Over the years afterwards, he made many improvements to the device, for which he was granted a patent. In his letter to Lee, May said, "A short time ago I became the owner of Psychograph No. 154 which is in fine mechanical condition and . . . I find myself using it more and more due to its size and portableness."[17]

The portability would have been a major advantage when May went to a business site to conduct employee tests. He next asked if there had been any later developments that might improve the machine further. Also, he wrote, "If there are special instructions on maintenance I will be pleased to have you send me a copy and I will be glad to remit for whatever charge there may be for same."[18]

May logged around forty-five cases during the year, half again more than the year before. That higher level continued into 1959 and even into 1960. However, hardly any of those cases appeared in the news. The few that did got no more than a passing mention in local newspapers. During this slow period, Luke and Helen moved again. The change perhaps reflected a need to lower their living costs. They moved to a home in the Wedgewood area, about three miles north of the University. May still had his basement laboratory space. However, granddaughter Mindi would eventually come to realize "the sadly truncated, almost refugee-status of his last lab."[19]

May received his next well-publicized case in early 1960. The build-up to the case began about five months before that. The events were somewhat reminiscent of the Will Forgeries scandal discussed in chapter 1. A middle-aged Ellensburg man decided to sell some property he had inherited as a young man. But he discovered it had been sold three years earlier for nonpayment of taxes. Records showed that the county owed him $182.37, the difference between the amount of unpaid taxes and what the property sold for. However, when he tried to pick up the check, he discovered that the money had already been claimed. The canceled check showed his purported signature and those of four witnesses.

Figure 18.1.   Luke with Granddaughter Mindi Reid. *Source*: **May-Reid Records.**

Further investigation disclosed that one witness, Thomas A. Rotta, had figured in numerous similar transactions. Besides several in King County, he'd done at least five in Kitsap County. One evidence package May received had "Paul C. Uhrich" as the victim.[20] In his report, May said, bluntly, "It is my opinion that the forged signatures of Paul Uhrich were written by Thomas Rotta." He noted that two witness signatures had probably been inked over light pencil traces. "The ink in the witness signatures show evidence of smearing in two directions, typical of ink being smeared in erasing the pencil outline."

Both May and the newspaper avoided giving too many details of Rotta's scheme, aside from the final forgeries. But in some ways, Rotta had it easier than the perpetrators of the Will Forgeries. That fraud required a breach of trust at the Bank of England. Rotta almost certainly started by simply reading the list, posted at a county seat, of properties scheduled for public auction due to nonpayment of taxes. A bit of research would identify properties where the overage was worth the trouble, and no one was likely to claim it. In fact, one potential claimant had died twenty-one years earlier, another nineteen. Authorities eventually charged Rotta with more than twenty counts of forgery or grand larceny. Rotta then agreed to plead guilty to one count each.

The Rotta case was well-covered by the Seattle newspapers but made little impression beyond the city. May's next newsworthy case took place in Everett, Washington. In late September, a fire gutted the Everett Elks Club. Initial reports said the fire had started at a deep fat fryer in the kitchen. Soon, however, there was speculation that the fryer blaze was secondary to a fire started by faulty wiring.

The Pacific Indemnity Company hired May to inspect the damage, which he did the day after the fire. He reported, "An inspection of the kitchen and the upper structure of the building left no doubt in my mind that the fire originated in the deep fryer."[21] May learned that the thermostat on the fryer had been changed a few weeks before the fire. "The cook had complained that he could not get the oil hot enough" with the old unit. Despite the burned exterior, May observed that the internal wiring on the fryer looked all right and showed no signs of failure.

Beyond all that, May also found that several people had handled the fryer after the fire had been put out. In his opinion, the fire scene contained too many variables that might have been altered since the fire. Such conditions would make it difficult to compare "the present characteristics of the thermostat with its characteristics before the fire."[22]

After that, the case dropped out of sight. Over the next three years, May's workload decreased again to about thirty cases per year. None would make much of a ripple in the news. Yet reporters still found May worth an interview, including one in the summer of 1962. An article in the *Post-Intelligencer* focused on May's recent work on document examination. Twice, "and fairly recently," the writer said, clients brought books that looked "old-old-old—and both bore this written signature, 'William Shakespeare.'"[23] May examined both the ink and the paper in these artifacts. From that, he "was able to convince these clients that the signatures were written a couple centuries after the greatest of dramatists was laid to rest."

By now, granddaughter Mindi Reid had grown old enough to retain specific memories of her life. And 1962 held a special place for her. In the spring, a World's Fair, formally the Century 21 Exposition, began its six-month run in Seattle. The fair transformed the city and gave it one of the most iconic landmarks in the world. And Grandpa Luke was there for family excursions. Major portions of the fair explored science and the world of the future. May had devoted his life to science . . . not just those areas useful to his work, but generally all of science. He was fascinated by it all.

In a memoir about Luke, Reid wrote, "I still find an odd comfort in the fact my grandfather lived to see the Space Needle rise above the industrial grey nonentity of Seattle's urban core."[24] She also said, "I grew up thinking it was the most normal thing in the world to have a laboratory in the basement—an essential element of 'Grampa-ness' a grandchild was entitled to." She loved all the exotic-seeming equipment.

For her fourth birthday, Luke pulled a "dirty" but delightful trick on her. She had shown a special interest in a small magnifier with an adjustable neck. One day, some time before her birthday, the precious tool disappeared from the lab. Luke claimed a burglar had broken in and, for some strange reason, stolen that one object. She was devastated, and too young to interpret grampa's straight-faced humor or twinkling eye. Of course, he then gave her the magnifier as a birthday present, a piece of memorabilia she still has.

May himself revisited some memories in the spring of 1963. He had originally met attorney Edmund Burke in connection with a murder case tried in Bozeman, Montana (chapter 13). Now, Burke had seen May's name in the classified section of the *American Bar Journal.* That had prompted "a note to inquire as to your good health and welfare since I last saw you in Seattle in 1946."[25] At that time Burke had switched from the naval reserve to the regular navy. Now he was about to retire after twenty years of active duty. He went on, "The oldest of our two sons, whom you would recall as a mere baby when you were at the house in Bozeman back in 1934, will graduate in law from the University of California this spring."

Their younger son was about to graduate from college so he and "Dorth," his wife Dorothy, hoped to travel a bit. "I shall always remain exceedingly grateful to you for the time which you spent with me in Montana just before I took office as County Attorney," Burke said. "Almost daily I have observed the deficiencies exhibited by those who lack basic training in investigative procedures."[26]

Burke went on, "Over the years, I have been saddened by the absolute lack of any recognition accorded to you for your foresight and the work you accomplished for the Navy and the Nation, especially during the pre-war and early war years. I still shudder to think of some of the dire consequences which this country might have suffered had that work not been accomplished."

He then invited May to come visit if he was ever in the Los Angeles area. In closing, Burke said, "Dorth joins in extending our warmest personal regards and best wishes to you." May's reply assured Burke that he had enjoyed the letter and appreciated "very much the sentiments therein expressed." He also said, "It is hoped that at some time in the not too distant future that we may have an opportunity to renew our friendship."[27]

Of course, by then May was more than seventy years old, in an era when that was considered quite elderly. Plus, he was probably in the early stages of the malady he would die from. Mindi Reid recalled that at her birthday party eight months earlier Luke was "painfully thin" with "translucent-skinned hands."[28] He was not likely to be traveling to Los Angeles.

May's last well-publicized case hit the newspapers at the end of the summer. And the main player harked back seven years to the contested will of Ethel G. Kleinlein. Recall that May had received a scarcely veiled bribe offer from Arnold M. Kleinlein, her ex-husband. Four years after losing out on his ex-wife's will, Kleinlein had tried again. A former cleaning lady in Seattle, Jennie Kleinlein, died and left an estate of about $360,000. Despite having the same last name, Arnold was no relation to Jennie. Yet, somehow, he showed up with a will that left the estate to him as "a friend." A physician's testimony asserted that Jennie was not mentally competent when the will was purportedly prepared, so May was not involved. The court awarded Jennie's estate to two of her grandchildren.

Arnold Kleinlein's only link to the 1963 will was as "a part-time chauffeur" for the deceased, Dr. S. Maimon Samuels.[29] That was supposedly enough to earn him a major share of Samuels's million-dollar estate. The purported will seemed to speak for both the doctor and his wife. Gratuitously, it even referred to the Jennie Kleinlein case. It said that an earlier will had tried to leave a "$360,000 estate to our friend Arnold Kleinlein, to whom both of us are deeply indebted for many kindnesses, but I understand the Courts have taken it from him. I trust there will be no interference of Judges and Courts with my will or with my executor."[30]

Naturally, the Samuels's surviving son and daughter fought this new submission. Kleinlein appeared totally confident, yet the signature on the claimed will was not well done. Three bankers testified that they would have questioned any check with such a signature. Then May gave his expert opinion that the signature was not genuine. May said the name on the will was a "slow drawing, rather than a fluently written, free-flowing signature."[31] A day after that, the *Post-Intelligencer* reported, "Clark Sellers of Pasadena, internationally-known handwriting expert, testified yesterday that in his opinion the signature offered on a will as that of S. Maimon Samuels is not Dr. Samuels' genuine signature."[32]

The judge threw out the bogus will, and then events took a bizarre turn. One of the lawyers for the Samuels's heirs insisted that the judge read aloud a letter that Kleinlein had slipped him during the course of the trial. "Should anyone offer or attempt to offer you any money to declare Dr. Samuels' will to be invalid," Kleinlein wrote, "I hereby agree to meet any offer made to you plus $360,000 cash to respect, honor and uphold the January, 1962 valid will."[33]

The judge said the matter was being further investigated, but a charge of criminal contempt of court was likely. Kleinlein, however, remained feisty and defiant. He told the *Post-Intelligencer,* "I've been robbed of a million dollars!" The next day, Kleinlein found himself in jail, charged with bribery, forgery, and criminal contempt. Two days after that, the court had three psychiatrists examine him. Satisfied that he was no flight risk, the judge reduced Kleinlein's bond and allowed him out on bail. Less than three weeks later, Arnold Kleinlein had a heart attack and died.

As Christmas approached, May received a letter from Clark Sellers. Sellers wrote, "One of the most important things that has happened to me in a long time, for which I am deeply grateful, was the opportunity of renewing our acquaintance and my affection for you through our joint participation in the Dr. Samuels case. There is nothing that quite takes the place of actually working together and pulling for each other."[34]

Despite his age, May continued to give talks to business and social organizations. One of his topics revisited the causes of crime, offering *Home Environment and Its Relationship to Crime.* He continued to speak to groups at least through 1963 but does seem to have cut back after that. In early 1964, the Pacific Northwest Security Association awarded May a commendation for his many years searching for truth and justice. The text said, "Few have sought it so diligently for so many years to prove equally innocence or guilt as has Luke S. May."[35]

May almost certainly suffered from leukemia for several years before the disease was finally diagnosed in the fall of 1964. In mid-November, an attorney in Phoenix, Arizona, wrote May about "a case involving allegedly forged signatures on two deeds purporting to convey certain real property."[36] He wondered what May's charge would be to examine the documents and later testify in court. Helen wrote the reply. "Mr. May has been seriously ill with leukemia for several weeks and is still critically ill. I regret that I am unable to assist you in the matter you mentioned."[37]

Three month later, a letter arrived from a detective agency in Boise, Idaho. A key document was "in the hands of the opposing counsel," so all they had was a copy.[38] The writer then identified the model of copy machine that had been used. "We would greatly appreciate learning if you could make a signature comparison from this copy and actual signatures of our client." Helen replied, "Mr. May has been seriously ill for several months and is not practicing at the present time."[39] She gave a similar answer to another request at the end of March.

Daughter Patricia described those final months in her memoir. "During those last days he told me that one comes to life to do a special job and to do one's best and when that has been accomplished, we go on," she recalled.[40] "A simple, meaningful definition of human purpose, really difficult to improve upon."

Figure 18.2. May Always Preferred Snappy Hats. *Source*: May-Reid Records.

He also urged her to "talk less, and *be* more." Good advice that Patricia admitted she had "often fallen short in practicing." Luke "enjoyed good conversation, but always maintained it at a quality level. . . . He detested gossip, but loved telling good jokes with such a mischievous warmth!"[41]

Despite the pain and his emaciation, she recalled, "his exceptional mind was as brilliant and fine as it had always been." But finally, she said, "he lapsed into a blessed coma [for] his final few hours." Luke S. May passed away on July 11, 1965.

His death was widely reported. The *Seattle Post-Intelligencer* said, "He was one of the first detectives to stress the importance of handwriting and of microscopic examination and chemical analysis of fingernails, hairs, bullets, and other physical evidence in the identification of criminals."[42] Newspapers all across the country picked up the death notice. Some published just a brief item while a few provided more details on his extraordinary career. May had set out "to do a special job" and to do his best. He had accomplished that and then gone on.

Retrospection

*A*bout eighteen months before May died, he received a letter from Jan Beck, a Berkeley-educated questioned documents examiner. Beck wrote him from Falls Church, Virginia, to ask about career opportunities in Seattle. He then had a good government position but was unhappy with certain aspects of the job. May studied the letter, then replied, "I would . . . all things considered, strongly advise against a change."[1]

That discouraged Beck for a while, but he did set up a private practice in Seattle a couple years after May died. Beck knew Clark Sellers through his professional society membership. Sellers was kind enough to write a letter of introduction to Helen May for him. After a time, Helen began accepting Beck's help in selling off Luke's equipment and library materials.

She did not, however, allow him to view the contents of one particular wooden one-drawer file cabinet. Helen sent that directly to the landfill, so we can only infer what was in it. It must have contained child-support papers about Florence Dorothy May, because we know Helen did not learn that Patricia had a half-sister until after Luke died. He had kept that a secret all those years.

Of course, May had to keep many secrets. For most of his cases, there would have been information he could share only with his client. That must have created a steady level of strain. In fact, the nature of his work involved a dichotomy. A detective wants truthful answers but occasionally lies, at least by omission, in seeking them. In "murder by the stars," May showed only the "confession" headline to the astrologer's youthful accomplice to trick him into talking. These and other subterfuges were "for the greater good" but would have surely been stressful.

We know that, given the right circumstances, May was willing to talk or write about some of his cases. And, from all accounts, he was an enthralling storyteller. But even then, he would have walked a fine line between explaining key details without revealing too much for some events. Thus, May used made-up names in most of the cases in *Crime's Nemesis* and for some of those published in *True Detective Mysteries* magazine. Of course, his link with the magazine would have been another source of tension. Violence and sex sold copies, so the editors played up those features. May disliked that approach and found his monthly column much more to his liking.

His personal life exhibited similar oddities. Recall that early in his career May added six years to his age. He had good business reasons for that, of course. But he never corrected that untruth and even perpetuated it in his navy records. And May took great delight in daughter Patricia and later his granddaughter. Yet, as discussed in chapter 4, evidence strongly suggests that he deliberately cut off contact with his first daughter. While that was probably for her own good, it must have been very painful for Luke.

Naturally, not every contrast was so grave. May was not a particularly religious person, and there's no indication that he was a regular church-goer. Still, Patricia recalled that "Dad was a God-respecting man."[2] She had fond childhood memories of May reading her Bible stories at bedtime. And, finally, May projected an almost professorial image in interviews and on the witness stand. But, according to family memories, May was a fan of televised professional wrestling (rasslin') during its heyday in the 1950s. Patricia told her daughter that Luke would really get into the action, with grunts and gestures. Yet he surely knew it was an athletic exhibition, not a real competition. That was hardly what one would expect from a thoughtful criminological expert.

But for all these apparent contradictions, May was no "tortured soul." As we have seen, he retained a warm and gentle—although sometimes mischie-vous—sense of humor. Whatever frustration he felt when careless or inept investigators botched a case, he did not show it overtly. He never criticized them to the news media, and even his attempts to instruct officials in proper techniques remained strictly one-on-one.

Thus, secrets were an integral part of May's work. In fact, his case re-cords contain many details that were never reported in the news. As for those files, Helen's son-in-law, aided by Jan Beck, moved the bulk of the Luke S. May Papers to the University of Washington in early 1969. The university had requested the materials as part of its program to preserve historically im-portant sources. Beck recalled, "The archivist was positively ecstatic when he told me that U.W. had 'acquired the papers of Luke May and Anna Louise Strong in the same week.'"[3]

Strong had been elected to the Seattle school board in 1916 before being recalled three years later for her opposition to U.S. involvement in World War I. She became a world-famous author, committed advocate for Communism, and personal friend of Chinese leader Mao Tse-tung. She was radically different from Luke May, but one can understand the archivist's excitement.

May's records fill nearly sixty-five containers stretching more than eighty-three linear feet. As mentioned in chapter 1, the boxes hold many of his two thousand-plus case files. They also have many product sheets, technical references, and some magazine articles. There are also scores of newspaper clippings about May and his cases.

With the pronounced shift in case type after World War II, questioned document examinations made up more than half of May's lifetime workload. But along with those, May handled nearly 270 death cases, with more than three hundred victims. About a third of those cases were never closed. Many were not prosecuted because officials did not have enough evidence, even with the help May provided. For firearms cases, that often arose from a failure to track down the death weapon. For some cases, key witnesses refused to cooperate. And sometimes officers compromised the crime scene or the evidence.

Of course, officials mostly hired May only after their own efforts had come up short. Sometimes that indicated they did not have the resources, but often it also meant the case was especially difficult. Still, on the face of it, failing to solve a third of the death cases he worked on seems rather unimpressive. Yet national statistics from the FBI show that even now officers fail to clear about the same fraction of homicides. That's despite investigators who are supposedly highly educated and have modern techniques and equipment to work with.

May succeeded partly because of well-trained natural ability and also because he was determined to have the best possible tools for scientific crime investigation. He therefore either improved the techniques already available or developed his own. Tool mark analysis is the most obvious, since his Clark case set the precedent for their use in court. He was also one of the earliest to assess bullet trajectories and blood spatter to reconstruct crimes.

May did firearms tests for more than two hundred cases. He could read bullets to identify the make and model of virtually every commonly used handgun and rifle in the world. Goddard rightly gets credit for informing a national audience about bullet and shell casing markings. Yet Luke May was identifying specific weapons at least as early. The army had studied wound ballistics for a long time, but May was probably the first to use it for a civilian application.

May devised better methods to record latent fingerprints. Early on, he found that standard fingerprint powders were not very good. As a result, he made up his own. Along the way, he discovered several ways that fingerprints could be counterfeited. He then worked out methods for detecting such fakes. To record fingerprint images, he found ways to photograph them using special lighting, filters, and film types. That work went hand in hand with his other advances in photography, both for crime-scene images and for evidence records. From there, he improved the preparation of visual aids to be shown in court.

After firearms, blunt trauma wounds by clubs of various types figured in many of May's death cases. That brought his blood spatter work into play. His "pinning and threading" technique added substantially to his ability to re-create a crime. Trauma impacts also required extensive analysis of hair and fibers. May cataloged and recorded a wide array of such samples. He could read hair samples to make reasonable inferences about the sex and age of the hair source. Along those lines, May was one of the first to use fracture or end matching as in the Nosko murder case.

He analyzed materials further in the lab, such as the case where he recovered the hidden writing on a sleeping bag cover. But he was also early to identify various paint types and how they had been applied. May used both chemical and physical methods to develop leads in a number of bombing cases he handled. For questioned documents, May refined methods to study paper, typewriters, ink, and more. He became an expert in the use of ultraviolet light to study documents as well as other substances.

As early as 1915, May used what we call "profiling" to guide his search for likely suspects. He probably saw it as a refinement of the *modus operandi* approach to criminal identification. He knew profiling's limitations but found it useful to prioritize where to send his agents. In this, he was perhaps a half century ahead of his time.

The list of techniques he helped advance goes on and on. And the range of his cases was amazing. Besides all manner of death cases and questioned documents, he handled just about every kind of investigation one can imagine. Many were relatively mundane, like background checks, divorces, and smuggling. But he also had cases that involved arson, explosions, structural collapses, aircraft crashes, cattle rustling(!), and more. Of course, as noted in chapter 1, only a modest fraction of May's cases appeared in magazines and the larger newspapers. Those not covered included some of his death cases as well as bombings, sabotage, and other dramatic events.

Still, the publicity he did receive fueled requests for his advice on scientific criminology. That began with the Chicago crime lab. Recall that Wigmore said, "Your advice has been most valuable to us." And the RCMP crime lab historian said that May's letter "carried the most weight" in their development. We have no such testimonial for the FBI crime lab, but the link through Inspector James Egan seems most suggestive. And not only did he help establish the Oregon State Police, but through Ed Newell he helped found the state police in New Hampshire.

May prompted the formation of the first association of law enforcement officials in the Pacific Northwest and remained the organization's president for more than a decade. As president, he promoted plans to harness radio communications for law enforcement in the Northwest. He also led efforts to apply teletype linkages to police work.

Not only did he lecture at the University of Washington, Willamette University, and the University of Oregon, he ran the private criminology school in Seattle for many, many years. Last but not least, he reached the general public through his monthly column in *True Detective Mysteries* magazine.

May's success rate made him famous . . . in his heyday. Recall that he was even well-known in Europe before World War II. After the war, when he handled few headline-grabbing cases, his fame still drew attention and respect. Yet Luke May's name dropped from sight the day after his death notice appeared. Just short of two years later, the estate put his large gun collection up for auction. One or two newspaper articles used the phrase "his colorful, 50-year career" but gave no details. Gun collectors flocked to the auction, but no one published any follow-up articles about Luke May.

Then, on January 10, 1970, the *Seattle Times* carried a brief announcement under its "Deaths, Funerals" heading, thirty pages deep in the newspaper. It reported the passing of Helen K. May, "widow of the late, noted criminologist, Luke S. May."[4] Three weeks later, the Sunday edition of the *Times* published a two-page article about "Luke May—Seattle's Master Criminologist."[5] The writer summarized May's career, including several of his most notable cases. That item was not reprinted anywhere else, but it did spark a flurry of local letters remembering him. Alfred Schweppe, former dean of the University of Washington Law School wrote, "In terms of permanent social value, he was one of our distinguished citizens."[6]

Five more years passed before the *Times* published a one-column historical vignette about May's work. Another vignette in 1978 mentioned May but focused mainly on Peggy Paulos's role in the Bremerton massacre. And that was it. More than a decade would pass before any new material about May appeared in print. That was authored by Jan Beck and published in the *Journal of Forensic Sciences*. Other than that, May's contributions were virtually forgotten. In fact, Luke May is hardly ever mentioned in texts on forensic science when the overall history of the field is reviewed. A scant few reference the tool mark precedent set by the Clark case, but most do not even cite that. You may well ask: Why not?

One need not postulate some vast conspiracy. Two factors worked against him. First, the change in the crime-fighting field that began after the death of August Vollmer had become more pronounced by the time May passed away. The American Society of Criminology and big university programs had even co-opted the word criminology. That term was reserved for work that dealt primarily with the sociology and psychology of crime. Matters involving physical evidence—its collection, processing, and presentation—would be left to "criminalists."

"Criminologist Dies" was a common headline about May's passing. Yet the newly accepted usage of that term excluded most of what May had done during his career. He addressed the issue of crime causation and prevention in his talks, but, day-to-day, he handled evidence. And, according to one history of the field, a leading proponent of the new paradigm declared, "Occupational affinity did not necessarily make one a criminologist."[7] So the field where May thought he had spent his life had essentially disowned him. It was too late for him to become known as an innovative criminalist.

The second factor involves the normal methods for publishing accounts of technical advances. May, of course, never went to college. Nor did he have any formal affiliation with a traditional academic institution. Thus, he was never pressed to submit articles to any of the available academic publications. In fact, it probably never occurred to him to try to publish there. That meant that his only such publication was his tool mark paper in the *American Journal of Police Science*.

May did receive two patents, but such documents are of interest only to narrowly focused specialists. He self-published his manuals for investigative work and distributed them himself. *Crime's Nemesis* was "only" a popular account. And who would look at *True Detective Mysteries* magazine as a reference? Newspaper articles provided a window on his cases. However, they focused on his results, not on how those results were obtained. May's other main avenues of communication were conference lectures, one-on-one letters and visits, and popular-interest talks. Those left few traces for the historian.

But he advanced the field with every appearance in court, every bit of advice to his colleagues, and every discussion for the general public. Hopefully, this case-based account of Luke May's life shows why he deserves to be honored as one of the pioneers of scientific crime detection.

Appendix

Cases Overview

$\mathscr{T}$he history of Luke May's casework falls roughly into three periods: (1) before 1920, (2) from 1920 to World War II, and (3) during and after the war. The Luke S. May Papers do not contain a formal log of his cases before the move to Seattle in 1919–1920. So that period has been re-created from news reports, a small number of case files, and May's book, *Crime's Nemesis*.

After Luke and his wife moved to Seattle in 1919–1920, May began to log every case. For most, he included a case number, short descriptive title, the kind of investigation(s) performed, and often the name of the client. Dates were either recorded or could be inferred from the assigned case number. (For every case discussed in the book, dates were confirmed by newspaper reports.) During and after World War II, May continued to assign case numbers but no longer included a title and other information on the master log. Those details were retained only in the case files themselves. As mentioned earlier, I copied some of those files and took brief notes on many more. Again, newspaper reports were used to confirm and supplement the information from the Luke May Papers.

A combination of all this information was used to create the list shown below, which classifies his cases by type of investigation. Death cases have been further assigned into subcategories. Within those divisions, I have also tried to list the cause of death. Note that "Homicides" is used to describe deaths that resulted in charges for murder or manslaughter. Hit-and-run and other death-causing incidents are listed separately. "Bludgeon" may refer to any "blunt-force trauma" method—a blow with some weapon (tire iron, fist, etc.) as well as when the victim is slammed against a hard object.

1910–1919

Before 1915, May's cases were all in Utah and mostly in Salt Lake City. After he moved his headquarters to Pocatello, he handled cases all across southern Idaho, plus one death case in Philipsburg, Montana (about fifty miles southeast of Missoula). During this time, newspapers and May's few case files identify just twenty-two cases. However, other documents show that May was doing well financially in the period after about 1914. It thus seems certain that he and his agency handled many more cases for which we have no records. In any event, the cases we know about break out into the following groupings:

  6   General investigations (burglary, tracing stolen goods, audio surveillance, etc.)
  5   Tracking individuals ("persons of interest," fugitives, missing persons, etc.)
  1   Questioned document
10   Death cases, with 14 victims:
  9   Homicides: Firearms (5), knife (2), poison, bludgeon
  1   Self-defense: Firearms

1920–1923

After May moved to Seattle, most of his cases were in Washington. Many were in Seattle, but he also had cases in large and small towns all over the state. Several others were in Oregon, and he even investigated an accidental death case in California. In total, he logged 438 cases.

141   Questioned documents (32 percent)
113   General investigations
 85   Tracking individuals
 37   Liquor law violations
 22   Sabotage (arson, bombing, etc.)
 40   Death cases, with 44 victims:
 29   Homicides: Firearms (19), poison (3), knife (1), means not reported (6)
  3   Suicides: Firearms (2), means not reported
  1   Self-defense: Firearms

7 Accidents: Firearms (3), faulty gas heater, automobile, drowning at sea, not reported

1924–1927

During this period, May logged 366 cases. That was down quite a bit from the previous span. However, the number and percentage of QD and death cases increased. Also, May was no longer called to investigate incidents of sabotage. Again, most cases were in Washington (with many around Puget Sound), but he also had several death cases in Idaho, two in Oregon, and one near Peace River, Alberta, Canada.

152 Questioned documents (42 percent)
100 General investigations
55 Tracking individuals
12 Liquor law violations
47 Death cases, with 52 victims:
32 Homicides: Firearms (23), bludgeon (5), knife, strangulation (2), means not reported
4 Suicides: Firearms (4)
2 Self-defense: Firearms (2)
3 Hit-and-run, automobile
6 Accidents: Firearms (5), drowning

1928–1931

A total of 280 cases were logged. The number of cases for this four-year span was down even further, and May no longer showed any liquor-related investigations. The percentage of QD cases increased, but the big factor was the surge in death cases. The range of locations outside of Washington was considerable, with four cases in Idaho, and one each in Oregon, Utah, Wyoming, and Alaska.

137 Questioned documents (49 percent)
61 General investigations
16 Tracking individuals
66 Death cases, with 67 victims:

54   Homicides: Firearms (40), bludgeon (10), knife, poison, means not reported (2)
 4   Suicides: Firearms (3), dynamite
 3   Hit-and-run, automobile
 5   Accidents: Firearms (2), automobile, drowning

1932–1935

A total of 224 cases were logged. The further decline was at least partly because he did not take private cases in King County while he was chief of detectives for Seattle. He continued to handle cases at a wide variety of locations. That included ten death cases all across Montana, four in Idaho, three in Oregon, and even one from Tampa, Florida.

109   Questioned documents (49 percent)
 51   General investigations
  6   Tracking individuals
 58   Death cases, with 70 victims:
 46   Homicides: Firearms (36), bludgeon (7), knife (2), strangulation
  4   Suicides: Firearms (2), drowning, means not reported
  6   Accidents: Firearms (5), falling bricks
  2   Self-defense: Firearms (2)

1936–1939

A total of 195 cases were logged. The continued decline in the number of cases was probably the result of May's increasing involvement with the U.S. Naval Reserve. The vast majority of his cases were in the Puget Sound area, but he had others all across the state. He also had death cases in Montana (2) and Oregon (3). He even performed evidence tests for a death in San Juan, Puerto Rico.

122   Questioned documents (49 percent)
 30   General investigations
  6   Tracking individuals
 37   Death cases, with 45 victims:
 21   Homicides: Firearms (12), bludgeon (7), knife (2)

6   Suicides: Firearms (6)
8   Accidents: Firearms (5), a fall, accidental drug overdose, means not reported
1   Hit-and-run, automobile
1   Self-defense: Firearm

1940–1950

Around 290 case numbers were assigned (May sometimes posted a number but then apparently did not take a case). He recorded case numbers and types, client names, and locations in his log for 1940, but only the case numbers after that. An even higher fraction of his cases came from Seattle and around Puget Sound. Still, he logged one documents case each from northern Idaho; Kodiak, Alaska; and Vancouver, British Columbia. He also had one death case in central Montana.

228   Questioned documents (79 percent)
 42   General investigations
 12   Tracking individuals
  8   Death cases, with 13 victims:
  3   Homicides: Firearm, bludgeon, knife
  1   Suicide: Firearm
  3   Accidents: Airline crash, strangulation, gas explosion
  1   Hit-and-run, automobile

1951–1965

About 470 cases numbers were assigned. Of the cases we know something about, all but one were in Seattle or around Puget Sound. The single exception, in Ritzville, Washington, was discussed in chapter 17. The only death case for the period was discussed in chapter 18.

400   Questioned documents (85 percent)
 54   General investigations
 15   Tracking individuals
  1   Death case, with 1 victim: Self-defense: Firearm

Notes

$\mathcal{T}$he Luke S. May Papers provided the core resource for this book. They are stored at the University of Washington Special Collections in Seattle. The Papers are on restricted usage, requiring permission from Mindi Reid, Luke May's granddaughter, to access the repository. (To reach her, contact Special Collections at the University.) That resource is cited many, many times in the text. The full citation would be: *Luke S. May Papers.* Special Collections, University of Washington Libraries, Seattle. Thus, to streamline the Notes presentation, that resource is abbreviated as "*May Papers,* UW."

Another repository accessed for the book was the National Archives and Records Administration in St. Louis, Missouri. Fortunately, May's official retirement date for his naval service was in 1951, so his records became archival and are available (for a fee) to others beyond his immediate family. Again, a citation for those resources would be quite long: *Luke Silvester* [*sic*] *May, Military Personnel Records*, National Archives and Records Administration, St. Louis, Missouri. Again, to streamline the Notes, that resource is abbreviated as "*May Naval Records.*"

These two repositories contained more than 130 letters that proved very useful for this project. More than one hundred of them were quoted in the chapters and are cited here in the Notes.

More than eighteen hundred newspaper clippings relevant to this narrative were collected. More than a hundred of those were scanned from library copies or clippings held in the Luke May Papers. The remainder were downloaded from the fee-based digital archives managed at GenealogyBank.com and Newspapers.com. While many provided valuable background information, only those directly quoted in the chapters are cited here.

CHAPTER 1

1. Doyle, Arthur Conan. "The Problem of Thor Bridge." *The Strand*, London, November 1921.

2. Ibid.

3. Ibid.

4. Ibid.

5. Ibid.

6. Ibid.

7. "Light Employee is Found Dead." *San Diego Union*, November 24, 1930.

8. "Death Clue Search on at Shelton." Olympia (WA), *Olympian*, November 26, 1930.

9. May, Luke S. *Crime's Nemesis*. New York: The Macmillan Company, 1936.

10. Ibid.

11. Ibid.

12. Ibid.

13. Ibid.

14. Ibid.

15. Ibid.

16. Ibid.

17. Ibid.

18. Ibid.

19. Ibid.

20. Hall, Albert L. "The Missile and the Weapon." *American Journal of Police Science*, 2, no. 4 (1931): 311–21. [Reprint of original paper.]

21. Ibid.

CHAPTER 2

1. Poole, Thomas W. *A Sketch of the Early Settlement and Subsequent Progress of the Town of Peterborough*. Ontario: Office of the Peterborough Review, 1867.

2. Reid, Mindi. *Extracts from the Journal of Patricia Helen (May) Reid*. Unpublished typescript, Redmond, Washington, 2000.

3. Ibid.

4. Ibid.

5. "May Yield Half of a Crop." Lincoln (NE), *World-Herald*, August 1, 1894.

6. Bassett, Samuel Clay. *Buffalo County, Nebraska, and Its People*. Chicago: The S. J. Clarke Publishing Company, 1916.

7. "The Outlook for Nebraska." *World-Herald*, June 2, 1901.

8. "Conan Doyle's New Story," *World-Herald*, June 29, 1902.

9. "Sherlock Holmes at His Best." *World-Herald*, June 30, 1902.

10. Doyle, Arthur Conan. *The Hound of the Baskervilles.* New York: Grosset & Dunlap, 1902.

11. Ibid.

12. "593 Buildings Erected in Salt Lake This Year." *Salt Lake Telegram,* December 20, 1902.

13. "Greatest Building Year in History of Salt Lake; Contractors Say Next Season May Break Record." *Salt Lake Telegram,* October 30, 1903.

14. "Salt Lake's Outlook for 1905 Better Than at Any Time in Past." *Salt Lake Telegram,* December 22, 1904.

15. "Closing Exercises of Jordan School District." *Salt Lake Tribune,* June 3, 1908.

16. "Gordon Academy Has Good Record." *Salt Lake Telegram,* January 25, 1908.

17. "Oakland Adopts Bertillon System." Fresno (CA), *Morning Republican,* December 29, 1908.

CHAPTER 3

1. "Burglar Kills a Salt Lake Boy." *Salt Lake Telegram,* October 12, 1910.

2. Ibid.

3. May, *Nemesis.*

4. Ibid.

5. Ibid.

6. "Few Clues for Police to Follow." *Salt Lake Telegram,* October 15, 1910.

7. Ibid.

8. "Wall of Evidence Built Up." *Salt Lake Telegram,* October 17, 1910.

9. "Salt Lake's 'First Nighters'." Salt Lake City, *The Theater,* March 6, 1911.

10. "Trunkey Starts for Tennessee." Ogden, *Evening Standard,* November 8, 1910.

11. "New Corporations." *Salt Lake Telegram,* January 7, 1911.

12. "Trusted Domestic Robs Employers; Now Is in Jail." *Salt Lake Telegram,* April 13, 1911.

13. May, *Nemesis.*

14. "Further Admissions in Keyser Home Burglary." *Salt Lake Tribune,* April 14, 1911.

15. "No Charge Against Girl." *Salt Lake Telegram,* April 17, 1911.

16. "No Trace Yet Found of Bandits." *Salt Lake Telegram,* June 8, 1911.

17. "Stolen Money is Returned to Bank." *Salt Lake Telegram,* June 23, 1911.

18. May, *Nemesis.*

19. "Bits of Information." *Salt Lake Telegram,* June 27, 1911.

20. May, *Nemesis.*

21. "Society: May—McCullough Marriage." *Salt Lake Telegram,* November 21, 1911.

22. Ibid.

23. "Drug Clerk Confesses to Systematic Looting of Employers Stock." *Salt Lake Telegram,* February 23, 1912.

24. Ibid.

25. May, *Nemesis.*

26. Ibid.

27. "Six-Prong Buck is Evidence of Skill of Local Nimrod." *Salt Lake Telegram,* November 5, 1912.

28. "Japanese Detective Walks into Marked Money Trap." *Salt Lake Telegram,* January 8, 1914.

29. "May in New Position." *Salt Lake Telegram,* January 14, 1914.

30. "Identifying Crooks by Pores of Their Skin." Anaconda (MT), *Standard,* March 22, 1914.

31. "Detective Work." *Salt Lake Tribune,* March 2, 1914.

32. "May Opens New Agency." *Salt Lake Telegram,* May 12, 1914.

33. "Wanted—Detective Representatives: Local young men." Washington, DC, *Evening Star,* June 21, 1914.

34. "Detective Bureau." Ogden, *Evening Standard,* October 1, 1914.

35. "Detective Service Headquarters Here." *Salt Lake Telegram,* December 10, 1914.

36. Ibid.

CHAPTER 4

1. "Bertillon System Soon to Be Put in Operation at Police Headquarters." *Salt Lake Telegram,* December 9, 1914.

2. "American Prison Delegates Meet." *San Francisco Chronicle,* October 10, 1915.

3. May, *Nemesis.*

4. Ibid.

5. Ibid.

6. "Five Arrested on Murder Charge." Idaho Falls, *Idaho Register,* March 30, 1915.

7. "Woman's Death Ends Trial." *Idaho Register,* April 23, 1915.

8. Clark, Solon. 1915. Letter to Luke May dated June 28. *May Papers,* UW.

9. Smith, C. Douglas. 1915. Letter to Luke May dated June 1. *May Papers,* UW.

10. "Detectives to Locate." Boise, *Idaho Statesman,* August 8, 1915.

11. "Articles of Incorporation." *Idaho Statesman,* January 8, 1916.

12. "Finger Print Photograph." *Twin Falls Chronicle,* February 27, 1916.

13. "Heaviest Snowfall Recorded." Idaho Falls, *Idaho Register,* March 28, 1916.

14. Fultz, Hollis B. (as told to). "Seeking a Slayer in the Craters of the Moon." *True Detective Mysteries,* May 1932.

15. "New Sweden Citizens Active." *Idaho Register,* June 30, 1916.

16. "Gun Outfit at Salmon . . . Murder and Robbery. . . ." Salmon (ID), *Herald,* July 7, 1916.

17. "Murderer of Breckenridge Confesses." *Idaho Register,* July 7, 1916.

18. "Caught Bad Man." *Idaho Register,* April 4, 1916.

19. Stevens, James M. 1916. Letter to Luke May dated November 28. *May Papers,* UW.

20. "Electricity and Wireless Solve Secret Service Problems." *The Electrical Experimenter,* June 1916.

21. Hawley, James H. *History of Idaho: The Gem of the Mountains.* Chicago: The S. J. Clarke Publishing Co., 1920.

22. "Murder Search On." Portland, *Oregonian,* March 29, 1917.

23. May, *Nemesis.*

24. Ibid.

25. Ibid.

26. "Ruth Portrays Cousin's Death as Accidental." Boise, *Idaho Statesman,* May 29, 1917.

27. "Dan Ruth is on Trial for Killing Yale Man." *Idaho Statesman,* November 13, 1917.

28. McAdams, Harrison. 1919. Letter to Luke May dated June 2. *May Papers,* UW.

29. Bevel, Tom, and Ross M. Gardner. *Bloodstain Pattern Analysis,* 3rd ed. Boca Raton, FL: Taylor & Francis Group, CRC Press, 2008.

30. "Florence May vs. L. S. May," *Case Number 18307,* Third District Court, Salt Lake County, Utah. June 1914–November 1918.

31. Ibid.

32. Ibid.

33. Ibid.

34. Ibid.

35. "Pocatello News." Boise, *Idaho Statesman,* January 24, 1919.

36. "Detective Skill Defies the Haunts of Nature." *The Investigator* 1, no. 1. Chicago: F. Dalton O'Sullivan Publishing, July 1919.

CHAPTER 5

1. "Returned Heroes Slain by I.W.W." *Salt Lake Tribune,* November 12, 1919.

2. McDougall, Isaac E. 1921. Letter to Luke May dated January 20. *May Papers,* UW.

3. "To Celebrate Armistice Day." *Seattle Times,* October 31, 1919.

4. "Idaho Sleuths Trail Murderers of Service Men." Boise, *Idaho Statesman,* February 29, 1920.

5. "Peace Officers on Fingerprint System in Idaho." *Idaho Statesman,* February 1, 1920.

6. "Pocatello Detective is Given Promotion." *Idaho Statesman,* March 24, 1920.

7. "Lumber Mill Burns at Chehalis, Wash." Portland, *Oregonian,* March 30, 1920.

8. May, Luke. 1920. Letter to C. L. Brown dated April 3. *May Papers,* UW.

9. "Outlaw May Have Murdered His Companion." *Seattle Times,* April 5, 1920.

10. May, Luke. April 13, 1920. "Scott-Cady Case File." *May Papers*, UW.

11. Ibid.

12. May, *Nemesis*.

13. "Father Shot and Killed by Stepson." *Seattle Times*, May 18, 1920.

14. May, Luke. June 4, 1920. "Friedman Case File." *May Papers*, UW.

15. Ibid.

16. Ibid.

17. "Killing Charge Dropped." *Seattle Times*, October 3, 1920.

18. Allen, Herman, 1920. Letter to Luke May dated May 7. *May Papers*, UW.

19. "Incendiary is Sentenced." Portland, *Oregonian*, September 30, 1920.

20. Stevens, Jay. 1920. Letter to Luke May dated October 16, *May Papers*, UW.

21. May, Luke. January 17, 1921. "Colagino Case File." *May Papers*, UW.

22. "Slayer Found Guilty." *Seattle Times*, January 26, 1921.

23. Wright, E. 1921. Letter to Luke May dated April 20. *May Papers*, UW.

24. Warnick, Lee. 1921. Letter to Revelare Secret Service dated April 20. *May Papers*, UW.

25. May, Luke. 1921. Letter to Sheriff Lee Warnick dated April 22. *May Papers*, UW.

26. May, Luke. May 5, 1921. "Sheriff Warnick Case File." *May Papers*, UW.

27. May, Luke. 1921. Letter to Clay Allen dated May 11. *May Papers*, UW.

28. "Drag Lake Union for Body!" *Seattle Times*, May 25, 1921.

29. May, Luke. June 3, 1921. "Mahoney Case File." *May Papers*, UW.

30. "State's Case Almost All Presented in Trunk Trial." *Seattle Times*, September 27, 1921.

31. Ibid.

32. Agent 35-S. August 2, 1921. "Progress Report." *May Papers*, UW.

33. Ibid.

34. Ibid.

35. May, Luke. August 9, 1921. "Great Northern Lumber Co. Bomb Case." *May Papers*, UW.

36. Ibid.

37. May, Luke. 1921. Letter to George Woodruff dated August 9. *May Papers*, UW.

38. "Explosion Plot Failure." Portland, *Oregonian*, August 17, 1921.

39. Allen, Herman. 1920. Letter to Luke May dated September 1. *May Papers*, UW.

CHAPTER 6

1. "Bachelor Murdered, Woman Missing." *Seattle Times*, December 22, 1921.

2. "Two Dead and One Shot in Quarrel." *Seattle Times*, August 4, 1918.

3. May, Luke. December 28, 1921. "Hochbrunn Case File." *May Papers*, UW.

4. Ibid.

5. May, Luke. 1922. Letter to George Dean dated January 7. *May Papers,* UW.

6. "Clara Skarin Held in Murder Case!" *Seattle Times,* September 3, 1922.

7. "Confesses Killing," *Bellingham Herald,* September 7, 1922.

8. Ibid.

9. "How Science is Leading the Battle Against Crime in the Northwest." *Seattle Times,* January 22, 1922.

10. Ibid.

11. Ibid.

12. Ibid.

13. "To Check Criminal." *Seattle Times,* April 8, 1922.

14. "Radio Will Be Used to Catch Northwestern Auto Speeders." *Bellingham Herald,* October 25, 1922.

15. "Will Team Work End Our Crime Waves?" Portland, *Oregonian,* December 17, 1922.

16. "News of the Week." Springfield (MA) *Republican,* February 2, 1922.

17. "Mastodon of the Microscope Family." *Seattle Times,* July 16, 1922.

18. May, Luke. 1921. Letter to George Dean dated December 30. *May Papers,* UW.

19. Osborn, Albert S. 1922. Letter to Luke May dated July 25. *May Papers,* UW.

20. "Almost Branded as Murder; Is Freed by Expert's Tests." *Seattle Star,* October 29, 1921.

21. Balthazard, V. "Identification of the Projectiles: Improvement of the Technique." *Annales de Médecine Légale,* vol. 2 (1922): 345–50. [Translated from the French.]

22. May, Luke. August 14, 1922. "Rorison Case File." *May Papers,* UW.

23. "Pocatello Society." Boise, *Idaho Statesman,* November 12, 1922.

24. "New Apartment Building Will be Ready Nov. 1." *Seattle Times,* October 22, 1922.

25. "11-Year Old Girl is Brutally Murdered." Trenton (NJ), *Evening Times,* March 9, 1923.

26. May, *Nemesis.*

27. Ibid.

28. "Evidence Gathered in Crime." Albany (OR), *Evening Herald,* March 12, 1923.

29. "State is to Ask Whitfield's Death." Portland, *Oregonian,* May 2, 1923.

30. "Blood on Clothes Declared Human." *Oregonian,* May 5, 1923.

31. May, *Nemesis.*

32. "Steamer Rainier is Rammed in Straits." *Bellingham Herald,* July 28, 1923.

33. "Ship Found Adrift." *Seattle Times,* July 29, 1923.

34. May, Luke. July 31, 1923. "Maru Case File." *May Paper,* UW.

35. "Curriculum and Organization." *Northwest College of Criminology,* Seattle, 1923–1924.

36. May, *Nemesis.*

37. "Two Held for Murder." Portland, *Oregonian,* September 6, 1923.

38. May, *Nemesis.*

39. Ibid.

40. "Dr. Covell Bound Over." Portland, *Oregonian,* September 29, 1923.

41. "Cripple Plots Crimes." Portland, *Oregonian,* October 10, 1923.

42. May, *Nemesis.*

43. Ibid.

44. "Code Slayer to Go into Court on Cot." Washington, DC, *Evening Star,* October 15, 1923.

45. "Luke May of Seattle—Real Craig Kennedy." *Portland News,* October 12, 1923.

CHAPTER 7

1. "Mystery Murder in Star Office: Reporter is 'Killed' by Bullet." *Seattle Star,* November 30, 1923.

2. Ibid.

3. "'Murder Gun' in Star's Mystery is Identified." *Seattle Star,* December 3, 1923.

4. "Last-Minute Trick Nabs Star's 'Mystery Slayer." *Seattle Star,* December 5, 1923.

5. May, Luke. February 9, 1924. "Mattice Case File." *May Papers,* UW.

6. Ibid.

7. "Father of Late Oculist Obtains $30,000 Verdict." *Seattle Times,* March 10, 1925.

8. Ibid.

9. Armbruster, Kurt E. *Before Seattle Rocked: A City and Its Music.* Seattle: University of Washington Press, 2011.

10. Davis, Rosemary Reeves. *The Rosenbluth Case: Federal Justice on Trial.* Ames: Iowa State University Press, 1971.

11. May, Luke. 1924. "Cronkhite Case File." *May Papers,* UW.

12. "Search for Missing Tacoma Woman Fails." *Seattle Times,* June 16, 1924.

13. May, *Nemesis.*

14. Ibid.

15. "Tacoma Murder Suspect Hidden." *Seattle Times,* July 18, 1924.

16. "Conner's Pal Testifies." Portland, *Oregonian,* October 24, 1924.

17. Ibid.

18. Revelle, Thomas P. 1928. Letter to Luke May dated April 14. *May Papers,* UW.

19. "Opium and Bolos Are Found in Joss House." *Seattle Times,* January 22, 1925.

20. "Joss House Gives Up Dope, Ten Bolos." *Seattle Post-Intelligencer,* January 22, 1925.

21. May, Luke. February 16, 1925. "Anna Case Case File." *May Papers,* UW.

22. May, Luke. 1922. Letter to James Seldon dated January 10. *May Papers,* UW.

23. May, Luke. April 11, 1925. "Hallen Case File," *May Papers,* UW.

24. May, *Nemesis.*

25. May, Luke. 1925. Letter to James W. Selden dated April 24. *May Papers,* UW.

CHAPTER 8

1. "Embezzler Easy Oil Stock Victim." *Seattle Times,* March 25, 1925.

2. Ibid.

3. Ibid.

4. Stout, Wesley W. "Fingerprinting Bullets." *Saturday Evening Post,* June 13 and 20, 1925, 6–7, 18–19.

5. "Sues Son for Forgery." *Seattle Times,* May 17, 1925.

6. May, Luke. 1925. "Hanna-Sisco Case File." *May Papers,* UW.

7. "Pictures Used as Clue." *Seattle Times,* August 2, 1925.

8. "Missing Man, Traced to Canada, Vanishes." *Seattle Times,* September 27, 1925.

9. May, Helen Klog. About 1955. *Pride of Forty Mile: Recollections of an Alaskan Childhood.* Unpublished typescript. Received from Mindi Reid, 2014.

10. Gilbert, Warren J. 1925. Letter to Luke May dated July 14. *May Papers,* UW.

11. May, Luke. 1925. Letter to prosecutor Warren J. Gilbert dated July 17. *May Papers,* UW.

12. Horning, Charles M. 1926. Letter to Luke May dated January 9. *May Papers,* UW.

13. May, Luke. 1926. Letter to Charles M. Horning dated January 21. *May Papers,* UW.

14. May, Luke. 1926. Letter to Charles M. Horning dated February 15. *May Papers,* UW.

15. Horning, Charles E. 1926. Letter to Luke May dated March 1. *May Papers,* UW.

16. "Autoists Sue Hoquiam for Bridge Collapse." *Seattle Times,* January 21, 1926.

17. May, Luke. January 16, 1926. "Hoquiam Case File." *May Papers,* UW.

18. City Engineer. January 29, 1926. "Little Hoquiam River Bridge." *History and Status Report,* Hoquiam, Washington. *May Papers,* UW.

19. May, Luke. 1926. Letter to J. H. P. Callahan dated February 1. *May Papers,* UW.

20. "Criminologist Speaks at Club." *Seattle Times,* March 6, 1926.

21. "Old and New Favorites On Local Screens This Week." *Seattle Times,* February 21, 1926.

22. Conles, J. R. "Topics of the Times." Eugene (OR), *Morning Register,* June 27, 1926.

23. May, Luke. March 1926. "Hungate Case File." *May Papers,* UW.

24. Technician G. H. K. March 10, 1926. "Experiment to Determine the Effect Produced on 32-20 Bullet Driven into Bone." *May Papers,* UW.

25. May, Luke. 1926. Letter to Bert McManus dated March 10. *May Papers,* UW.

26. Adams, J. A. March 24, 1926. Transcribed phone message to Luke May. *May Papers,* UW.

27. May, Luke. 1926. Letter to Sam M. Sumner dated March 29. *May Papers,* UW.

28. "Dismissal of Hungate Case is Requested." Wenatchee (WA), *World,* April 1, 1926.

29. "Sun Spots." *Wenatchee Sun,* April 2, 1926.

30. "W. A. Gaines Niece Slain!" *Seattle Times,* June 17, 1926.

31. "Woman Killed in Grove Near Seattle Lake." *Miami Herald,* June 18, 1926.

32. "Gaines Innocent." *Seattle Times,* June 21, 1926.

33. "Gaines' Murder Probe Opens." *Bellingham Herald,* June 25, 1926.

34. "Gaines Is Charged With Paying Undue Attention to Girl." Bridgeport (CT), *Telegram,* August 13, 1926.

35. White, Magner. "May Hunts Criminals With a Microscope." *American Magazine,* September 1926.

36. Ibid.

CHAPTER 9

1. "'That Man Shot Me,' Witness Says Marshall Charged." *Seattle Times,* March 23, 1927.

2. "Man Escapes, Was to Hang." Evansville (IN), *Courier and Press,* May 2, 1927.

3. "Program is Ready for Meeting Here of Peace Officers." *Eugene Guard,* February 7, 1927.

4. "May Suggests Courts Employ Crime Experts." *Seattle Times,* March 13, 1927.

5. "Sheriff Creates New Bureau." *Seattle Times,* May 1, 1927.

6. Crossman, Edward C. "Science Turns Detective." *Scientific American,* January 1927.

7. May, Luke. 1927. Letter to writer Edward C. Crossman dated January 20. *May Papers,* UW.

8. Crossman, Edward. 1927. Letter to Luke S. May dated March 19. *May Papers,* UW.

9. May, Luke. 1927. Letter to Edward Crossman dated June 20. *May Papers,* UW.

10. Crossman, Edward. 1927. Letter to Luke S. May dated August 5. *May Papers,* UW.

11. Ibid.

12. "Woman Slayer on Trial for Her Life." *Seattle Times,* September 27, 1927.

13. "Sheriff Gives Colvin Data in Extortion Case." *Seattle Times,* November 24, 1927.

14. "Pressure Applied." *Bellingham Herald,* January 18, 1928.

15. "Chemists Hunt Bagwell Case Death Causes." *Seattle Times,* March 16, 1928.

16. Stier, Robert. 1928. Letter to T. C. Barnhart dated March 23. *May Papers,* UW.

17. May, Luke. May 18, 1928. "Bagwell Case File." *May Papers,* UW.

18. Ibid.

19. "Ford Motors Used as Marine Engines." *Seattle Times,* March 18, 1928.

20. Ibid.

21. "Slain Woman's Letters Found." *Boston Herald,* September 26, 1928.

22. May, Luke. October 6–7, 1928. "Weekend Excursion." *May Papers,* UW.

23. Ibid.

24. Ibid.

25. "Professor Drowns." *Bellingham Herald,* October 8, 1928.

26. Jones, Augustus. 1928. Letter to Luke S. May dated December 19. *May Papers,* UW.

27. May, Luke. December 11, 1928. "Clark Case File." *May Papers,* UW.

28. May, L. S. September 25, 1934. *Comparison Magnascope.* Patent No. 1,974,654.

29. Ibid.

30. "Witness Lied, Court Holds." *Seattle Post-Intelligencer,* May 8, 1929.

31. Ibid.

32. Spencer, Edward W. 1929. "The New Edition." Review of *Questioned Documents,* by Albert S. Osborn. *Marquette Law Review* 13, no. 4 (June 1929): 260–61.

CHAPTER 10

1. "Dooley and Fasick Given 25–50 Years Behind Bars." *Seattle Times,* February 28, 1925.

2. "Body is Identified." *Bellingham Herald,* November 15, 1926.

3. "Fasicks' Trial for Murder of Harris Sought." *Seattle Times,* November 21, 1926.

4. "Knife Murder Clue." *Bellingham Herald,* January 19, 1927.

5. Ibid.

6. Ibid.

7. Peyser, Ethan Allen. 1927. Letter to Luke S. May dated January 25. *May Papers,* UW.

8. *State v. Fasick,* 149 Wash. 92, 270 Pac. 123 (1928).

9. Ibid.

10. Ibid.

11. Ibid.

12. Ibid.

13. Ibid.

14. Ibid.

15. May, *Nemesis.*

16. Ibid.

17. "Long Term Imposed." *Bellingham Herald,* March 2, 1929.

18. *State v. Clark,* 156 Wash. 543, 287 Pac. 18 (1930).

19. Ibid.

20. "Decision Reversed," *Bellingham Herald,* April 29, 1930.

21. May, *Nemesis.*

22. Heinrich, Edward O. 1929. Letter to Luke S. May dated March 26. *May Papers,* UW.

23. Ibid.

CHAPTER 11

1. Egan, James S. 1929. Letter to Luke S. May dated May 19. *May Papers,* UW.

2. Ibid.

3. Ibid.

4. Wigmore, John H. 1929. Letter to Luke S. May dated May 21. *May Papers,* UW.

5. Heinrich, Edward O. 1929. Postcard to Luke S. May dated June 12. *May Papers,* UW.

6. Wigmore, John H. 1929. Letter to Luke S. May dated July 2. *May Papers,* UW.

7. "Spokane Man Shot, Woman Chloroformed, Auto Burned." *Bellingham Herald,* May 23, 1929.

8. Ibid.

9. Ibid.

10. "Spokane Authorities Puzzled by Yarns." Olympia (WA), *Olympian,* May 25, 1929.

11. "Link is forged to Prove Murder Charge." Olympia (WA), *Olympian,* October 10, 1929.

12. Brower, Floyd. 1929. Letter to Luke May dated October 30. *May Papers,* UW.

13. "'Puppy Love' Crime Draws 3-Year Term." *Seattle Times,* December 15, 1929.

14. "Hair is Examined." *Bellingham Herald,* November 9, 1929.

15. May, Luke. November 10, 1929. "Woodall Case File." *May Papers,* UW.

16. Adams, J. A. 1930. Letter to Luke May dated February 27. *May Papers,* UW.

17. "Luke May Voices Confidence in 'Lie Detector' Findings." *Seattle Times,* November 29, 1929.

18. "Stranglers Leave Clue in Fingerprints, Say Experts." *San Francisco Chronicle,* June 12, 1929.

19. Flacco, Anthony and Jerry Clark. *The Road Out of Hell: Sanford Clark and the True Story of the Wineville Murders.* New York: Diversion Books, 2009.

20. "Wineville To Be Christened 'Mira Loma.'" Riverside (CA), *Daily Press,* October 16, 1930.

21. "Husband Faces Charges of Murder at Emmett Due to Wife's Death." Boise, *Idaho Statesman,* December 13, 1929.

22. May, *Nemesis.*

23. Ibid.

24. "Emmett Getting Back to Normal." *Idaho Statesman,* April 14, 1930.

25. "Murderer of Wife Sentenced to Hang." *Miami Herald,* April 16, 1930.

26. "Pardon Board Finally Frees John McClurg." *Idaho Statesman,* April 10, 1940.

27. "Luke May Will Speak." *Seattle Times,* January 5, 1930.

28. "Police School Slated." Portland, *Oregonian,* January 20, 1930.

29. "1st Will Ignores Daughter Who Gets All in 2nd." *Seattle Times,* January 17, 1930.

30. May, *Nemesis.*

31. Ibid.

32. Ibid

33. Wigmore, John H. 1930. Letter to Luke S. May dated January 2. *May Papers,* UW.

34. Ibid.

35. May, Luke. "The Identification of Knives, Tools and Instruments, A Positive Science." *American Journal of Police Science* 1, no. 3 (May–June 1930): 246–59.

36. May, Luke. "President's Message," *Journal of Proceedings,* Tenth International Convention, Northwest Association of Sheriffs and Police, Vancouver, British Columbia (June 22–25, 1930).

37. May, *Nemesis.*

38. "Unbalanced by Nagging, to be Lindsay's Plea." *Seattle Times,* December 13, 1931.

39. May, *Nemesis.*

40. "On the Job." *Seattle Times,* January 6, 1931.

CHAPTER 12

1. May, Luke. 1931. Letter to Edward C. Crossman dated January 15. *May Papers,* UW.

2. Ibid.

3. "Crime Can't Beat the Microscope." *Seattle Times,* January 25, 1931.

4. Ibid.

5. Ibid.

6. Ibid.

7. "Specialists Will Lecture at Willamette University Police School." Portland, *Oregonian,* March 1, 1931.

8. May, Luke. March 30, 1931. "Mooney Case File." *May Papers,* UW.

9. "Serious Charges May Follow Five Traffic Deaths." *Seattle Times,* April 3, 1931.

10. Bright, Earl G. "Crime Pays for Luke May—But Not Criminals." *Ketchikan Daily Tribune,* May 2, 1931.

11. Ibid.

12. Ibid.

13. Ibid.

14. Ibid.

15. Harrison, Harry H. "The Watchman Case . . . An Oregon Mystery." Portland (OR), *Oregonian*, May 17, 1936.

16. "How to Create a Future for the Past." *Bainbridge Review*, Bainbridge Island, WA, June 9, 2008.

17. Reid, Mindi. *Extracts from the Journal of Patricia Helen May Reid.* Unpublished typescript, Redmond, Washington, 2000.

18. "Modern Methods of Tracking Criminals Shown at Seattle." *Bellingham Herald*, June 23, 1931.

19. "State Bureau Gets Indorsement [*sic*] of Convention." *Bellingham Herald*, June 27, 1931.

20. May, Luke. 1931. Letter to Henry M. Newson dated December 17. *May Papers*, UW.

21. Newson, Henry M. 1931. Letter to F. J. Mead dated October 19. *May Papers*, UW.

22. May, Luke. 1931. Letter to F. J. Mead dated October 30. *May Papers*, UW.

23. Letter, Luke S. May to Major Henry M. Newson, RCMP, Ottawa (October 30, 1931).

24. Ibid.

25. Ibid.

26. Ibid.

27. Ibid.

28. Saunders, Garry. "Fiftieth Anniversary of the Crime Detection Laboratories, 1937–1987." *Gazette Magazine* 49, no. 11, Ottawa, Ontario (1987).

29. "Olympia Bank Closes Doors Friday." Olympia (WA), *Olympian*, January 23, 1932.

30. Fultz, Hollis. 1932. Letter to Luke S. May dated January 26. *May Papers*, UW.

31. May, Luke. "How I Solved the Strange Kelso Killing." *True Detective Mysteries*, January 1932.

32. Bucklin, A. L. H. "Talking Needles." *True Detective Mysteries*, November 1925.

33. Ibid.

34. Fultz, Hollis B. "Smiling Sam Hanna's Sinister Secret." *True Detective Mysteries*, April 1932.

35. Fultz, Hollis. 1932. Letter to Luke S. May dated January 26. *May Papers*, UW.

36. "Luke May Receives 'Tips' About Kidnapped Lindy Baby." *Seattle Times*, March 18, 1932.

37. Teale, Edwin W. "Blackmailers and Forgers Betrayed by Their Pens." *Popular Science*, April 1932.

38. Ibid.

39. Moore, Harry C. 1932. Letter to State Board of Health dated April 28. *May Papers*, UW.

40. Meyer, Harvey K. 1932. Letter to Luke S. May dated May 11. *May Papers*, UW.

41. "Claims Upon Burke Estate Partly Paid," *Seattle Times*, October 7, 1932.

42. "Expert in Antique Jewelry to Divide Burke Collection," *Seattle Times*, January 29, 1934.

43. "Chiefs of Police Open Convention." Portland, *Oregonian*, June 15, 1932.

44. "May Reveals How Markings on Bullet Trapped Killer." *Seattle Star*, January 30, 1933.

45. Egan, James S. 1929. Letter to Luke May dated November 1. *May Papers*, UW.

46. "Trial Progresses." *Bellingham Herald*, November 2, 1932.

47. May, Luke. 1933. Letter to E. V. Ahern dated February 13. *May Papers*, UW.

48. Ahern, E. V. 1933. Letter to Luke S. May dated March 8. *May Papers*, UW.

49. "Storm Hurls *Akron* into Ocean." *Seattle Star*, April 4, 1933.

50. "Famous Criminologist Now is Proud Father." *Seattle Star*, April 4, 1933.

51. Reid, *Extracts*.

CHAPTER 13

1. "Tennant's Death is Mourned by All Seattle," *Seattle Times*, April 18, 1933.

2. "Reporters Recall Tennant." *Seattle Times*, April 18, 1933.

3. Hunt, Lester M. "Crime Expert Appointed by Mayor Dore." *Seattle Post-Intelligencer*, April 27, 1933.

4. Ibid.

5. Ibid.

6. Hoover, J. Edgar. 1933. Letter to Luke S. May dated May 18. *May Papers*, UW.

7. Wakefield, Claude E. 1934. Letter to Mayor John F. Dore dated January 26. *May Papers*, UW.

8. "Advertisement: Scientific Murder Investigation." *Popular Science Magazine*, May 1933.

9. May, Luke. *Scientific Murder Investigation*. Privately printed, 1933. *May Papers*, UW.

10. May, Luke. *Detective Science: Field Manual of Criminology*. Privately printed, 1933. *May Papers*, UW.

11. Newell, Edward. 1979. Letter to Professor William Hunt dated April 30. *May Papers*, UW.

12. "Weapons of Gangland Rounded Up in Seattle." *Seattle Times*, October 27, 1933.

13. "Police Chief Denies May's 'Crime Wave.'" *Seattle Times*, November 24, 1933.

14. "George Coyne is Acquitted of Murder." Olympia (WA), *Olympian*, October 25, 1933.

15. May, Luke. April 1934 "Baughn Case File." *May Papers*, UW.

16. May, Luke. 1934. Letter to C. L. McCauley dated April 14. *May Papers*, UW.

17. Queets, Brander. "Six Murders in Six Minutes." *True Detective Mysteries,* June–October 1936. [Luke May "as told to" Queets, published in five parts.]

18. Ibid.

19. Ibid.

20. Newell, Edward. 1983. Letter to Patricia (May) Reid dated May 14. *May Papers,* UW.

21. Queets, "Six Murders."

22. Ibid.

23. "Luke May Quits as Detective Bureau Chief." *Seattle Post-Intelligencer,* June 30, 1934.

24. "Wounded Man Denies Grocer fired on Him." *Seattle Times,* May 26, 1934.

25. Meek, Frank E. 1934. Letter to Luke S. May dated April 13. *May Papers,* UW.

26. "Continuing Crime Organization Asked." Olympia (WA), *Olympian,* December 14, 1934.

27. "Lindbergh and Wife Tell Jury of Baby's Kidnaping." *Seattle Times,* January 3, 1935.

28. "Negro to Describe Finding of Slain Lindbergh Baby; Experts Draw Net Tighter." Boise, *Idaho Statesman,* January 17, 1935.

29. "Harry Lawton Named Head of Crime Council." *Seattle Times,* January 16, 1935.

30. "Luke May to Speak Before Clergymen." *Seattle Times,* February 2, 1935.

31. "Expert to Speak at Crime Meets." Portland, *Oregonian,* February 10, 1935.

32. Burke, Edmund Jr. 1935. Letter to Luke S. May dated February 2. *May Papers,* UW.

33. Fultz, Hollis B. "Behind the Scenes with a Great Criminologist." *True Detective Mysteries,* May 1935.

CHAPTER 14

1. Newell, Edward. 1983. Letter to Patricia (May) Reid dated May 14. *May Papers,* UW.

2. Ibid.

3. Ibid.

4. "Kidnapped Heir Signs Ransom Note." *Boston Herald,* May 26, 1935.

5. "G-Men Are No More; They Have joined FBI." Trenton (NJ), *Evening Times,* June 29, 1935.

6. Newell, May 14, 1983.

7. May, Luke. "Luke May's Department." *True Detective Mysteries,* June 1935.

8. Ibid.

9. Shuttleworth, John. 1935. Letter to Luke May dated October 7. *May Papers,* UW.

10. Cruickshank, Forbes. 1936. Letter to Luke May dated January 6. *May Papers,* UW.

11. May, *Nemesis.*

12. "The World of Books: 'Crimes Nemesis.'" Springfield (MA) *Daily Republican,* March 30, 1936.

13. "Name Changed by Police Group." Portland (OR), *Oregonian,* June 17, 1936.

14. "New Laws Make Crime Profitless." Portland (OR), *Oregonian,* June 17, 1936.

15. "Fear of Kidnaper Big Aid to Police." *Oregonian,* June 17, 1936.

16. "Four-Year Police School Will Be Opened at U of W." *Seattle Times,* January 10, 1936.

17. Newell, Edward. 1936. Letter to Luke May dated July 1. *May Papers,* UW.

18. Ibid.

19. Ibid.

20. Gousseff, J. 1936. Letter to Luke May dated November 14. *May Papers,* UW.

21. May, Luke. "Luke May's Department." *True Detective Mysteries,* January 1936.

22. Ibid.

23. May, Luke. "Luke May's Department." *True Detective Mysteries,* May 1936.

24. "Alonzo Deen Cole v. Phillips H. Lord, Inc.," *Case on Appeal, New York State Supreme Court, Appellate Division—First Department,* Corporate Press, Inc. (1942).

25. May, Luke. 1936. Letter to Folmar Blangsted dated October 24. *May Papers,* UW.

26. Blangsted, Folmar. 1936 Letter to Luke May dated December 1. *May Papers,* UW.

27. May, Luke. Letter to Folmar Blangsted dated December 8, 1936. *May Papers,* UW.

28. "Upcoming Programs." *San Diego Union,* February 2, 1937.

29. "Coast Guard, Navy Officers Honored with Lodge Dinner." *Seattle Times,* March 18, 1937.

30. "Luke S. May Buys Home on Capitol Hill." *Seattle Times,* March 21, 1937.

31. Reid, *Extracts.*

32. May, Luke. "Luke May's Department." *True Detective Mysteries,* May 1937.

33. Ibid.

34. May, Luke. August 10, 1937. "Azling Poison Case." *May Papers,* UW.

35. Pearson, Drew and Robert S. Allen, "Britain and France Yield to Ease European Tension." *Seattle Times,* December 16, 1937.

CHAPTER 15

1. *The Denali,* 105 F.2d 413, 420 (9th Circuit Court of Appeals, 1939).

2. "Screams Heard, Says 'Tub' Trial Witness." *Seattle Times,* March 8, 1938.

3. Battle, George Gordon. "The Mind of the Juror as Judge of the Facts" by Albert S. Osborn. *Virginia Law Review* 25, no. 1 (November 1938): 117–20.

4. "Lie Detector Is Not Infallible." Council Bluffs (IA), *Daily Nonpareil,* March 24, 1938.

5. Gardner, Robert. "No Such Word as Gratitude in the World of Politics." Los Angeles *Daily Pilot,* March 6, 2005.

6. May, Luke. 1937. Letter to Edward C. Newell dated October 21. *May Papers,* UW.

7. Newell, Edward C. 1979. Letter to William Hunt dated April 30. *May Papers,* UW.

8. Newell, Edward C. 1938. Letter to Luke S. May dated June 15. *May Papers,* UW.

9. Ibid.

10. May, Luke. "Luke May's Department." *True Detective Mysteries,* October 1938.

11. Ibid.

12. May, Luke. "Luke May's Department." *True Detective Mysteries,* December 1937.

13. "War Deaths at Walla Walla." Klamath Falls (OR), *Evening Herald,* December 1, 1938.

14. Ibid.

15. "Second Big Opium Cache Seized." *Bellingham Herald,* September 1, 1938.

16. Reid, *Extracts.*

17. May, Luke. "Luke May's Department." *True Detective Mysteries,* June 1939.

18. Ibid.

19. May, Luke. "Luke May's Department." *True Detective Mysteries,* October 1938.

20. "$1,300,000,000 Navy Bill Asks 95 New Ship." *Seattle Times,* November 5, 1939.

21. "Record-Length Hearing on Fisk Will Continues." *Seattle Times,* January 15, 1940.

22. "Teacher Upheld in $200,000 Fisk Will Suit." *Seattle Times,* March 24, 1940.

23. May, Luke. "Luke May's Department." *True Detective Mysteries,* January 1940.

24. Ibid

25. Ibid.

26. "Mlle. Curie to Speak at Athletic Club." *Seattle Times,* March 3, 1940.

27. May, Luke. 1941. Letter to W. S. Wharton dated December 5. *May Papers,* UW.

28. "Luke S. May Now With U.S. Navy." *Bellingham Herald,* November 16, 1941.

29. Reid, *Extracts.*

30. "Radio Newscasts." *Voices of World War II,* University of Missouri (2001–2004).

31. Reid, *Extracts.*

CHAPTER 16

1. "Japan, Rebuked, Bolts League." *Seattle Times,* February 24, 1933.

2. Saunders, Richard L. "Preparation of the US Navy Intelligence Officer." *Master of Military Studies Thesis,* Marine Corps Command and Staff College, Quantico, Virginia, 1996.

3. Allen, Clay. 1933. Letter to Intelligence Officer, Thirteenth Naval District dated August 5. *May Naval Records.*

4. May, Luke. 1934. Letter report to commandant, Thirteenth Naval District dated January 5, forwarded to Office of Naval Intelligence. *May Naval Records.*

5. Ibid.

6. Bureau of Navigation, U.S. Navy. 1934. Telegram to 13th Naval District dated October 20. *May Naval Records.*

7. May, Luke. 1939. Letter to Commandant, Thirteenth Naval District dated November 8. *May Naval Records.*

8. Frost, D. Adams. 1934. Letter to Walker Buckner dated December 10. *May Papers,* UW.

9. Packard, Captain Wylan H. *A Century of U.S. Naval Intelligence.* Washington, DC: Department of the Navy, 1996.

10. Bureau of Navigation. 1936. Letter to Luke May dated January 22. *May Naval Records.*

11. Packard, *Naval Intelligence.*

12. Treasury Department. 1941. Letter to Luke May dated October 23. *May Naval Records.*

13. Packard, *Naval Intelligence.*

14. Ibid.

15. Fenner, E. B. 1938. Letter from Thirteenth Naval District to U.S. Navy, Bureau of Navigation, dated November 18. *May Naval Records.*

16. Packard, *Naval Intelligence.*

17. "Japanese Launching South China Drive." Olympia (WA), *Olympian,* November 15, 1939.

18. Freeman, C. S. 1940. Letter to Bureau of Navigation dated September 18. *May Naval Records.*

19. Freeman, Charles S. 1941. Letter to Bureau of Navigation dated April 23. *May Naval Records.*

20. Showers, Donald "Mac." *Video Interview,* National World War II Museum, New Orleans, Louisiana, 2013.

21. Cummings, D. E. 1941. Letter to Luke May dated November 14. *May Papers,* UW.

22. Wharton, W. S. 1941. Letter to Luke May dated November 14. *May Papers,* UW.

23. May, Luke. 1941. Letter to Eugene J. Kerrigan, dated December 5. *May Papers,* UW.

24. Luckel, F. W. 1942. Letter to DIO, Thirteenth Naval District dated November 17. *May Naval Records.*

25. "Fletcher, New 13th District Chief, Prefers Duty at Sea." *Seattle Times,* November 22, 1942.

26. "Widespread Attacks." *Seattle Times,* December 7, 1942.

27. Dea, David. 1943. Letter to Mr. and Mrs. Luke S. May dated March 17. *May Papers,* UW.

28. Dea, David. 1943. Letter to Mr. and Mrs. Luke S. May dated May 4. *May Papers,* UW.

29. Dea, David. 1943. Letter to Mr. and Mrs. Luke S. May dated August 29. *May Papers,* UW.

30. "Kiska Isle Retaken." *Seattle Times,* August 21, 1943.

31. Train, Harold C. 1943. Letter to naval personnel dated September 15. *May Naval Records.*

32. Davis, Hartwell C. March 30, 1943. "Luke Silvester May." *Report on the Fitness of Officers,* 13th Naval District. *May Papers,* UW.

33. Forrestal, James. 1943. Letter to Luke May via commandant, Thirteenth Naval District dated September 25. [Signed, but never officially delivered.] *May Naval Records.*

34. Chief of Naval Personnel. 1943, Letter to commandant, Thirteenth Naval District dated September 27. *May Naval Records.*

35. Fletcher, Frank Jack. 1943, Letter to chief of naval personnel dated October 7. *May Naval Records.*

36. Ibid.

37. Chief of Naval Personnel. 1944. Letter to Luke May dated April 3. *May Naval Records.*

38. Davis, Hartwell C. 1944. Letter to Myron Avery, office of judge advocate general dated April 17. *May Naval Records.*

39. May, Luke. 1944. Letter to chief of naval operations dated May 18. *May Naval Records.*

40. Chief of Naval Operations. 1944. Letter to Luke May dated June 5. *May Naval Records*

41. Ibid.

42. "Air, Sea Forces Heap Ruin on Japan's Inner Defense With Humiliating Attacks." Olympia (WA), *Olympian,* September 5, 1944.

43. Packard, *Naval Intelligence.*

CHAPTER 17

1. Reid, *Extracts.*

2. Lloyd Shorett, Lloyd. 1944. Letter to Henry Kreis dated November 26. *May Papers,* UW.

3. Baillargeon, Cebert. 1945. Letter to Luke May dated January 6. *May Papers,* UW.

4. "America's Sherlock Holmes Returns." Dayton (WA), *Chronicle-Dispatch,* October 25, 1945.

5. "Ex-Mrs. Wingard Files Balm Suit." *Seattle Times,* April 3, 1945.

6. Griffin, Tracy E. 1945. Letter to Luke May dated April 16. *May Papers,* UW.

7. Sykes, Irene Hibbs. 1945. Letter to Luke S. May dated August 1. *May Papers,* UW.

8. May, Luke. 1945. Letter to Mrs. Irene Hibbs Sykes dated August 7. *May Papers,* UW.

9. Reid, *Extracts.*

10. Ibid.

11. Ibid.

12. May, Luke. August 29, 1945. "Twin Creek Acres Expenses and Sale Account." *May Papers,* UW.

13. May, Luke. 1946. Letter to Miles Poindexter, Greenlee, Virginia dated March 22. *May Papers,* UW.

14. "Along Film Row." *Seattle Times,* January 10, 1947.

15. Marsh, Willard. "Crime's Nemesis." *Seattle Times,* March 23, 1947.

16. Marsh, Willard. "Trap for the Guilty." *Seattle Times,* April 6, 1947.

17. Kelley, Thomas D. 1947. Letter to Luke May dated July 2. *May Papers,* UW.

18. "Eight Dead in Seattle Crash: Blame Brakes." *Ellensburg Daily Record,* December 1, 1947.

19. May, Luke. December 18, 1947. "Airliner Crash File." *May Papers,* UW.

20. May, Luke. 1948. Letter to W. K. Andrews dated March 18. *May Papers,* UW.

21. Behncke, David L. 1948. Letter to Luke May dated August 2. *May Papers,* UW.

22. Ibid.

23. May, Luke. 1948. Letter to David L. Behncke dated August 14. *May Papers,* UW.

24. "Faulty Landing Method Blamed." *Seattle Times,* May 20, 1949.

25. "Crash Pilot Cleared of Recklessness." *Seattle Times,* May 25, 1950.

26. Crouch, Joel. 1948. Letter to President David Behncke dated December 29. *May Papers,* UW.

27. Reid, *Extracts*.

28. "P.T.A. Urges Fund to Probe Youth's Death." *Seattle Times*, October 22, 1948.

29. "Criminologist Continues on Mystery Case." Klamath Falls (OR), *Herald and News*, December 18, 1948.

30. "Hanging Case Baffles Quiz." Portland, *Oregonian*, December 22, 1948.

31. "20th Century's Top Stories: The Fred Cohen Murder." Bremerton (WA), *The Sun*, December 31, 1999.

32. Sauvageau, Anny and Vernon J. Geberth. *Autoerotic Deaths: Practical Forensic and Investigative Perspectives*. Boca Raton: CRC Press, 2013.

33. May, Luke. March 22, 1949. "Phillips Case File." May *Papers*, UW.

34. "Million-Word Trial Ends Here Friday." Ritzville (WA), *Journal-Times*, October 16, 1952.

35. "Lind Rancher Wins Verdict After Appeal." Ritzville (WA), *Journal-Times*, January 13, 1955.

36. "Gas Believed Cause of Fatal South End Blast." *Seattle Times*, July 14, 1950.

37. May, Luke. July 26, 1950. "Buttnick Explosion File." *May Papers*, UW.

38. Ibid.

39. "Firm in Gas Blast Sues for $25,281." *Seattle Times*, October 16, 1950.

40. May, Luke. January 30, 1950. "Thomson Will Case." *May Papers*, UW.

41. "Beneficiary Fears B. C. Will is Fraud." *Seattle Times*, December 12, 1950.

42. Chief of Naval Personnel. 1951. Letter to Luke May dated February 6. *May Papers*, UW.

43. Turner, Ralph. March 19, 1951. "Book Dedication: *Forensic Science and Laboratory Techniques*." Photocopy of title page found in Luke May personal library.

44. "Engaged." *Seattle Times*, October 14, 1952.

45. Blangsted, Folmar. 1954. Letter to Luke May dated February 7. *May Papers*, UW.

46. May, Luke. 1954. Letter to Folmar Blangsted dated March 5. *May Papers*, UW.

47. Blangsted, Folmar. 1954. Letter to Luke May dated March 14. *May Papers*, UW.

48. May, Luke. 1954. Letter to Folmar Blangsted dated March 17. *May Papers*, UW.

49. Blangsted, Folmar. 1954. Letter to Luke May dated August 20. *May Papers*, UW.

50. Lynch, Frank. "Inside Job—Story of a Private Eye" *Seattle Post-Intelligencer*, April 14, 1954.

51. Lynch, Frank. "Case of the Forged Names on the Will" *Seattle Post-Intelligencer*, April 16, 1954.

CHAPTER 18

1. "Criminologist to Testify in Murder Trial." *Seattle Times,* January 8, 1955.
2. Ibid.
3. "Pellet Holes in Ceiling Shown Jury." *Seattle Times,* January 10, 1955.
4. "'Good Friend' Loses Bequest of $240,000." *Seattle Post-Intelligencer,* February 5, 1955.
5. "Judge Rules on Two Wills Left by Alaskan's Widow." Fairbanks (AK), *Daily News-Miner,* February 7, 1955.
6. Youngblood, C. T. 1955. Letter to Luke May dated April 15, 1955. *May Papers,* UW.
7. Morn, Frank. *Academic Politics and the History of Criminal Justice Education.* Westport, CT: Greenwood Press, 1995.
8. "Crime Blame Placed on Public in Vollmer's Book." *Oakland Tribune,* September 21, 1936.
9. "May Speaks to Soroptimists." *Seattle Times,* March 6, 1926.
10. "Luke May to Speak Before Clergymen." *Seattle Times,* February 2, 1935.
11. May, Luke. January 9, 1956. "Record of Phone Conversation." *May Papers,* UW.
12. Ibid.
13. May, Luke. February 14, 1957. "Bag Cover Examination." *May Papers,* UW.
14. Ibid.
15. Daly, W. J. 1957. Letter to Luke S. May dated March 19. *May Papers,* UW.
16. Guthman, Ed. "No Record of Auto Sale by Beck, Jr., Says Union Aide." *Seattle Times,* November 16, 1957.
17. May, Luke. 1958. Letter to C. D. Lee, Lee & Sons dated November 20. *May Papers,* UW
18. Ibid.
19. Reid, Mindi. "Childhood Memories of Criminologist Luke May, by his Granddaughter." *Online Encyclopedia of Washington State History,* HistoryLink.org, Seattle, November 9, 2003.
20. May, Luke. February 19, 1960. "Rotta Forgery Case." *May Papers,* UW.
21. May, Luke. September 30, 1960. "Elks Club Fire." *May Papers,* UW.
22. Ibid.
23. Lynch, Frank. "The Mysterious Case of the Forged Will." *Seattle Post-Intelligencer,* June 15, 1962.
24. Reid, "Childhood Memories."
25. Burke, Edmund Jr. 1963. Letter to Luke May dated March 1. *May Papers,* UW.

26. Ibid.

27. May, Luke. 1963. Letter to Captain Edmund Burke dated June 4. *May Papers,* UW.

28. Reid, "Childhood Memories."

29. May, Luke. September 1963. "Samuels Will Case." *May Papers,* UW.

30. Ibid.

31. "Luke May Heard in Will Testimony." *Seattle Post-Intelligencer,* September 13, 1963.

32. "2 More Handwriting Experts Claim Will Signature Not Valid." *Seattle Post-Intelligencer,* September 14, 1963.

33. "His Letter to Court Released: 'I've Been Robbed,' Kleinlein Says As Will Fight Lost." *Seattle Post-Intelligencer,* September 20, 1963.

34. Sellers, Clark. 1963. Letter to Luke May dated December 16. *May Papers,* UW.

35. "Commendation: Luke S. May." Pacific Northwest Security Association, Seattle, January 24, 1964. *May Papers,* UW.

36. Weinstein, Shepard M. 1964. Letter to Luke S. May dated November 12. *May Papers,* UW.

37. May, Mrs. Luke. 1964. Letter to Shepard M. Weinstein dated November 16. *May Papers,* UW.

38. Valleau, Henry. 1965. Letter to Luke May dated February 18. *May Papers,* UW.

39. May, Mrs. Luke. 1965. Letter to Henry Valleau dated February 25. *May Papers,* UW.

40. Reid, *Extracts.*

41. Ibid.

42. "Luke S. May, 79, Crime Detector." *Seattle Post-Intelligencer,* July 13, 1965.

RETROSPECTION

1. May, Luke. 1964. Letter to Jan Beck dated January 2. *May Papers,* UW.

2. Reid, *Extracts.*

3. Beck, Jan. Personal communication, 2016.

4. "Death, Funerals." *Seattle Times,* January 10, 1970.

5. Rumley, Larry. "Luke May—Seattle's Master Criminologist." *Seattle Times,* February 1, 1970.

6. Reddin, John J. "Master Sleuth Remembered." *Seattle Times,* March 8, 1970.

7. Morn, *Academic Politics.*

Bibliography

$\mathcal{A}$round 140 books were consulted during the preparation of this manuscript. Also, about 225 reports, journal and magazine articles, and government documents were collected during the research for this project. The list below contains sources that provided the most extensive background or verified important elements.

Akenson, Donald Harman. *Irish in Ontario: A Study in Rural History*, Second Edition. Montreal: McGill-Queen's University, 1999.

Alder, Ken. *The Lie Detectors: The History of an American Obsession*. New York: Simon & Schuster, 2007.

Baldwin, David, and John Birkett, Owen Facey, Gilleon Rabey. *The Forensic Examination and Interpretation of Tool Marks*. Chichester, UK: John Wiley & Sons, Ltd, 2013.

Battles, Kathleen. *Calling All Cars: Radio Dragnets and the Technology of Policing*. Minneapolis: University of Minnesota Press, 2010.

Beck, J. "Luke May of Seattle—'America's Sherlock Holmes.'" *Journal of Forensic Sciences* 37, no. 1 (1992): 349–55.

Burton, Judge William R. (ed.). *Past and Present of Adams County, Nebraska*. Chicago: S. J. Clarke Publishing Co., 1916.

Carleton, Simon C., and Isadore Goldstein, "A New Scientific Method of Identification." *New York State Journal of Medicine* 35, no. 18 (1935): 901–6.

Chisum, W. Jerry, and Brent E. Turvey. *Crime Reconstruction*, Second Edition. Waltham, Massachusetts: Academic Press, 2011.

Clark, Richard. *Capital Punishment in Britain*. Birmingham, UK: Ian Allen Publishing, 2009.

Collins, Audrey. "The Will Forgeries: A Forgotten Sensation." Surrey, Great Britain: National Archives, February 8, 2013.

Copeland, Tom. *The Centralia Tragedy of 1919: Elmer Smith and the Wobblies.* Seattle: University of Washington Press, 1993.

Crossman, Edward C. *Gun and Rifle Facts.* Chicago: Outers' Book Company, 1923.

Doyle, Arthur Conan. *The Complete Sherlock Holmes.* New York: Barnes & Noble, 2003.

Dunning, John. *On the Air: The Encyclopedia of Old-Time Radio.* New York: Oxford University Press, 1998.

Evans, Colin. *The Second Casebook of Forensic Detection.* Hoboken: John Wiley and Sons, Inc., 2004.

Fohlin, Ernest V. *Salt Lake City, Past and Present.* Salt Lake City: Skelton Publishing Co., 1908.

Francis, John. *History of the Bank of England, Its Times and Traditions.* New York: Office of the Banker's Magazine, 1862.

Freele, William F., and Edna R. Killmeyer. *The History of the Oregon State Police.* Salem: Department of State Police, 1981.

Gault, Robert H. "Hans Gross." *Journal of the American Institute of Criminal Law and Criminology* 6, no. 5 (January 1916): 641–42.

Grams, Martin, Jr. *Gang Busters: the Crime Fighters of American Broadcasting.* Churchville, MD: OTR Publishing, 2004.

Gray, Peter R. A. "The Expert Witness Problem." *International Journal of Speech, Language and the Law* 17, no. 2 (2010): 63–90.

Hamby, James E., and James W. Thorpe, "The History of Firearm and Toolmark Identification." *Association of Firearm and Tool Mark Examiners Journal* 31, no. 3 (Summer 1999): 266–84.

Heard, Brian J. *Handbook of Firearms and Ballistics: Examining and Interpreting Forensic Evidence.* Chichester, UK: John Wiley & Sons, Ltd., 2008.

History of the County of Peterborough, Ontario. Toronto, Canada: C. Blackett Robinson Publishers, 1884.

History of the Salt Lake City Police Department. Salt Lake City: Police History Project, 2013.

"Hypnotised [*sic*] to Kill." *The Advertiser,* Adelaide (Australia), January 22, 1924.

Inman, Keith, and Norah Rudin. *Principles and Practices of Criminalistics: The Profession of Forensic Science.* Boca Raton: CRC Press, 2001.

James, Stuart H., and Paul E. Kish, T. Paulette Sutton. *Principles of Bloodstain Pattern Analysis: Theory and Practice.* Boca Raton, FL: CRC Press, 2005.

Jones, Phill. "Rise of a Forensic Scientist: Edward O. Heinrich." *History Magazine* (June/July 2009): 9.

Keegan, John (ed.). *Encyclopedia of World War II.* New York: Gallery Books, 1990.

Kneubuehl, Beat P. (ed.). *Wound Ballistics: Basics and Applications.* New York: Springer Publishing, 2011.

Levinson, Jay. *Questioned Documents: A Lawyer's Handbook.* San Diego: Academic Press, 2001.

MacKay, Donald. *Flight from Famine: The Coming of the Irish to Canada,* Reprint Edition. Toronto, Canada: Dundurn Press, 2009.

Maffeo, Steven E. *U.S. Navy Codebreakers, Linguists, and Intelligence Officers against Japan, 1910–1941*. Lanham, MD: Rowman & Littlefield, 2016.

Malton, Sara. *Forgery in Nineteenth-Century Literature and Culture*. New York: Palgrave Macmillan, 2009.

Masland, John W., and Laurence I. Radway. *Soldiers and Scholars: Military Education and National Policy*. Princeton University Press, 1957.

McClelland, John Jr. *Wobbly War: The Centralia Story*. Tacoma: Washington State Historical Society, 1987.

Miller, J. Mitchell (ed.). *21st Century Criminology: Reference Handbook*, Vol. 1. Thousand Oaks, CA: Sage Publications, 2009.

Morison, Samuel Eliot. *The Oxford History of the American People*. New York: Oxford University Press, 1965.

Muehlberger, C. W. "Col. Calvin Hooker Goddard 1891–1955." *Journal of Criminal Law and Criminology* 46, no. 1 (1955–1956): 103–4.

"Murders by I.W.W." *The Age* (Melbourne, Australia), November 14, 1919.

Nichols, Ronald. "The Scientific Foundations of Firearms and Tool Mark Identification—A Response to Recent Challenges." *Journal of Forensic Sciences* 52, no. 3 (May 2007): 586–94.

Parker, Alfred E. *Crime Fighter: August Vollmer*. New York: MacMillan, 1961.

Saltvig, Robert. "The Tragic Legend of Laura Law." *The Pacific Northwest Quarterly* 78, no. 3 (July 1987): 91–99.

Sanders, Joseph. "Science, Law and the Expert Witness." *Law and Contemporary Problems*, vol. 72 (Winter 2009): 63–90.

Segrave, Kerry. *Lie Detectors: A Social History*. Jefferson, NC: McFarland & Company, Inc., 2004.

Sheldon, Charles H. *A Century of Judging: A Political History of the Washington Supreme Court*. Seattle: University of Washington Press, 1988.

Stevens, Serita, and Anne Bannon. *Book of Poisons*. Cincinnati: Writer's Digest Books, 2007.

Streissguth, Thomas. *The Roaring Twenties*. New York: Facts on File, Inc., 2007.

Theoharis, Athan G. (ed.). *The FBI: A Comprehensive Reference Guide*. Phoenix, AZ: The Oryx Press, 1999.

Tilstone, William J., and Kathleen A. Savage, Leigh A. Clark. *Forensic Science: An Encyclopedia of History, Methods, and Techniques*. Santa Barbara, CA: ABC-CLIO, 2006.

Timmerbeil, Sven. "The Role of Expert Witnesses in German and U.S. Civil Litigation." *Annual Survey of International & Comparative Law* 9, no. 1 (2003): 163–87.

West, Nigel. *Historical Dictionary of Naval Intelligence*. Lanham, MD: Rowman & Littlefield Publishing Group, Inc., 2010.

Index

Page references for photographs are *italicized.*

accident investigations:
  airplane, 233–235;
  automobile, 156, *157*;
  firearms, 94–95, 160–161, 195;
  gas explosion, 238;
  hit-and-run, 124–125, 152, 195;
  summarized, 263–265
American Legion, 58–59, 181
American Society of Criminology, 200, 245, 260
ancestors, ix, 18–19, 23, 25, 33, 38, 103–104, 232
arson and fires, 61, 64, 101, 172, 249, 258, 262
audio surveillance and transmission, 37, 39, 50, 92, 262
autopsy, 68, 82, 86, 123, 147, 176, 198;
  of shooting victim, 10, 47, 63, 91, 95, 204

Balthazard, Victor, 35–36, 62, 78–79, 205
Bertillon, Alphonse, 12, 40;
  identification system, 15, 27, 43
blood:
  evidence, 5, 63, 125, 147, 206;

spatter, 60, 145, 151, 205–206, 257–258;
test for human, 14, 51, 82, 100, 108, 115, 164;
types, 15, 108
bloodstains, 4, 52, 75, 161, 178, 206
boating, ix, 116, 122, 124, 126, *127*, 128, 194, 209, 235;
  Seattle Yacht Club, 116, 194, 235
bombs and bombing:
  cases, 61, 70, 129, 167, 170, 201, 258;
  war-related, 196–197, 203, 211, 224
bootleggers and bootlegging. *See* illegal liquor
Bremerton Massacre, 174–178, 191–192, 259
bridge failure assessment, 109, *110*, 111
bullet comparison, 62, 79, 90;
  damaged slug, 66, 72, 80, 100–101, *104*, 173;
  death weapon verified, 65, *73*, *98*, 117, 157, 201;
  development of, 10, 35, 106, 155;
  for specific weapon, 63, 113, 144, 179;
  model identified by, 73, 133, 166;
  testing, 78, 109, 113, 116, 131;
  using dimensions, 63, 65–66

bullet trajectories, 4, 51, 178, 257;
  wounds and, 60, 63, 91, 95–96, 122,
  144, 195
Bureau of Forensic Ballistics, 105–106,
  143
Bureau of Investigation. *See* FBI.

Caldwell, Harry H., 27–28, 43, 55, 120,
  146, 199–200
Centralia Massacre, 57–61
chemical testing, 9, 86–87, 123–124,
  162, 246, 254
Chief of Detectives Luke May, 169–
  170, 172, 178, 264
code breaking, 86, 194, 220, 225, 227
comparison microscope, 79, 105–106,
  129.
  See also Revelaroscope and
  Magnascope
coroner's jury, 44, 85, 96, 114, 235
crime prevention, 84, 118, 173, 179,
  181, 202, 245, 260
crime reconstruction, 6, 29, 147–148,
  151, 198
crime scene investigation, 30, 86, 134,
  137, 141, 176;
  compromised, 63, 204;
  method development, 8, 12, 26, 108
crime science pioneers, other:
  Atcherley, Llewelyn W., 203;
  Galton, Francis, 13, 40;
  Goddard, Henry, 9–10;
  Goldstein, Isadore, 191;
  Hall, Albert L., 15;
  Henry, Edward Richard, 13;
  Herschel, William James, 13;
  House, Dr. Robert E., 187;
  Landsteiner, Karl, 14, 108;
  Locard, Edmond, 39–40;
  Lombroso, Cesare, 11–12, 26;
  Marsh, James, 9;
  Piotrowski, Eduard, 52, 205;
  Simon, Carleton, 191;
  Spilsbury, Bernard, 26;

  Teichmann, Ludwig, 14;
  Uhlenhuth, Paul, 14
crime shows. *See* movies; radio;
  television
Crime's Nemesis, 7, 14, 188, 191, 233,
  260–261;
  specific cases, 31, 51, 82, 97, 256
criminalistics, 8, 200, 260;
  pioneers, 14, 239–240
criminology, viii, 8, 15, 163, 260;
  books, 7, 14, 36, 166;
  education, 26, 218, 240;
  milestones and pioneers, 55, 141,
  146, 199;
  school, 76, 84, 193;
  talks, 82, 111, 148
Crossman, Edward C., 27, 55, 105,
  120–121, 146, 155, 158, 201

Davis, Hartwell C., 223, 225–226
Director of Naval Intelligence, 215–216,
  225
District Intelligence Officer (DIO),
  197, 217–219, 221, 223, 225
divorce and child support, 41, 53–54,
  99, 255
Doyle, Arthur Conan, 1, 3, 13–14,
  23–24

Egan, James S., 142, 189, 258;
  and J. Edgar Hoover, 165–166, 170;
  and Luke May, 142, 159, 185, 188,
  210
embezzlement, 103, 246
end matching, 83, 163, 230, 258
estate work, 130, 149, 165, 237, 239,
  244–245, 251
evidence:
  admissibility, 79, 135–136, 138, 140,
  181;
  improperly handled, 57, 63, 124,
  176, 179, 204
expert witness, 75, 118, 140, 199;
  acceptance of, 15, 36, 79;

firearms, 120, 141;
  questioned documents, 55, 126, 239,
  244, 251;
  tool marks, 138, 181

FBI, 161, 170, 183, 191, 257;
  agents, 142, 184;
  crime lab, 166, 258;
  history, 26–27, 94
fingerprint evidence, 27, 138, 165, 178;
  as key clue, 63, 89, 109, 208;
  history of, 12, 15, 39;
  method improvements, *46*, 55, 75,
  182, 257
firearms identification, 26, 62, 89, 104,
  120;
  basics and development, 72, 78–79,
  105;
  history, *10*, 15;
  specific weapon, *64*, 65, 100, 102
firearms makes:
  Colt, 62–63, 65–66, 89, 95, 113,
  133, 158, 190;
  Iver Johnson, 100;
  Luger, 96–98;
  Savage Arms, 89;
  Smith & Wesson, 72–73, 113;
  Thompson, 141;
  Walther, 194;
  Warner Arms, 73;
  Winchester, 3–4, 121, 159
fires. *See* arson and fires.
forensic science, viii–ix, 36, 40, 239–
  240, 259;
  and medicine, 35, 40, 52, 205;
  methods, 8, 14–15
forgery, 68, 111, 122–123, 166–167,
  244;
  as capital offense, 10–11;
  real estate, 106, 248–249;
  wills, 11, 55, 149, 239, 244.
  See also questioned documents;
  handwriting.
Fultz, Hollis, 151, 162–163, 182, 236

Gang Busters radio show, 191–192
Goddard, Major Calvin, 105, 120, 158,
  189, 199, 257;
  and Chicago crime lab, 141, 143,
  149, 244
Great Depression, 162, 167, 245
Gross, Hans, 14, 26, 52

habitual criminal, 43, 144, 177
hair and fibers, 28, 78, 100, 125, 152,
  258
handwriting analysis, 11, 26, 99, 119,
  202;
  in murder case, 48, 68, 126, 180;
  in suicide or accident, 5, 107, 160;
  techniques, 78, 164.
  See also questioned documents.
Harris, John L., 42, 54;
  in Seattle, 60, 90, 94;
  later career, 99, 108, 147, 189, 201
Heinrich, Edward O., 28, 55–56, 105–
  106, 146;
  and Luke May, 120, 140, 143
homicide, 115, 170.
  See also murder *categories*
Hoover, J. Edgar, 94, 165, *170*, 183,
  191
horse raising, ix, 21, 232, 235

illegal liquor, 69–70, 76, 92, 112 122,
  262–263;
  moonshine, 4, 49, 57, 75, 80, 108,
  125;
  Prohibition, 3, 56, 110, 132, 172;
  state laws, 43, 53
Industrial Workers of the World
  (IWW), 57–61, 70, 81
Institute of Scientific Criminology, 76,
  84, 115, 129, 171, 188, 218
insurance company cases, 64, 91, 147,
  156, 201, 238
International Association for
  Identification, 43, 55, 120, 146, 200

international ties, 187, 189–190, 203, 207, 209–210
Irish emigration, 17–18

Kirk, Paul L., 146, 200, 240

law enforcement, 59, 70, 75, 188;
    community, 152, 161, 187;
    education, 148, 245;
    inadequacies, 63, 102, 109, 160;
    meetings, 61, 75, 88, 210;
    successes, 150, 179–180, 188
leisure activities, 39, 92, 116, 256;
    fishing, 126, 128;
    outdoors, 153
    shooting, 20, 130, 194.
    See also horse raising; boating
lie detector. *See* polygraph.
Lindbergh kidnapping, 164, 180–181, 188, 214
Luke May's Department, 185, 187, 190–191, 194, 202–203, 205–206, 209, 259

Magnuson, Warren G., 181–*182*
Mahoney Trunk Murder, 66–69
maritime cases, 84, 197–198, 263
marriages, 36, 45, 107
May, Luke S. *See specific topics*
May, Luke S., photos, *vii, 32, 221, 236, 253*;
    family, *22, 248*;
    work, *50, 77, 93, 202*
May, Luke S., siblings and children:
    brother Vincent, 20, 33, 38–39, 173, 238–239;
    daughter Florence Dorothy, 39, 41, 53–54, 255;
    daughter Patricia, viii, 168, 193, 201, 205, 211, *231*–232, 235, 240, 247, 252, 254–256;
    sister Margaret, 20–21, 24;
    sister Mary, 20, 24
Maylon Detective Service, 33, 35–37, 39–41

modus operandi, 202, 258
moonshine and moonshiner. *See* illegal liquor.
movies, 32, 92, 112;
    crime-related, 184, 191, 209, 232;
    May's cases,187, 192, 240
murder by firearm, 51, 71, 73, 79, 163;
    during a quarrel, 63–65, 96, 121, 132, 173;
    during a theft, 29, 47, 100, 109, 117, 157, 159, 166
murder by other means, 114, 198;
    clubbing, 57, 108, 125–126, 145, 147, 150, 179;
    knife, 49, 81, 83, 163, 203, 207;
    poison, 44, 67, 85–88, 123
murders with multiple victims, 57, 61–62, 174, 190, 204

naval intelligence, 207, 213–223, 225–228
Naval Reserve, 197, 205, 215, 217, 226, 239, 264;
    off-duty activities, 172, 185, 192–193, 250;
    rank, 171, 210, 226
Newell, Edward C., 171, 176, 178, 183–185, 189–190, 201, 259
Northwest Association of Sheriffs and Police, 75–76, 106, 165;
    and James Egan, 142, 159;
    conferences, 120, 185;
    May talks, 112, 150.
    See also Pacific Coast International Association of Law Enforcement Officers
Northwest College of Criminology. *See* Institute of Scientific Criminology.
Northwestern University, 141, 143, 199, 220, 231

Oregon State Police, 158–159, 161, 168, 201, 259
Orfila, Matthieu, 9, 14

Osborn, Albert S., 27, 55, 78, 130, 147, 199, 201

Pacific Coast International Association of Law Enforcement Officers, 188, 202, 210, 235
paint analysis, 152, 258
photographs and photography, 26, 43, 45, 66, 91;
  crime scene, 176, 178;
  development, 12, 62, 106;
  published, 89, 110, 140, 151;
  techniques, 50, 55, 107, 162, 163, 258;
  tool marks, 134, 140
poison, 9, 44, 123–124, 195, 203, 262, 264–265
police radio. *See* radio
polygraph, 146, 187, 194, 199, 229–230, 237, 247
powder burns, 4–5, 63, 95, 191.
  See also firearms identification.
profiling, 49, 137, 185, 258
publications, 87, 170, 260;
  journals, 76, 105, 149, 163, 259;
  key books, 9, 13–14, 27, 36, 105, 130, 200;
  magazines, 3, 27, 50, 54, 115.
  See also Crime's Nemesis; True Detective Mysteries magazine

questioned documents, 130, 199, 207, 233, 237, 258;
  case load, 70, 81, 118, 229;
  history, 14.
  See also forgery; handwriting

radio, 50, 119, 211, 218;
  in police work, 75–76, 146, 172, 209, 259;
  programs, 191–192
RCMP, 161–162, 168, 258
resettlement in the U. S., 19–21
residences and property, 66, *67*, 81, 99, 210;
  before Seattle, 20–21, *25*, 36;
  cases involving, 106, 130, 165;
  for relatives, 104, 168, 173, 238–239;
  home and lab, 115, *193*, 218;
  office, 66, 81, 83, 229;
  personal island, 153, 159, *160*, 210;
  transactions, 90, 210, 229, 232, 238
Revelaroscope and Magnascope, 76, *77*, 78, 104, 129
Roaring Twenties, 92, 112

sabotage, 70, 258, 262–263;
  war-related, 215–*216*, 222.
  See also bombs and bombing
Saint Valentine's Day Massacre, 141
Sellers, J. Clark, 41–42, 45, 61, 116, 162;
  in Seattle, 60, 81, 90, 251–252;
  later career, 94, 121, 146
Showers, Donald McCollister "Mac," 220, 227
Society for the Advancement of Criminology. *See* American Society of Criminology
suicide, 4–5, *6*, 78, 151, *152*, 203, 262–265;
  claimed or suspected, 45, 156, 204, 235
Supreme Court, Washington state, 132, 138–140, 150, 165, 178, 244;
  reversals, 102, 134–136, 237

television, vii, 240
Tennant, Charles, 68, 114, 169
Thirteenth Naval District, 197, 211, 215–*216*, 218–219, 221, 223, 225–226, 244
tool marks, 37, *38*, 131, 136, 140, 150, 257, 259;
  cases, 34, 133, 138–*139*, 181, 233
tracking individuals, 34, 48, 55, 106–107, 119, *120*, 165, 262–265
True Detective Mysteries magazine, 47, 163, 182, *186*, 195, 256, 260
truth serum, 187, 194, 243

ultraviolet light, 164, 209, 258
University of Oregon, 82, 118, 148, 259
University of Washington, ix, 6, 165,
    178, 256, 259, 267;
    criminology, 115, 189, 259;
    students, 58, 240

Vollmer, August, 94, 142, *200*, 240,
    244;
    firsts, 28, 146;
    lectures, 55, 75, 189

Wigmore, John Henry, 141, *142*, 143,
    149, 258
Wobblies. *See* Industrial Workers of the
    World.
World War I, 52, 55, 58, 132, 141, 163,
    206, 217, 222–223, 225, 257
World War II, 222–223, 228;
    prelude, 196–197, 206, 213, 216;
    preparation, 206, 214, 219
wound ballistics, 5, 257